GLOBAL LAWYERING SKILLS

Second Edition

■ ■ ■

Mary-Beth Moylan
Asscociate Dean for Experiential Learning, Professor of Lawyering Skills
McGeorge School of Law, University of the Pacific

Stephanie J. Thompson
Director of Academic Support, Professor of Lawyering Skills
McGeorge School of Law, University of the Pacific

Contributing Authors

Lindsey D. Blanchard

Adrienne Brungess

Ederlina Co

Daniel J. Croxall

Gretchen Franz

Kathleen Friedrich

Jennifer A. Gibson

Hether C. Macfarlane

Maureen Moran

Jeffrey E. Proske

Richard Schickele

Edward H. Telfeyan

Maureen Watkins

AMERICAN CASEBOOK SERIES®

American Casebook Series is a trademark registered in the U.S. Patent and Trademark Office.

© 2013 LEG, Inc. d/b/a West Academic Publishing
© 2018 LEG, Inc. d/b/a West Academic
      444 Cedar Street, Suite 700
      St. Paul, MN 55101
      1-877-888-1330

West, West Academic Publishing, and West Academic are trademarks of West Publishing Corporation, used under license.

Printed in the United States of America

ISBN: 978-1-68328-317-1

DEDICATION

The second edition of this book could not have happened without support of Annette Bethea and the support of the families of our GLS faculty.

We would also like to thank Raquel Aldana, our former Associate Dean for Faculty Scholarship, Michael Colatrella, our Associate Dean for Academic Affairs, and Michael Hunter Schwartz and Jay Mootz, our present and immediate past Deans, for administrative support of our program and this project.

Finally, we would like to thank teaching assistants Tim Keaton, Dannica Molina, and Wiemond Wu for their editorial assistance.

SUMMARY OF CONTENTS

TABLE OF CONTENTS

GLOBAL LAWYERING SKILLS

SKILLS

Second Edition

CHAPTER 1

INTRODUCTION

■ ■ ■

By Mary-Beth Moylan

A. WHAT ARE GLOBAL LAWYERING SKILLS?

The purpose of this book is to encourage the acquisition of both a wide range of lawyering skills (global in breadth) and an understanding of an international or transnational perspective (global in reach). Lawyers practicing law in the United States or in other countries need a set of core skills to enable them to adequately represent the interests of their clients. Whether you plan to practice corporate litigation, government agency law, real estate transactional work, criminal prosecution or defense, entertainment law, family law, or international human rights law, or to establish your own general practice in a small town, you need to be armed with core legal research, writing, and communication skills. You also will need an understanding of how cross-cultural considerations impact the practice of law and an understanding of how ethics play a part in the daily work of all lawyers.

Through each chapter of the book, we introduce you to a core skill and expect that your professor will supplement the introductory materials and exercises with additional materials and exercises to fine tune your skills. Your professor may also give you information that helps relate the skill to a regional practice or local rule in your jurisdiction. For example, in our chapter on Citation, we speak generally about the importance of citing authorities accurately and consistently, and we introduce some of the citation manuals that are used in the United States. However, if you attend law school and plan to practice in a state where a particular citation manual is used exclusively in your state courts, your professor may provide additional information and exercises relating to that citation manual.

Similarly, our chapters on legal research, writing, and communication skills are not tailored to specific legal markets. We will focus on the core research, writing, and communication skills. Your professor will enhance your understanding of law practice in particular regions of the country, or abroad, by focusing your assignments more heavily on either book or electronic research, depending on the typical practice in law firms and organizations in your region.

Written and oral communication skills can also be regionally nuanced, and your professor's explanations or samples of practical writing from your legal market—whether in Boston, Massachusetts; or Atlanta, Georgia; or Chickasaw, Oklahoma; or Guelph, Ontario—will greatly aid your understanding of how to be ready for the practice of law when you graduate. Being prepared for practice means both having mastered the core skills in a lawyer's toolkit, and knowing how and when to employ them in your everyday encounters with legal problems. The authors of this book believe that a combination of study, simulation, and live-client experiences is the best way to acquire this preparation.

Additionally, exercising your lawyering skills in an ethical manner is of critical importance to a successful career as a lawyer. Not only do State Bar organizations require ethical practice and discipline lawyers who fall short of professional standards, but lawyers who leave ethics at the courthouse door often find themselves isolated by their community and deeply dissatisfied in their work. Those lawyers who contemplate the ethical dimension of their client's legal problem and who interact in a civil manner with opposing counsel are able to solve the legal problem most effectively for their client. Moreover, the clients on both sides usually walk away from their experience with the legal system with a more positive attitude about the process—a benefit to the profession as a whole.

B. WHY DO LAWYERS NEED A GLOBAL PERSPECTIVE?

This book provides you with a global perspective on the practice of law. Most chapters contain a section that discusses the cross-cultural considerations relating to the skill being discussed, and there are chapters focused on international and foreign legal research as well. Why, you may ask, do you need to read these sections? The answer is two-fold: first, transnational problems do arise in domestic legal cases, and second, having cross-cultural awareness will make you a better counselor and advocate even if the legal problem has nothing to do with international law.

While it is true that not everyone will practice international law or even encounter the need to research foreign law, all lawyers will encounter legal problems that have cross-border implications or consequences and will need to understand how cross-border issues can arise in domestic litigation or transactions. Take for example a small business in Lincoln, Nebraska. The owner has purchased goods to sell from a supplier abroad. The shipment of the goods is delayed as the result of a strike in the foreign country and the owner in Nebraska has suffered a loss as a result. The owner comes to you and asks whether she can recover. You, of course, first ask if there is a contract and determine which law governs the terms of the contract to assess if there has been a breach. Even in making that assessment you would have to understand that there are multiple jurisdictions that may have an interest in this transaction because the legal problem crosses an international border.

The problem described above may be governed by the United Nations Convention on Contracts for the International Sale of Goods (usually referred to as CISG). If so, you would need to read and analyze articles of the treaty. If the agreement is governed by the law of one of the home countries for a contracting party, the strike may or may not be an excuse for failure to timely deliver. For example, if the foreign jurisdiction is France, where strikes are a part of daily life, the existence of the strike has a different consequence than if the foreign jurisdiction is China, where strikes are highly unusual. As a lawyer for the owner in Nebraska, you will not be expected to know the law of France or China, or the particular rules governing certain international agreements under the CISG, but to serve your client well you should know the right questions to ask about the cross-border implications of the legal problem. Knowing how to research the law of these countries may also help you.

We live in a global world, and having awareness of differences in laws and cultures will make you as a U.S. lawyer a better advocate and better counselor. When you graduate from law school and become a practitioner, you will have clients with backgrounds quite different than your own. If you open up your own practice, you may see not only a wide range of subject matter, but also a wide demographic of client profiles. One week you may assist a ninety-year-old man from Great Britain with an amendment to his will. The next week you may work with a twenty-five-year-old entrepreneur from Brazil to start up a Jiu Jitsu Dojo and Café. Later in the month you may assist a fifty-year-old Iraqi-American woman with a discrimination claim against her employer. Your ability to serve the needs of all of these clients may turn on your ability to recognize your own cultural assumptions and to listen closely to the cultural differences that may be impeding your clients' understanding of the legal process in the United States.

Even if you go to work for a large firm that specializes in intellectual property litigation, your ability to understand the cultural differences that inform notions of property will greatly aid you in communicating with other lawyers representing clients who may have violated U.S. copyright laws. We are all a product of the culture in which we were raised and live. Awareness of both our own cultural biases and those of our clients, co-workers, and opponents makes us more useful to our clients and more successful in our practice.

C. HOW IS THIS BOOK ORGANIZED?

This book takes you from an overview of U.S. and foreign legal systems, to the basics of U.S. practice-based writing, starting with office memoranda and client correspondence, and moving to persuasive writing for both trial and appellate courts. Along the way, the book provides chapters on professionalism, oral argument, alternative dispute resolution, contract drafting, and research and citation.

Every chapter in this book is focused on a particular writing, research, or advocacy topic. Some of the chapters relate to one another. For example, the chapters covering "writing skills" progress from objective to persuasive writing, but many of the same skills are required for quality writing whether the approach is objective or persuasive. We have tried to reference back to relevant portions of previous chapters when appropriate, but you are encouraged to read the writing chapters in the order presented to get a complete introduction to legal writing skills.

The "personal skills" chapters, including professional identity, client interviewing and counseling, as well as alternative dispute resolution chapters, are interspersed to reflect that these skills are required throughout a lawyer's practice. These chapters can be read in any order and should be referenced regularly when working on simulations or when working in live-client clinics later in your law school career.

Each chapter follows a basic structure that includes the purpose of the skill (why lawyers need the skill), substantive instruction in the skill set (how lawyers use the skill), cross-cultural observations (what different manifestations of the skill may arise in different countries or settings), and practical problems to exercise the use of the skill.

Your professor will give you examples of each skill that best reflect the practice in your region, or that are most consistent with the format that your professor prefers. Practice does vary to some extent, so this book will present some examples, but it leaves to the individual professor the job of presenting examples and samples of complete documents.

We hope that your Global Lawyering Skills book is a starting point from which you can expand the breadth of your legal writing, research, and advocacy skills. With an ever-changing more globalized world, it is critical that lawyers of tomorrow learn a wide range of skills, and practice cross-cultural competence along with the basics of research and writing.

PRACTICE EXERCISE

Using the definition of "Civility" found in Sophie Sparrow's article, *Practicing Civility in the Legal Writing Course: Helping Law Students Learn Professionalism,* and reproduced below, please write a brief description of an experience you have had where a person lacked civility. Your description should refer to the definition of civility and explain how the conduct you witnessed diverged from the definition.

> Civility "begins with the assumption that humans matter, that we owe each other respect, and that treating each other well is a moral duty." Civility means valuing the reactions, views, and cultures of others. It implies the ability to disagree without violence or insult.[1]

As a start to thinking about the role of culture and the use of rules in the legal profession, draft a one page essay applying this rule to your own real life situation.

---

[1] Sophie Sparrow, *Practicing Civility in the Legal Writing Course: Helping Law Students Learn Professionalism*, 13 LEGAL WRITING J. 113, 119 (2007).

CHAPTER 2

DOMESTIC AND FOREIGN LEGAL SYSTEMS

■ ■ ■

By Hether C. Macfarlane

Most students come to law school with at least a rudimentary idea of how the U.S. legal system operates, even if it is based solely on movies and television shows. There is more, however, to the law than what appears on the screen. The law is part of the society in which we live, and it both reflects and molds our society. Therefore, in order to practice effectively in the United States, law students need to understand the structure and sources of domestic law. In addition, because law practice grows more global every day, U.S. law students also need to have some understanding of the other legal systems in the world; this understanding needs to include the basic concept that U.S. law is not the only form of law or the most developed form of law.

The two most influential legal systems in the world are the Common Law and Civil Law[1] systems. In addition to understanding those systems to a greater or lesser degree, 21st Century U.S. lawyers need to have some familiarity with 1) the European Union, whose members are largely Civil Law nations, 2) religiously-based legal systems, primarily Islamic, and 3) international law itself.

- **The Common Law system,** which is the legal system of the United States, originated in England and owes its expansion across the globe to the influence of the British Empire. It is based on precedents established in judicial opinions written by judges, who were the creators of much of the law we study in the first year of law school. This is not to say that common law countries lack statutes; but the defining characteristic of a common law system is the importance of judicial decisions, both in creating law and in interpreting statutory law. The judicially-created law and interpretations of statutes become part of the law in a Common Law system.

- **The Civil Law system** is used in the majority of countries in the world. Its law is statutory and codified. It is a system that developed in Europe based on Roman Law, Canon Law,

---

[1] "Civil Law" in this sense should not be confused with the U.S. distinction between "civil" and "criminal" law.

and customary law. Although each country has a more or less unique version of Civil Law, all of the Civil Law systems of Europe, Latin and South America, and Asia have more in common with each other than they have with the Common Law system.

- **The European Union** (EU) is a supranational organization whose law is based on treaties, EU legislation, and decisions of the European Court of Justice, and whose legal procedures reflect the overwhelming influence of the Civil Law countries that form the majority of its twenty-eight current members (as of 2017).[2] Given the role of the European Court of Justice, however, some aspects of the European Union system are beginning to resemble Common Law systems.

- Some countries follow, at least in part, a **religiously based legal system**, such as the Shari'a Law of Islamic countries.

- Finally, there is **International Law**, the legal system regulating the actions and relations of nations that applies worldwide and is based on treaties and customary law.

A. THE U.S. SYSTEM

The U.S. legal system is actually two legal systems, that of the federal government and that of each of the constituent states of the union.[3] Each of these systems has the same sources of law: a constitution, statutes enacted by legislatures, regulations developed by agencies, and cases decided by courts. The four sources are listed here in the hierarchical order of their importance. Thus, a constitution is the ultimate source of law, and no statute or case can override a constitution. A statute is law enacted by the legislature that is binding on all courts in that jurisdiction. While a court can declare a statute unconstitutional, it cannot rewrite a statute[4] and must apply a statute as the legislature enacted it. Administrative regulations usually come from the executive branch of government and have the force and effect of statutes so long as they have been created in

---

[2]   The United Kingdom voted in a referendum on June 23, 2016 to leave the EU. Negotiations for this "Brexit" began on March 29, 2017 when the U.K. formally notified the EU of the U.K.'s intention to leave. Negotiations are expected to last for at least two years. Until then, the U.K. remains a full member. *See* European Union Newsroom, http://europa.eu/newsroom/highlights/special-coverage/brexit_en (last visited Feb. 10, 2018).

[3]   Some Native American tribes have their own legal systems, which are often applied by tribal courts on reservation lands.

[4]   There is at least one state where the state constitution has been interpreted to allow a State Supreme Court to "reform" or rewrite a state statute to make it constitutionally sound. *See* Kopp v. Fair Political Practices Commission, 11 Cal. 4th 607 (1995) (permitting the rewriting of a California statute to save its constitutionality when the intention of the enacting body was clear and reformation would be preferred to invalidation). In California, however, federal courts are not permitted to rewrite statutes. *See* California Prolife Council PAC v. Scully, 989 F. Supp. 1282 (E.D. Cal. 1998).

accordance with the powers granted to the agency by the legislature.[5] Finally, case law comes from the judicial branch. Despite the emphasis on reading cases in the first year of law school, case law is at the bottom of the hierarchy, and any law created by a judicial decision can be changed or eliminated by the enactment of a statute.

Because judicial decisions are fundamental to the U.S. common law system, however, the first place to look to understand that system is the similar judicial structures of the federal and state governments. These structures are arranged hierarchically, with numerous trial courts at the bottom of the hierarchy, several intermediate appellate courts in the middle (in systems with intermediate appellate courts), and one appellate court of last resort at the top. Losing litigants have the right to one appeal of an adverse decision, usually to the intermediate appellate court, but to the highest court if there is no intermediate court. If the system includes intermediate appellate courts, litigants who lose in that level of court have no right to appeal to the highest court but must instead ask that court's permission to appeal.

1. THE FEDERAL JUDICIAL STRUCTURE

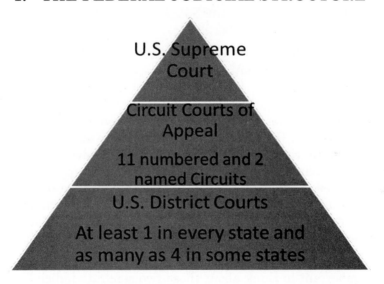

U.S. Supreme Court

Circuit Courts of Appeal

11 numbered and 2 named Circuits

U.S. District Courts

At least 1 in every state and as many as 4 in some states

The Courts of Appeal in the federal system are generally referred to as "circuits." Eleven of them are numbered (one through eleven); the other two

---

[5] While most agencies are formed by the executive branch, some are created by the legislature or the people themselves in states that have a constitutionally sanctioned initiative process. Some examples of non-executive created agencies are the Federal Election Commission and the California Fair Political Practices Commission, which were both created by Political Reform Acts in 1974. The federal agency was created by an act of Congress, while its state counterpart was created by an initiative and vote of the people of California. Whether created through executive or legislative power, the regulations promulgated by agencies are limited by statute.

are named as the District of Columbia Circuit and the Federal Circuit. District courts, the trial courts in the federal system, are named geographically as, for example, the U.S. District Court for the District of Massachusetts if there is only one district in a particular state, or the U.S. District Court for the Eastern District of California if there is more than one district in a state. Decisions of a particular U.S. District Court are appealed to the Circuit Court of Appeal that covers the state in which that trial court sits. Decisions of all of the circuits may be appealed to the U.S. Supreme Court.

2.   SAMPLE STATE JUDICIAL STRUCTURES[6]

California	New York	South Dakota
• California Supreme Court • Court of Appeal (6) • Superior Court (58)	• Court of Appeal • Appellate Division of the Supreme Court (4) • Supreme Court (62)	• South Dakota Supreme Court • None • Circuit Court (7)

State court systems are generally structured the same way as the federal court system. Decisions of trial courts in the states are appealed to the intermediate court whose geographical jurisdiction includes the location of that trial court. Decisions of intermediate appellate courts are in turn appealed to the highest court in the state. Nine states do not have any intermediate appellate courts. Delaware, New Hampshire, and South Dakota are examples of states without intermediate appellate courts. In these states, losing litigants in the trial courts have the right to appeal directly to the state's highest court.

It is important to think about these two separate judicial systems as sitting side by side rather than as the federal system sitting above the state systems. Each system is primarily responsible for cases where the applicable law originates from the legislature or judicial branch associated with either the state or the federal government. Thus, state courts decide

---

[6]   New York has 62 counties, each one with at least one trial court. In New York City, the supreme court handles both civil and criminal matters. Outside New York City, the supreme court handles civil matters, and the county court handles criminal matters, so there are more trial courts than there are counties. For more information, see the NY court system's very informative website: NY State Unified Court System, http://www.courts.state.ny.us/courts (last visited Feb.11, 2018).

cases primarily involving state law, and federal courts decide cases primarily involving federal law. In instances where one system has to apply the law of the other system, the resulting decision does not create law for the "foreign" system.

Judicial decisions based on the law of that court's jurisdiction can and do create law in that jurisdiction. Thus, federal judges may create law for the federal system, and state court judges may create law for their state. That outcome is the essence of a common law system. But one of the hallmarks of any legal system should be predictability: people need to be able to predict the legal effect of their actions or there is no real legal system. Common law systems create this predictability through the doctrine of *stare decisis*, a Latin phrase meaning to stay with what has been decided. Under this doctrine, in most circumstances a court should decide similar cases with similar facts in the same way. On the other hand, if the court believes the old rule is not workable, it may refuse to stand by its previous decision. Courts hesitate to abandon *stare decisis* but will do so when (1) the rule may be changed without inflicting a significant hardship on those who have relied on it, (2) related principles have developed to the point where the rule no longer has a real substance, or (3) the facts have changed so much or come to be viewed so differently by society that the old rule is no longer justified. The flexibility for the court to overrule prior precedent keeps the law from becoming set in stone and out of touch with society.

Closely related to the concept of *stare decisis* is the doctrine of precedent. Indeed, the two terms are often used interchangeably. According to the doctrine of precedent, lower courts are required to follow the precedents of the courts above them in the hierarchical structure discussed above. Precedent is a vertical concept; decisions of courts at the same level as the court considering a case or at a lower level cannot create law for that court, although they can suggest what the law is.

Another concept that goes along with *stare decisis* and precedent is the concept of mandatory or binding authority. Since courts can create law to be applied by the courts below them in each judicial system, when a judge or a lawyer looks to find the applicable law, he looks to cases decided by higher courts in that particular judicial system. So, a lawyer representing a litigant in a U.S. District Court looks to cases decided by the U.S. Supreme Court and by the Court of Appeal whose jurisdiction includes the state in which the District Court sits.

For example, mandatory authority for a case to be heard in the U.S. District Court for the District of Oregon comes from either the Ninth Circuit Court of Appeal or the U.S. Supreme Court, while mandatory authority for a case to be heard in the U.S. District Court for the Eastern District of New York comes from either the Second Circuit Court of Appeal or the U.S. Supreme Court. The situation is somewhat different in state courts in that states with intermediate appellate courts often treat all of those courts as separate parts of one united court. In these states, mandatory authority for a case in a state trial court comes from any of the intermediate appellate courts in the state, not just the intermediate appellate court in whose geographical jurisdiction the trial court sits, and from the state supreme court.

Any discussion of mandatory authority is incomplete unless it includes the mandatory nature of the other sources of law: constitutions, statutes, and regulations. For the federal system, the U.S. Constitution, all federal statutes, and all validly enacted federal regulations are mandatory authority. The same is true of state sources of law as mandatory authority in that state's courts. If a source of law does not fit into one of these categories, it cannot be mandatory and is treated as merely persuasive authority. The statutes, regulations, and cases from a different jurisdiction are persuasive authority outside their own jurisdiction even though they are mandatory authority inside their own jurisdiction. Thus, the reasoning in an Illinois case may persuade a Florida judge to decide his case in the same way if there is no mandatory Florida authority, and a judge in Utah may look to the interpretation of a Vermont statute to help her interpret the meaning of a similar Utah statute. But in neither case is the court bound by the "foreign" decision or statute.

To summarize, when determining the law that applies to your case, the first step is to determine which legal system's law, federal or state, applies. The constitution, statutes, and regulations of that system may provide the legal answer, or the answer may lie in cases from that system that have established the law or interpreted the enacted law. If case law is involved, it must come from a court above the one considering your case to be mandatory authority. If there is no mandatory authority, you will need to find persuasive authority that can support the outcome you want in your case.

B. THE CIVIL LAW SYSTEM

The majority of countries in the world today have Civil Law legal systems. These systems originated on the European Continent and spread to the rest of the world, either through colonization or voluntary adoption. While the laws of the many Civil Law countries vary enormously one to the other, they all share two defining characteristics. First, the law in Civil Law countries is highly conceptualized. A Civil Law lawyer looks to apply a general principle, which has been deduced from lesser principles. For a Civil Law student, the point of legal reasoning is to find the single "right" answer to the problem by looking to the relevant general principle, not to find the best argument to support a proposition. Second, Civil Law countries have a written legal code that was designed to be a systematic, authoritative, and comprehensive statement of the law of that country. Because common law systems lack this systematic nature, Civil Law lawyers often regard common law systems as having, in fact, no real legal system at all.

These codes cover private civil law (in the sense that we use "civil law" in the United States in opposition to "criminal law") and commercial law. Private civil law is itself divided into the law of persons (natural and legal), the family, inheritance, property, and obligations (which includes contracts, torts, unjust enrichment, and moveable property). These divisions owe their universality to similar divisions that existed in Roman Law, and Roman Law is a required course in the legal curriculum of Civil Law countries.

When Civil Law lawyers think of Roman Law, they have in mind the Corpus Juris Civilis, compiled at the order of the Emperor Justinian in the 6th century C.E. The Corpus Juris was itself a codification of the civil law inherited and much annotated, and in Justinian's mind much corrupted, from the Roman Empire of antiquity. Few if any actual laws survived from the classical Roman era, so the Corpus Juris comprised four different parts:

- **The Institutes:** essentially a textbook of elementary principles of law, written by Gaius, a teacher from the classical era, which set out the basic framework noted above, much as a Nutshell or a commercial outline would today. Unlike those modern texts, the Institutes were given the force of law.

- **The Digest** (or Pandecta): a compilation of excerpts from the writings of classical jurists, primarily from the 2nd and 3rd centuries C.E. The compilers of the Corpus Juris edited and occasionally revised these excerpts. The Digest is the largest and the core part of the Corpus Juris Civilis. The excerpts were comments on the words of Roman enactments or solutions of actual or hypothetical cases from the period.

- **The Codex:** a compilation of previous imperial decrees, also edited and revised by Justinian's drafting committee. The decrees dated primarily from the 4th, 5th, and 6th centuries C.E.

- **The Novels, or *Novellae Constitutiones:*** Justinian's own enactments dating from the completion of the other three parts of the Corpus Juris.

Europeans in the territory of the ancient Roman Empire were unaware of the Corpus Juris Civilis until the early 12th century, when a copy of the Corpus Juris was discovered in Italy. Up to that time, these European communities, as well as those that were never part of the Empire, were governed by customary law, which continued to exist up to the time of the creation of various national Codes in the 19th century. Once the Corpus Juris came to light, however, students of the law throughout much of Europe studied it, and scholars from every nation based their writings on interpretations of it.

Codification of the law was primarily a result of the revolutions of the 18th and 19th centuries and the creation of the nation states of Europe. Although Prussia drafted a code in 1794, the first and most influential code for large parts of Europe and the Americas was the French Code Napoleon of 1804. Like many of the other Continental codes, the motive behind the Code Napoleon was the revolutionary desire to remove the vestiges of the old feudal regimes and replace them with a systematic set of laws that protected the individual from both despotic rulers and the caste of judges, who often ignored the law. As a result, Civil Law systems are designed to restrict the power of the judiciary to create or change the law, which marks a major difference with common law systems. Other codifications, such as those of Germany and Italy, resulted from the need to create a single legal system for a country that had incorporated new territory or that resulted from the unification of previously distinct areas with differing legal systems. Finally, Civil Law countries in the Middle and Far East adopted codification as a way of introducing Western law, often at the prompting of imperial powers.

Generally, the codes of most Civil Law countries follow to a greater or lesser degree either the French or the German Codes. The French drafters needed to reconcile the local customs of the north of the country with the law of the south, which was more influenced by Roman Law. The drafters were primarily practitioners, who wanted to create a clear legal system that would provide answers to the problems that were most likely to arise in the future. The Code comprised mainly rules or principles with a fairly narrow scope, leaving many gaps that could be filled in through interpretation. The drafters of the German Code of 1898, on the other hand, were professors, who relied on almost a century of study of both Roman Law and German customary law. The resulting code was a system of concepts, principles, and rules rather than detailed provisions. The drafters believed that all problems that arose later would be capable of solution by applying these concepts and principles.

C. THE EUROPEAN UNION: A DEVELOPING SYSTEM GROWING FROM CIVIL LAW

The European Union (EU) describes itself as an economic and political partnership among twenty-eight European member states, each of which has its own government and territory. It is an outgrowth of the European Coal and Steel Community, founded in 1951 and based on the idea that a common economic policy among the six founding countries would make war in Europe less likely because of economic interdependence.[7] Its guiding framework includes a single market and, for most of its members, a single currency, the Euro. The EU's goals include fostering human rights in Europe and abroad.

The EU resulted from a series of treaties signed by the various members, beginning with the Treaty of Paris in 1951, the Treaty of Rome in 1957, which created the European Economic Community, the Maastricht Treaty of European Union (TEU) in 1993, and the Reform Treaty of Lisbon in 2009 (the Treaty on the Functioning of the European Union or TFEU). All of these treaties comprise the "constitution" of the EU. The powers of the EU are limited to those given to it by its member states in these foundational treaties.

The EU has a rather complex structure because of its nature as a partnership. There are six basic organs of the EU:

- **The European Council,** composed of the heads of state or government of all of the member states. It meets four times a year and sets broad policies. Its decisions are reached by consensus, unless one of the founding treaties requires a vote. This body has no authority to create law.

- **The Council of the European Union** represents the interests of the individual member states and is composed of representatives of those states. The actual representative varies with the issue under consideration; for example, if the topic involves agriculture, the representative is the agriculture minister of each state, whereas if the topic involves foreign affairs, the representative is the foreign minister of each state. This Council must approve all EU legislation.

- **The European Parliament** is elected directly by the citizens of the member states. Although the Members of Parliament (MEPs) are elected in national elections, they organize themselves along party, rather than national, lines. The Parliament cannot propose legislation, but it can suggest amendments to legislation and vote proposed legislation up or down. Most legislation must be approved by both the Parliament and the Council.

- **The European Commission** represents the interests of the EU itself. It proposes legislation, manages the day-to-day

---

[7] The Nobel Peace Prize Committee awarded its 2012 Peace Prize to the European Union, which "for over six decades contributed to the advancement of peace and reconciliation, democracy and human rights in Europe." Nobelprize.org: The Official Web Site of the Nobel Prize, http://www.nobelprize.org/nobel_prizes/peace/laureates (last visited Dec. 19, 2017).

task of implementing EU policies and the EU budget, enforces EU law (along with the European Court of Justice), and represents the EU internationally. The twenty-eight Commissioners, one from each member state, are nominated by their governments and serve five-year terms, during which they are independent of their home country. The Commission drafts legislation and proposes it to the Parliament and the Council.

- **The Court of Justice of the European Union** (ECJ) interprets EU law to ensure that it does not exceed the power allotted to the EU in the treaties and that it is applied equally in all member states. The ECJ consists of one judge from each member state and eight additional judges who serve as Advocates-General. An Advocate-General is assigned to each case to present an independent opinion to the panel of judges, who may accept or reject that opinion. Decisions of the ECJ are not binding precedent for later cases either in the ECJ itself or in national courts, but over the years the ECJ has developed a body of law that more closely resembles common law than civil law.

- **The Economic and Monetary Union** and **the European Central Bank** are responsible for handling inflationary and deflationary pressures and maintaining the stability of the Euro. Nineteen of the twenty-eight member states have adopted the Euro as their currency; the remaining ten states have continued to use their national currency.

The "law" of the European Union consists of the foundational treaties, which are the "primary law" of the EU. The "secondary law" of the EU consists of legislation affecting all member states, divided between "regulations," which are directly binding on the member states, and "directives," which set goals that the member states must reach, although they may choose their own method to implement them. Those possible methods include legislation, constitutional amendments, or internal regulations. The Commission and the ECJ are responsible for enforcing secondary law by determining whether a member state has complied with a directive and ordering compliance if that state has not acted.

D. LEGAL SYSTEMS BASED IN ISLAM[8]

"Islamic law" has two meanings. The first refers to the law based on the religious sources of Islam. The second connotes the law as it exists in

---

[8] The legal systems of many countries include laws based in the dominant religion of the country. These religiously based systems stem from Islamic, Judaic, Hindu, Buddhist, and Confucian beliefs. Most of them affect primarily family or contractual matters, although a few countries base their entire legal system on religion. The religious system covering the widest

the many countries in the modern Islamic world. These are entirely separate bodies of law. The second meaning of Islamic law relates to codes, statutes, and regulations of the modern nation states whose populations are predominantly Muslim. This area stretches from Africa, across the Middle East and many countries in the southern area of the former Soviet Union, and down through Asia into Indonesia and the Philippines. There is not room here to discuss the laws of the many countries comprising that part of the world, but most of these countries inherited a civil law system from former European colonial rulers. Therefore, this discussion focuses solely on the first meaning of "Islamic law."

This first meaning is usually identified in the United States as Shari'a. The word means the "Whole Duty of Man," a path ordained by Allah by which people can reach salvation, which is the goal of all devout Muslims. This path forms the basis for all law in an Islamic society but does not identify every legal rule of the society. The jurisprudence of Shari'a is based on four main sources:

- *The Qur-an.* The Qur-an is not a statement of law but rather is the word of Allah revealed to the Prophet Mohammed. It is the ultimate source of all law in the Islamic world. Some verses of the Qur-an state clear rules, while others are basically moral exhortations on which Islamic society later based legal rules. The other three sources of law nevertheless derive from the Qur-an and its principle that, like Allah himself, Islamic law is a single whole.

- *The Sunna* (the sayings and practice of the Prophet Mohammed and his companions). Through the Sunna, Islamic law imported the legal system that existed in Mecca and Medina at the beginning of Islam by recording in specific verses, or hadiths, what the Prophet approved of, rejected, or was silent about.

- *ijma* (the consensus of scholars and jurists). As Islamic society developed, legal issues arose to which the Qur-an and the Sunna did not provide clear solutions. The answers were provided not through legislation but rather through the interpretations of legal scholars. These interpretations are referred to as fiqh and are the result of the scholars' attempts to understand the ultimate meaning of God's law, or Shari'a. Many schools of interpretation developed in the several centuries after the death of the Prophet. These schools have

---

geographic area and affecting the largest number of people is Islam, so this text concentrates on Islamic law. To learn more about religiously based legal systems worldwide, see Marylin Johnson Raisch, "Religious Legal Systems in Comparative Law—A Guide to Introductory Research" at http://www.nyulawglobal.org/globalex/Religious_Legal_Systems.html (last visited Feb. 11, 2018).

developed over time into four distinct schools, each of which is predominant in different parts of the Islamic world.

- *qiyas* (reasoning by analogy to the first three sources). This source of law relates to "new" issues as they arise. For example, the Qur-an prohibits use of alcohol. Reasoning by analogy, use of drugs is similarly prohibited under Shari'a.

Modern Islamic legal systems are a combination of the law as derived from the religious texts and the rules necessary for the functioning of a nation state, a form of governance that did not exist at the time Islam came into being. The needs of these different states account for the many differences in the laws of countries in the Islamic world.

E. INTERNATIONAL LAW

International Law is the system of law governing the relationships between nation states and between nation states and other international actors, such as international organizations. It is a legal system without an executive or legislative branch. Its judicial branch—the International Court of Justice (ICJ), based in The Hague—is like U.S. courts in that it is limited to deciding disputes submitted to it and cannot reach out to take up a dispute. However, unlike U.S. courts, the ICJ has no way to enforce its judgment if a state refuses to comply with the Court's decision.

Nevertheless, there is a recognized body of law referred to as "international law." Without a legislative branch, its sources are different from those we have considered so far. The sources of international law are enumerated in Article 38 of the Statute of the ICJ as quoted here:

(1) The Court [ICJ], whose function is to decide in accordance with international law such disputes as are submitted to it, shall apply:

  (a) International conventions, whether general or particular, establishing rules expressly recognized by the contesting states;

  (b) International custom, as evidence of a general practice accepted as law;

  (c) The general principles of law recognized by civilized nations;

  (d) Subject to the provisions of Article 59, judicial decisions and the teachings of the most highly qualified publicists of the various nations, as subsidiary means for the determination of rules of law.[9]

---

[9] Statute of the International Court of Justice art. 38, Jun. 26, 1945, 59 Stat. 1055.

This list is exhaustive, and it is generally considered hierarchical, with treaties as the most important source of international law and judicial decisions and the teachings of publicists as merely subsidiary.

- "International conventions" in Article 38(1)(a) of the Statute of the ICJ refers to treaties between any two sovereign states—bilateral treaties—or among three or more sovereign states—multilateral treaties. International lawyers use the terms "treaty" and "convention" interchangeably. The essence of an international treaty is the consent of the parties to it to be bound by its provisions. Although a treaty is based on agreement, a state is not free to disregard its treaty obligations simply because it no longer agrees with the terms of the treaty. Rather, under the doctrine of *pacta sunt servanda,* signatories to a treaty are bound by the treaty and must perform their obligations under it in good faith.

- "International custom" is the second source of International Law. Article 38(1)(b) refers to such custom as "evidence of a general practice accepted as law." This formula has two parts: "a general practice" and "accepted as law." "General practice" in turn has two parts. To be considered "general," international custom must be a rule followed by most states; a few states or a mere majority of states is not sufficient. States may exempt themselves from this customary law if they persistently object to the custom while it is being formed. States that fail to persistently object to customary law as it forms are bound by it once it becomes established. A "practice" refers to the conduct of states, which can be either active or passive. The practice must be consistent to form part of customary law. Finally, to be "accepted as law," the practice must be one that states follow because they believe themselves to be required to do so by international law. This sense of obligation is referred to as *opinio juris.*

- The "general principles of law" in Article 38(1)(c) refers to principles of national law, not general principles of international law. These principles are secondary to those of customary international law and treaties, and they are used primarily to fill in gaps in International Law, which is not as completely developed as national legal systems. There appear to be three categories of general principles that have been recognized by the ICJ. In the first category are principles that are universally recognized, such as the requirement of good faith, and the principle that someone may not profit from her own wrongdoing. The second category involves principles addressing the administration of justice, such as *res judicata* and the passage of time as a defense to some claims. The third category involves principles necessary to fill gaps and may involve analogies to domestic laws to solve unusual problems such as disputes involving international organizations or between states and private corporations.

- Fourth, Article 38(1)(d) permits the ICJ to look to the decisions of courts and "the teachings of the most highly qualified publicists of the various nations" to determine the substance of international law. These sources are subsidiary to the other Article 38 sources. The publicists whose teachings the ICJ may look to are only those who are "highly qualified," and their teachings are merely evidence of the substance of International Law, not an independent source of law. Finally, this section of Article 38 is limited by its opening phrase, "Subject to the provisions of Article 59." Article 59 makes it clear that the decisions of courts are not binding precedent in International Law, but also codifies the principle of *res judicata* by stating that the ICJ's decisions are binding on the parties to the case. Although International Law, like the Civil Law, rejects *stare decisis*, in reality the ICJ and other international tribunals regularly look to prior decisions to maintain consistency in their rulings.

F. CROSS-CULTURAL CONSIDERATIONS

You are reading this chapter as part of your education to become a lawyer in the United States. Whether you know any lawyers or not, you probably have an idea of what at least some lawyers do and how the legal profession is organized. American lawyers represent clients in court and by counseling them about business and personal transactions. American lawyers work in firms ranging in size from solo practitioners to multinational firms with hundreds of lawyers. They also work inside businesses as in-house counsel and for national, state, and local governments. Lawyers may ultimately become judges, either through election or selection by a governor or the President. All lawyers must pass a bar examination to practice law; some states require admitted lawyers to belong to the state bar association, while others make bar association membership voluntary. Despite these differences, however, the United States has a single class of lawyers, each of whom may move from the private to the public sector and back without any restrictions.

Your understanding of what Civil Law lawyers do, however, is probably more limited. The organization of the legal profession is very different in Civil Law jurisdictions. Law is an undergraduate degree in Civil Law countries. When Civil Law students graduate from university, they must choose a career path and generally stick to it for the rest of their lives. Their choices are to become a judge, a public prosecutor, a government lawyer, an advocate, or a notary. In some countries, law graduates must go through a period of practical training in which they work for the judiciary, the government, and in private practice; in other countries, they simply make the choice when they finish university. They enter their chosen field at the bottom and work their way up. One result of this system is that judges are not the experienced and admired people they are in the United States.

An advocate is most like a U.S. lawyer. Advocates advise clients and represent them in court. They may also help them with business planning and managing property. Until recently, both partnerships and corporate law departments were forbidden or extremely limited in Civil Law countries, although that situation is changing. Law firms are often small, although the expansion of international trade and business transactions has led to an increase in the size of law firms, particularly in Europe.

The most dramatic difference between the U.S. and the civil law legal professions involves notaries. In the United States, a notary need not be a lawyer, although in New York a lawyer can become a notary without having to take a special examination, thus, many New York lawyers become notaries. A U.S. notary's function is to attest to the identity of the person signing a document. A Civil Law notary is a much more important person, and must be a law school graduate. The number of notaries is very limited, and they often have quasi-monopolies on the provision of legal services. Civil Law notaries draft important legal documents, such as wills, contracts, and corporate charters. They also authenticate instruments, known in the Civil Law world as "public acts." A notary's authentication of a legal instrument establishes that the instrument is genuine and that it accurately represents what the parties said and agreed to. Finally, notaries act as a kind of official depository. They are required to keep a copy of every instrument they prepare.

PRACTICE EXERCISE

There is a treaty on the formation and interpretation of treaties themselves, the Vienna Convention on the Law of Treaties. Using any search engine you would like, locate the text of this Convention. According to the Convention, how may a state express its consent to be bound by the terms of a treaty?

CHAPTER 3

INTERCULTURAL COMPETENCE

■ ■ ■

By Maureen Watkins and Adrienne Brungess

Most, if not all, human interaction is intercultural to some degree. As composites of family, ethnic, religious, and societal backgrounds, people are walking prisms of their experiences and values. The integrated filters that are calibrated and tuned over a lifetime guide and affect how people interact with and respond to each other. In an increasingly globalized society, the need for intercultural competence is essential.

Intercultural competence is the appropriate and effective management of interaction between people who represent different or divergent affective, cognitive, and behavioral orientations to the world in terms of nationality, race, ethnicity, tribe, religion, or region.[1] By being mindful of one's own cultural background while being aware of and flexible to the other party's background as well, it is possible to communicate more effectively and, consequently, to achieve the desired outcome.[2] In this context, the term culture pertains to enduring yet evolving intergenerational attitudes, values, beliefs, rituals, and customs, and behavioral patterns into which people are born and live.[3] To achieve intercultural competence is to understand one's own cultural matrix, recognize differences, and be open to new experiences.[4]

A. THE ICEBERG CONCEPT OF CULTURE[5]

As depicted in the image below, there are both perceptible and invisible aspects of culture. What can be observed as culture is typically behavior, while what motivates such behavior lies below the surface. Readily perceptible manifestations of an individual's culture include language, religion, gender, age, ethnicity, and dress, to name a few.

---

[1] Brian H. Spitzberg & Gabrielle Changon, *Conceptualizing Intercultural Competence*, THE SAGE HANDBOOK OF INTERCULTURAL COMPETENCE 7 (Darla K. Deardorff ed., 2009).

[2] *Id.* at 13.

[3] *Id.* at 6.

[4] *Id.* at 14; *See* Global Competencies Model. Bill Hunter et al., *What Does it Mean to be Globally Competent?*, 10 J. STUD. INT'L EDUC. 267, 278 (2006).

[5] EDWARD T. HALL, BEYOND CULTURE (1976); Robert T. Moran et al., *Intercultural Competence in Business*, THE SAGE HANDBOOK OF INTERCULTURAL COMPETENCE 298 (Darla K. Deardorff ed., 2009); Prof. Dr. Uwe Kils, *Iceberg* [photograph] (2005), available at http://en.wiki pedia.org/wiki/File:Iceberg.jpg (last visited Feb. 16, 2018).

The subconscious realm of culture is comprised of a myriad of values and assumptions woven over time. These concepts are so inextricably linked to an individual's sense of self that he may not be consciously aware of them. Cultural values are fundamental beliefs that are learned very early and are the basis of many behaviors.[6] Examples of cultural values include fealty, punctuality, or honesty. Cultural assumptions are expectations about preferred and expected ways of being that influence values, beliefs, behaviors, and communications.[7] "All men are created equal" is an example of a cultural assumption. Someone who does not share this assumption and considers himself to be superior to others, might, for example, treat his subordinates badly and not tolerate any feedback. The first step toward intercultural competence is examining and truly knowing one's own cultural values and assumption. From there, it is necessary to be open to and tolerant of the differences in dealings with members of other cultural groups.

Behavior

Language, gender. Ethnicity, dress, religion, race, arts, cooking, crafts, celebrations, games, etc.

Values & Assumptions

Notions of modesty, concept of self, decision-making processes, concepts of time, education, raising children, morality, social hierarchy, friendship, beauty, work ethic, concepts of physical space, individualism or group norms, roles in relation to age, sex, status, occupation and kinship, concepts of justice, dealing with pain, death, etc.

1.   CULTURAL SELF-AWARENESS

Being aware of and actively familiar with one's own cultural makeup is a prerequisite to being able to gauge another individual's reactions. This familiarity entails having actively assessed the bases for one's motivations, such as religion, family values, ethnicity, societal conditioning, gender roles, and the role of the elderly.[8] To a certain extent, geographic origin, which is also linked to certain cultural norms, affects an individual's

---

[6]   Robert T. Moran et al., *supra* note 5, at 298.

[7]   *Id.*

[8]   GEERT HOFSTEDE & GERT JAN HOFSTEDE, CULTURES AND ORGANIZATIONS: SOFTWARE OF THE MIND (2005); HALL, *supra* note 5.

cultural composition. This is particularly noteworthy in connection with high-context and low-context cultures.[9]

Edward T. Hall, who is considered by many anthropologists as the "father of intercultural communication," coined the terms high-context and low-context cultures to describe the degree to which the communication's meaning is imbedded in the context versus the code or message in which it is conveyed.[10] This gives an indication of how people interact and communicate with other members of their culture. These associations reflect a deeper set of social norms and assumptions that motivate such behavior.

An individual from a low-context culture will generally expect to find the meaning of the communication in the message itself. People from low-context cultures are typically direct in their mode of expression. They are explicit and rely largely on the verbal communication itself rather than on non-verbal cues. The individual, rather than the group, is emphasized in low-context cultures.[11] Western society is often associated with low-context cultures, as in, for example, Canada, the United States, Australia, New Zealand, and Europe.

Unlike individuals from low-context cultures, high-context culture individuals generally seek the meaning of a communication in the context and surroundings of the communication rather than the words themselves. Crucial information is imbedded in the context of the exchange. Indeed, information is not always verbalized, and the discussion can move around the actual point like a circle. In some instances, the main issues may be only inferred and perhaps never discussed directly. In high-context cultures, there is more of a collectivist approach rather than a focus on the individual.[12] High-context cultures place great value on traditions, on history, and on maintaining relationships.[13] Areas generally associated with high-context cultures include Asia, the Middle East, Africa, and much of the rest of the world.

As discussed above, individuals from high and low-context cultures communicate differently. These approaches also manifest themselves in very different conflict styles. Being aware of these differences is essential to being an effective negotiator and conflict manager.

---

[9]   HALL, *supra* note 5.

[10]   R. S. Zaharna, *An Associative Approach to Intercultural Communication Competence in the Arab World*, THE SAGE HANDBOOK OF INTERCULTURAL COMPETENCE 184 (Darla K. Deardorff ed., 2009); HALL, *supra* note 5, at 98.

[11]   HALL, *supra* note 5, at 231.

[12]   Zaharna, *supra* note 10, at 184.

[13]   Gert Jan Hofstede, *The Moral Circle in Intercultural Competence: Trust Across Cultures*, THE SAGE HANDBOOK OF INTERCULTURAL COMPETENCE 92 (Darla K. Deardorff ed., 2009); *see also* GEERT HOFSTEDE, CULTURE'S CONSEQUENCES: INTERNATIONAL DIFFERENCES IN WORK-RELATED VALUES (2d ed. 2001)[hereinafter HOFSTEDE, CULTURE'S CONSEQUENCES].

Contrast Between Low-Context and High-Context Cultures Conflict Styles[14]

Key Questions	Low-Context Conflict	High-Context Conflict
Why	Use of linear logic; separation of parties from the problem	Use of spiral logic; integration of conflict and parties to a conflict
When	Individualistic oriented; violations of individual expectations create conflict potentials	Group oriented; violations of collective expectations create conflict potentials
What	Overtly display meanings through direct communication forms; direct approach; action and solution oriented	Implicitly imbeds meanings at different levels of context; indirect, non-confrontational attitude; "face" and relationship oriented
How	Explicit communication codes; open, direct strategies	Implicit communication codes; ambiguous, indirect strategies

B. INTERCULTURAL COMPETENCE FOR LAWYERS

Developing intercultural competence is an important part of becoming an effective communicator. Being culturally self-aware is the first step in the process and a prerequisite to navigating communications between high-context and low-context cultures. This ability is especially important in the practice of law. Lawyers are called upon to be advisors, adversaries, confidants, and advocates, to name a few. To advise or persuade effectively, the lawyer must know her audience. This means that the lawyer must also be aware of cultural aspects that could affect either the way her message should be delivered or the way it could be perceived, and she should provide for such eventualities.

---

[14] HALL, *supra* note 5; John Barkai, *Cultural Dimension Interests, the Dance of Negotiation, and Weather Forecasting: A Perspective on Cross-Cultural Negotiation and Dispute Resolution,* 8 PEPP. DISP. RESOL. L.J. 403, 409–10 (2008).

1. CROSS-CULTURAL INTERACTIONS AND COMMUNICATIONS

The attorney's goal in all client interactions and communications is not to overwhelm the audience with technical information and complex legal advice. Rather, the goal is "to generate a flow of accurate information and reach a mutually agreed-upon decision."[15] Further, client interaction is fraught with hidden dynamics[16]; these dynamics are even more complex when communicating with a client from an unfamiliar culture. Attorneys who ignore the important role culture plays in communication will ultimately have more difficulty establishing trust with the client and eliciting critical information.

Clients probably already feel inhibited when meeting with an attorney, especially if it is for the first time. A client may feel embarrassment or shame about the circumstances at issue, or may be intimidated by lawyers or the legal system.[17] The client may also not speak English well, or may be inhibited as a result of other social and cultural constraints. Therefore, the lawyer must be culturally educated to facilitate a meaningful relationship with the client. "As more shared meanings and mutual understanding occur, the client will be more likely to share honest and complete information with the lawyer."[18]

Attorneys should demonstrate empathy when working with clients to overcome the challenges posed by intercultural exchanges. Additionally, the lawyer should endeavor to establish common ground and illustrate similarities to facilitate trust.[19] To accomplish this, the lawyer must abandon pre-conceived notions and stereotypes about differing cultures and try to understand the client's experience from the client's perspective. Further, the attorney must be cautious about non-verbal cues that may be perceived as aggressive or inappropriate, and should not make assumptions about a client's non-verbal cues. Moreover, attorneys must be aware that certain communication forms that are acceptable within a particular social group may not be acceptable from an outsider.[20] Education about cultural differences, including the different expectations in low and high-context cultures, is a good place to start, but since every person is a unique product of multiple influences, generalizations about a client's background are likely insufficient and incomplete. Instead, reflective

---

[15] Mark. K. Schoenfield & Barbara Pearlman Schoenfield, *Interviewing & Counseling Clients in a Legal Setting*, 11 AKRON LAW REVIEW 313 (Fall 1977) (available at https://uakron.edu/dot Asset/f36260e3-b1e8-4aef-8795-7b33b650a857.pdf, last visited December 5, 2017).

[16] STEPHAN H. KRIEGER & RICHARD K. NEUMANN, JR., ESSENTIAL LAWYERING SKILLS 120 (5th ed. 2015).

[17] *See* id.

[18] Joan B. Kessler, *The Lawyer's Intercultural Communication Problems with Clients from Diverse Cultures*, 9 NW. J. INT'L L. & BUS. 64, 71 (1988–1989).

[19] *Id.* at 72.

[20] *Id.* at 73–74.

listening and respectful inquiry are the best methods for a lawyer to employ.

Consider this example:

"[L]isten carefully to a client's answer to the greeting, 'How are you?' The response 'I am blessed' is a . . . client's clearly intentional deviation from the majority culture's standard answer of 'fine' or 'good.' It is a hint to the finely attuned ear, or in some cases a declaration against the obstinate dominant culture, that the client is a person . . . of faith. It would be insensitive for the lawyer to think the response weird or unintelligent, when instead it is a reflection of a highly developed ethic having potentially important consequences to the consultation."[21]

It is important to remember, and frequently reflect on the fact that not all clients will share your vocabulary, verbal skills, level of education, or experiences. Acknowledging the client's story and mirroring the client's behavioral prompts and non-verbal communication will help facilitate the trust necessary for effective client representation.

It is also paramount that the attorney communicate respect for the client by listening actively, showing empathy and openness, and by steering the communication with patience; tolerance and flexibility are key.[22] The client should feel that she was able to communicate freely with counsel and provide the necessary details and perspective. Do not speak to the client with a tone that may be perceived as arrogant or condescending; additionally, do not appear scolding or judgmental, and be respectful of the client's emotional responses. And communicate clearly to the client that you understand her goals and expectations.[23]

Another critical area where culture plays a role is in strategizing about a resolution to the client's problem. Just as the attorney brings to the situation her cultural context, so does the client bring his cultural identity, ethnicity, race, gender, and social values. There is often a power imbalance in the typical attorney-client relationship that could lead the attorney to make certain assumptions about the client and how she would like her problem to be resolved. Here, especially, the attorney should refrain from making assumptions and focus rather on cultural context indicators to enhance her understanding of the client. In some circumstances, the attorney may need to accept a decision by a client that may seem imprudent in the attorney's value system. Here, it is important for the

---

[21] Nelson P. Miller, *Beyond Bias—Cultural Competence as a Lawyer Skill*, MICHIGAN BAR JOURNAL 39 (June 2008) (available at https://www.fordham.edu/download/downloads/id/3026/beyond_bias_cultural_competency.pdf, last visited December 5, 2017).

[22] *See* Kessler, *supra* note 18, at 77.

[23] Miller, *supra* note 21, at 40.

attorney to take note of the client's stated objective, rather than her own notions of what constitutes a successful outcome.[24]

As Justice Sotomayor explained in her article, "A Latina Judge's Voice," it is important to understand how culture and personal experiences affect perspective and bias.[25] An attorney who knows her own cultural matrix is in a better position to calibrate her interaction with the client for the most effective and fruitful responses.

For example, a culturally competent attorney uses an array of tiered questions to elicit nuanced information from a low-context client. In this situation, a question like, "Is there anything else you'd like to know?" or "Did that make sense to you?" would likely be ineffective. The client might be reluctant to express either a gap in understanding or to convey that the information conveyed was inadequate. The client's reluctance to respond to the second question may be linked to a concern about offending the attorney. Conversely, a low-context client may well benefit from further discussion of the possible ramifications of certain conduct that may not have been immediately apparent in the situation.

In culturally diverse situations, it is important to eliminate barriers that could impede establishing the relationship of trust that is the basis of the attorney-client relationship and essential for representing the client effectively. For example, the parties' body language can be potentially misread and, consequently, misinterpreted. A primary example of this phenomenon is the role eye contact plays in various cultures. In most low-context cultures, looking at someone straight in the eyes and maintaining eye contact indicates honesty and open communication. Contrastingly, in other cultures, many of which also are low-context environments, such conduct is considered rude and inappropriate. In these cultures, averting one's eyes is a sign of respect. Therefore, the attorney must be mindful of assumptions based on body language.[26]

As another example, consider the potential mixed message that may arise as a result of nodding in conversation. The act of nodding while someone is talking is a common custom; however, its significance varies among cultures. In some cultures, nodding while someone is speaking indicates agreement with the speaker, while in other cultures, nodding merely indicates that the listener is listening. In this situation, it is

---

[24] AM. BAR ASSOC. STANDARD 2.4 ON CULTURAL COMPETENCE (2006). *See* AM. BAR ASSOC. STANDARDS FOR PROVISION OF CIVIL LEGAL AID, STANDARD 2.4 ON CULTURAL COMPETENCE (2006).

[25] Sonia Sotomayor, *A Latina Judge's Voice*, 13 BERKELEY LA RAZA L.J. 87, 91–92 (2002).

[26] *See* Susan J. Bryant & Jean Koh Peters, FIVE HABITS FOR CROSS-CULTURAL LAWYERING, *available at* http://www.mcgeorge.edu/Documents/Conferences/5_Habits_for_Cross_Cultural_Lawyering_Bryant_and_Peters.pdf (last visited December 5, 2017); *see also* Susan J. Bryant & Jean Koh Peters, *The 5 Habits: Building Cross-Cultural Competence in Lawyers*, 8 CLINICAL L. REV. 33 (2001).

important to double check whether the communication with the client is both heard and understood.

2. CROSS-CULTURAL PRESENTATIONS

"[C]ultural competency is an essential skillset for the 21st century attorney who seeks to deliver effective advocacy and serve justice."[27] This requires that the attorney know her audience and anticipate how information is going to be perceived and processed and, ultimately, valued.[28] "Attorneys who regularly work with clients, witnesses, or opposing counsel who are foreign nationals or members of discrete ethnic groups recognize that those individuals' beliefs and understandings regarding law, the relationship of the individual to the government, individual legal rights and responsibilities, the form of the legal system, [and] particular doctrines . . . may vary at times . . . from the views and beliefs of mainstream American culture."[29]

Here too, a finely tuned cross-cultural filter is indispensable. When representing a culturally diverse client, the attorney is effectively translating the client's reality in a convincing way in the legal process. To convey the client's reality, the attorney must have become knowledgeable about the client's cultural values and assumptions. Only then can the narrative reflect the client's position.[30]

The attorney's rhetorical strategies, when implemented effectively, significantly impact the attitudes and outcomes of a case.[31] Therefore, the attorney must be culturally sensitive when developing these strategies. Consider the effect of something as simple as mispronunciation of party names. Names are ancestrally significant for many minority and immigrant clients,[32] as are roles played in the community and family. Therefore, attorneys should ensure that foreign names are pronounced correctly and that appropriate respect is demonstrated. Moreover, attorneys must try to help the audience connect emotionally with the client's plight, but must accomplish this without tokenizing the client, or

---

[27] Travis Adams, *Cultural Competency: A Necessary Skill for the 21st Century Attorney*, 4 WILLIAM MITCHELL LAW RAZA L.J. 4 (2012) available at http://open.mitchellhamline.edu/cgi/view content.cgi?article=1010&context=lawraza (last visited December 6, 2017).

[28] *See also* Chapter 8 on Knowing Your Audience.

[29] Marilyn J. Berger, John B. Mitchell, Ronald H. Clark, PRETRIAL ADVOCACY: PLANNING, ANALYSIS, & STRATEGY 6 (WOLTERS KLUWER 2017).

[30] AM. BAR ASSOC. STANDARDS FOR PROVISION OF CIVIL LEGAL AID, STANDARD 2.4 ON CULTURAL COMPETENCE (2006).

[31] Michelle Ramos-Burkhart, *Do You See What I See? How a Lack of Cultural Competency May Be Affecting Your Bottom Line*, THE JURY EXPERT (May/June 2013) available at http://www.thejuryexpert.com/wp-content/uploads//1305/JuryExpert_1305_SeeWhatISee.pdf (last visited December 6, 2017).

[32] *See* Clare McLaughlin, *The Lasting Impact of Mispronouncing Students' Names*, NEATODAY.ORG, September 1, 2016 available at http://neatoday.org/2016/09/01/pronouncing-students-names/ (last visited December 6, 2017).

imposing the attorney's own values, or the values of the predominant culture, in place of the client's.

The culturally-aware attorney will revisit these skills and continue to educate herself to achieve cultural competence. Therefore, attorneys should frequently self-reflect and review critically their own presentation style and strategic decisions to determine where additional efforts and education will be beneficial.[33] In the global arena, the legal industry demands lawyers possess these critical skills for success.[34]

3. CROSS-CULTURAL NEGOTIATIONS

The dance of negotiation is done in every culture, but the music and the steps may vary significantly between cultures.[35] In negotiations, the interplay between low-context and high-context individuals can be very delicate and potentially disastrous. A cross-culturally competent negotiator should calibrate her strategy in alignment with her client's while keeping a keen eye on the mannerisms and motivations of her counterparts. By understanding how others process information, how they tend to operate, and how they go about making decisions, the attorney is in a much better position to manage the negotiation process to her client's benefit.

At the outset, communication styles will invariably affect the negotiation process.[36] As discussed above, individuals from low-context cultures tend to be direct, explicit, and rely on verbal rather than on non-verbal forms of communications. People from high-context cultures convey information not only through verbal communication but also through the context, relying on non-verbal cues to supplement the meaning of the communication.[37]

The high-context and low-context communication styles are also linked to other values and behavioral norms that invariably affect the course of negotiations.[38] For example:

---

[33] *Id.*

[34] *Id.*

[35] Wendi L. Adair & Jeanne M. Brett, *The Negotiation Dance: Time, Culture, and Behavioral Sequences in Negotiation*, 16 ORG. SCI. 33 (2005).

[36] *See also* Chapter 23 on Interviewing the Client.

[37] Zaharna, *supra* note 10, at 184.

[38] HALL, *supra* note 5, at 101, 105–16; HOFSTEDE, CULTURE'S CONSEQUENCES, *supra* note 13; HOFSTEDE & HOFSTEDE, *supra* note 8.

Cultural Value	Low-Context Culture	High-Context Culture
Time	More present and future oriented, values change over time	More focused on history, traditions, maintaining status quo
Risk Propensity	Less averse to risk	Tend to avoid risk
Disclosure of Information	Some disclosure, direct, confrontational attitude; action and solution-oriented	Minimal disclosure, indirect; non-confrontational attitude, face, and relationship-oriented
Group vs. Individual	Individualistic oriented	Group-oriented, collectivist
Nature of Agreements	Want agreement in writing	Value personal commitments; a "good deal" is also a long-term business relationship

Building a relationship with the other participants is key to successful negotiation and cultural awareness is vital to this effort. A negotiator who lacks cultural education may find herself unaware of the problems causing communications to deteriorate and may not understand the reactions and strategies of opponents as a result. When planning for cross-cultural negotiation, it is important to consider the cultural implications of your conduct and communication. For example, the pace of a negotiation process and the length of time the process takes varies dramatically among different cultures. Some cultures value certain ceremonies and exchange of pleasantries before addressing substantive issues. Additionally, not all cultures value physical contact, hand-shaking, kissing, etc., the same way; the lawyer should know what to expect before entering the negotiation.[39]

To negotiate effectively when there are cross-cultural considerations, avoid making assumptions or relying on generalizations about cultural norms. Pay attention and look for cues and guidance from the other participants and ask questions when appropriate. Speak slowly if a participant is not a native English speaker. Confirm your understanding by repeating concepts or mirroring back what you think you heard. Acknowledge if you make mistakes or demonstrate cultural insensitivity

---

[39] *See* Salli A. Swartz, Marcelo E. Bombau, Ingrid Busson-Hall, *Cross-Cultural Negotiations—Or—Have You Ever Been Yelled at by an American Attorney in a Negotiation?*, AMERICANBAR.ORG (2017) available at https://www.americanbar.org/publications/international_ law_news/2013/spring/crosscultural_negotiations_have_you_ever_been_yelled_at_by_american_ attorney_negotiation.html (last visited December 6, 2017).

and learn from it. And demonstrate respect and courtesy; avoid condescension and judgment.[40]

The lawyer as negotiator plays an essential role as translator of not only his client's wishes but also of the other party's underlying interests. Being interculturally competent enables the lawyer to advance the dance of negotiation along, ideally avoiding cultural pitfalls that impede the communication process.

C. CONCLUSION

As societies become more mobile and the economy becomes increasingly global, the skill of intercultural competence is essential. Individuals are unique composites of their cultural, ethnic, and societal backgrounds. Consequently, most communication is intercultural by definition. Being able to navigate cross-cultural communications appropriately and effectively is especially important in the practice of law. Attorneys are often referred to as "counsel" because an attorney is, among other things, a counselor. However, to give effective, sage advice, the attorney must first understand her client. In today's world, the most effective attorney must also have intercultural competence.

---

[40] *Id.*

CHAPTER 4

PROFESSIONALISM AND PROFESSIONAL IDENTITY

■ ■ ■

By Lindsey D. Blanchard, Daniel J. Croxall, and Jeffrey E. Proske

Law school does a great job of teaching law students what the substantive law is and how to apply it to everyday human affairs. However, lawyers need to have more than a deep understanding of the law to be successful. When you become a lawyer, you become a member of a profession with obligations to the court (as a member sworn to support the Constitution and to discharge your duties to the best of your abilities), to clients (as their trusted counselor and advisor), and to the community (as a leader). Therefore, in addition to mastery of substantive areas of law, your ability to practice law effectively depends on a number of factors: emotional intelligence, discipline, perspective, self-directedness, interpersonal skills, and most importantly, a sense of purpose in the leadership role lawyers play in the administration of justice and the rule of law.

Your cultivation of these skills and concepts will not only affect your effectiveness as a lawyer, it will also affect your professional identity—i.e., the kind of lawyer you become and the kind of lawyer that others perceive you to be. Some lawyers have developed a reputation for being trustworthy, dedicated, reliable, and hard-working. Others have not. But, those identities do not begin to take shape on the day you graduate from law school, on the day you are sworn into the bar, or on your first day of work. Rather, your professional identity begins to take shape on your first day of law school, during your first interactions with your professors (from whom you will seek professional references during your job search) and classmates (who are your future colleagues). And, it continues to take shape throughout your law school career through the choices you make about which courses to take, which clubs to join, and which networking events to attend. This chapter discusses the Top Ten practices you should begin to develop, as well as other considerations you should begin to contemplate, now, as you start the process of developing your own professional identity.

A. DEVELOPING AND NURTURING YOUR PROFESSIONAL REPUTATION

Lawyers, like other licensed professionals, have a special role in society in as much as they are trained to become advocates for others as well as being officers of the court, sworn to uphold the law. In keeping with this role, the law recognizes that each individual lawyer is entitled to certain privileges: the attorney-client privilege, which protects communications between the lawyer and her client from being used against the client's interests; and the attorney work product doctrine, which permits a lawyer to shield her thought processes and written work related to a client's representation from disclosure. Because the measure of responsibility accorded to each individual lawyer in our society is so high, lawyers are individually licensed by bar associations, which are responsible for ensuring that their member lawyers conduct their work in accordance with the highest ethical principles. Thus, a lawyer is individually responsible to ensure that her conduct comports with the highest ethical standards.

While many lawyers work as employees of law firms, non-profit organizations, government agencies, or corporations, they are still individually responsible for ensuring that the work they do, irrespective of the organization for which they work, comports with the highest standards of the profession. Accordingly, a lawyer must seek to develop a reputation as a person who clients, colleagues, courts, and the community can rely upon for honesty, competence, and diligence.

Understanding this framework for your professional identity as a lawyer is fundamental to developing and nurturing your reputation as a lawyer. Your reputation hangs on your ability to conduct yourself with honor and integrity in your work, and on your reputation among your colleagues for honesty and integrity in your dealings with them. This framework extends to every area of life, including your personal life, your social media presence, and your correspondence with others in every format, from Twitter to e-mail, to texts, to the briefs you submit to a court.

While the process of building a reputation as a lawyer may be mysterious to first-year law students, there are several ways to go about doing so, even in the first year of law school. First, consider joining one or more student organizations at your law school. Every law school has a host of student groups, some focused on specific areas of law, others on community service, and still others on student governance or purely social purposes. Joining student organizations is a great way to meet your peers and to start building your reputation among them. Second, consider joining national and local bar associations. Many bar associations, like the American Bar Association, offer free or reduced membership rates for law students. Joining bar associations is a time-honored way for law students and newly-minted lawyers to become part of the larger legal community. Bar associations also provide numerous opportunities for their members to participate in continuing legal education to assist them in keeping up with emerging changes in the law. Third, joining service organizations engaged in community outreach programs can be a marvelous way to get a foothold in the community, and to start developing a reputation as a community-spirited person. In most cities, there are many organizations dedicated to assisting people in need, such as the elderly, immigrants, artists, and people experiencing homelessness. Finally, developing a professional presence on social media by creating profiles on various platforms such as LinkedIn, Facebook, and Twitter, can give you access to a massive global network of professionals, and can help you make yourself known to the world at large.

Keeping a keen eye on your reputation will serve you in the profession for a lifetime. Clients, courts, and the community will regard you as a reliable, competent, and honest counselor. Failing to keep a keen eye on your reputation can achieve the opposite result.

B. FINDING MENTORS

The practice of law is complex, and it involves a steep learning curve to master the various skills involved in doing it well, from financial management, to effective client counseling, to the strategic dimensions of client problem solving that accompany any area of practice. While it is certainly possible to develop these skills through trial and error, a better approach is to learn from those who have trod the path before you so you do not have to make otherwise avoidable mistakes. Finding mentors in the profession is critical to mastering these skills, and the first year of law school is a good time to start.

Many law students find the prospect of approaching lawyers and judges intimidating. They do not want to bother busy professionals with their questions. However, many of these lawyers and judges welcome the opportunity to engage with law students and young lawyers, and to offer them guidance and mentorship. Every law school has a network of alumni whose careers span the spectrum of practice areas and who would willingly take the time to discuss the profession with you. Your law school's alumni association and career development office should be a prime source for you to seek out mentors in the profession.

The best way to overcome any intimidation you might feel about reaching out to a lawyer for mentorship is to simply call or write to them to express interest in their career. Most lawyers are gratified to learn that a law student has an interest in the work they have devoted their career to, and will happily make time to meet with them. One effective way to make a connection with a potential mentor is to ask them for an informational interview where you speak with the lawyer about how she came to the role she plays in the profession, and seek advice about steps you can take to follow a similar path. In addition to obtaining the benefit of your mentor's insights and guidance, you may also learn a great deal about what it is like to practice in the mentor's field, which will help you learn if that area of practice would be a fit for you.

Every lawyer was once in your shoes, and many lawyers with long experience in the profession look for ways to mentor new members of the profession. Let yourself benefit from mentoring opportunities when they present themselves. By engaging with mentors, you learn from their experience, you expand your circle of wise advisors, and you develop lifelong friendships.

C. BECOMING AN EMPATHETIC PROBLEM SOLVER

When we consider the qualities of great lawyers in history, we often celebrate traits such as integrity, courage, discipline, and tenacity. These are each important qualities of effective lawyers. However, the best lawyers are first and foremost counselors who train themselves to understand as richly as possible every dimension of a client's experience and the problem the client has come to them to have solved.[1]

Clients seek the assistance of lawyers often in the most challenging times of their lives, and they come to lawyers with a limited understanding of the legal context of their problems. Often, their understanding of the work lawyers do comes from popular media sources that do not present the full array of tools at a lawyer's disposal to resolve a problem. Therefore, it is incumbent upon lawyers to develop the skills that permit them to discover all of the dimensions of the client's problem in order to craft a strategy for solving the problem in a way that addresses all of the elements of the client's needs.

The key to being an effective counselor is empathy. The Oxford English Dictionary defines empathy as the "power of mentally identifying oneself with (and so fully comprehending) a person."[2] Employing an empathetic approach with clients invites them to open up and share more fully. A lawyer's office can be a very intimidating place for a client, and any steps you can take to minimize the client's anxiety about the counseling experience will help you learn as much as possible about their situation so you can craft an effective solution. For example, a client who has suffered a financial and emotional loss might conclude that the only resolution available would be through litigation and a judgment for money damages. However, money damages may not address the emotional loss the client

---

[1]   *See* Chapter 3 on Intercultural Competence.
[2]   THE NEW SHORTER OXFORD ENGLISH DICTIONARY (1993).

has suffered. A more complete and effective resolution of this client's problem would certainly address not only the financial loss, but also the emotional loss. A lawyer who employs the tools of an empathetic problem solver can craft a resolution for the client that delivers not only a financial recovery, but also some measure of redress for the emotional loss. Developing the skill of being an empathetic lawyer takes time and practice, but it is essential to becoming an effective lawyer.

D. BEING DILIGENT AND CAREFUL

Being a lawyer is a lot of work. You will have to balance dozens of files at once, likely for different clients with different needs—all of whom will expect your best performance. And the work will not be easy. It will involve researching complex issues and critically analyzing the law and, depending on your practice area, clearly and concisely conveying your legal analyses and arguments in writing, drafting complicated contracts, or writing nuanced policies. All of these tasks will need to be performed in compliance with statutes of limitations, court rules and deadlines, and contract requirements—or the work could be for naught. If you do not file a claim on behalf of your client within the statute of limitations, the claim will be barred. If you submit a document to court that does not comply with the word limit or is submitted late, it could be rejected. And, if you attempt to renew a contract on behalf of your client by email rather than the prescribed certified mail, the contract could lapse.

Meeting these demands requires a lawyer to be diligent and careful. A lawyer must constantly ask herself: Have I canvassed the law relevant to my client's issue, carefully read and understood it, and thoughtfully applied it to my client's situation? Have I complied with all court rules regarding formatting and submission requirements? Have I failed to address any important considerations in this contract negotiation? Have I carefully reviewed this contract to ensure that a misplaced comma has not changed the intended meaning of a particular clause? Have I calendared all relevant deadlines so that all of this work is completed on time? Without hard work and attention to detail, the answer to some of these questions will be "no," and at a significant cost to your client.

Law school provides you with a glimpse into this world. Completing the reading and writing assignments for your various classes on time and to the best of your ability will be difficult. It will require you to be diligent and careful. You must ask yourself: Have I carefully read and understood the assigned materials for today's classes? Have I thought about how the concepts I learned would apply to different hypotheticals that my professor might pose in class? Have I conveyed the results of my research and analysis in writing in a clear, concise, and grammatically-correct manner? Have I reviewed the instructions for formatting and submitting my assignment? Have I calendared all relevant deadlines so that all of this work is completed on time?

If your answer to any of these questions is "no," it will reflect solely on you. As discussed above, however, the stakes are raised in practice when you are acting on behalf of a client. Therefore, you need to develop the strong work ethic and attention to detail required to answer each of these questions with a "yes" so you will be prepared for the even greater demands—and consequences—you will face as a practicing attorney.

E. TIMELINESS

In a recent national survey of over 24,000 lawyers from various practice areas and work settings, timeliness—i.e., "[a]rriv[ing] on time for meetings, appointments, and hearings"—was ranked as the second-most necessary competency for new lawyers to possess, just behind the ability to keep information confidential.[3] This makes sense, given the signal of disrespect a late arrival sends to clients, colleagues, and the court, and the potentially devastating consequences of such behavior. Arriving late to an appointment with a client says that you are either disorganized or have better things to do, neither of which engenders trust and either of which may cause the client to find a lawyer who will take the matter more seriously. Arriving late to meetings with your colleagues says that your time is more important than theirs and is likely to strain the working environment. And, arriving late to a court hearing tells the court that you are unable to follow court orders, and could result in your matter being struck from the calendar or in you being held in contempt of court.

How can you avoid these pitfalls in your career? Make timeliness a habit, and start now. The bottom line is that there really is no excuse for being the person who is always running late and wasting other people's time, so don't be that person. Treat your get-togethers with friends like they are appointments with clients, treat your study group sessions like they are meetings with colleagues, and treat your classes like they are hearings with the court. In each of those scenarios, abide by the maxim that to be early is to be on time, to be on time is to be late, and to be late is just not acceptable. And, on the (what should be) rare occasion that you are running late, find a way to get a message to whomever is waiting for you, and apologize when you arrive.

F. ADHERING TO THE GOLDEN RULE

You know the Golden Rule: treat others as you would like to be treated. Do not make the mistake of thinking this rule does not apply to you now that you are in law school or once you become a lawyer. And, if you have

---

[3]   INSTITUTE FOR THE ADVANCEMENT OF THE AMERICAN LEGAL SYSTEM, FOUNDATIONS FOR PRACTICE: THE WHOLE LAWYER AND THE CHARACTER QUOTIENT 26 (July 2016).

forgotten about this rule somewhere along the way, now is a good time to start holding yourself accountable. Your success as a lawyer—in both the short and long term—will depend on your ability to build and maintain relationships, and the fastest way to burn a bridge with someone is to treat that person in a discourteous or disrespectful manner.

So, treat *everyone* with the courtesy and respect that you expect in return; today: your classmates and professors, law school staff and administrative personnel, mentors and alumni, judicial and law firm personnel who assist you in setting up externships and interviews, and everyone else with whom you interact; tomorrow: your colleagues, superiors, subordinates, assistants, opponents, judicial personnel . . . the list is endless. But, you get the idea: no person's role is too insignificant to deserve your respect.

You will not always find it easy to follow the Golden Rule as a practicing attorney. For example, you may encounter an opposing counsel who seems to be intentionally delaying resolution of a dispute, refuses a reasonable request for an extension of a deadline, or treats you with condescension. It can be difficult not to respond in kind to this sort of disrespectful behavior. But, try to avoid hitting "send" on that anger-induced reply email or raising your voice in frustration. Take a deep breath, remind yourself of your end-goal of reaching the best result for your client, and re-evaluate your response. Responding in kind will only exacerbate the situation, but adhering to your own standards of conduct will allow you to remain in control.

G. OWNING UP TO MISTAKES

Many junior attorneys have experienced the dread of turning an assignment in to a supervising attorney and then discovering a mistake. It happens. The goal, of course, is to not submit assignments containing mistakes, but that is not always possible. What should a junior attorney do once he discovers a mistake in work product he has created? The answer is much harder than it sounds: you must immediately inform the supervising attorney. If you do not, it puts the case and your employer at risk. Be up front. Be candid.

One of the main reasons to be forthcoming when you have made a mistake (other than general ethical behavior) is that junior associates typically do not have the experience or frame of reference to adequately determine if a mistake requires corrective action. Typical mistakes that junior associates tend to make include substantive errors in memoranda and motions, billing mistakes, failure to read local rules and procedures, inadvertently disclosing confidential information, and failing to ask questions when something is unclear. Of course, this list is by no means exhaustive. So, which of these mistakes is most important? Least important? It depends. And as a junior attorney, your supervising attorney is the only person with the perspective and authority to make that determination.

The key to reporting an error is timeliness. It feels awful to go to the person or persons you work for and say, "I screwed up." It is easy to put it off until tomorrow or even next week. Do not fall into that trap. Some errors can be fixed if caught quickly. Some more weighty errors require significant thought and discussion to figure out how to best remedy the situation. Either way, you should report the error as soon as possible so that it can be cured as soon as possible if necessary. One last thing: it helps to have a suggested "fix" for the error when you speak to your supervising attorney about the error. Try to include your suggested remedy immediately after reporting the error. Self-reporting takes guts, but it is absolutely essential to maintain credibility with your bosses and to appropriately represent your clients.

H. SELF-DIRECTEDNESS

The flip side of the owning-your-mistakes coin is self-directedness. It can be irritating and inefficient when a supervising attorney has to constantly provide direction to junior attorneys, even for menial tasks. While it is definitely important to ask questions of more experienced attorneys, like clarifying directions on assignments, doing so can also become a distraction and make a junior attorney appear needy or incompetent. Junior attorneys should refrain from asking supervising attorneys questions that the junior attorney could have quickly and easily found with a little effort. How can junior attorneys determine what kinds of questions are appropriate?

The general rule has to be that if you do not know, ask. That is the baseline. But there are certainly times where questions are not important enough to ask a supervising attorney or the answer can be found elsewhere instead of interrupting a supervising attorney. They are busy people. Questions pertaining to office procedures, supplies, printing instructions, and the like can easily be handled by someone other than a supervising attorney. On the other hand, junior attorneys are better off asking a question than to spend hours researching an issue that the supervising attorney did not have in mind when assigning the task. So, the more substantive a question is, the more appropriate it is to seek guidance from a supervising attorney. Law or legal-based questions, of course, should be asked of senior attorneys. But a junior attorney should always consider whether the question can be handled by someone other than a supervising attorney before going to that attorney, such as another attorney of similar seniority, paralegals, legal secretaries, and the like. If the answer can be found easily, take the initiative and show that you are a self-directed employee. If it cannot or you are not sure, ask the supervising attorney.

I. SOCIAL MEDIA BEHAVIOR

Some of the following is common sense. Most readers understand the importance of online behavior and how it can impact a career. There are at least two important considerations that budding lawyers must confront: past social media content and formulating a professional identity going forward. These concerns are equally important for your job search and interviewing process, as well as after you land a job.

Do not think for a second that modern legal employers will not look at, and actively search for, your online presence. And, no matter how well you think you have hidden spring break photos from six years ago, they can still be found. What can you do? If you have social media content that you are not comfortable with a potential legal employer viewing, you should delete the post at the very least. There are also programs and services beginning to pop up that claim to be able to "scrub" your online history. The best scenario is that all of your past online content is benign. If that is the case, then you have nothing to worry about. If it is not the case, consider how you can delete, remove, or modify content that might be objectionable to a future employer.

Going forward, there are steps you can take to make your social media presence appealing to a potential legal employer. Consider creating and posting content that is relevant to a particular area of the law that might appeal to legal employers you have identified. Stories abound of law students who blogged or otherwise commented on a legal topic and landed jobs out of law school in that same area. In fact, with modern blog platforms, it is not particularly challenging to set up a blog to create content that an employer might find intriguing. Even if you decide to keep legal content out of your online presence going forward, consider social media a marketing tool. Use it to show who you are, what you enjoy, and what your legal interests are. Someone will notice, and that person just might be your future employer.

J. FINDING YOUR PASSION

Law students are often encouraged to follow their passion in choosing an area of study and a career path in law school. Some law students enter law school with a highly developed interest in a specific area of law, and that passion will guide them through law school and into their professional lives. Others have a passion for social justice, or for certain types of legal practice, such as trial advocacy or transactional work. However, most law students do not have such clearly-defined passions when they start law school. Rather, most law students enter law school knowing only what they have learned from film and television about the work lawyers do, and they often feel they need to aspire to similar missions in their career path.

The reality of the profession is that there is a vast array of pathways for lawyers, most of which are never depicted on television and in the movies. It is important to approach the process of your legal education as an opportunity to explore the spectrum of career paths that others in the profession have taken before you, and to discover your highest and best use in the profession. Law school presents opportunities to discover interests and passions that you may not have been aware of before. The work you do in law school in learning the principles of law, the process of legal analysis, and the skills of oral advocacy and client counseling may spark insights into strengths and interests you did not know you had. Making yourself open to personal and professional growth in law school can lead you, sometimes unexpectedly, on a career path you would never have imagined before.

It is also important to approach your professional development with patience. Passion for a pursuit can come in many forms: passion for writing a well-reasoned, flawless brief; for concluding a well-crafted transaction; or for achieving an effective outcome for a client in a negotiation. It can propel you on a path for a lifetime, or for much briefer periods of time. Careers in the law are a lifetime in the making, and few lawyers end up in the same job in which they started when they graduated from law school. While passion can be a useful guide, it is equally important to focus on other motivators as well. Finding purposefulness in the work you do from day to day is key to success. If you feel the work you are doing on a day-to-day basis serves a larger purpose, then that is a legacy worthy of your effort.

PRACTICE EXERCISE

Choose two of the Top Ten practices discussed above that you believe you most need to work on. For each, write a paragraph that explains why you think you need to work on that skill or quality. Then, state a concrete, manageable goal for yourself that is related to development of that skill or quality, and develop a specific plan for achieving that goal. In other words, what steps will you take to reach your goal? Finally, pick a date midway through the semester at which you will evaluate your progress toward goal attainment.

For example, are you the person who is always running behind, and you know you need to work on timeliness? If so, one goal might be to not be late to your study group meetings anymore. And, to achieve that goal, you might take the following steps: (1) calendar all study group meetings; (2) set a reminder on your phone to alert you of upcoming meetings; (3) schedule your time so that you arrive five minutes early for each meeting; and (4) keep track of whether you were on time to each meeting. When it comes time for your self-evaluation, you will be able to determine whether you have achieved your goal. If you have not, you should think about why you did not achieve it and how you can adjust your plan going forward. Then, keep trying!

CHAPTER 5

RULES: AN OVERVIEW OF STATUTORY INTERPRETATION AND SYNTHESIS

■ ■ ■

By Adrienne Brungess

A. STATUTORY INTERPRETATION OVERVIEW

Sometimes a statute's language is straightforward and thus its meaning is clear. More frequently, however, statutory language contains ambiguity that must be resolved by a court. Statutory interpretation is the process by which courts interpret and apply legislation. There are a variety of tools judges use to determine the meaning of statutes, including traditional canons of statutory construction, legislative history, and analysis of the statute's purpose. Further, every state and the federal government have codified rules of statutory interpretation.[1]

Consider for a moment why a legislature might use ambiguous language when crafting a statute—ambiguities can allow for changes to the meaning of language over time and for adaptation of the language to new situations and technologies. Ambiguity allows courts to determine how particular language of a statute should be applied and enforced.

The process of interpretation begins with careful examination of the text of the statute and inferences based on the structure and composition of the statute.[2] Start by reading the statute carefully. Pay particular attention to the legislature's use of select words: "and," "or," "shall," or "may."

- "and" will tend to mean the statute has conjunctive (mandatory) components
- "or" probably means the statute has disjunctive components[3]

---

[1] Jacob Scott, *Codified Canons and the Common Law of Interpretation*, 98 GEO. L.J. 341, 350 (2010).

[2] NORMAN J. SINGER & J.D. SHAMBIE SINGER, 2A SUTHERLAND STATUTORY CONSTRUCTION § 47:1 (7th ed. 2007).

[3] *See* Chapter 6 on Legal Reasoning and Analysis.

- "shall" indicates a mandate

- "may" indicates a permissive component

Courts begin the statutory interpretation process with the foundational doctrine of "plain meaning." To define and apply a provision the legislature left undefined, courts look initially to the "plain" or "ordinary" meaning. If the plain meaning is evident and the words are clear, the court must enforce it according to its ordinary terms.[4] Thus, if the statutory language is clear, the court should not look outside the statute to the legislative history or purpose to define the term.[5] This foundational principle of interpretation is crucial to the court's interpretation because it provides the basis for application of the court's other interpretive tools.[6] To determine ordinary meaning, the court will typically start with a dictionary or common sense definition.[7]

In the case of ambiguity, courts apply canons of construction that serve as general rules or presumptions that help the court determine substantive meaning from the language, context, and structure of a statute.[8] "Thus, the canons form a body of interpretive common law that legitimizes sources and methods of legal reasoning, all with an eye toward how the legislature would want its intent to be effectuated."[9]

Courts will read the statute as a whole and in light of the broader context of an entire act. Ambiguity can be resolved when viewed with the rest of the statutory scheme and the same terminology may be used elsewhere in a context that is clearer; conversely, viewing a term in isolation may have effects that are incompatible with the rest of the statute.[10] Further, courts distinguish between terms of art that may have specialized meanings and other words that are ordinarily given a dictionary definition.[11]

There are two basic categories of canons: extrinsic tools that look outside the text to its underlying purpose and intrinsic tools that look for meaning in the structure of the text and conventional definitions.[12]

---

[4]   *See* Caminetti v. United States, 242 U.S. 470 (1917)

[5]   *See* Yule Kim, *Congressional Research Service Report for Congress—Statutory Interpretation: Principles & Recent Trends,* available at https://fas.org/sgp/crs/misc/97-589.pdf (Updated December 19, 2011) (last visited Feburary 14, 2018).

[6]   Brian G. Slocum, *Linguistics and 'Ordinary Meaning' Determinations,* STATUTE L. REV., Oxford University, 3, (Dec. 8, 2011) available at SSRN: http://ssrn.com/abstract=1970012 (last visited December 20, 2017).

[7]   *Id.* at 4.

[8]   Scott, *supra* note 1, at 344.

[9]   *Id.* at 346.

[10]   SINGER & SINGER, *supra* note 2, at § 47:6; United Savings Ass'n v. Timbers of Inwood Forest Associates, 484 U.S. 365, 371 (1988).

[11]   SINGER & SINGER, *supra* note 2, at § 47:27–47:31.

[12]   *Id.* at § 45:14.

Primary sources, such as statutory definitions sections and case law, might include instructions regarding how particular terms should be interpreted. Definitions sections suggest what the legislating body intended a term to mean. Court opinions may consider the statute's legislative history, or review other useful authority, when interpreting a statutory provision.[13] This can include inquiry into the events that led up to a bill's introduction in the legislature and statements made, actions taken during the bill's consideration, and post-enactment history.[14] Such an extrinsic inquiry might be necessary when more than one meaning is reasonable or application of a particular intrinsic canon is unclear; generally this is only undertaken when the meaning of a statute is ambiguous.[15]

Courts also employ intrinsic canons that analyze the meaning of ambiguous statutory text by reviewing all the language of the statute and statutory scheme. Consider first the "Whole Act Rule." This rule provides that the text of the entire statute, as a whole, must be considered when interpreting ambiguous language. Therefore, if a word is used multiple times in the same statutory enactment, it is presumed to have the same meaning each time. Provisions should not be interpreted inconsistently with other provisions in the same statute.[16] Next, courts may apply the "Rule to Avoid Surplusage." The foundational principle of this rule is that every word or phrase in the statute is meaningful and necessary; any interpretation that would render a word or phrase meaningless should be rejected.[17]

Some additional commonly applied intrinsic canons, which are more complicated to employ, include:

- *expressio unius:* The inclusion of one thing indicates exclusion of others. Where the statute provides a list of designated things, all omissions should be considered intentionally excluded.[18] This canon is often applied when the statutory language uses words like "includes" or "such as."

  o For example: A state prisoner brought a habeas action under a federal code section (§ 2254). The Federal Rules of Criminal Procedure do not apply to habeas petitions

---

[13]   Slocum, *supra* note 6, at 5–6.

[14]   SINGER & SINGER, *supra* note 2, at § 48:1.

[15]   *Id.*

[16]   *See* William N. Eskridge, Jr., *The New Textualism & Normative Canons*, YALE LAW SCHOOL FACULTY SCHOLARSHIP SERIES, PAPER 4795, available at http://digitalcommons.law.yale.edu/fss_papers/4795 (2013).

[17]   Katherine Clark & Matthew Connolly, *A Guide to Reading, Interpreting, & Applying Statutes*, available at https://www.law.georgetown.edu/academics/academic-programs/legal-writing-scholarship/writing-center/upload/statutoryinterpretation.pdf, p. 7 (The Writing Center at GULC 2006).

[18]   Scott, *supra* note 1, at 352, note 42; *see also* SINGER & SINGER, *supra* note 2, at § 47:23.

brought by state prisoners; a different statute, § 2255, governs habeas petitions by federal prisoners. Under § 2255, a judge is allowed to conduct discovery under either the Federal Rules of Criminal Procedure or Civil Procedure. By contrast, § 2254 permits discovery only under the Federal Rules of Civil Procedure. The state prisoner argued that since no authority expressly prohibits application of the Federal Rules of Criminal Procedure to a state prisoner's petition, he should be permitted to apply them in his case. The court concluded such an interpretation conflicted with the maxim of *expressio unius*; the inclusion of the Federal Rules of Criminal Procedure in § 2255 was intentional and thus so was the omission of the same in § 2254.[19]

- *noscitur a sociis:* When a term is ambiguous, its meaning may be determined by reference to its relationship with other associated words and phrases. Thus, a word may be defined by an accompanying word.[20] This doctrine is applied when interpreting terms that are grouped together with other similar terms; the adjacent terms offer clues regarding how broadly or narrowly to interpret the ambiguous term.[21]

   o   For example: The False Claims Act (FCA) contains a "public disclosure bar" that forecloses private parties from bringing suits that are based on government agency's public disclosure of transactions in a government "report, hearing, audit, or investigation, or from the news media."[22] When a complainant supported his suit using a written response from the Labor Department to requests made under the Freedom of Information Act (FOIA), the Supreme Court applied this canon. The Court held that since the FCA does not define "report," the court should look first to the plain meaning. The Court then applied *noscitur a sociis*, determining that the response fell within the broad, ordinary meaning of "report." The Court concluded that FCA's inclusion of disclosure by way of "news media" indicated a broad scope to the disclosure bar.[23]

- *ejusdem generis:* Meaning "of the same kind." When a statute uses specific terms followed by general terms, the general

---

[19]   *See* Copeland v. Ryan, 852 F.3d 900, 906–07 (9th Cir. 2017).

[20]   SINGER & SINGER, *supra* note 2, at § 47:16.

[21]   Clark & Connolly, *supra* note 17, at p. 6.

[22]   31 U.S.C. § 3730(e)(4)(A) (2017).

[23]   Schindler Elevator Corp. v. United States ex rel. Kirk, 131 S. Ct. 1885, 1890–96 (2011).

terms are construed consistently with those objects enumerated by the preceding specific words. This is a common and intentional drafting technique that allows the legislature to avoid spelling out in advance every contingency in which the statute could apply.[24] This canon may be applied when interpreting loosely written statutes that list classes of persons or things.

o For example: Federal code section 18 U.S.C. § 1715 prohibits the mailing of pistols, revolvers, and "other firearms capable of being concealed on the person." A defendant was convicted under this statute for having mailed a 22-inch sawed-off shotgun. There was evidence at trial that the gun could be concealed. The Supreme Court determined that under the rule of *ejusdem generis*, the statute applied to sawed-off shotguns; the use of the word "firearms" followed by "pistols and revolvers" did not limit firearms under this statute to only pistols and revolvers. Although ordinarily general terms are limited to the specific terms the follow, it should not be used to defeat the purpose of the legislation, which in this case was to prohibit mailing of concealable weapons.[25]

- *reddendo singula singulis:* The limited or restrictive clauses in a statute refer to, limit, and restrict the immediately preceding clause or the last antecedent.[26] Where words are found at the beginning of a clause, it is not necessary that each word apply to all later branches of the clause. This canon is applied when the opening words of a section are general and the succeeding components regulate particular instances.

o For example: a criminal statute provided: "Kidnapping is the unlawful taking, restraining or confining of a person, by force or deception, with intent that the victim be held for ransom, as a hostage, confined against his will, or to be held to service against the victim's will."[27] The court applied the canon of *reddendo singula singulis*, confirming that when a statutory rule contains multiple antecedents, they are to be read distributively. In evaluating whether "intent" applied to all of the components that followed it, the court concluded: "there must be an intent to confine against the victim's will when he is taken, restrained or confined with intent that

---

[24] SINGER & SINGER, *supra* note 2, at § 47:17.

[25] United States v. Powell, 423 U.S. 87, 90–91 (1975).

[26] SINGER & SINGER, *supra* note 2, at § 47:26.

[27] N.M. Stat. Ann.§ 40A–4–1 (1953) (later amended and renumbered: 1978, § 30–4–1).

he be held for ransom, or as a hostage, but it is not
necessary that he be confined against his will when the
purpose of the taking, restraining or confining is that the
victim be held to service against his will. Merely to
confine or restrain against a person's will without the
requisite intention is not kidnapping."[28]

Legal analysts should be cautious, however, when attempting to
interpret statutory language. Each canon is "correct"; however, application
of different canons may lead to varying results. Further, it is not always
clear which canon to apply and the textual meaning is arguably incomplete
without some context of the statute's purpose or objective.[29] Therefore,
when applying canons of construction, consider what makes sense in the
situation and opt for simple construction, given the language provided, that
achieves that end.[30]

1.   CROSS-CULTURAL CONSIDERATIONS IN STATUTORY INTERPRETATION

Statutory interpretation canons are techniques implemented in
common law jurisdictions, such as the United States. Such interpretation
may be considered unnecessary in civil law countries.[31] Civil law countries
may not require this kind of interpretation; the words used by the
legislature are considered approximate. Thus, the text is considered a
starting point for the court, even if the text seems clear and the literal
meaning may not be decisive, thereby making formal canons
unnecessary.[32] Express words may logically have implied meanings;
although a word may cause ambiguity, the word itself may be insignificant
and therefore will be viewed in a verbal context.[33] Additionally, a civil law
court does not generally consider meaning in the abstract but rather in the
specific factual context of the case before it[34] (as a civil law court's decision

---

[28]   State v. Clark, 80 N.M. 340 (1969).

[29]   Karl N. Llewellyn, *Remarks on the Theory of Appellate Decision and the Rules or Canons
About How Statutes Are to be Construed*, 3 VAND. L. REV. 395, 400, 401–406 (1950) (identifying 28
different correct but conflicting canons of construction).

[30]   *Id.* at 401 (emphasis in original).

[31]   *See* Michael Murray, *Explanatory Synthesis and Rule Synthesis: A Comparative Civil Law
and Common Law Analysis*, 83–84 Bahçeşehir Üniversitesi Hukuk Fakültesi-Kazancı Hukuk
Dergisi 139, 141 (2011) (stating that in common law jurisdictions, judges are empowered to create
and change law through case adjudication and written opinions that act as legal precedent for
future cases; however, judges in civil law jurisdictions are not so empowered and are to read and
apply the law enacted by the legislature without change, with judicial decisions having no binding
effect on later cases).

[32]   *See* Francis Bennion, BENNION ON STATUTE LAW 83 (3d ed. 1990) available at www.
francisbennion.com Doc. No. 1990.002.082.

[33]   *Id.* at 84.

[34]   *Id.* at 93–94.

does not have the same precedential value that it would have in a common law jurisdiction).

Consider also the role of public values in judicial interpretation of statutes: the legal norms and principles of a society and the values that a particular culture considers just and good for all.[35] Public values vary among different cultures and thus when applied can lead to differing results.

PRACTICE EXAMPLE

A skilled legal analyst and advocate will consider how the court will interpret a statute when determining how to advise a client or when preparing for argument.

Read this statutory language:

> **18 U.S.C.A. § 924(c)(1)(A)** Except to the extent that a greater minimum sentence is otherwise provided by this subsection or by any other provision of law, any person who, during and in relation to any crime of violence or drug trafficking crime (including a crime of violence or drug trafficking crime that provides for an enhanced punishment if committed by the use of a deadly or dangerous weapon or device) for which the person may be prosecuted in a court of the United States, uses or carries a firearm, or who, in furtherance of any such crime, possesses a firearm, shall, in addition to the punishment provided for such crime of violence or drug trafficking crime
>
> **(i)** be sentenced to a term of imprisonment of not less than 5 years;
>
> **(ii)** if the firearm is brandished, be sentenced to a term of imprisonment of not less than 7 years; and
>
> **(iii)** if the firearm is discharged, be sentenced to a term of imprisonment of not less than 10 years.

Your client's facts: Police officers found a handgun locked in the glove compartment of Smith's truck; he was using the truck to transport marijuana for sale. Under this statute, is Smith subject to the mandatory sentence, if found guilty of drug trafficking?

B. SYNTHESIZING RULES FROM CASE LAW

Since statutory language is frequently vague and contains ambiguities, you will need to find judicial opinions that interpret and apply the statutory language. Alternatively, there may not be a statute on point at all, and the topic may be governed by case law only. In either situation, it is common to find several cases relevant to the topic and jurisdiction that

---

[35] William Eskridge, Jr., *Public Values in Statutory Interpretation*, 137 U. PA. L. REV. 1007, 1008 (1989).

address different factual situations or evolving interpretations of a legal principle. To determine the applicable legal principle, you need to combine the information from the various cases to generate a complete rule you will ultimately use to analyze your assigned legal question. This is the process of synthesis: integrating legal principles from several sources.

Once you have located the cases that govern your legal issue, it is important to first determine the legal principle from each of those cases. Occasionally, the court will articulate a clear rule of law. When the court has articulated a rule clearly, the text can be synthesized by first locating the common language from all of the cases on point and then considering what is different or similar in each opinion. However, when the court does not articulate a clear rule, you may have to infer the legal principle based on the facts, holding, reasoning, or policy.

Once you understand the cases that govern your legal issue, you must next understand how the cases work together. Rules frequently evolve as more cases make their way through the appellate court system. Synthesis requires you to identify what the different opinions have in common. It is also important to focus on components that have predictive value for the factual situation you are being asked to analyze. Failure to synthesize governing case law leads to piecemeal application of case holdings, rather than application of rule components that consider the rule's evolution over time. A case may still contain "good law" while one part of its reasoning has been further developed or adjusted to consider different facts or policy considerations. Piecemeal application of case holdings usually leads to flawed conclusions.

A good place to start is by arranging the cases you have located hierarchically and chronologically. Also, separate binding case law from persuasive authority.[36] Charting your sources can help organize the relevant portions of the opinions and allows you to see the commonalities.

---

[36] DEBORAH SCHMEDEMANN & CHRISTINA KUNZ, SYNTHESIS—LEGAL READING, REASONING, AND WRITING 43 (2d ed. 2004).

For example:

	Case 1	Case 2	Case 3
Date of Opinion			
Jurisdiction			
Key Facts			
Holding			
Reasoning			
Legal Principle from the case that has predictive value for your legal issue			

The following steps can help you synthesize your rule. First, consider the language used in each opinion—if the courts all use identical language, that language should ultimately be part of your final synthesized rule. Next, determine what language is similar, but not identical. Determine whether a broader term can accurately encompass the similar terminology used; if it can, use that new term in your synthesized rule.[37] If not, choose among the different terms and include what is necessary to ensure the rule remains accurate based on the case holdings and predictive based on the legal question you are evaluating.

Next, look for language that appears only in one or some of the opinions. Consider how this language works with the rule you have crafted so far and whether addition of the language would change how your rule is applied—e.g., would a case that does not include that language have been decided differently if that language had been applied? If the answer is no, then this language can be added. If the answer is yes, then the new language probably creates a disjunctive rule element and should be phrased appropriately.[38] The new language may result from a new factual situation that appears in a later case and thus the court was not required to consider it in earlier cases. Look past the court's holding and consider its reasoning and why the court altered the earlier version of the rule.

Ultimately, the synthesized rule should be stated simply and concisely so the reader can easily understand it. The rule should have predictive value for the next factual situation that arises—i.e., your client's situation. Most importantly, it must accurately reflect the governing law in the relevant jurisdiction such that when applied the rule will accurately predict the outcome of the next case.[39] Note also that a secondary source that discusses the legal topic you are analyzing may provide a synthesized

---

[37] *See Id.*

[38] *See Id.*

[39] *See* Paul Figley, *Teaching Rule Synthesis with Real Cases*, 61 J. LEGAL EDUC. 245 (2011).

rule, as well as references to the case law that provides the rule's components. Starting with a secondary source, like an encyclopedia or a law review article, may provide you a broad rule overview, and fuse together language from the relevant authorities, thereby providing foundational concepts you can develop and enhance with your own case research and analysis.[40]

1.   CROSS-CULTURAL CONSIDERATIONS IN RULE SYNTHESIS

Synthesis of precedent seems logical in the common law context. But what purpose does such synthesis serve in a civil law jurisdiction where *stare decisis* does not apply? The role synthesis plays will vary depending on the jurisdiction. Just because there is no common law does not necessarily mean the court will ignore precedent; it may still be valuable to the civil law judge's consideration of a case.

Although not binding, a civil law judge may find prior decisions persuasive with regard to defining or interpreting a rule. Also, a civil law court may rely on prior decisions as illustrative of reasoning and policy; thus, the precedent could be used as rationale without being relied upon as binding.[41] In such circumstances, rule synthesis does not create the legal authority governing the case but instead is used to explain and provide examples of situations to illustrate how the law has been applied. This kind of explanatory synthesis is demonstrative rather than controlling and can still be useful to the legal analyst and the court.[42] In this way, explanatory synthesis has greater flexibility; cases can be used for their storyline and the legal advocate is not limited to selecting cases strictly because they are mandatory.[43]

Furthermore, judicial culture and case reporting practices can limit the use of rule synthesis in legal analysis. Common law system opinions generally describe the background of the case with detail and include a discussion of the court's rationale, supported by citation to authority. Civil law system opinions are inconsistent with regard to background detail and rationale, and may not cite to authority at all.[44] This makes case synthesis difficult, particularly for use as a source of legal reasoning.

PRACTICE EXAMPLE

Your client's facts: Your client, Mrs. Johnson, made a public statement disparaging her neighbor, Mr. Thompson, a candidate for public office, and

---

[40]   *See* Chapter 25 on Research Strategies.
[41]   *See* Murray, *supra* note 31, at 146–149.
[42]   *Id.* at 149.
[43]   *Id.* at 154.
[44]   *Id.* at 156.

accusing him of criminal activity. At the time she made the statement, she was angry with him and she believed the statements to be true. However, she later discovered the statement was false and he had not engaged in any criminal activity. Mr. Thompson is now threatening to sue for defamation. Your assigning senior attorney has told you that Mr. Thompson will have to show that Mrs. Johnson acted with "actual malice" when she made the statements. The case would be filed in California state court.

Can Mr. Thompson prove actual malice? Create a synthesized rule from the following cases and make a prediction.

Case 1: *New York Times Co. v. Sullivan*, 376 U.S. 254 (1964).

Facts: Defendant The New York Times published an editorial advertisement communicating information about an elected commissioner of a city in Alabama. The advertisement contained an inaccurate information about the wrongs the city police and elected officials had committed against civil rights leaders, students, and organizations. Sullivan, an elected commissioner of the city, brought a civil libel action.

Holding: The evidence presented by Plaintiff Sullivan was constitutionally insufficient to support judgment in his favor.

Reasoning: Public discussion of the character and qualifications of candidates for public office is critical. Open discourse works to the benefit of society and the advantages derived from this public debate far outweighs the inconvenience that may be caused to private persons. "The occasional injury to the reputations of individuals must yield to the public welfare. . . ."

Legal Principle: A public official cannot recover damages for a defamatory falsehood relating to his official conduct unless he proves that the statement was made with "actual malice," that is, the statement was made with knowledge that it was false or with reckless disregard of whether it was false or not.

Case 2: *McCoy v. Hearst Corp.*, 42 Cal. 3d 835 (1986).

Facts: Defendant newspaper published allegations that Plaintiff McCoy engaged in corrupt police and prosecutorial activities. It was later determined the information given to the reporters who published the story was false.

Holding: Plaintiff failed to prove that Defendant acted with actual malice.

Reasoning: Defendant reasonably believed the information reported was true. The fact that it failed to investigate further and the fact that it may have harbored ill will toward Plaintiff was not sufficient to prove malice.

Legal Principle: Investigatory failures and evidence of ill will does not necessarily amount to "actual malice" for purposes of defamation.

Case 3: *Live Oak Publishing Co. v. Cohagan*, 234 Cal. App. 3d 1277 (3d Dist. 1991).

Facts: Plaintiff newspaper published a letter from Defendant reader as an advertisement, which later turned out to contain false information. Defendant claimed she believed the statements made in the letter were true.

Holding: Plaintiff could not establish actual malice.

Reasoning: Defendant actually believed the statements to be true when she made them. Although there was proof that she harbored some animosity, that ill will toward Plaintiff was only circumstantial evidence of actual malice. Ill will without knowledge of falsity does not amount to actual malice.

Legal Principle: Evidence of ill will is not sufficient to establish actual malice without knowledge of falsity of the statement made.

CHAPTER 6

LEGAL REASONING AND ANALYSIS TOOLKIT

■ ■ ■

By Stephanie J. Thompson

A. THE TOOLKIT GENERALLY

This chapter will introduce you to the various tools needed for effective legal reasoning and analysis in all types of legal writing. Subsequent chapters will provide you with different strategies on how to use these tools for the different types of legal writing, including objective writing, persuasive writing, and correspondence.

The key to using these tools is to be flexible and to learn what works best for you. If you are a holistic type of writer and learner, then you should take a holistic approach to using these tools. If you are a checklist or step-by-step writer and learner, then you should take that type of approach to using these tools.

B. ORGANIZATIONAL PARADIGMS

Lawyers and law-trained readers are busy. They like structure and have an expectation of how information will be delivered. As such, organizational structures—or writing paradigms—are used by most lawyers. These paradigms provide a consistent and expected structure to all forms of legal writing. When a busy lawyer picks up an objective memorandum written by a legal intern or a busy judge picks up a motion or memorandum of points and authorities submitted to the court, they already know (or expect) that the information the writer is conveying will have a certain organization. This allows lawyers, judges, and other law-trained readers to read and evaluate a document as quickly as possible.

1. THE OBJECTIVE PARADIGM

The acronym used for the objective legal writing paradigm is CREAC.[1] It stands for Conclusion, Rule, Explanation, Application, and Conclusion.

---

[1] It is important to note that there are various acronyms used for the objective legal writing paradigm, such as TREAC, IRAC, TREAT, CRAC. While the acronyms are different, the basic organizational structure is the same for each of these acronyms.

These components are explained in more detail below. However, it is important to first understand where CREAC is used. CREAC is not the organizational structure for an entire objective document. Instead, CREAC is used for each individual legal issue addressed in the Discussion section of an objective document. For example, if you are writing a formal memorandum (Chapter 10) or short-form memorandum (Chapter 11), you will have a Discussion section; this section is where CREAC is used.

Within the Discussion section, you may have multiple CREACs. Based on the issues you are addressing, you will need to decide how many CREACs to use. The general rule is to use one CREAC for each individual legal issue. This is not always a simple determination. To make this determination, you must completely understand the legal issues and rules you are addressing and the types of rules you are working with.[2]

For example, if the rule for the legal issue you are evaluating has four elements, then you likely will have four CREACs—one CREAC for each element. Or, if the legal rule for the legal issue you are evaluating does not have elements, but has two legal terms that require separate analysis or have specific legal definitions, then you likely will have two CREACs. But if the legal issue only has one component or a straightforward application of a legal rule, then you likely will have only one CREAC. Chapter 9 discusses objective writing in depth.

2. THE PERSUASIVE PARADIGM

The acronym used for the persuasive legal writing paradigm is CRAC.[3] It stands for Conclusion, Rule, Analysis, and Conclusion. As with the objective paradigm CREAC, it also is important to first understand where CRAC is used in your document and how many CRACs should be used. Just as CREAC is not the organizational structure for an entire objective memorandum, CRAC is not the organizational structure for an entire persuasive document. Instead, CRAC is used for each individual legal issue being addressed in the Argument section of a persuasive document.

For example, if you are writing a pre-trial motion or an appellate brief, you will have an Argument section; this section is where CRAC is used. Also, as with CREAC, the number of CRACs you will use in your Argument section will depend upon the legal issues and legal rules being analyzed in your Argument section. Chapter 16 discusses persuasive writing in depth.

While these paradigms provide a consistent and expected organization or structure to all forms of legal writing, the substance that is provided in each of the components of the paradigms will vary greatly based on the law

---

[2]   *See* Chapter 5 on Rules for more information on rule structures and rule synthesis.

[3]   There also are various acronyms used for the persuasive legal writing paradigm, such as TRAC, IRAC, TRAT. While the acronyms are different, the basic organizational structure is the same for each of these acronyms. Additionally, the acronym CRAC is often pronounced "C-RAC."

that is being applied, the facts of the client's case, and the different types of reasoning used based on your strategic decisions.

C. THE TOOLS IN THE TOOLKIT

The goal of this section is to introduce you to the various tools that can be used in your analysis of a legal issue and in your CREACs and CRACs. The strategies for using them will be discussed in the chapters dedicated to specific types of legal documents. Before you can use any of the tools effectively, however, you need to understand the tools themselves.

1. THE RULE OF LAW

Legal analysis is anchored by the rule of law. Without a rule, there cannot be legal analysis. Finding and writing the rule of law may be the most important step in building your legal analysis.

a. Finding and Synthesizing the Rule

The rule of law comes from primary authority. Primary authority consists of constitutions, statutes, cases, and administrative decisions and regulations. If the authority does not fall into one of these four categories, then it is not primary authority.

To determine the applicable rule of law, you will conduct research to find the relevant primary authorities. Once you have found the relevant primary authorities, you will need to determine if those authorities provide a clear and simple rule, or if you need to combine, or synthesize, several primary authorities to develop a complete rule.

Synthesis typically is the binding together of several cases to create a complete rule of law or expression of policy. Synthesis is not merely mentioning one case after another. For example, it is not synthesis to describe Case A, Case B, Case C, Case D, and then Case E. That is nothing more than an amplified list; the rules from the cases need to be bound together. To synthesize, step back and evaluate what the cases really have in common. Focus on the reasoning and key facts that the cases have in common to find and explain a collective meaning that is not apparent from the individual cases themselves.[4]

b. Identifying the Type of Rule

There are various types of rules. Knowing the type of rule you have is critical to your organization of how you write the rule, explain the rule, apply the rule, and decide how many paradigms (CREAC or CRAC) you will need to organize your analysis. A clear rule structure is fundamental to clear communication. The four most common types of rules are discussed

---

[4] *See* Chapter 5 on Rules for more discussion of rule synthesis.

below, but be aware that not all rules fall into one of these types of rules—
a rule may be a combination of these types of rules or something that has
yet to be categorized. The goal of identifying the type of rule is to help you
organize the analysis of the rule and to help you analyze your rule, not to
give it a label.

c. Simple Declarative Rule

A simple declarative rule is a rule that has no sub-parts, exceptions,
or other considerations. Essentially, the rule speaks for itself.

The following is an example of a simple declarative rule:

> It is illegal for anyone under the age of sixteen to operate a motor
> vehicle.

d. Conjunctive Rule

A conjunctive rule, or an "and" test, requires the satisfaction of all
parts, elements, or mandatory components of the rule. The rule cannot be
satisfied unless all of the parts, elements, or mandatory components of the
rule are satisfied. Sometimes, however, the court will say it is considering
"factors," but it may actually mean elements. You will need to read the
court's opinion critically and evaluate the context clues to determine if the
rule is a factors test or actually a conjunctive rule.

The following is an example of a conjunctive rule:

> A structure in the nature of a fence is covered under the spite fence
> statute if it unnecessarily exceeds six feet in height *and* its size, scale,
> *and* positioning on the land can be reasonably interpreted as a fence
> (emphasis added to highlight the conjunctive nature of the rule).

This is a conjunctive rule because for the rule to be satisfied the
structure must exceed six feet in height *and* its size, scale, *and* positioning
on the land can be reasonably interpreted as a fence. Thus, the rule is not
satisfied if it only meets the height requirement or if any one or more of the
size, scale and positioning requirements are not met. All parts must be
satisfied for the rule to apply.

When working with a conjunctive rule, there are important strategy
considerations to keep in mind. Specifically, for the party trying to apply
the rule to the facts, all parts of the conjunctive rule must be satisfied for
it to apply. However, the party opposing the application of the rule only
needs to disprove or defeat one element to prevail.

e.   Disjunctive Rule

A disjunctive rule, or an "either or" test, requires the satisfaction of only one part of the rule. The rule can be satisfied if only one or the other part of the test is met.

The following is an example of a disjunctive rule:

> One factor in determining whether a classification of persons qualifies as a quasi-suspect class under the Equal Protection Clause of the United States Constitution is whether the class of persons is a recognized minority group *or* is politically powerless (emphasis added to highlight the disjunctive nature of the rule).

This is a disjunctive rule because this factor can be satisfied if either the class of persons is a minority *or* if the class of persons is politically powerless; both are not required. From a strategy perspective, the party applying the rule can prove either the first part or the second part of the rule to prevail. The party opposing the application of the rule, however, needs to disprove or defeat both parts of the rule to prevail.

f.   Factors Tests and Balancing Tests

A factors test requires the court to evaluate various factors. "Factors" are distinguished from "elements" in that factors *may* be met for a rule to be satisfied, while elements *must* be met for a rule to be satisfied. In a factors test, typically a list of things to consider is provided. The key in a factors test is that no one listed factor carries more weight than any other listed factor. Indeed, the list may not even be exhaustive, but may only be intended to guide the decision on the issue presented. Each of the factors is considered with regard to the facts of the case to determine whether the rule has been satisfied or whether it is determinative of the issue presented.

A factors test allows for maximum flexibility because the factors that are most important in a given case will change with each factual situation and with the necessary considerations related to that situation.

The following is an example of a factors test:

> The determination of whether a worker is an employee or an independent contractor depends upon whether the employer has the right to control the worker, both as to the work done and the manner and means in which it is performed. Factors that may be considered for this determination are: whether the worker is engaged in an occupation or business distinct from that of the employer; whether the work is a part of the regular business of the employer; whether the employer or the worker supplies the instrumentalities, tools, and the place for the person doing the work; whether the employer requires the worker to purchase his own equipment or materials; whether the worker completes his work with or without supervision; whether the work requires a specialized skill; the length of time for which the services are to be performed; the degree of permanence of the working relationship; the method of payment, whether by time or by the job; and whether the parties believe they are creating an employer-employee relationship.

In applying this factors test, the court may look at some or all of these factors and may even consider factors not included in this list.

Balancing tests, on the other hand, require a choice between factors, with the one or more entitled to greater weight controlling the outcome of the issue.

In a balancing test the court must balance the rule's listed factors. The court would look at the quality of the support for each factor, the number of points that support one side or the other, and the overall factual and policy-based impact the competing factors has on the case.

The following is an example of a balancing test:

> In ruling on a motion to exclude evidence, the probative value of the evidence must be weighed against its potential prejudicial effect.

In using this balancing test, the court would look at the positive value of the offered evidence and balance it against the claimed prejudice it would create against the objecting party. The court would then rule on the admissibility of the evidence based on its determination of which of the potential effects of the evidence has more validity or is of greater concern.

2. WRITING THE RULE OF LAW

Depending on the type of rule you are working with, the length of your rule may range from one sentence to two paragraphs. A simple declarative rule typically is one sentence, or maybe two sentences. A factors test, however, may take at least a paragraph to comprehensively lay out the all of the factors for the reader.

The key to writing good rules is to be flexible—let the rule itself dictate how you write it and how long it will be. The goal in writing any rule is to communicate to your reader the substance of the rule itself, any applicable exceptions to the rule, and anything else a judge might consider in evaluating the rule.

3.   EXPLAINING THE RULE OF LAW

Most rules cannot be completely understood with a single sentence or a simple statement of the rule. It can happen on occasion, typically with a simple declarative rule, but the more normal course requires some type of explanation for each rule you include in your writing. Most readers expect an example of how the rule has been applied or interpreted by the courts. Remember, you have done all of the research on a particular issue and, as such, you have a level of knowledge about that issue that your reader does not have. You must assume that your reader only knows what you tell her.

There are two general types of rule explanation: a case illustration[5] or a parenthetical.

a.   Case Illustration Explanation of the Rule of Law

A case illustration is a detailed description of a precedent case that provides the reader with an example of how the rule was applied by the court in another case. In describing the precedent case, the case illustration should include information regarding the issue before the court, the facts, the holding, the reasoning, and the conclusion of the precedent case. Keep in mind, however, that a case illustration is not a case summary. Instead, when providing information about the issue before the court, the facts, the holding, the reasoning, and the conclusion of the precedent case, the information provided should be focused only on the particular legal issue being explained as relevant to your analysis.

Assume, for example, that you have a case where the speed at which your client was driving her car at the time of her accident was relevant. You found a rule regarding the speed at which a car can lawfully be driven in relation to the posted speed limit. This rule has various elements and exceptions. Based on the facts of your case, and the topic of your CREAC, you decide to provide a case illustration to give a specific example of when driving at the posted speed limit is legally unreasonable. The precedent case you decide to use discusses the entire rule regarding the speed at which a car is driven in relation to the posted speed limit, including a

---

[5]   Case illustrations also are frequently called "in-text" illustrations. This book uses the term case illustration.

discussion of when driving at the posted speed is unreasonable. Your case illustration, however, will only focus on the driving at the posted speed is unreasonable part of the rule because that is the only issue relevant to your client's case. That is, when providing information about the issue before the court, the facts, the holding, the reasoning, and the conclusion of the precedent case, the information provided will be focused only on the court's discussion of when driving at the posted speed is unreasonable.

The following is an example of a case illustration:

> Driving at the posted speed limit is unreasonable when conditions require a lesser speed. *Harris v. Ball*, 79 Cal. 2d 555 (1975). In *Harris*, the parents of a ten-year-old child sued the driver of a vehicle that struck and seriously injured the child as she was crossing a county road at a school bus stop. It was raining heavily at the time. The road was hilly, and there was a curve a short distance before the bus stop in the direction from which the defendant was traveling. The defendant was very familiar with the road as he lived about two miles past the site of the accident. He was driving at the posted speed limit of 40 mph. When the defendant saw the flashing lights of the school bus, he slammed on the brakes and swerved to the left to avoid hitting the bus, striking the child as she crossed the road. *Id.* at 556.
>
> In holding that the defendant was negligent even though he was driving at the posted speed limit, the court reasoned that he had been traveling at a speed that was too great to enable him to stop in time to avoid hitting the bus, even though it was in compliance with the posted speed limit. His vision was reduced because of the heavy downpour. In addition, the court reasoned, because he was familiar with the road and living nearby, he must have been aware of the presence of the school bus stop. Given these facts, his speed at the time of the accident was unreasonable. *Id.* at 557.

b. Parenthetical Explanation of the Rule of Law

A parenthetical is like a case illustration in that it provides the reader with an example of how the rule was applied in another case, but it is much shorter than a case illustration. A parenthetical can be thought of as a quick "hey-by-the-way" example, rather than an example you want the reader to focus on, such as a case illustration. Because it is a short example, a parenthetical usually is not a complete sentence but only a short descriptive phrase that provides the holding of the court and the relevant facts. Additionally, it is called a parenthetical because it is included in parenthesis at the end of a citation.

For example, a rule with a parenthetical may read as follows. The first sentence is the rule and the information in the parenthesis is the parenthetical explanation:

> A structure in the nature of a fence is covered under the spite fence statute if it unnecessarily exceeds six feet in height and its size, scale, and positioning on the land can be reasonably interpreted as a fence. *Dowdell v. Bloomquist*, 847 A.2d 827 (2004) (holding a row of four trees with a height exceeding 60 feet and spanning 40 feet along the neighbor's property line was a structure in the nature of a fence).

If you find that you cannot communicate your "hey-by-the-way" example in the concise manner required for a parenthetical, then do not force it into a parenthetical. Step back and ask yourself what it is that you are trying to provide to your reader with the explanation. If you only want to give a quick example, use a parenthetical. If you want to provide a more detailed example, use a case illustration. If you are using analogical reasoning (discussed below), in most instances you would need to use a case illustration, because a parenthetical would not provide enough detail to permit a close comparison of the facts and of the court's reasoning.

4. ANALYSIS OF THE RULE OF LAW

a. Rule-Based (or Deductive) Reasoning

Rule-based reasoning, also known as deductive reasoning, justifies a result by simply establishing and applying a rule of law. This type of reasoning is most commonly used when working with a simple declarative rule. The result is the result because the law mandates it. There typically is not any in-depth analysis in rule-based reasoning, but a simple application of the rule to the facts.

Rule-based reasoning requires three parts: (1) the rule of law being applied, (2) the conclusion you are proving based on the application of the rule of law, and (3) the relevant facts from your client's case that are needed to prove your conclusion.

b. Analogical Reasoning

Analogical reasoning is analysis that compares the facts of a client's case to the facts and applies the reasoning of a precedent case. This can be done to show that the client's case is similar to a precedent case or to show that the client's case is distinguishable from a precedent case.[6]

---

[6] Analogical reasoning used to distinguish a precedent case sometimes is called counter-analogical reasoning.

Courts tend to decide cases the same way other courts have decided cases for the same reasons. These are the principles of precedent and stare decisis at work.[7] This means if a court has already ruled on a given legal issue and another case arises with the same legal issue with comparable facts, then the holding and reasoning from the previous case (the precedent case) will apply to the new case.

Thus, if you can demonstrate that the client's case is factually similar to a precedent case and that the reasoning of the precedent case applies to the facts of the client's case, then you can make an informed prediction (objective writing) or a persuasive argument (persuasive writing) about how the case likely will or should turn out. Similarly, if you want an outcome that is different from the precedent case, you can show why the client's case is factually different and why the reasoning of the precedent case does not apply to the client's case, and thus make an informed prediction (objective writing) or a persuasive argument (persuasive writing) about how the case likely will or should turn out.

For analogical reasoning to be complete, two things must be done. First, the facts of the client's case and the facts of the precedent case must be compared. This may be done to show that the facts are similar or it may be done to show that the facts are different; but, a factual comparison must be included. While this may not seem hard to do, keep in mind that these must be specific factually-detailed comparisons, not generalizations. And, in truth, some of the best reasoned analyses and arguments are developed by showing similarities or differences in the facts of cases. So, do not overlook the possibility of there being factual similarities or differences where none are immediately apparent.

The second part of analogical reasoning, however, is more complex. This part requires you to demonstrate how the reasoning of the precedent case applies in your case and how the reasoning supports the outcome you are predicting or arguing. This is the key to analogical reasoning.

For example, if you were walking across campus on a lovely spring day and a professor walked by you and said, "We are similar; we are both wearing green shirts today," and then walked away, you might think the professor was quite strange. What was the point of the random shirt comparison? Was the professor just odd? Was there a reason he pointed out the comparison? However, it would have made more sense if the professor said, "We are similar; we are both wearing green shirts today" and followed that comment with, "and it is a good thing because it is St. Patrick's Day and we do not want to get pinched." In this scenario, you would understand *why* the professor made the comparison. It would be more than a random

---

[7]   *See* Chapter 2 on Domestic and Foreign Legal Systems for more information on these concepts.

shirt comparison, but a comparison that was based on a specific reason and led to a specific outcome.

This example demonstrates the point that factual comparisons alone are irrelevant and can be confusing. There must be a reason for the comparison for it to make sense. For example, if the reason for the above comparison was wearing green on St. Patrick's Day, then it makes sense that the professor compared the color of an article of clothing. However, if the professor commented that you both have short blonde hair; it would not make any sense at all in light of it being St. Patrick's Day. Thus, the factual comparison must be also related to the underlying reason for the comparison to make sense.

In legal writing, the underlying reason for the comparison comes from the reasoning of the precedent case. Without this direct connection to the reasoning from the precedent case, your reader will ask, "What's the point?"

c. Policy-Based Reasoning

Policy-based reasoning applies the purpose underlying a rule to justify a result. Policy-based reasoning is most often used to bolster an argument that already is supported by legal authorities. It also is used to demonstrate the policy implications of a particular result. Additionally, where there are not any applicable legal authorities, policy-based reasoning may be used to predict the type of law that may be created in the future.

To use policy-based reasoning, you must determine the purpose underlying the law. It might come from a court's opinion, the purpose section of a statute, legislative history, or published legal commentary on a rule of law. It should not, however, come from your own personal view of society; it must be based in law.

CHAPTER 7

THE PROCESS OF LEGAL WRITING

■ ■ ■

By Mary-Beth Moylan

A. THE PURPOSE OF LEGAL WRITING

The primary purpose of legal writing is consistent with the purpose of all writing—to communicate ideas. Some forms of legal writing also have the purpose of creating legal obligations. Other forms have the purpose of informing individuals of their rights. Still other forms predict outcomes, make demands, or attempt to persuade the reader to support a client's argument or position. No matter what purpose, or combination of purposes, an attorney has for drafting a document, the process of writing starts with identifying the audience, researching the law, and structuring the document to achieve the necessary purpose of the writing.

This chapter takes you through an outlining process that can be useful when commencing the drafting of any number of legal documents. It also discusses the importance of attribution in legal writing.

B. STARTING THE PROCESS OF LEGAL WRITING

Outlining is a necessary part of good legal writing. Some writers struggle to move immediately to an outline stage. Instead, they need to brainstorm on the paper or "free-write" to get their ideas flowing. There are many names for this type of initial writing process. Some call it brainstorming, free-writing, zero-draft, dump list, or stream of consciousness drafting. By whatever name, if you have historically done free-flow writing without an outline, or have let yourself free-write first before committing to an outline, you may want to continue with this same practice before you settle into an outline. For some writers, the process of letting the ideas flow is cathartic and inspirational. As long as you take the stream of consciousness draft and pull a thesis from your ideas, this approach is a fine first step in the outlining process. However, it is not even close to the final step. In the legal writing process, you need to move beyond the free flow of ideas into an organized outline.

In most outlining processes, you want to start from a thesis. What is the point that you seek to make with your written expression? In a term paper for an undergraduate class, you might start with an introduction that sets forth your thesis and then have separate sections for each of the sub-points that prove your assertion. You would plan to end with a conclusion that ties the whole paper together. The same basic principles apply to outlining for legal documents. The first question you should ask when you are starting your outline is "what is the point I seek to make with this document?"

To find the main point or points, you can ask yourself "what conclusion do I want my reader to reach when she reads this document?" For some people creating a list of the legal issues and the results desired is a good starting point. For others, a free-write in a narrative form is helpful to crystallize what the document is about. Once you have used your own method to develop the main point for your document, your outline should begin to form. The list of legal issues, or the narrative writing about the legal problem, will start you on your way to key terms and concepts that will be the foundation of your outline.

For most legal documents, there are main points and sub-points that support the general thesis. Each main point and sub-point in a legal document must be supported by legal authority and/or factual evidence. Even in a transactional document, the author should have a legal or factual basis for each provision that he chooses to include.

As other chapters in this book describe, there are a number of useful organizational paradigms that can be employed for crafting different types of legal documents. In objective legal writing, your organization should follow some variant of the CREAC paradigm (Conclusion, Rule, Explanation, Application, Conclusion), and in persuasive legal writing, your organization should follow CRAC (Conclusion, Rule, Analysis, Conclusion). These organizational paradigms can be incorporated into your outlining process. Additionally, for every major issue, your outline should include a point heading and then each of the components of the paradigm: CREAC for objective documents and CRAC for persuasive documents.

C. THE INITIAL OUTLINE

The best way to start outlining for legal documents is to take a legal problem and look at the different ways that the legal analysis of that issue can be presented in an outline form. Each heading that you create should correspond to a discrete point arising in the legal problem. So, if you have a problem that involves both a procedural question relating to a statute of limitations and a substantive question relating to whether there has been a breach of a duty to perform under a contract, you should have two outline headings as a starting point: one for the statute of limitations and one for the breach of duty. Regardless of whether the issues are substantive or procedural issues, each discrete point in the legal analysis should have an outline heading.[1] Your outline might look something like the following example.[2]

Outline for *Bert v. Ernie*

I.   Did Bert wait too long under the Code of the relevant jurisdiction to bring a breach of contract cause of action against Ernie for failure to care for Bert's pigeons?

II.   Did Ernie breach his contract with Bert when he failed to feed or care for Bert's pigeons while Bert was on vacation?

Within each of the main point headings, your outline should then set out the sub-points that support an answer to the main question presented. At this point, the sub-points should appear as questions or descriptive headings. Keep in mind, however, that some points of the outline may require sub-parts and others may not. For the case of *Bert v. Ernie*, the statute of limitations question may not have sub-parts, but the substantive breach of contract question might. So, in the next phase, your outline could look like this:

Outline for *Bert v. Ernie*

I.   Did Bert wait too long under the Code of the relevant jurisdiction to bring a breach of contract cause of action against Ernie for failure to care for Bert's pigeons?

II.   Did Ernie breach his contract with Bert when he failed to feed or care for Bert's pigeons while Bert was on vacation?

A.   Was Ernie's failure to feed the pigeons for one day a breach of his agreement with Bert?

B.   Is a defense of justification applicable here since Ernie was in the hospital on the day that he failed to feed the pigeons?

D. THE ANNOTATED OUTLINE

The next step in the outlining process for any kind of legal document is to convert your initial outline into an annotated outline. An annotated outline is one that is fleshed out with legal and factual support. For each main point you plan to make, and for each sub-point that helps to support

---

[1]   The outline heading may be in statement or question form. The example below demonstrates the question form.

[2]   The case and all citations used in the outlining examples in this chapter are completely fictitious. Any similarities to real or imaginary people are coincidental. Any similarities to real case citations are also unintended.

that point, you should include case law, statutory law, or administrative law, and factual documentation that you plan to use in the analysis. This means thinking through which legal authorities help you, as well as those that you want to distinguish. For some writers the annotation process is just a process of jotting down the names and citations for cases they plan to use. For others, the annotations can be very detailed and may include case briefings for each of the cases and notes about how the case will be used to support the point. A bare bones annotated outline might look something like the one below.

Very often you will spend a good deal of time organizing your authorities and figuring out what to include in your annotated outline and what to set aside. In this respect, outlining is the culmination of the research process. After finding all possible relevant authorities, viewing the draft of the annotated outline is helpful. Consideration can then be given to which are the best sources for your pending analysis. Potential problems that still need to be addressed can also be identified at this point.

Similarly, the annotation process offers a chance to sift through your factual support and align the facts you have with the legal requirements of a claim or defense. When organizing your factual support, consideration should be given to which witnesses support a point and where in the documented record the factual support is found. If no court document supports your assertion, you may find that an additional declaration or affidavit must be drafted.

In the *Bert v. Ernie* case, an annotated outline might look like this:

Outline for *Bert v. Ernie*

I.   Did Bert wait too long under the Code of the relevant jurisdiction to bring a breach of contract cause of action against Ernie for failure to care for Bert's pigeons?

Legal support: Statute of Limitation—30 Code of Applicable Jurisdiction § 12546 (2017)—providing that all claims for breach of contract must be brought within 2 years of the breach; *Garcia v. Flower Power, Inc.*, 123 Regional Reporter 456 (2004)—interpreting the statutory period for filing an action to commence as soon as the plaintiff demonstrates that she knew of the breach.

Factual support: Letter from Bert to Ernie complaining about his substandard care of pigeons dated October 1, 2015; Complaint filed January 6, 2018.

II.   Did Ernie breach his contract with Bert when he failed to feed or care for Bert's pigeons while Bert was on vacation?

A.   Was Ernie's failure to feed the pigeons for one day a breach of his agreement with Bert?

    Legal support: *Case v. Law*, 789 Regional Reporter 123 (2007)—explaining the basic standard for breach of contract.

    Factual support: Deposition of Ernie; Deposition of Bert; Complaint filed January 6, 2018; Answer filed February 20, 2018.

B.   Is a defense of justification applicable here since Ernie was in the hospital on the day that he failed to feed the pigeons?

    Legal support: *Legal Eagles v. Hospital Assn. of America*, 457 Regional Reporter 32 (2009)—finding a justification for failing to perform when there was an emergency and performance became impossible.

    Factual support: Deposition of Ernie; Deposition of Bert; Record of Hospital Admittance; Complaint filed January 6, 2018; Answer filed February 20, 2018.

Of course, in most cases that you are writing about, the legal analysis will require the use of many more legal and factual authorities than the above sample provides. A typical annotated outline will contain numerous cases and often numerous and inter-relating statutory sections. Be prepared to spend a fair amount of time ensuring that you have a complete annotated outline before launching into the drafting phase.

E. DRAFTING FROM AN OUTLINE

Depending on the level of detail you have included in your annotated outline, drafting can be a more or less time-consuming process. Many writers who work with very detailed annotated outlines find that once they arrive at the drafting phase, the legal document almost writes itself. The outline is the template from which the document is written. With a detailed outline, you have at your fingertips the authorities you plan to use in the annotations and you are reminded of your main points and sub-points by the headings. Therefore, the drafting process may only involve writing out the connections that you are already thinking about between facts and law. For those with a detailed annotated outline, writing is mechanical, and the outline becomes the only reference material needed at the drafting stage.

That said, new legal writers often make the mistake of thinking that drafting a legal document is a linear process. It is not. In legal writing, cycling back to your outline and readjusting it throughout the drafting process is appropriate and sometimes necessary. Once you start to write out the analysis, you may find a point that you thought was adequately supported by two sub-points, really requires a third sub-point to help explain your analysis. Or, as you write about an authority that you thought provided support to your main point, you may find that upon a second or third reading it does not say exactly what you thought it said. Even more common, a new case may be decided during your writing process that may alter your analysis. Since you need to be updating legal research regularly, there is a fairly good chance you will find something new and helpful (or unhelpful) during the drafting process.

Finding new authority, or realizing a different structure is preferred, does not always mean a redrafting of the initial outline; but, it is sometimes beneficial to rework your thoughts in an outline form first. The outline is a tool. The goal is to first prepare for your writing, and then continue to use its structure to refine your thinking as you write.

Additionally, as the successful writer cycles back through her outline, and drafts and re-drafts, she also needs to be constantly checking for the thesis of the document. As discussed above, each main issue must have a thesis to be supported. In addition, in most situations each paragraph should have a clear topic or thesis sentence.[3] Each sentence should express a single idea that supports that topic or thesis sentence. Checking and double-checking that each sentence and paragraph is doing its job is the task of the writer when moving from outline to draft. Not infrequently, a drafter will get lost in her work because the stream of consciousness writing takes over and the intentional use of topic and thesis sentences is lost. Cycling back through the individual paragraphs and sentences in each section and sub-section and checking to see that each is doing its job is the best way to ensure for clear written communication.[4]

F. ATTRIBUTION

Legal writing must be supported by legal authority. You must look to other sources and include those sources in your legal analysis. In journalism, the taking of work from another is strictly forbidden without attribution. In fact, in numerous instances disgraced journalists have lost their jobs and reputations because of paraphrasing the work of another too closely.[5] In legal writing, to an even greater extent than in journalism, you

---

[3] In some situations, paragraphs can be sub-sets of a series of paragraphs all tied to the same topic or thesis. In these situations, you might have a series of supporting sentences that form a paragraph, but do not have a separate thesis.

[4] The details of editing are covered in Chapter 28, White-Glove Inspection. For the purposes of this chapter, it is important to note that the process of writing is one not only of outlining and writing, but also of rewriting.

[5] The New York Times, Media Decoder, *CNN and Time Suspend Journalist After Admission of Plagiarism*, August 12, 2012, http://mediadecoder.blogs.nytimes.com/2012/08/10/time-magazine

must paraphrase and sometimes quote rules from prior decisions. Ideas that are expressed by jurists in other cases must be used to advance your client's case. You must cite to the authorities that you are paraphrasing, and you must quote any material that is directly taken from another case, a law review article, or any other published source. Attribution makes legal analysis stronger because it demonstrates to the reader that the analysis is supported by authority. So, failure to give attribution weakens the legitimacy and dilutes the strength of the argument.

Attribution is not only legally required, it is ethical practice. Attorneys who plagiarize are not credible. With all parties and the judges very often reading the same universe of cases, it is not difficult for a lifted quotation or an unattributed paraphrase to be noticed. When opposing counsel or the court become aware that an attorney is taking ideas from elsewhere and claiming them for her own, her reputation as an ethical and trustworthy resource is diminished. Since the job of every attorney is to persuade the decision maker of the correctness of her client's position, a loss of trust by the decision maker is a serious obstacle to the attorney's ability to do her job. Moreover, under the ABA Model Rules of Professional Conduct, all attorneys have a duty of candor to the court.[6] Disclosing the source of a statement or rule is an important aspect of this duty.

The best way to make sure that you do not inadvertently fail to attribute to a source is to reference citations as you go in your outlining and drafting process. If you wait until the end to put in citations and other sources of authority, you may omit one or more references. Citing as you outline and draft is the safest and most efficient course.

G. CROSS-CULTURAL CONSIDERATIONS

1. WRITING EXPECTATIONS ACROSS AUDIENCES

Different expectations of formality in writing exist across jurisdictions, levels of court, and legal firms or organizations. The basic process of your writing should be the same no matter the audience or the type of document. However, how long you spend on an outline or on perfecting your every sentence will be different if you are writing a brief to the U.S. Supreme Court or a short memo to a partner. Additionally, your tone will also be

---

-to-examine-plagiarism-accusation-against-zakaria (last visited Feb. 12, 2018); The Toronto Star, *Plagiarism and fabrication undermine news media credibility*, August 9, 2012, http://www.thestar.com/entertainment/books/article/1238375-plagiarism-and-fabrication-charges-undermine-news-media-credibility (last visited Feb. 12, 2018); PBS Independent Lens, *A Fragile Trust: Plagiarism, Power, and Jayson Blair at the New York Times*, http://www.pbs.org/independentlens/films/fragile-trust/ (last visited Feb. 10, 2018).

  6 ABA MODEL RULE OF PROFESSIONAL CONDUCT, RULE 3.3, https://www.americanbar.org/groups/professional_responsibility/publications/model_rules_of_professional_conduct/rule_3_3_candor_toward_the_tribunal.html (last visited Feb. 10, 2018).

different depending on your audience. [7] The local culture of a court you are writing to, or the culture within your firm or practice area, may dictate the style you use, the citation manual you follow, and the level of formality with which you write. Be prepared to look at samples from colleagues and to adapt your final written product to conform to the local culture and custom.

2. INTERNATIONAL PRACTICE

If you find yourself practicing in a different country or in an international tribunal, the expectations for the content of your legal document might be quite different than in the United States. Common law systems require references to case law precedent in almost every type of formal legal writing. In contrast, since case law is not precedential in civil law systems, the focus in writing in a civil law system is on codes, as well as treatises and other interpretations of codified law.

The tone of legal documents in other countries may also be more formal and more formulaic. Again, be prepared to adapt your process and your style to the norms of the culture where you are practicing. [8] It does not benefit you or your client to write a document in a format that you find comfortable if it does not conform to the expectations of your reader.

---

[7]   *See* Chapter 8 on Knowing Your Audience.
[8]   *See* Chapter 3 on Intercultural Competence.

CHAPTER 8

KNOWING YOUR AUDIENCE

■ ■ ■

By Stephanie J. Thompson

A. IMPORTANCE OF KNOWING YOUR AUDIENCE

To be an effective legal writer, you must know your audience. Justice Antonin Scalia said, "I think there is a writing genius . . . which consists primarily, I think, of the ability to place oneself in the shoes of one's audience—to assume only what they assume, to anticipate what they anticipate, to explain what they need explained, to think what they must be thinking, to feel what they must be feeling."[1]

Being a successful legal writer is not just about the information you want to communicate, but more about what the audience wants to know, what the audience needs to know, and how the audience will interpret the information being communicated. As a writer, you always need to be thinking about the purpose for the creation of your document. What information do you want to relay to the audience? What conclusions do you want the audience to reach? What level of understanding do you want the audience to have about the issues being discussed? If you do not know what you want to achieve in writing your document, both generally and specifically, you will not be able to effectively communicate with the audience.

B. PRIMARY AUDIENCES AND SECONDARY AUDIENCES

For every document you produce as a legal writer, there will be more than one potential audience. When you are writing, you must always be thinking about both the primary audience—the intended audience—and the secondary audience—anyone else who might also read the document. For example, if you are drafting a memorandum for a supervising attorney, you should assume that other attorneys you work with also may read it. If you are drafting a letter to opposing counsel, you should assume that the judge may read it as an exhibit to a motion. If you are drafting any

---

[1] Scribes Award for Scalia (Full Pt 2) 6:10–6:38, available at https://www.youtube.com/watch?v=RdZSSO3mF3s (last visited Feb. 6, 2018).

document to the court, you should know that opposing counsel will read it. Finally, you should remember that your client may read everything you write, regardless of the primary audience. While a client may not be able to discern the difference between a good work product and a great work product, a client likely will be able to identify a poorly written, disorganized, or unpolished work product.

Thus, when determining your purpose for writing the document, think about both the primary audience and the secondary audience.

C. LAW-TRAINED AUDIENCES

Lawyers, judges, mediators, arbitrators, and other law-trained audiences are busy, likely to be hypercritical, and will question your analysis until you have convinced them; they will not give you the benefit of the doubt about anything. Additionally, law-trained audiences do not simply want the answer to the question; they want to know why the answer you have provided is the best answer.

When writing to a law-trained audience, you should keep the following principles in mind: (1) they do not want to do any additional work, but instead want a document that is self-contained both legally and factually, (2) they do not want to read a document more than once to know the answer or to understand the analysis, (3) they expect the organization of the document to provide the answers first and the analysis second, and (4) they only want documents that are clear and concise, that stay on topic, and that include only relevant information.[2]

1. SUPERVISING ATTORNEYS

As both a legal intern and a new attorney, your primary audience will be your supervising attorney. Frequently you will write a document and then the supervising attorney will edit and submit it to the primary audience as her own work product. Thus, regardless of the substance, to create an effective document for a supervising attorney, you need to understand how the supervising attorney writes stylistically and substantively, as the supervising attorney ultimately will make the document her own.

For example, you may work for one supervising attorney who hates headings to be in bold but prefers them to be underlined, and, at the same time, you work for another supervising attorney who loves headings in bold and hates them underlined. Or, you may work for one supervising attorney who only uses deductive reasoning while another prefers each point to be established by analogical reasoning. Recognizing these nuances between

---

[2] Michael J. Higdon, *The Legal Reader: An Expose*, UNIVERSITY OF TENNESSEE LEGAL STUDIES RESEARCH PAPER NO. 183, pp. 8–9, University of Tennessee College of Law, March 9, 2012 (SSRN-id2047423).

the supervising attorneys you work for, and remembering that the work product may not be reflective of your own writing style, will minimize the amount of editing a supervising attorney will perform on your work product. At the same time, however, you must also keep in mind the ultimate audience of the document, such as the client, opposing counsel, or the court.

2. OPPOSING COUNSEL

As an attorney, you will have extensive written communication with opposing counsel. This is true both in litigation and transactional practice. This communication may be in the form of a letter, an e-mail, a brief, a negotiation document, a proposed written contract, or a settlement agreement.

While the main purpose in writing to opposing counsel may be to persuade him that your client has the stronger position, this purpose needs to be balanced with professionalism. Your goal is to persuade opposing counsel without coming across as aggressive, demeaning, or condescending. Having a positive working relationship with opposing counsel can help maintain your professionalism and credibility as well as encourage settlement or other swift resolution of the case.

3. JUDGES AND ARBITRATORS

Judges and arbitrators are decision-makers. Your purpose in writing to a judge or an arbitrator is to convince him that he should rule in favor of your client. In doing so, however, you need to put yourself in the mindset of the judge who is busy, unfamiliar with the case, and only wants to know what he needs to know about the relevant law and facts. The judge does not want to read character attacks or overly aggressive arguments. Therefore, when writing to a judge or an arbitrator, focus on being concise and accurate and avoid being aggressive, hyperbolic, or condescending.

Additionally, judges rely on attorneys to be accurate in the information they provide to the court. The one question you never want the judge to ponder when reading your brief is "can that be right?" When a judge questions the accuracy of the information you provide, the judge is questioning your credibility. The Honorable Arthur Gilbert of the California Court of Appeal has said that attorneys frequently will "misstate what a case stands for" and he encourages attorneys to ask themselves, "Does the case say what I am saying it says? I mean really be honest with yourself." He had even stronger words for attorneys omitting unfavorable authority: "If there is a case that works against you, and it's there, to ignore it is ridiculous."[3]

The American Bar Association Model Rules of Professional Conduct, in Rule 3.3 on Candor to the Tribunal, provide that a lawyer shall not knowingly

- make a false statement of fact or law to a tribunal or fail to correct a false statement of material fact or law previously made to the tribunal by the lawyer;

- fail to disclose to the tribunal legal authority in the controlling jurisdiction known to the lawyer to be directly adverse to the position of the client and not disclosed by opposing counsel; or

- offer evidence that the lawyer knows to be false. If a lawyer, the lawyer's client, or a witness called by the lawyer, has offered material evidence and the lawyer comes to know of its falsity, the lawyer shall take reasonable remedial measures, including, if necessary, disclosure to the tribunal. A lawyer may refuse to offer evidence, other than the testimony of a defendant in a criminal matter, that the lawyer reasonably believes is false.

Judge Gilbert's comments, and the ABA Model Rules of Professional Conduct, not only address intentional misstatements of the facts or the law, but they also cover exaggerations of the facts or the law. The judge needs to be able to rely on attorneys and trust that what they are writing is accurate.

Finally, when writing to the court, attorneys need to be brief. Brevity is a characteristic that judges frequently encourage lawyers to utilize in their writing. United States Supreme Court Justice Clarence Thomas stated, "It should be obvious to you that people are really busy."[4] He further explained that, "When I used to write briefs, I always assumed that the judge had other things to read than what I wrote. So, I read it understanding that mine was not the most important thing he would read that day. So, if you assume that, how would you write it?"[5] Essentially, when writing to a judge or an arbitrator, your task is not to prove how much you know about a particular topic or how eloquent you are. Instead, it is

[3] Interview of the Honorable Arthur Gilbert, *Lawyers Stretching Precedent*, http://www.law prose.org/interviews/judges-lawyers-writers-on-writing.php?vid=gilbert_dont_stretch_precedents &vidtitle=Hon._Arthur_Gilbert_On_Lawyers_Stretching_Precedents (last visited Feb. 16, 2018).

[4] Interview of Justice Clarence Thomas, *Judges are Impatient*, http://lawprose.org/interviews/ judges-lawyers-writers-on-writing.php?vid=thomas_judges_impatient&vidtitle=Justice_Clarence_ Thomas_Judges_are_Impatient (last visited Feb. 16, 2018).

[5] *Id.*

about filtering complex information down to the most concise and important points that need to be considered.

4. MEDIATORS

Writing to mediators is different than writing to judges and arbitrators because mediators, for the most part, are not decision-makers. Instead, a mediator is an impartial third person who tries to help the parties negotiate a mutually acceptable resolution to their conflict.[6] Your purpose in writing to the mediator is not to convince him that he should rule in favor of your client, but to convince him that your client has the stronger case and that your proposed course of action is the better approach. If the mediator agrees with you, he may encourage the other party to move toward your proposed solution, and ultimately encourage a settlement of the dispute in your favor.

Mediators are not looking for the same type of legal argument you may put before the judge or an arbitrator. While mediators do need to know the basic law and facts of a case, mediators are more interested in learning about the possible settlement options, the barriers to settlement, and the discrete issues that are at the heart of the case; they do not want to hear about every legal argument, or disagreement, that the parties can raise. Attorneys frequently make the mistake of taking an existing document they filed with the court, such as a motion to dismiss or a motion for summary judgment, making a few edits and re-titling it "Mediation Brief." This approach does not provide the mediator with what the mediator really needs and does not reflect that the attorney thought about his audience.

Additionally, the secondary audience in a mediation needs to be treated almost the same as a primary audience. While the mediator is the primary audience, the secondary audience is the opposing party and opposing counsel. This secondary audience will be active participants in the mediation and you will want to convince them to see your side of the issues just as much as you want to convince the mediator. In the end, the mediator is not the decision-maker in mediation; the opposing party is the decision-maker. Failing to recognize this nuance could make settlement more difficult.

D. LAY-PERSONS GENERALLY

A lay-person is anyone who is not a member of the legal profession. When writing to a lay-person, you must explain complex legal issues in such a way that an average individual with no legal training will be able to comprehend. The two types of lay-persons you likely will write to are clients and opposing parties.

---

[6]   *See* Chapter 22 on the differences between mediators and arbitrators.

1. CLIENTS GENERALLY

While there are certain nuances that need to be mastered when writing to different types of clients, one central requirement is needed when writing to all clients—reliability. When a client makes a decision based on information his attorney provides, the client assumes that the information provided is correct, that the approach is ethical, and that all reasonable options have been presented.

Clients, for the most part, want answers. Like a medical patient at a doctor's office trying to determine what is wrong with them, lay-persons want to know what the problem is and how to solve it. They do not care as much about why it is what it is, what it is called, or even how the law supports it; instead, clients tend to be more results-oriented.

2. INDIVIDUAL CLIENTS

Individual clients can be the hardest audience to write to because of their varying levels of experience and understanding. You will spend years mastering "legal style and tone" only to learn that you need to eliminate most of it from your written communication with clients. Depending on the sophistication of an individual client, your tone and substance may vary. However, you should assume that most clients are not law-trained audiences and you need to avoid "sounding like a lawyer" to these clients— eliminate all legalese, in-depth legal analysis, and legal citations.

Legalese is a term that describes the technical and formal style of legal writing. This specific style of writing is understood by those in the profession, but may be difficult for lay-people to understand. Consider going to a doctor's office and being told that you have nasopharyngitis, rhino pharyngitis, or acute coryza. Those words may cause confusion, or even panic if you do not know what they mean. However, instead of telling you that you have nasopharyngitis, rhino pharyngitis, or acute coryza, the doctor could have avoided confusion and unnecessary panic by simply telling you that you have a common cold.

The same principle applies to legal writing. For example, instead of telling a client that she may be barred by a statute of limitations, simply tell her that she has a limited amount of time to file a complaint and that she may not be able to sue if she does not file her complaint by a certain date. Thus, the focus needs to be on communicating the information in a manner that is understandable to the client.

Written communications with clients also should utilize a more colloquial or conversational tone. This approach does not mean that you should fill your e-mails with emoticons and shorthand, but it does mean that your style of writing should be inviting, respectful, and reflect an awareness of your audience's knowledge and experience.

Finally, one of the most offensive things an attorney can do to a client is be condescending. In a study of clients and lawyers, the clients named "superior attitude," "indifference," "impatient," and "impersonal" as some of the most negative characteristics of attorneys and "friendliness," "professionalism," and "courtesy" as some of the most positive characteristics.[7]

3. CORPORATE CLIENTS

Corporate clients are different than individual clients. When working with corporate clients, you might interact with a range of people with varying levels of education and experience and in a variety of different jobs, such as CEOs, in-house counsel, human resources directors, or other high-level executives. Typically, representatives of corporate clients are educated and well-versed in business and, in some cases, the law. While it is still desirable to write to these clients with some of the same style techniques as with individual clients—eliminate legalese and use a conversational tone—you often can include more in-depth legal analysis, with citations, and a more sophisticated explanation of the issues and options.

4. OPPOSING PARTY

While it is an ethical violation to directly contact the opposing party if the opposing party is represented by counsel,[8] situations may arise when the opposing party is not represented. For example, if you represent a tenant who wants to send a demand letter to his landlord, the landlord may not have an attorney. Differing thoughts exist on how to approach this type of letter. Some attorneys will intentionally write the letter with legalese, citations, and in-depth legal analysis. This approach is effective when the attorney knows that the landlord will get an attorney and, even though the letter is addressed to the landlord, the primary audience actually is the landlord's attorney. Or, it may be done for intimidation. While this intimidation tactic is not always seen as an ethical practice, it is a strategy used by many attorneys. The better approach probably is to write the letter to your primary audience—the landlord—in a manner that he can understand, but make it persuasive so the secondary audience—the attorney—will understand and appreciate your demand.

5. POTENTIAL CLIENTS

Many attorneys use the internet to its fullest potential—blogging, other forms of social media, posting online articles, and giving online presentations and seminars. Viewers of these services can be anyone in the

---

[7] Daniel J. McAuliffe, Shirley J. Wahl, *Relationship with Client*, 2 ARIZ. PRAC., CIVIL TRIAL PRACTICE § 5.7 (2d ed. Nov. 2012).

[8] ABA MODEL RULE 4.2 COMMUNICATION WITH PERSON REPRESENTED BY COUNSEL (2012).

world, including existing clients, potential clients, opposing counsel, judges, arbitrators, mediators, law students, and lay-persons who are trying to better understand a particular legal concept. Knowing that the audience of online publications and presentations can be both law-trained audiences and lay-persons, the materials need to be written in a way that they can be understood by all types of audiences, or they need to be written with a targeted audience and purpose in mind.

E.   RESEARCHING YOUR AUDIENCE

The Honorable William Bauer of the 7th Circuit Court of Appeal said, "You're going to address a lot of different personalities and people with different backgrounds. And, nobody really divorces themselves from the final analysis and from their own backgrounds."[9] His point is that you need to know whom your audiences are before you begin to write. With the limitless information available on the internet, it is relatively easy to learn about your audience.

For example, if you are working on an employment discrimination case and you learn that the judge hearing your motion to dismiss was just recently appointed to the bench after a long career as a criminal defense attorney, you may want to approach the depth of information provided in your motion differently than if you learned the judge was a former employment discrimination attorney. Similarly, if you are engaged in mediation and the mediator has thirty years of experience, you may approach the mediation differently than if this was going to be the mediator's first mediation.

Information you generally would want to know about all types of audiences includes their education, work history, life experiences, and anything else that could help you better understand them as an audience. This information will be particularly easy to find for judges, mediators, and arbitrators as there are websites dedicated to them.[10] And, it is likely that opposing counsel has her own website that you can research, in addition to the information provided on state and local bar association websites.

Information about your client most likely will come from your direct communications with him, but you can supplement that information with

---

[9]   Interview with the Honorable William J. Bauer, *Writing for All Judges*, http://www.law prose.org/interviews/judges-lawyers-writers-on-writing.php?vid=bauer_writing_for_judges&vid title=Hon._William_J._Bauer_On_Writing_for_All_Judges (last visited Feb. 16, 2018).

[10]   Federal Judicial Center, Biographical Directory of Federal Judges, 1789—present, http:// www.fjc.gov/history/home.nsf/page/judges.html (last visited Feb. 2, 2018); The Recorder, Judicial Profiles, http://www.law.com/jsp/ca/judicial_profiles.jsp (last visited Feb. 2, 2018); ARC Mediation, Mediator Profiles, http://www.arcmediation.com/mediator_profiles (last visited Dec. 2012); LinkedIn, American Arbitration Association Arbitrators, http://www.linkedin.com/title/arbitrator/ at-american-arbitration-association (last visited Feb. 2, 2018); JAMS, Neutrals, https://www.jams adr.com/neutrals/search (last visited Feb. 10, 2018); American Arbitration Association, Arbitrators & Mediators, https://www.adr.org/aaa-panel (last visited Feb. 10, 2018).

general internet searches. While some clients are comfortable telling their attorney everything, others are not, and independent research may be necessary. Finally, most of the information you will learn about the opposing party will come from your client and general internet searches.[11] During the discovery-phase of litigation, however, you will be able to learn more about the opposing party.

F. CROSS-CULTURAL CONSIDERATIONS

While this discussion has focused on generalizations regarding the different types of audiences attorneys will encounter in the practice of law, relying on generalizations and stereotypes when it comes to cultural issues or the personal experiences of your audience could inhibit communication. Thus, in addition to generally understanding the type of audience you will communicate with, you also should evaluate your audience's culture and experiences. This may include gender, race, national origin, age, sexual orientation, marital status, religion, political affiliation, socio-economic status, as well as personal struggles and other life experiences. Recall, Judge Bauer's statement that "Nobody really divorces themselves . . . from their different backgrounds."[12] Thus, the more you can know about your audience, and their backgrounds, the better you can communicate with them.

It is important to be aware that every culture has its own set of values that affect behavior and decision-making. You should not assume that your own viewpoint, or the viewpoint of your client, is universally accepted by all cultures. Cultural norms are generally defined by assessing high and low-context factors.[13] "Context is best defined as the array of stimuli surrounding a communication event including body gestures, tone of voice, physical distance between interlocutors, time of day, weather, situation, societal norms, geographic place of communication, and other external factors."[14] High-context cultures rely heavily on contextual clues when assessing a message, whereas low-context cultures place greater importance on the content of the message itself, and afford less consideration to the surrounding context.

---

[11] Discovery is the process before trial where attorneys obtain information from the opposing party through demands for production of documents, depositions of parties and potential witnesses, interrogatories (questions and answers written under oath), and requests for admissions of fact. This is broad right of disclosure to allow the parties to go to trial with as much knowledge as possible and that neither party should be able to keep secrets from the other.

[12] Interview with the Honorable William J. Bauer, *Writing for All Judges*, http://www.law prose.org/interviews/judges-lawyers-writers-on-writing.php?vid=bauer_writing_for_judges&vid title=Hon._William_J._Bauer_On_Writing_for_All_Judges (last visited Feb. 2, 2018).

[13] Edward T. Hall, BEYOND CULTURE (1976); *see also* Chapter 3 on Intercultural Competence.

[14] Filipp Sapienza, *Culture And Context: A Summary Of Geert Hofstede's And Edward Hall's Theories Of Cross-Cultural Communication For Web Usability*, http://www.filippsapienza.com/ CultureContextEnglish.html, Copyright © 2017 www.filippsapienza.com (last visited Feb. 16, 2018).

An individual from a high-context culture may take longer to make decisions, and those decisions may be significantly impacted by factors such as the formality of the process, the age or gender of the participants, whether certain ceremonies were established and followed, and the participants' non-verbal communication. Additionally, high-context cultures may value the interaction over accomplishing the task, and may be willing to spend more time navigating the process, placing great emphasis on forming relationships. Conversely, someone from a low-context culture will want to stick closely to an agenda, navigate the process quickly and without ceremony, and communicate directly and efficiently using plain language. In a low-context culture, there tends to be less confusion about the parameters of the final product.

Some things to consider when engaging with an audience with a different cultural background than your own include: How direct should communication be? Are there ceremonial traditions that are expected? What are the cultural attitudes about gender, age, education, and socio-economic factors? What are the norms related to dispute resolution? How is conflict treated? How do members of the culture address and respond to people in positions of authority? Are members of the culture likely to disclose private information, or engage in a public display of conflict? A skilled attorney will educate herself and explore these factors to most effectively communicate with different audiences and navigate the process.

PRACTICE EXERCISE

Using the search engine of your choice or one of the sources suggested in this chapter, research a judge in your local jurisdiction or a judge identified by your professor. Make a list of the information that would help you "know your audience" if you were submitting a brief to this judge.

CHAPTER 9

OBJECTIVE LEGAL WRITING

■ ■ ■

By Stephanie J. Thompson

A. PURPOSE OF OBJECTIVE LEGAL WRITING

Objective legal writing is predictive writing. It is neutral analysis used to evaluate the law and the facts from both sides of an issue and to evaluate the strengths and weaknesses of a client's situation. It also is used to predict the likely outcome of a particular legal issue and recommend a course of action. The purpose of objective legal writing is not to persuade the reader to agree with a particular position or argument, but instead it is to inform the reader of the likely analysis and outcomes associated with the legal issue or issues being evaluated.

Objective legal writing must be impartial and unbiased. Assume that your reader will rely on your analysis and predictions. If you emphasize the analysis too much one way or the other, or employ persuasive writing strategies, then the reader may not fully appreciate the risks associated with the analysis and recommendations provided. Instead, think of objective legal writing as a well-supported list of pros and cons.

Objective legal writing frequently is used to help supervising attorneys determine the next steps in a case, develop a strategy, or answer a research question. It also is used by attorneys to communicate these next steps or recommendations to clients. And, it is used by law clerks who work for judges to inform the judge of the facts, the law, and the analysis of a particular issue before the court.

B. TYPES OF OBJECTIVE LEGAL WRITING

Objective writing generally comes in three forms—memorandums, correspondence, and bench briefs. Each of these documents are written with a specific purpose in mind for a specific audience but they may ultimately evolve into something more. For example, a formal memorandum to a supervising attorney may become the basis of an advice letter for a client. The advice letter to the client may become the basis of a motion to the court. Or, a law clerk's bench brief to inform and advise the judge may become the published decision of the court. Each of these types of objective writing are described generally below but further information is provided in chapters specifically dedicated to each type of objective legal writing (see Chapter 10 on Formal Memorandums, Chapter 11 on Short-Form Memorandums, Chapter 15 on Professional Correspondence, and Chapter 21 on Judicial Writing).

1. MEMORANDUMS

Memorandums are in-house communications between legal interns and attorneys, between attorneys, or between attorneys and clients. They generally come in two forms—a formal memorandum and a short-form memorandum.

A formal memorandum is a comprehensive document that provides the reader with all of the information necessary to objectively evaluate a complex legal issue. This information is provided with the assumption that the reader is not familiar with the facts, the law, the legal issues, or the analysis.

A formal memorandum contains the following five components: (1) Question Presented, (2) Brief Answer, (3) Facts, (4) Discussion, and (5) Conclusion. This is a traditional form of objective legal writing and, while the format may change depending upon the assigning attorney, most attorneys expect to see the above components in formal memorandum. Chapter 10 discusses formal memorandums.

A short-form memorandum provides analysis on a specific topic or topics where the reader already has some knowledge of the underlying issue or facts. A short-form memorandum will not contain all of the formal memorandum components. Instead, it only includes the components the reader needs. If a short-form memorandum is written to an attorney who has knowledge about the facts of the case, it may only include the Question Presented, the Brief Answer, and Discussion sections. If the short memorandum is only answering a research question, it may only include the Question Presented and the Discussion sections. Or, if the short-form memorandum only is addressing one narrow factual issue, it may only include the Facts and the Discussion sections. Essentially, the components included in a short-form memorandum depend upon the purpose of the memorandum and the knowledge and needs of the reader. Chapter 11 discusses short-form memorandums.

2. CORRESPONDENCE

Written correspondence is a staple in the practice of law. Attorneys communicate in writing on a regular basis with other attorneys, clients, judges, experts, witnesses, and others. Written correspondence in the practice of law can take many forms, including advice letters, demand letters, and e-mails. The advice letter is the form of correspondence that falls into the objective legal writing category.

Advice letters are the correspondence an attorney sends to clients to inform them about the attorney's understanding of the scope and nature of the representation, to provide them with specific legal findings based on research performed, and to advise them on the various options available to achieve specific objectives. Chapter 15 discusses professional correspondence, including advice letters.

3.   BENCH BRIEFS

Most judges have a law clerk or staff of law clerks to research the issues before the court and draft opinions regarding the court's decision on a particular issue. Specifically, law clerks read the briefs associated with a particular motion before the court, research the issues, and write a bench brief for the judge. A bench brief is similar to a formal or a short-form memorandum—it identifies the issues before the court, summarizes the facts, provides objective legal analysis of the issues supported by research, and recommends an outcome. Law clerks do not make the decision for the judge, but instead seek to inform the judge of the legal analysis at issue with a particular motion before the court, advise the judge of the most likely outcome under the law, and provide the judge with any additional information the law clerk thinks would be helpful to assist the judge in making her decision. Chapter 21 discusses judicial writing.

C. THE STRUCTURE OF OBJECTIVE WRITING

Lawyers and law-trained readers are busy. Thus, they expect objective documents to be presented in a familiar manner. Therefore, most lawyers use organizational structures—or writing paradigms. These paradigms provide a standardized structure for all forms of legal writing. When a busy lawyer picks up an objective memorandum written by a legal intern or a busy judge picks up bench brief written by a judicial clerk, they already know or expect that the information the writer is trying to convey will be presented in a certain manner. This allows lawyers and law-trained readers to read and evaluate the analysis as quickly as possible.

1.   THE OBJECTIVE WRITING PARADIGM

The acronym used for the objective legal writing paradigm is CREAC.[1] It stands for Conclusion, Rule, Explanation, Application, and Conclusion. Each of these sections is explained in more detail below. However, it is

---

[1]   It is important to note that there are various acronyms used for the objective legal writing paradigm, such as TREAC, IRAC, TREAT, CRAC, IRAC. While the acronyms are different, the basic organizational structure is the same for each of these paradigms.

important to first understand where CREAC is used. CREAC is not the organizational structure for objective documents as a whole.

Instead, CREAC is used for each individual legal issue addressed in the Discussion section of an objective document. For example, if you are writing an objective memorandum (see Chapters 10 and 11) or an advice letter (see Chapter 15), there will be a section of those documents where your objective analysis is provided. This is frequently called the Discussion section or the Analysis section. This is where CREAC is used.

As a general rule, there should be a separate CREAC for each individual legal issue. This is not always a simple determination. To make this determination, there must be a complete understanding of the legal issues and rules to be addressed. For example, if the legal test being applied has four elements, then there will be four CREACs in the Discussion section—one CREAC for each element of the legal test. Or, if the legal test being applied does not have elements but has two legal terms that require separate analysis or have specific legal definitions, then there will be two CREACs in the Discussion section. But, if the rule only has one component or a straightforward application, then there will only be one CREAC in the Discussion section.

One way to determine the number of CREACs to use is to evaluate each legal issue and determine if there are sub-issues or sub-sub-issues for that legal issue. This is where outlining the legal issues and outlining the legal rules is essential. You must know how your issues and rules breakdown to be able to determine how many CREACs to include in the Discussion section.

For example, if the legal issue being addressed by the objective document relates to a criminal defendant's due process right to a fair trial, the following legal principle would apply:

> Under the U.S. Constitution, a criminal defendant's due process right to a fair trial may be violated as a result of the State's failure to preserve potentially exculpatory evidence. *Arizona v. Youngblood*, 488 U.S. 51, 58 (1988). To establish a due process violation for failure to preserve potentially exculpatory evidence, the defendant must establish that (1) the State acted in bad faith when it failed to preserve the evidence; (2) the evidence was suppressed or destroyed by the State; (3) the evidence had an exculpatory value that was apparent to the State before it was destroyed; and (4) the defendant is unable to obtain comparable evidence by other reasonably available means. *Id.* All four elements of the test must be met to establish a due process violation. *Id.*

If this is the legal principle, then there would need to be four CREACs in the Discussion section, one for each of the elements.

On the other hand, if the legal principle addressed by the objective document relates to whether an artwork that uses a celebrity's image is a violation of the celebrity's right of publicity or instead is protected by the First Amendment, the following legal principle would apply:

> A work is entitled to First Amendment protection when it "adds significant creative elements so as to be transformed into something more than a mere celebrity likeness or imitation" and does not take away from the celebrity's right of publicity. *Comedy III Prods. Inc. v. Gary Saderup Chapter. Inc.*, 25 Cal. 4th 387, 391 (2001). This is known as the "transformative test." The transformative test balances whether the work shows creative, expressive, and transformative elements with whether the value of the work derives primarily from the celebrity's fame. *Id.* The court developed this balancing test to resolve the conflict between the right of publicity and First Amendment rights. *Id.* at 404. The transformative test considers "whether the new work merely supersedes the objects of the original creation, or instead adds something new, with a further purpose or different character." *Id.* A work is protected by the First Amendment only if it contains "significant transformative elements or [if] the value of the work does not derive primarily from the celebrity's fame." *Id.* at 407.

If this is the legal principle, then there would be only one CREAC in the Discussion section to evaluate the balancing test holistically.

When using organizational paradigms, be flexible. While the organizational paradigm provides the structure that law-trained readers expect, the paradigms can be modified when dictated by the need for clarity.

2. THE CREAC COMPONENTS

A complete CREAC has five components. These components are Conclusion, Rule, Explanation, Application, and Conclusion. Each of these components is explained below.

a. Conclusion

Objective legal writing always begins with the objective conclusion. There is no surprise or suspense to be developed. Instead, law-trained readers want to know the objective conclusion first before they read the analysis. Thus, the conclusion, or the C in the CREAC, is the objective conclusion being predicted with the CREAC. It is not the ultimate conclusion for the entire objective document. It may not even be the ultimate conclusion for the Discussion section. Instead, it only is the conclusion for the specific legal issue being addressed by that specific CREAC. Sometimes, the conclusion is one sentence, but its length should be based what is needed to completely (but concisely) articulate the conclusion on the specific issue that is the subject of the CREAC.

b. Rule

The rule, or the R in the CREAC, is the specific legal principle applied to the legal issue addressed by the CREAC. The rule is derived from primary authority: a constitution, statutes, cases, or administrative regulations. It frequently is derived from a synthesis of several of these sources (see Chapter 5). Because rules come from primary authority, all rules must be supported by a citation to the legal authority from which the rule was derived.

Substantively, the rule must provide a complete rule on the particular point of law addressed by the CREAC. This includes the rule itself, as well as any exceptions to the rule, and anything else that a court might consider when applying this rule. It should not, however, provide a history lesson on how the rule was developed.

When writing a rule, keep in mind that it does not need to be a particular length. It is not required to be only one sentence; in fact, multiple sentences tend to be better. What is included in the rule depends exclusively on what the reader needs to know about the rule as it relates to the issue addressed by the CREAC. Thus, every rule will be approached differently based on the specific legal issue addressed by the CREAC and by the overall objective document.

c. Explanation

The explanation, or the E in the CREAC, is where the reader is provided with a detailed example or further explanation of the rule stated in the R of the CREAC. The purpose of the explanation is twofold.

First, the explanation should give the reader a better understanding of how the rule, the R in the CREAC, is interpreted and applied. Remember, you have done all of the research on a particular rule and you have a certain level of knowledge about the rule that your reader does not. You should assume that the reader only knows what you tell her. Thus, for your reader to understand how the rule is interpreted and applied, you need to provide her with that information in the explanation (the E in the CREAC).

Second, the explanation is used to set up the application (the A in the CREAC). For example, if you plan to provide a factual comparison between the facts of your case and the facts of a precedent case, you need to first provide a discussion of that precedent case, including the relevant facts, in the explanation section of the CREAC.

There are two main types of explanations that can be used in the explanation section of the CREAC—the case illustration and the parenthetical. These are discussed in more depth in the Legal Analysis Toolkit Chapter (see Chapter 6). The general rule for explanations is that there is no length or number requirement and the amount of information to be included in the explanation is dictated by what is needed to explain the rule to the reader. Thus, the amount of information provided in an explanation section will change with every explanation section (the E in the CREAC), every CREAC, and every objective document.

d. Application

The application, the A in the CREAC, is where you apply the rule provided in the R of the CREAC to the facts of the client's case. The most common types of legal analysis used to apply the rule to the client's facts are deductive reasoning, analogical reasoning, and policy-based reasoning. These are discussed in more depth in the Legal Analysis Toolkit Chapter (see Chapter 6), but the following paragraphs contain short descriptions of each.

Deductive reasoning justifies a result by directly applying a legal principle to the facts of the client's case. The result is the result simply because the law mandates it. There is no in-depth analysis, rather a straightforward application of a simple legal principle to the facts of the client's case. For example, if the rule is that a person must be 16 years old to drive a vehicle and the client's facts show that the driver at issue was 18 years old, then the deductive reasoning would be a simple application of that rule to the facts. Depending upon the complexity of the rule and the facts of the client's case, the deductive reasoning (the A in the CREAC) may be as short as one sentence but may also be as long as a paragraph.

Analogical reasoning applies the facts and reasoning of a precedent case to the facts of the client's case. This is done to show that the circumstances of the client's case are similar to the circumstances of the precedent case and, therefore, the likely outcome of the client's case will be the same as the precedent case. Or, it may be used to show that the circumstances of the client's case are different from the circumstances of the precedent case and, therefore, the likely outcome of the client's case may be different from the outcome in the precedent case. Analogical reasoning tends to be a longer form of analysis.

Policy-based reasoning applies the purpose underlying a rule to justify a result. Policy-based reasoning is most often used to bolster an analysis that already is supported by legal authorities and to demonstrate the policy implications of a particular prediction. Additionally, where there are not any applicable legal authorities, policy-based reasoning may be used to predict the type of law that may be created in the future. It is important to note that when using policy-based reasoning, the policy being applied must be based in law, not personal opinion or a general view of society.

e.   Conclusion

The CREAC paradigm begins and ends with a conclusion or the C in the CREAC. While the closing C and the beginning C should not simply be a cut-and-paste of the same sentence, they should generally be the same. If the two conclusions are substantively different, then you likely got lost somewhere in your CREAC. As discussed above, the conclusion only is the conclusion for the specific legal issue being addressed by the specific CREAC, not an overall conclusion for the entire memorandum. Sometimes, the conclusion is one sentence, but its length should be based what is needed to completely (but concisely) articulate the conclusion on the specific issue that is the subject of the CREAC.

CHAPTER 10

THE FORMAL MEMORANDUM

■ ■ ■

By Gretchen Franz

A. FORMAL MEMORANDUM GENERALLY

A formal memorandum is objectively written to evaluate and predict the likely outcome of one or multiple legal issues involved in a potential case. The formal memorandum is primarily informative in nature—it flushes out and balances the strengths and weaknesses of both sides of an issue. It presents and analyzes the law and facts to predict how a court may decide the legal issue. Although the formal memorandum is objective in nature, it most often will recommend a course of action—how best to present the client's arguments and attack the opposition's arguments.

The formal memorandum is most often written for a supervising attorney. It is written for the benefit of that attorney who has usually requested an answer to a specific legal question. The supervising attorney will expect to read an evaluation of the controlling law, the likely outcome of how that law affects the facts of the case, and a recommendation of how to proceed. While the primary purpose of the formal memorandum is to inform others about the merits of the case, the memorandum can also serve as the basis for the following tasks:

- Advising the client of the strengths and weaknesses of his potential case.

- Preparing other documents—e.g., demand letters, client letters, negotiation/settlement and/or mediation materials, and briefs filed with the court.

- Creating strategy for representing the client and pursuing litigation.

This chapter explains the goals and substance of the components of a formal memorandum. You will very likely be drafting a formal memorandum in your course, and your professor will provide you with detailed instructions and possibly a checklist for your own assignment.

B. COMPONENTS OF A FORMAL MEMORANDUM

While the format and structure of a formal memorandum may differ depending on the circumstances in which it is being written, it generally contains the following components:

- Heading
- Question Presented[1]
- Brief Answer
- Facts
- Discussion
- Conclusion

Formal Memorandum Outline for One Issue Problem

The memorandum for a single issue problem will have a Caption, headings, and a single Conclusion, Rule, Explanation, Application, Conclusion paradigm. The following provides an example of what the outline of a one issue problem might look like.

---

[1] The Issue or Issue Statement is sometimes used synonymously with the Question Presented.

MEMORANDUM	
TO:	Name of Person Who Assigned the Memorandum
FROM:	Your Name
DATE:	Date Memorandum Was Written
RE:	File Number, Case/Client Name, and Short Description of Subject of Memo

QUESTION PRESENTED
BRIEF ANSWER
FACTS
DISCUSSION

Umbrella Paragraph*

CREAC

Conclusion

Rule

Explanation

Application

Conclusion

CONCLUSION

*An umbrella paragraph may or may not be useful for a single-issue memorandum. The purpose of the umbrella paragraph is to present information that is preliminary or defines the scope and structure of the analysis that follows. The umbrella paragraph usually contains a roadmap that provides the reader with an orientation to the order in which the issues will be discussed. For a single-issue memorandum, no roadmap may be necessary.

For a multi-issue memorandum, the umbrella paragraph will usually contain the roadmap and provide the reader with an outline of the order in which the issues will be addressed, as well as any common rules or preliminary considerations that should be contemplated.

Formal Memorandum Outline for Two or More Issues Problem

The memorandum for two or more issues will also include a Caption, Headings, and a single Conclusion, Rule, Explanation, Application, Conclusion paradigm for each issue. The following provides an example of what the outline of a two or more issues problem might look like.

MEMORANDUM	
TO:	Name of Person Who Assigned the Memorandum
FROM:	Your Name
DATE:	Date Memorandum Was Written
RE:	File Number, Case/Client Name, and Short Description of Subject of Memo

QUESTIONS PRESENTED

I. First Question Presented

II. Second Question Presented

BRIEF ANSWER

I. Brief Answer to First Question Presented

II. Brief Answer to Second Question Presented

FACTS

DISCUSSION

Umbrella Paragraph

I. Predictive Point Heading for Issue I

CREAC

Conclusion

Rule

Explanation

Application

Conclusion

II. Predictive Point Heading for Issue II

CREAC

Conclusion

Rule

Explanation

Application

Conclusion

CONCLUSION

1. QUESTION PRESENTED

The Question Presented identifies the legal issue or subject the memorandum evaluates. There may be a single issue, a single issue with subparts, or multiple issues unrelated to one another. The Question Presented identifies the relevant statute or common law rule, sets out the specific legal issue, and includes the facts relevant to the legal issue. There are two standard ways to craft the Questions Presented: the Under-Does-When Question Presented and the Narrative Question Presented.

Both forms of the Question Presented may be phrased specifically or generally. When phrased specifically, the Question Presented identifies the persons, places, or things in relation to a particular case. Most frequently, the Question Presented will be written specifically—to address the specific issue the assigning attorney has requested be evaluated with regard to a particular client or case. The examples provided below are written specifically.

A Question Presented phrased generally characterizes an issue generically. The general question presented is appropriate when the assigning attorney has asked for an evaluation of an issue without reference to a particular client's case.

a. Under-Does-When Question Presented

The most common Question Presented is one sentence ending with a question mark. This Under-Does-When Question Presented construction contains the following components:

- Under: This provides the reader with the relevant statute or law.

- Does: This provides the reader with the legal issue evaluated in the Memorandum.

- When: This provides the reader with the facts that are relevant to the legal issue. All facts that the court will consider in deciding the legal issue should be included. It will sometimes be cumbersome to include all the relevant facts. In that case, the facts should either be summarized or categorized.

Examples:

- Background: The Illinois Dog Bite Statute provides that a person who owns or harbors a dog is not liable for damages when the dog injures a person, if the person was (1) not lawfully present on the premises and (2) the dog acted with provocation.

- Facts: Zach Tyler climbed over his neighbor's locked fence gate that had a prominent two-foot square sign—STAY OUT!—and entered Sharon Mason's yard. Sharon's dog, Tino, was sleeping under a tree. Zach kicked Tino in the stomach. The dog woke up and growled. Zach kicked the dog two more times, and the dog growled after each kick, and then bit Zach in the leg.

In this factual scenario, there are two issues to evaluate under the Illinois Dog Bite Statute: (1) lawful presence and (2) provocation.

The issues can be presented in separate Questions Presented:

First: Under-Does-When Question Presented:

Under the Illinois Dog Bite Statute (*relevant statute or law*), was Zach Tyler lawfully present (*legal issue evaluated in memorandum*) when he entered Sharon Mason's yard by climbing over a locked fence gate that had a prominent two-foot square sign that read "STAY OUT!"? (*facts relevant to the legal issue of whether Zach Tyler was lawfully present under the Illinois Dog Bite Statute*)

Second: Under-Does-When Question Presented:

Under the Illinois Dog Bite Statute (*relevant statute or law*), did Zach Tyler provoke Tino the dog (*legal issue evaluated in memorandum*) when he kicked the dog in the stomach multiple times and the dog growled after each kick? (*facts relevant to the legal issue of whether the dog acted with provocation*)

Or, because the issues both relate to the Illinois Dog Bite Statute, the Question Presented can be crafted as one question with two subparts:

Under the Illinois Dog Bite Statute (*statute or law relevant to sub-issues*):

(a)   Was Zach Tyler lawfully present (*legal issue evaluated in memorandum*) when he entered Sharon Mason's yard by climbing over a locked fence gate that had a prominent two-foot square sign that read "STAY OUT!"? (*facts relevant to the legal issue of whether the boy was lawfully present*), and

(b)   Did Zach Tyler provoke Tino the dog (*legal issue evaluated in memorandum*) when he kicked the dog in the stomach multiple times and the dog growled after each kick? (*facts relevant to the legal issue of whether the dog acted with provocation*)

---

b. Narrative Question Presented[2]

Another construction for writing the Question Presented is referred to as the Narrative Question Presented. The goal of the Narrative Question Presented is to provide the issue in the framework of a story. Unlike the Under-Does-When Question Presented, which is crafted as one sentence, the Narrative Question Presented is multiple sentences. It should be under one hundred (100) words and the last sentence should end with a question mark. Like the Under-Does-When Question Presented where multiple Questions Presented (or one Question Presented with sub-parts) are required for multi-issue Memoranda, multiple Narrative Questions Presented (or one with sub-parts) are required for multi-issue Memoranda.

Example:

Under the Illinois Dog Bite Statute, a dog owner is not liable for damages when her dog injures a person if the person was not lawfully present and if the dog was provoked. Zach Tyler climbed over a fence with a sign that read "STAY OUT" and entered Sharon Mason's yard. He kicked Sharon's dog multiple times in the stomach. The dog growled after each kick and then bit Zach in the leg. Was Zach Tyler lawfully present and did he provoke Tino the dog? (NOTE: 85 words)

---

2. BRIEF ANSWER

The Brief Answer responds to the Question Presented and includes a short explanation to support that answer. The Brief Answer should mirror the structure of the Question Presented. If there is more than one Question Presented, each Question Presented should have a corresponding Brief Answer. Likewise, if the Question Presented has sub-parts, the Brief Answer should as well. The format of the Brief Answer is the same whether the Under-Does-When or Narrative Question Presented construction is used.

If the Question Presented is phrased in general terms, the Brief Answer should be phrased in general terms as well. Conversely, if the Question Presented is specific, the Brief Answer should also be specific.

Each Brief Answer has three components:

1. Short statement of the answer:

    - Yes or No. (There are rare instances when the Question Presented can be definitively answered with a yes or no. This is not the norm. It may occur if there is a simple

---

[2] The Narrative Question Presented is adapted from The Advanced Question Presented materials provided in the Advanced Legal Writing and Editing seminars taught by Bryan A. Garner and Law Prose, Inc. (Nov. 2007).

legal issue—i.e. Can John purchase alcohol in California? In California, a person must be 21 to purchase alcohol. John is 23. Thus, the Brief Answer for this issue would begin with a definite Yes. Conversely, if John is 15, the Briefly Answer would be begin with a definite No.)

- Probably Yes/Likely Yes.

- Probably No (Probably Not)/Likely No (Likely Not).

2. Statement of the applicable rule or rules.

3. Summary of how the relevant law applies to the facts of the case. Briefly summarize the reasoning that supports the conclusion regarding the Question Presented.

Examples:

If this is your Question Presented	Then this might be your Brief Answer
1. Under the Illinois Dog Bite Statute (*relevant statute or law*), was Zach Tyler lawfully present (*legal issue evaluated in memorandum*) when he entered Sharon Mason's yard by climbing over a locked fence gate that had a prominent two-foot square sign that read "STAY OUT!" (*facts relevant to legal issue*)?	1. Probably No. (*short statement of answer*) Under the Illinois Dog Bite Statute, a person is lawfully present if the person is in an area that appears open to the public, and if the person was given no or inadequate notice that entry to the area is forbidden or dangerous (*statement of applicable rule or rules*). In this case, the locked fence gate probably made it appear that the area was not open to the public. In addition, the prominent sign that stated "STAY OUT!" likely provided adequate notice that entry to the front yard was forbidden. Because the area did not appear open to the public, and Zach Tyler was provided adequate notice that entry was forbidden, he was likely not lawfully present. (*summary of the reasoning including relevant facts and application of the rule or rules*)
2. Under the Illinois Dog Bite Statute (*relevant statute or law*), did Zach Tyler provoke Tino the dog (*legal issue evaluated in memorandum*) when he kicked the dog in the stomach multiple times and the dog growled after each kick? (*facts relevant to the legal issue of whether the dog acted with provocation*)	2. Probably Yes. (*short statement of answer*) Under the Illinois Dog Bite Statute, a dog is provoked if it is physically touched and indicates a dislike to that touch. (*statement of applicable rule or rules*) In this case, Zach Tyler kicked the dog three times in the stomach. The dog indicated her dislike of the kicking, by growing after each kick. Because Zach Tyler physically touched the dog, and she responded by growling after each kick, Tyler probably provoked the dog. (*summary of the reasoning including relevant facts and application of the rule or rules*).

3.   FACTS

The goal of the Facts is to tell the reader the story of what happened that led to the conflict or issues evaluated in the memorandum. The Facts section should contain the facts that are legally relevant to the issue(s) evaluated in the memorandum. Legally relevant facts are those facts that are necessary to determine how the law applies to the issue. However, the legally relevant facts should not be presented in isolation. They should be surrounded with background facts that provide context to the legally relevant facts to complete the story.

a. Audience

When crafting the facts, remember that the reader is most likely the supervising attorney. The goal is to objectively present the facts to the reader in one consolidated narrative. It is good to keep in mind that the memorandum may later be used as a basis for other documents. While this should not encourage the writer to present the facts persuasively, it should help the writer anticipate the opposition's arguments by identifying the facts most beneficial to the client—and those that may better support the opposition's position.

b. Fact Selection

The first paragraph of the Facts introduces the reader to the framework of the story. To do this, the first paragraph should

- Identify the client and other important people or entities involved in the case.

- Explain the client's problem or the goal that the client wants to achieve.

- Provide the time, date, and location of all relevant events.

- Briefly reference the procedural history of the case.

The body of the Facts should be focused on telling the full story. It is here that the focus needs to be on including the legally relevant facts. The legally relevant facts are dispositive facts—those that will affect the outcome of the application of the law. All facts that are used in the Discussion section are legally relevant facts. However, if only the legally relevant facts were included, the story would likely seem incomplete. As such, any facts that are necessary to provide context to the story should also be included. These facts should be specific and flow together with the legally relevant facts to tell the story in such a manner that the reader understands what actually happened.

When selecting the facts to include, there are a few things to keep in mind. First, the facts must include the "good" facts (favorable for the client) and the "bad" facts (favorable for the opposition). It is easy to include the good facts. It is equally important, however, to include facts that may be detrimental to the client's case and actually support the opponent's argument. The "bad" facts are important because they alert the writer to arguments that demonstrate the client may have difficulty achieving her goal. Addressing the bad facts may also help evaluate whether there is an argument that minimizes the impact of those facts. The "bad" facts must be included in the Facts section and addressed in the analysis of the issue to adequately and objectively advise the reader of the merits of the case. Remember that not all advice is good news for the client.

Also, when selecting facts, make sure they are facts. Only facts should be included in the Fact section. Do not include the legal analysis or legal conclusions—they are not facts. The Facts section also should not include law, legal commentary, or the writer's interpretation of the facts.

c.   Writing the Facts

The facts must be written objectively. The purpose of a formal memorandum is to be predictive, not persuasive. Save persuasive techniques for demand letters, briefs, and motions. Another thing to keep in mind when writing the facts is to ensure they are accurate based upon the knowledge of the facts at the time the memorandum is written. The facts should be detailed, not summarized or generalized. The details provide for an in-depth analysis of the issue. However, do not embellish the facts or comment upon the facts. A change in facts can drastically affect how the law applies. This can result in a flawed analysis.

Additionally, present the facts in a well-organized manner. The facts may be organized in different ways—chronologically, topically, or a combination of the two. The manner in which the facts are organized depends upon the issue(s) involved. If there is one issue, the most straightforward way to present the facts is in chronological order. If, however, there are multiple issues, and different facts are needed for the different issues, the facts can be presented topically, by issue. If there are multiple issues with differing facts, the facts can also be presented chronologically according to each issue.

d.   Writing Tips

- To help determine which facts are legally relevant, carefully read the legal authorities relevant to the issue. Specifically, check to see which facts the courts noted in the reasoning. This will help determine which facts in the client's case are relevant to the resolution of the issue.

- After writing the Discussion section, carefully note which facts were relied upon in the analysis. Check to make sure any facts relied upon in the Discussion section are included in the Facts section of the Memorandum.

- Conversely, after writing the Discussion section, re-read the Facts section. If there are facts that were not included in the analysis that might be helpful to evaluating the issue, be sure to discuss them in the Discussion section.

4. DISCUSSION

The Discussion is the crux of the Memorandum. The purpose of this section is to explain the relevant legal rules and how the rules apply to the facts of the client's case, and to make a predictive conclusion based upon the analysis. The Discussion should explain all relevant applications of the law—those that support the client's case and any counter-arguments the opposition can make.

a. Umbrella

The Discussion most often begins with an Umbrella paragraph that provides an overview of the memorandum and organization of the Discussion. Not all memoranda require an Umbrella paragraph. This paragraph is included when the law or synthesized rules for the issue has multiple parts and the analysis has more than one step. If there is more than one main issue addressed in the Memorandum, each will likely have its own Umbrella paragraph. Generally, the Umbrella begins with the overall conclusion reached regarding the particular issue addressed in the memorandum. It also includes the overall organization of the Discussion section and the basic reason for the conclusion, if it can be stated succinctly.

b. Predictive Point Headings

In predictive writing, point headings are used as an organizational tool. They keep the writer and the reader on track with the issue or issues being evaluated. Point headings tell the reader that there is a change in an issue or sub-issue. The predictive point heading generally includes the predictive conclusion regarding that issue and the succinct reason supporting that conclusion.

c. CREAC

The body of the Discussion of each issue or sub-issue should follow the CREAC paradigm. If the memorandum analyzes multiple issues, address each issue separately. It may help to number the different issues and include a predictive point heading for each main issue. If the memorandum has an issue with sub-issues, use predictive sub-point headings to distinguish between the sub-issues.

Conclusion: The conclusion is the ultimate prediction regarding the Issue or Sub-Issue.

Rule(s):   State the specific legal principle to be applied to the legal issue being addressed by the CREAC.

Explanation: Explain the rule(s). Depending on the type of rule explanation, this will be (1) a rule statement plus a case illustration; or (2) a rule statement plus a short statement of the court's reasoning; or (3) a rule statement plus a parenthetical; or (4) just a rule statement (when the rule speaks for itself). Choose the type of rule explanation that will support the application of the rule to the facts of the case. (See Chapter 6: Legal Reasoning and Analysis Toolkit for a discussion of the different types of rule explanations).

Application: This section should discuss and resolve the application of the law pertaining to the client's case. Analyze the issue by applying the rules to the facts using analogical reasoning, deductive reasoning, and/or policy-based reasoning. (See Chapter 6: Legal Reasoning and Analysis Toolkit, for a discussion of the different types of analyses)

Conclusion: Provide the predictive answer to the issue or sub-issue, and a succinct reason supporting that prediction.

5. CONCLUSION

The final Conclusion in a formal memorandum summarizes the analysis regarding each issue identified in the Question(s) Presented of the Memorandum. This is not the C in the CREAC, but a separate section that summarizes the analysis and conclusions of all of the issues identified in the Question(s) Presented and addressed in the Discussion section. To do so, the Conclusion needs to remind the reader of the conclusion for each issue (the C in the CREAC) with a summary of the legal reasoning and the facts that support the conclusion.

C. EDITING CHECKLIST FOR THE FORMAL MEMORANDUM

After drafting each component of the formal memorandum, use an Editing Checklist to proofread your Memorandum. The checklist should help evaluate whether all of the required components include the requisite substance and whether the format of the memorandum is in order. You may either craft your own checklist from this chapter or your professor may provide a checklist for you.

D. CROSS-CULTURAL CONSIDERATIONS

The formal memorandum is deeply entrenched in United States legal practice. Likewise, each international or foreign law practice has some sort of internal written product to evaluate legal issues. The proper format for predictive legal writing will depend on the country and the legal setting. Additionally, the cultural expectations of domestic legal employers may be different from one another. Specific law firms or other legal employers may have different formats for the formal memorandum. The writer must learn the "culture" of the legal employer and the expectations it has regarding predictive memoranda.

PRACTICE EXERCISE

Choose a memorandum that you have written, or your professor has provided to you, and do the following in the margins: (1) identify the C, R, E, A, and C for each Issue; (2) identify the different types of rule explanations in each E of the CREAC, (3) identify the different types of analyses used in each A of the CREAC, and (4) verify that the rule explanations align with the manner in which the rule is used in the analysis.

CHAPTER 11

THE SHORT-FORM MEMORANDUM

■ ■ ■

By Hether C. Macfarlane

A. LONG V. SHORT-FORM MEMORANDA

Chapter 10 introduced the components of a formal objective memorandum of law. This book starts with a formal memorandum for several reasons. First, a formal memorandum is the best way for you to demonstrate your understanding of statutes, cases, and legal analysis. Second, as noted in Chapter 10, the formal memorandum is deeply ingrained in the American legal culture, and potential employers want to know that you know how to write one. A formal memo shows that you are able to evaluate both sides of a problem and present a neutral analysis. Memos you write for this class are therefore often your best writing samples—after you edit and revise them—when you look for a summer job or an internship or externship. Finally, employers still often have summer associates and interns/externs write formal memos for precisely the same reason that your legal research and writing professor did: to be able to judge your understanding of the law and your skills of legal analysis. Of course, employers also want to get the important information that a busy attorney may use as the future basis for other documents such as advice and demand letters, or even persuasive briefs. So, all law students need to know how to write such a memo.

The reality today, however, is that practicing lawyers write fewer and fewer formal memoranda. One reason for this change is economic: one estimate is that a formal memorandum can cost between $5,000 and $20,000 to produce.[1] Clients are increasingly scrutinizing the bottom line and are unwilling to pay for the kind of training of young lawyers that firms achieved in the past through the production of formal memos. In addition, writing a full memorandum takes a long time (as you have learned by writing at least one of them yourself), and firms are coming to believe that a young lawyer's time can be better spent in doing the research and reaching a conclusion. Finally, both busy lawyers and busy clients are less willing than they were in the past to take the time to read through a formal memorandum. They are increasingly relying, therefore, on short-form

---

[1] I am grateful to Lisa Healy, Associate Professor of Legal Writing at Suffolk University Law School, for sharing this information with me.

memoranda and e-mails to convey an answer to a legal problem posed by a client.

B. WHAT SECTIONS TO INCLUDE IN A SHORT-FORM MEMO

Because this shift to shorter memoranda is still evolving, lawyers and legal research and writing faculty have not yet agreed on the components of a short-form memorandum.

One approach is to combine the Question Presented, the Brief Answer, and the Conclusion into an **Executive Summary** that comes before the Facts and the Discussion section. The Executive Summary provides the reader a quick way to learn the issue the memo addresses as well as the writer's analysis and conclusions. An effective Executive Summary does not include citations, and it needs to include five elements:

1. The issue or issues addressed in the memo

2. A summary of the rules applied in the memo

3. A summary of the writer's reasoning in the memo

4. The writer's ultimate predictions (or conclusions) in the memo

5. A recommendation for future action

The Executive Summary should be about half a page, and the reader should be able to read it in no more than a minute.

Another approach is to combine the Question Presented and the Facts section into an **Introduction.** This section begins with a statement of the issue the writer has been asked to address and then provides the facts of the client's case. Because this section does not include a conclusion or prediction, the memo needs to include a Conclusion section after the Discussion.

Sample first sentence for either approach: This memo addresses the possible liability in Illinois of a dog's owner when the animal bites a child after the child has kicked the dog several times."

C. SHORTENING THE DISCUSSION SECTION

The Discussion section is the longest part of a formal memorandum, and it remains the most important part of a short-form memorandum. Therefore, the Discussion section cannot be eliminated completely. Nor is it reasonable to completely exclude case illustrations from the text. That approach creates the danger that the writer will destroy the clarity of the of the analysis by failing to include sufficient facts of the precedent cases, by failing to supply the court's reasoning in the precedent cases, or by failing to apply that reasoning to the facts of the client's case.

Instead of simply eliminating elements of the formal memorandum's Discussion section, the solution to shortening it is to find ways to make the E portions of the CREACs more concise.

1. CHOOSE WHICH RULES NEED NO EXPLANATION

A very complete formal memo might provide some explanation of every applicable rule, including rules that are primarily background for the rule that is most important to the topic. These background rules will not need explanation in a shorter memo. For example, a rule that states that the speed limit on the local interstate highway is 65 mph needs no explanation and can be applied directly to the fact that the client was driving 80 mph at the time of the accident.

2. EDIT THE CASE ILLUSTRATIONS

The situation is different if the most relevant rule needs to be explained, such as a statute saying vehicles may not be driven at a speed that is greater than what is reasonable under the conditions prevailing at the time. What speed is "reasonable" then depends on the facts of the case.

Assume that your client has been sued for negligence as the result of a car accident in which she hit a pedestrian at an intersection. Your client can prove her speed at the time was 35 mph on a road with a 40-mph speed limit. The accident occurred early in the morning, and the road was enveloped in a dense fog. You have found several cases that involved adverse road conditions, one of which is *Harris v. Ball*.[2] The two examples that follow show a full case illustration and an edited case illustration.

---

[2]   The facts of this case are adapted from Gleich v. Volpe, 346 N.Y.S.2d 806 (N.Y. 1973). The citation for Harris v. Ball is fictitious.

The following is an example of a full case illustration:

> Driving at the posted speed limit is unreasonable when conditions require a lesser speed. *Harris v. Ball*, 79 Cal. 2d 555, 557 (1975). In *Harris*, the parents of a ten-year-old sued the driver of a vehicle that struck and seriously injured the child as she was crossing a county road at a school bus stop. It was raining heavily at the time. The road was hilly, and there was a curve a short distance before the bus stop in the direction from which the defendant was traveling. The defendant was very familiar with the road as he lived about two miles past the site of the accident. He was driving at the posted speed limit of 40 mph. When the defendant saw the flashing lights of the school bus, he slammed on the brakes and swerved to the left to avoid hitting the bus, striking the child as she crossed the road. *Id.* at 556.
>
> In holding that the defendant was negligent, even though he was driving at the posted speed limit, the court reasoned that he had been traveling at a speed that was too great to enable him to stop in time to avoid hitting the bus. His vision was reduced because of the heavy downpour. In addition, the court reasoned, because he was familiar with the road and lived nearby, he must have been aware of the presence of the school bus stop. Given these facts, his speed at the time of the accident was unreasonable. *Id.* at 557.

The following is an example of an abbreviated case illustration:

> Driving at the posted speed limit is unreasonable when conditions require a lesser speed. *Harris v. Ball*, 79 Cal. 2d 555, 557 (1975). The defendant in *Harris* was driving at the posted speed limit on a rainy afternoon on a road with which he was very familiar. Shortly after exiting a curve in the road, he saw the flashing lights of a school bus ahead. Unable to stop before hitting the bus, he swerved to the left and struck a child who was crossing the road in front of the bus. *Id.* at 556. In holding that the defendant was negligent, the court in its reasoning noted the heavy rain, the defendant's familiarity with the location of the school bus stop, and the defendant's inability to stop quickly enough to avoid the accident as evidence that these conditions meant driving at the posted speed limit was not reasonable at the time. *Id.* at 557.

The abbreviated case illustration is shorter because the writer condensed both the facts and the court's reasoning. At the same time, however, all of the necessary facts and reasoning remain in the abbreviated case illustration. Indeed, the shorter version would likely be appropriate in either a long-form or a short-form memo.

3.   USE PARENTHETICAL ILLUSTRATIONS

The shortest way to explain a rule is to use a parenthetical illustration. The skill of writing parenthetical illustrations is useful for both short-form objective memoranda and for persuasive arguments. But it is definitely a skill, and it takes practice to develop.

The following is an example of a parenthetical:

> Driving at the posted speed limit is unreasonable when conditions require a lesser speed. *Harris v. Ball*, 79 Cal. 2d 555, 557 (1975) (holding that a driver's speed was unreasonable even though he drove at the posted speed limit because a heavy rain storm made him unable to stop in time to avoid a collision at a familiar school bus stop).

The entire explanation here consists of a statement or thesis about the law, a citation to a case, and a short description of the case that supports the statement. A parenthetical explanation is even shorter than the abbreviated case illustration because it weaves the relevant facts together with the court's reasoning instead of stating them separately. Nonetheless, this explanation still includes both of those necessary elements without sacrificing clarity of meaning.

Guidelines for Parenthetical Explanations[3]

A parenthetical explanation must follow a rule statement or statement about a rule.

A parenthetical must consist of a single sentence. If the explanation requires more than one sentence, a parenthetical is inappropriate.

A parenthetical must be placed after the court and date at the end of a full citation or after the page number in a short-form citation; insert one space but do not insert any punctuation.

A parenthetical generally must begin with a lower case present participle (a verb form ending in "ing") that explains some action of the court such as "holding," "reasoning," "concluding." This participle must refer to an action of the court, not an action of one of the parties. There are two exceptions to the rule to begin a parenthetical with a present participle: (1) when the explanation consists of a quotation from the case, and (2) when the writer uses a series of cases to provide short examples. For example, for a statement of law concerning the age at which states have punished young people for crimes as if they were adults, each case citation could be followed by a parenthetical that simply stated that defendant's age.

---

[3]   Adapted from MICHAEL R. SMITH, ADVANCED LEGAL WRITING 56–59 (3d ed. 2013).

A parenthetical should have no ending punctuation unless the parenthetical consists of a complete sentence in a quotation.

Remember that a parenthetical is an explanation (the E in the CREAC), not a statement of a rule. The rule belongs in the sentence that precedes the citation, not in the parenthetical. Finally, be sure that the text of the parenthetical relates to the context for which you are citing the case, not just to the case itself.

Compare the parenthetical below to the previous parenthetical example:

> Driving at the posted speed limit is **unreasonable** when conditions require a lesser speed. *Harris v. Ball* (holding that a driver **violated the law** when he drove at the posted speed limit in a heavy rain storm and was unable to stop to avoid a stopped school bus when he was familiar with the location of the bus stop).

While the driver certainly violated the speed law, the context of the parenthetical was the reasonableness of his speed, not the violation of the law, so this parenthetical would be ineffective in explaining the term "reasonable" in the statute.

These techniques should allow you to write a Discussion section that is shorter than such a section in a formal memorandum but complete enough for the reader to understand the analysis.

D. E-MAILED LEGAL ANALYSIS[4]

Email (or e-mail) is a feature of all lawyers' lives, both professional and personal. Lawyers use email to request information from clients or provide information to clients, to communicate with courts and opposing counsel, and to ask questions of other lawyers in their firm. They may use email to engage in negotiations with counsel for other parties. Other forms of professional correspondence are covered in Chapter 15. The focus of this section, however, is on email as a method of communicating legal analysis to an assigning lawyer who has asked for it.

You should use email to communicate legal analysis only if the analysis is very short; if the topic is such that you need multiple hard-copy pages to complete the requested analysis, write it as a formal or short-form memorandum that you then attach to the email. Writers help readers orient themselves to the points in and flow of memos by using page

---

[4] Sources include Kristen E. Murray, *You Know What I Meant: The Science behind Email and Intent*, 14 LEGAL COMM. & RHETORIC: JALWD 119 (Fall 2017); Richard K. Neumann, Jr., J. Lyn Entrikin & Sheila Simon, LEGAL WRITING 235–38 (3d ed. 2015); Mary Barnard Ray, THE BASICS OF LEGAL WRITING 247–51 (rev'd 1st ed. 2008); Wayne Schiess, WRITING FOR THE LEGAL AUDIENCE 33–44 (2003).

numbers. Because it is impossible to put page numbers in an email, readers may have difficulty orienting themselves in a message longer than can appear on two screens of a computer or tablet. The tendency of everyone today to read on smaller cell phone screens also increases the need to use emails for only short legal analysis. Indeed, research has shown that people are more likely to give up in the middle of an electronic memo than they are with a hard copy.[5]

As far as format goes, make sure that the email is addressed to the correct person. The subject line should be both specific and clear. In the body of the email, start with a statement of the issue you were asked to address, followed by a one or two-sentence conclusion. You may or may not need to state any essential facts, usually depending on how long it has been since you received the original request. If only a short period of time has passed, you can omit any factual statement as the recipient will probably be engaged in the client's case already. As for the analysis, use a brief form of CREAC, with a particularly brief E section. If you believe the recipient will not be able to understand the analysis without an extended E section, you should write a memo and attach it to an email that merely communicates that memo. Finally, it is likely that you will not need to include a separate conclusion section, just as you may not have included one in a short-form memorandum as discussed above.

Because of the absence of page numbers, email memos need to include other methods to help readers stay oriented. Be sure to put spaces between paragraphs, as you cannot indent the beginning of a paragraph using the tab key. Headings, topic sentences, and roadmap paragraphs are just as, if not more, important in an email memo than they are in a traditional memo. Because it is not possible to center headings in an email, they should stay at the left margin and appear in bold, not in all-caps. In roadmap paragraphs, use numerals, rather than words, or use bullets. An email memo can take advantage of hyperlinks to allow the reader to jump straight to any authorities mentioned in the analysis, so those authorities do not need to be attached to the memo.

The professionalism guidelines that govern communicating legal analysis in a print memo apply as well to emailed legal analyses. Grammar and punctuation remain necessities; emoticons and abbreviations such as OMG and IMHO are inappropriate. In addition, writers need to be particularly aware of tone. Email is particularly poor at conveying emotion. What "sounds" like zealous reasoning to the writer may easily come across to the reader as hostility and anger. Written communication cannot convey your emotion in the way face-to-face communication can through facial expression, gesture, and tone of voice, and email seems to be particularly susceptible to being misunderstood without these in-person elements. If

---

[5]   Kendra Huard Fershee, *The New Legal Writing: The Importance of Teaching Law Students How to Use E-Mail Professionally*, 71 MD. L. REV. ENDNOTES 1 (2001).

your mood while drafting an email actually is angry or hostile, either save that draft until much later after you have reviewed it, or don't send that email at all. And remember that your recipient may forward the email to others, who may send it on. Numerous examples exist of emails intended for one person that later "go viral" on the internet.

Finally, email correspondence needs to be treated the same as all other professional communication in terms of confidentiality and protecting the attorney-client privilege. Therefore, even email sent within your firm should contain a notation of attorney-client work product.

The next page shows an example of legal analysis appropriate to be sent by email. Assume that all citations include hyperlinks to the cited source.

Sent To: Geoffrey Martin, Senior Partner

From: Sara Liu, Summer Associate

Subject: Research re: domestic partner & wrongful death action

Date: August 19, 2012

Dear Geoffrey,

You asked me whether a same-sex domestic partner can bring a claim for wrongful death in California.

Yes, a domestic partner can bring the claim. Wrongful death is strictly a statutory cause of action in California, not a common law cause of action; therefore, a party must be included in the statute to have a right to sue. *Scott v. Thompson*, 184 Cal. App. 4th 1506 (4th Dist. 2010). The applicable statute is California Code of Civil Procedure § 377.60(a) (West Supp. 2012). In 2002, the statute was amended to include "domestic partners" among family members who may bring such a claim. A copy of the statute is attached to this e-mail.

A problem would arise, however, if the domestic partnership were not registered with the Secretary of State's office, as required by California Family Code § 297(b)(9) (West 2004). Without the registration, the surviving partner would not have standing to sue. *Armijo v. Miles*, 127 Cal. App. 4th 1405 (2d Dist. 2005).

Please let me know if you have any further questions.

Sara

CONFIDENTIALITY NOTICE: The contents of this email message and any attachments are intended solely for the addressee(s) and may contain confidential and/or privileged information and may be legally protected from disclosure.

CHAPTER 12

RECEIVING AND IMPLEMENTING FEEDBACK

■ ■ ■

By Adrienne Brungess and Stephanie J. Thompson

A. INTRODUCTION

Psychologists have reached "substantial consensus that students' progress in higher education can be facilitated by, or indeed is wholly contingent on, their ability and willingness to share responsibility for their learning."[1] "The key to learning is feedback. It is nearly impossible to learn anything without it."[2] A student's mindset will dictate the student's interpretation of and response to critical feedback. If, for example, you view critical feedback as an indication that you are not "smart" enough, you will find it more difficult to grow from the criticism and implement it effectively. Alternatively, if you view criticism as an opportunity to become more intelligent and proficient in the area in question, you are far more likely to make meaningful progress.[3] Getting feedback is one of the best learning opportunities in law school. Therefore, before attempting to digest the feedback you receive on written work, try to approach the endeavor as an opportunity to strengthen your legal writing and analytical skills, rather than as an indictment of your character.

Students tend to receive more extensive feedback on legal writing assignments than on other assessments before or during law school[4] and the breadth of the feedback can seem overwhelming. You should not be surprised when you encounter lengthy feedback when your work is returned. The thoroughness of the feedback reflects that your professor wants only your success, and to help you reach your full potential. Your

---

[1] Robert A. Nash & Naomi E. Winstone, *Responsibility-Sharing in the Giving & Receiving of Assessment & Feedback*, FRONTIERS IN PSYCHOLOGY, 2, (Sept. 6, 2017) (*citations omitted*) available at https://www.frontiersin.org/articles/10.3389/fpsyg.2017.01519/full (last visited December 4, 2017).

[2] STEVEN LEVITT, THINK LIKE A FREAK (2014).

[3] *See generally*, Carol S. Dweck & Ellen L. Leggett, *A Social-Cognitive Approach to Motivation and Personality*, 95 PSYCHOL. REV. 256 (1988).

[4] Carrie Sperling & Susan Shapcott, *Fixing Students' Fixed Mindsets: Paving The Way For Meaningful Assessment,* 8 LEGAL WRITING JOURNAL 39, 60 (2012) available at http://www.legal writingjournal.org/2015/05/19/fixing-students-fixed-mindsets-paving-the-way-for-meaningful-assessment/#chapter2 (last visited December 4, 2017).

professor's goal is to facilitate your growth as a writer and a professional and feedback on your work is a key to your success. Your goal must be mastery of the subject, rather than a high score or grade. Convince yourself you are equal to the challenges posed before immersing yourself in your professor's feedback. Remember that legal writing differs significantly from the kinds of writing most students have practiced before. When approaching tasks and implementing feedback, you should realistically assess your abilities and actively seek out resources to help in the areas where you are struggling. If you are more concerned about appearing unintelligent to your professors or peers than you are about mastering the process, you are unlikely to reach your potential.[5]

Consider the following when you review and implement your feedback:

- Accept your responsibility in the learning process and acknowledge that you must play an active role in this endeavor.[6] "[S]imply receiving feedback—no matter how high in quality—can never lead students to improve unless they actively receive, digest, and act upon it . . ."[7] Therefore, your active engagement is essential.

- Approach the critical feedback with optimism; you must believe that the feedback will enhance your mastery of the subject.[8] You did not come to law school with these skills, but you have the ability to acquire and even master them, with practice, open-mindedness, and experience.

- Devote substantial time and effort to reach your potential as a legal writer. It will be more time consuming for some students than for others; do not allow yourself to be frustrated by this. It is a marathon effort, not a sprint.

- If you are confused about a comment, do not allow the confusion to derail you. First, review your course materials and notes, or examples your professor may have provided; seek out the resolution on your own. If you are still confused, ask your professor for assistance. But do not remain silent or guess, or worse, ignore what your professor intended in effort to protect your ego; your professor welcomes questions and discussion about your work product. Discuss and share with your peers (as is permitted by your course rules); try to engage with a colleague who has strengths in areas where you need to improve.

---

[5] *See* Dweck, *supra* note 3; Sperling & Shapcott, *supra*, note 4, at 48–49.

[6] Nash & Winstone, *supra* note 1, at 3.

[7] *Id.*

[8] Sperling & Shapcott, *supra* note 4, at 68.

- Be deliberate about your strategy to catalog and implement the feedback you receive; do not take an ad hoc approach to this process. Focus on efforts that you can control, such as your research planning, pre-writing, time management, editing and revision process, etc.[9] rather than on the score or grade assessed.

B. IMPLEMENTING FEEDBACK

Evaluating the feedback provided to you by a professor requires different approaches if you are using it for a re-write or if you do not have a revision. Both approaches are described below.

1. FEEDBACK FOR A REVISION

Below is a suggested series of steps you can take to incorporate the feedback your professor has given you to consider for your re-write.

1. Take a deep breath. Remind yourself that the feedback is designed to identify where and how you can improve. It is a fantastic learning opportunity!

2. Read a clean copy of your assignment before you read your professor's feedback. For most students, the last time they read their paper would have been a couple of weeks earlier—right before they turned it in. Give yourself the context of what your professor read before you read your professor's feedback.

3. Now you are ready for your professor's feedback. Before you get started, develop a checklist or other accountability method to ensure you have addressed all of the professor's comments and edits. This might be as simple as you checking off each point directly on the document your professor returned to you. Ensuring that you have incorporated all of the feedback provided to you by your professor is especially important when you are revising a document because the professor will usually investigate into whether you incorporated all of her feedback.

4. Next, group the feedback given into two main categories: technical and substantive.

5. Now separate those categories into smaller categories. Prioritizing these tasks effectively is critical to your revision effort and will give you confidence that you are submitting your best final work product. By dividing the feedback into

---

[9] *Id.* at 78.

separate tasks, you will feel less overwhelmed and have shorter do-able tasks.

a. Technical

    i. Format and assignment requirements (margins, font, etc.)

    ii. Structure (organization—CREAC, CRAC, nested, etc.)

    iii. Grammar

    iv. Punctuation

    v. Spelling

    vi. Citation

b. Substantive (you may want to sub-divide this again, if needed)

    i. Introduction or Question Presented & Brief Answer

    ii. Discussion or Analysis

    iii. Facts

    iv. Rules

    v. Headings and Point Headings

    vi. Analysis

    vii. Conclusion

    viii. Overall Conclusion

6. At this point, decide the order in which you will incorporate the technical feedback. This likely will be the easiest feedback to address and the least time consuming.

7. Next, prioritize the tasks and goals related to all feedback for everything in the substantive category, and establish time parameters for each task you will complete. For example, you would assign yourself one hour to just review and correct all grammar, punctuation, and spelling. Or, a half hour to confirm your structure is correct—did you use CREAC, CRAC, or another writing paradigm correctly—are all of the component parts included and in the correct order; if not, make a note to correct it. And, this can become even more specific—one hour to just work on one specific CREAC or one sub-CREAC; or even smaller—one hour for just the analogical reasoning portion of one sub-CREAC. This type of focused review of feedback will allow you to carefully evaluate just one thing at a time. Trying to incorporate all of the feedback

given in one sitting will be overwhelming and frustrating because it will require you to focus on too many things at once. This all but guarantees you will miss something.

8.   During this process, you should also consider when you are able to complete each task. For example, you may want to work on the feedback for the Facts section last because you know you may be changing the facts used in the analysis section. Doing so may cause a change to the facts that should be included in the Facts section. The same is true for citation, especially short citations. If you know you will be moving things around in the Discussion or Analysis sections, then you probably want to correct the citations after you have modified those other sections. This is an important part of the planning process and it will help with efficiency in incorporating feedback.

2.   FEEDBACK WITHOUT A REVISION

When a paper is returned that will not be revised, most law students look at the grade and then never look at the paper again. This is a mistake. Even if you are not going to re-write the paper, the feedback provided by your professor offers an important learning opportunity. How you approach this feedback, however, is different from how you would approach feedback when you are revising. When reviewing feedback on written work where no revision is required, consider this method:

1.   Like above, group the feedback into two main categories: technical and substantive.

2.   Review the technical. Review all feedback that relates to grammar, punctuation and spelling. What common errors do you see? Are you making the same mistakes repeatedly? Or, instead, are there only occasional typos? Or are there frequent typos? This review will demonstrate where you should focus on your next writing project. Do you need to talk with your professor about a specific grammar or punctuation issue that you seem to get wrong repeatedly? Do you need to make sure you have more time to really white-glove your paper before you turn it in?[10] Grammar, punctuation and spelling should be near perfect in all your written work product, so it is important to determine what mistakes you are making so you can fix them and not repeat them.

3.   Next, review the feedback on your citations. What are your citation strengths? What errors are you making? Are your full

---

[10]   *See* Chapter 28 for details on the "White-Glove Inspection" that should be the final review of every piece of written work you submit.

cites correct, but you seem to make the same mistakes for short cites? Or are your cites correct but you do not seem to be citing frequently enough? Again, determine the common mistakes you are making. First, review your citation manual and the rules related to citation form or content you may have struggled with. If you are unable to determine how to correct these mistakes, then you should speak with your professor. Like the other technical writing components, citations will be used in most legal writing assignments, so it important that you assess what is going wrong and remedy the problem for the next assignment.

4. Next, review the substance. Because you are not going to be incorporating the assignment-specific feedback into a rewrite, any fact specific feedback should not be your focus. The focus now is to address common themes—Did you correctly use the writing paradigm? If not, how will you ensure you use it correctly in the future? Were your rules stated and synthesized correctly? If not, how will you ensure that this problem does not recur? Then, complete this step with all components: the depth of analysis, structure of analysis, use of facts, counter-arguments, etc. Assess what went well and where you need to improve.

5. At the end of this review process, you should create a one-page document from the feedback provided identifying and prioritizing areas of focus for your next assignment. This document should include a checklist of the feedback that indicated strengths and the areas where you received critical feedback. Review this document while you are writing your next paper.

CHAPTER 13

INTERVIEWING THE CLIENT

■ ■ ■

By Kathleen Friedrich

A lawyer has three main goals in client interviewing and counseling: (1) to gather information from the client, (2) to build and maintain rapport with the client, and (3) to inform and advise the client. This chapter provides an overview of the lawyering skill of interviewing a client.

A. PURPOSE OF CLIENT INTERVIEWING

The primary purpose of the legal interview is to gather and exchange information between the client and the lawyer. Whether the client seeks advice, assistance in a transaction, or representation in litigation, the client needs to realize four objectives from his communications with a lawyer. First, the client needs to talk about his situation, matter, or problem in his own words. Second, the client needs to get answers about his situation, matter, or problem. Third, the client needs to understand the scope of legal services available to him. And finally, the client needs to determine his need and eligibility for those services. Likewise, the lawyer needs to get accurate and complete information about the client's matter to inform the client about the legal options available, help the client choose the best option or, where appropriate, encourage the client's participation in resolving the problem.

B. VALUE OF GOOD COMMUNICATION SKILLS

Communication experts tell us that people who engage in active listening skills during face-to-face communications build rapport with the other person. A person shows that she is an active listener and connects with the speaker when she does the following: makes lots of eye contact (80 percent of the conversation time or more); uses gestures such as head nods and smiles; if sitting, has a forward body lean toward the speaker, or if standing, is squarely facing the speaker; and has warmth in her voice when attending and responding to the speaker.

On the other hand, a person does not connect with the speaker and risks failing to establish rapport if he does the following: makes little eye contact (40 percent of the conversation time or less); uses few gestures; has a backward body lean or a body angled 30 degrees away from the speaker;

and lacks warmth in his voice. Studies have shown that people who display active listening skills are more persuasive, more trustworthy, better informed, and more sensitive to the needs of the client.[1]

C. ESSENTIAL COMMUNICATION SKILLS

Dale Carnegie once wrote, "When dealing with people, remember you are not dealing with creatures of logic, but with creatures of emotion, creatures bristling with prejudice and motivated by pride and vanity." [2] Carnegie's lesson reminds us that lawyering, like other professional skills that deal with human relationships, is not only about logical analysis. Lawyering cannot be a purely cerebral function, but must include the role that emotions play in the law. Attorney-client communications are no exception: this skill requires a balance of the logical mind with the emotional heart. Furthermore, development of strong communication skills requires recognition that there is a science and an art to communicating with one's client.

The overriding responsibility of the lawyer is to create an atmosphere that leads to a full exchange of all necessary information between the lawyer and the client. When the lawyer is successful at creating an environment where the client feels comfortable and feels that the lawyer can be trusted with good, bad, or even embarrassing information, the client will freely share that information. If the lawyer does not create an inviting environment where the client feels that the lawyer cares about the client and the client's situation, the client will not share everything and may even give untruthful responses to the lawyer's questions.

Thus, fundamental to the successful client interview is the establishment and maintenance of rapport between the lawyer and client where the client feels understood and supported by the lawyer such that he can trust the lawyer with vital information. This is easily stated but sometimes difficult for lawyers to do. The lawyer should bring everything the lawyer has learned (in and out of the classroom) about human communication to the task of client interviewing. As a lawyer gains more experience in interviewing clients, the lawyer will become more skilled at building the relationships and the contexts conducive to successful interviews. However, there is no better way for the lawyer to create rapport than to be a good listener.

---

[1] MATTHEW MCKAY, MARTHA DAVIS, & PATRICK FANNING, MESSAGES: THE COMMUNICATION SKILLS BOOK (3d ed. 2009).

[2] Dale Carnegie is well-known as the developer of famous courses in self-improvement, salesmanship, and interpersonal skills. He was the author of HOW TO WIN FRIENDS AND INFLUENCE PEOPLE (1998), a blockbuster self-help book about the power of persuasion.

1. COMMUNICATION INCLUDES NON-VERBAL OR SILENT MESSAGES

One of the fundamental skills of an effective lawyer is listening. Listening involves receiving and evaluating sounds and attaching meaning to them. A client conveys two messages to the lawyer during an interview: (1) messages containing content (facts and legal issues); and (2) messages revealing feelings (emotions and concerns).[3] Messages containing content are expressly verbalized with words while messages revealing feelings are expressed non-verbally through such means as facial expressions and body gestures. These non-verbal messages are also called silent messages. Studies show that the typical speaking rate is 125 to 150 words per minute[4]; but, the listening-thinking rate is about 400 words per minute.[5] The interviewer should make use of the time in the speaking-thinking ratio to consider both the content (or verbal) messages and the feelings (or non-verbal) messages.

2. DEVELOPING THE SKILL OF ACTIVE LISTENING

Whenever people listen, they are at various levels of attentiveness. Communication experts teach us that active listening is the highest and most effective level of listening. This level requires the greatest concentration and sensitivity on the part of the listener; it is the level where the potential for understanding, trust, and effective communication between the speaker and the listener is optimal.

Generally, the lawyer should be exercising active listening skills for most of the initial client interview. There are some exceptions to this rule. For instance, the lawyer may need to interrupt and guide the interview so that the lawyer efficiently gathers the relevant information needed to assist the client. In addition, the lawyer will frequently need to evaluate the verbal and non-verbal messages from the client during the course of the interview.

The active listener tries to get a deeper understanding of the speaker. This listener is not only attentive to the words being spoken but is also trying to identify with the speaker and align her own thoughts and feelings more closely with the speaker. In doing so, the listener must actively suspend her own thoughts and feelings and give attention solely to listening. It figuratively means "putting yourself in the other person's

---

[3] ALBERT MEHRABIAN, SILENT MESSAGES: IMPLICIT COMMUNICATION OF EMOTIONS AND ATTITUDES (1981).

[4] Jiahong Yuan, Mark Liberman, Christopher Cieri, *Towards an Integrated Understanding of Speaking Rate in Conversation*, Department of Linguistics, Linguistic Data Consortium, University of Pennsylvania, available at http://languagelog.ldc.upenn.edu/myl/ldc/llog/icslp06_final.pdf (2006).

[5] Ronald Carver, *How good are some of the world's best readers?*, 20 READING RESEARCH QUARTERLY 389–419 (1985).

shoes." The active listener must not only listen for the content of the message but, just as importantly, for the intent and feeling of the message as well. It requires the listener to show both verbally and nonverbally to the speaker that she is listening. The listener demonstrates attentiveness using a number of verbal and non-verbal signals discussed below.

The active listener is extremely perceptive. This listener looks for verbal and visual cues that might signify that the other person would like to say something. When one of these cues appears, the active listener gives the floor to the other person. The active listener listens not only to what is said and how it is said, but is also perceptive to what is not being said.

The active listener is also a skillful questioner and uses questions to encourage the speaker to extend the conversation and clarify the message. The active listener senses when it is appropriate to probe into areas that need to be developed further to get a better total picture of what the speaker is trying to communicate.

The active listener employs three very important skills: sensing, attending, and responding. These are skills most of us have intuitively developed in our communications with others throughout our lifetimes. Sensing is the ability of the active listener to recognize and appreciate the silent message that the speaker is sending, that is, vocal intonation, body language, facial expression and so forth.[6]

Attending refers to the verbal, vocal, and visual messages that the active listener sends to the speaker indicating attentiveness, receptiveness, and acknowledgement of the speaker and the message. This includes eye contact, open body language (squarely facing the speaker with no folded arms), affirmative head nods, appropriate facial expressions, verbal expressions such as, "Yes," "I see," "Go on," "Continue," and "Keep going," and avoidance of nervous, bored or angry gestures.

Attending also includes the establishment of a receptive listening setting, such as an atmosphere of privacy that is away from interruptions and distractions such as telephone calls, people talking, or people within earshot. It includes not violating the speaker's "personal space," as well as eliminating such communication barriers as a large desk between the speaker and the listener. Desks, tables, and other objects placed between the lawyer and the client can inhibit free sharing of information. Barriers can also make it appear to the client that the lawyer is hiding or trying to take a dominant power position during the interview. As an active listener, the lawyer pays attention to creating a comfortable physical setting for the interview. The lawyer removes stacks of books, files, or other physical barriers between the client and herself.

---

[6]   ALBERT MEHRABIAN, NONVERBAL COMMUNICATION (1972).

Responding refers to the skill of engaging the speaker to get feedback on the accuracy of the speaker's content and feeling. For example, an active listener is responding when the listener comments, "I sense that the defendant's conduct upset you." The active listener is also responding when the listener tries to keep the speaker talking, seeks clarification of the speaker's message, asks questions to gather more information, tries to make the speaker feel understood, and tries to get the speaker to better understand himself and his problems or concerns.

D. PREPARING FOR THE INITIAL INTERVIEW

Preparing for a client interview is important because a lawyer should devote herself to being an active listener during the interview.

In some cases, the lawyer will be responsible for scheduling the interview directly with the client and in some cases, that responsibility will be delegated to office staff. The person scheduling the interview should discuss whether the client will be charged a consultation fee, should instruct the potential client to bring relevant paperwork to the first meeting, and should inform the potential client what to expect at the interview, including how long it will last.

The lawyer should plan where the interview will occur, keeping in mind which physical space will optimize gathering information and establishing rapport.

Before the interview occurs, the lawyer should review any intake notes and conduct any preliminary legal or factual research. Again, the lawyer who can anticipate and review legal issues beforehand, can effectively and efficiently guide the interview so that she obtains from, and shares with, the client as much relevant information as possible.

E. ORGANIZATION OF INITIAL INTERVIEW

The lawyer is responsible for the content of the interview (what information is exchanged) and the process of the interview (how information is shared). Without steamrolling the client, the lawyer should guide the conversation so that it is productive and has momentum. The client does not know what information the lawyer needs and, without guidance, may include irrelevant information and omit crucial information.

Just like a story or a legal memo, client interviews should have a structure. There should be a beginning, a middle, and an end. If a lawyer finishes gathering facts and begins to advise the client about the client's rights and then suddenly returns to gathering more facts and then has to change the earlier advice given, the client will be confused and perhaps see the lawyer as disorganized and perhaps even incompetent.

A useful structure for a client interview is as follows: (1) the lawyer provides her proposed agenda for the meeting at the outset; (2) the client provides an overview of the matter and the client's uninterrupted, extemporaneous version of the facts; (3) the lawyer follows up by asking questions to obtain more details to key issues; (4) the client identifies his goals that relate to his legal matter; and (5) the lawyer concludes the interview with clarity about the next steps, if any, to be taken by the lawyer and the client.

1.   BEGINNING THE INTERVIEW

The lawyer should determine how the client wishes to be addressed. Each client is different and some may appreciate the formality of using a title with a surname until the lawyer-client relationship is formally established. On the other hand, some clients may appreciate the use of first names because it may signify to that client that the lawyer and client are equals in a common enterprise.

The lawyer should greet the client and escort the client to the place where the interview is to take place. If the lawyer welcomes the client, it allows the client to engage in some small talk as an icebreaker to what is to follow. It will provide the lawyer with valuable information about the client's attitude and emotions. This information will allow the lawyer to assess how she will conduct the interview with this individual client.

For instance, for the angry client, the lawyer may need to allow an opportunity for the client to vent about why he is angry. Or if the client is shy and quiet, the lawyer might want to plan for long pauses for the client to be able to effectively express himself in the interview. Some lawyers have very strong people skills that they mastered before attending law school. For others, it is a skill that the lawyer must repeatedly practice before it becomes intuitive or second-nature.

The lawyer should tell the client the proposed agenda for the interview, especially if the client has never met with a lawyer before. The lawyer should confirm what to expect at the meeting and how long the meeting will last. This will give the client some confidence that the lawyer is taking charge of the conversation. It will help the client to understand the purpose of the interview and what will likely occur during the interview so that the client can at least mentally assess how much information he will have time to convey to the lawyer.

The beginning of the interview is also a good time to discuss any protocols or rules to be followed during the meeting. For instance, if the lawyer has invited an associate to join the interview, the lawyer should explain this to the client. In addition, many lawyers find that the beginning of the interview is the appropriate time to explain the attorney-client privilege.[7] The lawyer should be sensitive to explain this privilege to the client using language that is appropriate to that client. The business client who has had prior interactions with a lawyer will not need as detailed an explanation as the unsophisticated client who is making his first visit to a lawyer's office.

Some practitioners are convinced that advising the client that all communications between the lawyer and client will be held in complete confidence will comfort the client to such an extent he will feel compelled to disclose all of the information he possesses, no matter its nature—good, bad, or even extremely personal and embarrassing. This view over-simplifies the art and science of attorney-client communications. Clients are inhibited from sharing certain information for a number of reasons. Explanation of this privilege is generally not a facilitator of communication.

Rather, the free flow of information is facilitated by rapport between the lawyer and client. Clients will disclose their secrets to the lawyer when they feel there is sufficient rapport with the lawyer that they can trust the lawyer with such information, that they will not be embarrassed by or harshly judged by the content of the information. Nonetheless, it is the better practice to make sure that the client understands the nature of the privilege and has some ground rules for the conversation.

2. INFORMATION-GATHERING

Some lawyers will begin this stage of the interview by gathering basic statistical information about the client such as address, occupation, and education. Some lawyers like to begin the interview this way because these questions are generally not emotionally-charged and thus allow the lawyer to ease more slowly into what brought the client into the lawyer's office. However, this question-short answer back and forth is not effective in building rapport because it does not allow the client to tell his story. The lawyer is usually talking more than the client.

The better method of beginning this stage of the interview is to invite the client to describe what brought the client to the lawyer. The use of open-ended questions to begin the interview allows the client to do the talking so that the lawyer obtains the client's version of the circumstances/problem/dispute/matter.

If the lawyer does not know, a good introductory question is "What brings you to my office today?" Or "How can I help you?" Even better, the lawyer can focus the client and at the same time demonstrate active

---

[7]   Model Rules of Professional Conduct Rule 1.6 (a) provides: "A lawyer shall not reveal information relating to the representation of a client unless the client gives informed consent, the disclosure is impliedly authorized in order to carry out the representation or the disclosure is permitted by paragraph (b)."

listening skills by stating that the lawyer has a general idea what the client came to discuss and giving the floor to the client to share more. Some examples are: "My secretary tells me that you are having a problem with your landlord. Tell me more about the problem with your landlord." Or, "I understand you are looking for legal advice because you are planning to start a new business. What kind of business are you starting?"

3. TIPS FOR GUIDING THIS STAGE OF INTERVIEW

Respond directly to relevant statements and pay less attention to what is not relevant. This is a gentle, hopefully non-intrusive way to steer the client toward areas which give necessary and useful information. Not all clients pick up on these cues; in those cases, it may be necessary for the lawyer to be more directive with her questions.

Interrupt tactfully. When the conversation goes too far astray and shows little sign of returning to a useful course, you should interrupt gently and return the client to the relevant areas of discussion. For example, "I understand that you and your brother did not get along when you were growing up, but now we need to focus on who is the better person to act as the legal guardian for your elderly mother."

One of the marks of an effective professional is the ability to ask useful questions in a productive way. The lawyer should focus on areas in which she needs information to understand the client's problems and the pertinent facts. The lawyer should develop a strategy for asking questions. The lawyer should frame questions in ways that lead to a productive conversation.

The lawyer should be aware of the different forms of questioning, understand their respective advantages and disadvantages, and use the appropriate form of questioning based on the goal of the interview and the kind and quality of the information sought from the client. The lawyer should ask open-ended questions when she wants the client to explain, elaborate, talk freely, or tell a story about what happened to him. Some examples of open-ended prompts are "Please describe X"; "Tell me more about Y"; "What happened next?"

The lawyer should use close-ended questions when she wants shorter responses that provide concrete, factual information or yes-or-no answers. Close-ended questions are used to direct or steer the interview and should be used to verify information or to follow up on information. Use follow-up questions,[8] leading questions,[9] and summary questions to probe for details and clarify or verify information.

4.   PROBING STAGE

The lawyer needs to be inquisitive. This quality can also be indirectly useful in building rapport with the client; curiosity about the client's matter shows an interest in the client. Moreover, the client does not know what the lawyer needs to know to properly assess the matter. The client may need prompting with questions to provide essential information. While there is no replacement for knowledge of necessary areas of inquiry in the various areas of the lawyer's practice, there are interview guides and checklists to aid in identifying the information the lawyer needs from the client.[10]

While use of guides for a limited purpose may in some instances be appropriate, lawyers should be careful about relying on guides or checklists to conduct interviews while the interview is happening. They should remain active listeners, engage in eye contact with the client, and abandon the guide or checklist if the client's story does not fit within that framework.

A standard check list for a client interview that can be used for a variety of legal problems includes the following:

1.   Ask for raw facts and the client's source of knowledge about the problem;

2.   Ask for factual details to assess potential legal claims and defenses;

3.   Ask about writings, pleadings, or other documents;

4.   Ask about witnesses—who saw, heard, felt, or said anything;

5.   Clarify ambiguities and fill in missing information;

---

[8]   Follow-up questions keep the conversation moving forward and allow for clarification and elaboration of details. Follow up questions either elicit a yes or no answer or with a why? However, there are occasions when some client information calls for a unique follow-up question.

[9]   Leading questions are questions that suggest the particular answer or contain the information the examiner is looking to have confirmed. Leading questions may often be answerable with a "yes" or "no" (though not all yes-no questions are leading). In client interviews, their usefulness is generally restricted to quickly confirming information already provided by the client.

[10]   Most jurisdictions publish practice guides on various legal subjects that contain issue checklists or interview guides that can be useful in organizing an interview and identifying key issues to explore. Legal Solutions by Thomson Reuters advertises "guidance on the practice of law with comprehensive legal forms and practice manuals." See for example: FAMILY LAW, (The Rutter Group California Practice Guide), Chapter 1 entitled "The First Client Interview"; TEXAS PRACTICE GUIDE, EMPLOYMENT PRACTICE, Chapter 1:45 entitled "Checklists" and; ELDER LAW, 2016–2017 ed. (Vol 56), Massachusetts Practice Series, which "provides checklists, practice tips and forms to assist the elder law practitioner."

6. Direct the client's attention to areas which the client may have overlooked; and

7. Unless the lawyer concludes that she has built insufficient rapport to delve too deeply into private, sensitive areas, ask the client any remaining questions before moving to the next stage.

5. ADVISING THE CLIENT

This is the stage where the lawyer gives information to the client. How much information the lawyer can provide to the client at this stage of the relationship depends upon how complex the matter is and how much information the client has been able to provide to the lawyer. One way to begin this stage is to repeat a summary of the story back to the client. No two people hear the same thing the same way, so, to avoid misunderstanding later in the representation, the lawyer should confirm what she thinks she has heard.

The lawyer should make sure that the client has been allowed to identify all of his issues and concerns. Here is an example of such a catchall question: "Is there anything else you wish to tell me before I advise you?"

During this stage, the lawyer should ascertain the client's goals. If the client has not already disclosed why he is coming to see a lawyer, ask what the client wants. A lawyer can pose this question in various ways: "Why do you think you need a lawyer?" "What do you think I can do to help you?"

In some circumstances, the client may not be able to articulate what he thinks the lawyer can do. This type of client may be unsophisticated about the legal system; he may think that he has a legal problem and views lawyers as problem solvers and so this client will turn to the lawyer to offer solutions to his circumstances. Some clients may only want to know their legal rights in a situation; others will want to know the range of possible solutions to their problems; and still others will be insistent that they only want to discuss one solution. Which one of many solutions is best for the client requires the skill of counseling which is discussed in the next chapter.

In advising the client about potential remedies, the lawyer should not merely identify and explain legal options but should also explore non-legal solutions. Sometimes a non-legal solution will be the cheapest and most efficient way to solve the problem. This advice may mean the lawyer does not create a long-term attorney-client relationship where the lawyer can generate attorney fees, but it may be the most ethical approach, and it may generate future goodwill with this client.

The lawyer should explain the law, procedures, and other technical information in everyday language—not simplistically, but simply. The lawyer should avoid legal and other technical terms. If it is necessary to use them, the lawyer should explain what they mean.

The lawyer should allow the client to ask questions. The lawyer should make sure that she has answered the client's questions to the best of her ability.

F. CONCLUDING THE INTERVIEW

Ending an interview is an art in itself. It is not just a matter of standing up, shaking hands, and saying "good-bye." The lawyer should recognize the natural ending to the interview. When an interview is pressed beyond its natural ending, it can become nonproductive. In some cases, this may require the lawyer to interview the client more than once to obtain all of the facts that the lawyer needs and for the lawyer to provide the client with the information the client wants.

At the conclusion of the interview, it must be clear what legal services the client is seeking and whether the lawyer has decided to undertake the client's matter. In some cases, it will be clear to the lawyer that a referral to another professional is appropriate. Such a referral will conclude the interview and generally will also conclude the attorney-client relationship. In other cases, the client seeks legal advice. If the matter is simple enough, such advice can be provided in the interview, again resulting in closure of the attorney-client relationship. In other instances, legal advice may require further factual or legal research.

Just like any professional in other walks of life would do, the lawyer should provide the client with an estimate of the time it will take to conduct the research and what the lawyer will charge for such services. In addition, there may be further information that the client has available that the lawyer will need to review before rendering legal advice.

It is the responsibility of the lawyer to clarify with the client whether the attorney-client relationship is continuing beyond the interview. If the client is seeking legal assistance or representation beyond the initial interview, the lawyer needs to confirm the on-going nature of the attorney-client relationship, discuss the fees and costs for such assistance and services, and clarify what actions, if any, will be taken by the lawyer and what actions, if any will be taken by the client.[11]

---

[11] Model Rules of Professional Conduct Rule 1.5 sets forth rules regarding types of fee agreements that must be in writing. As a matter of good practice, it is always wise to prepare a confirming letter that the lawyer is not undertaking any further legal work on behalf of the client beyond the initial interview.

G. EFFECTIVE INTERVIEWING TECHNIQUES

A lawyer's verbal and non-verbal behavior should indicate that she cares about what the client is saying. Here are some techniques for effective interviewing:

1. Engage in appropriate eye contact. Visually connect with the client without staring so as not to make the client feel uncomfortable.

2. Do not engage in distracting behavior, such as gazing out the window, answering the telephone, thumbing through unrelated papers, or tapping your fingers.

3. Demonstrate comfortable body language which shows interest in and concern for the client and the client's situation. Avoid indicating defensiveness (e.g., arms crossed) or boredom (e.g., yawning) or invading the client's physical space or "comfort zone" (e.g., touching the client or getting nose-to-nose with the client).

4. Encourage the client to talk with short phrases and open-ended questions like "Take your time; tell me everything that happened." "Tell me more about X, Y, Z." "After that, what happened next?"

5. Be aware of the amount of your note taking. After the client has given you an overview of the situation and you are ready to confirm information and conduct some follow-up, jot down important information and key words but not a verbatim transcript. Make notes about areas to which you want to return in the future. Do not get lost in taking notes so that you completely lose eye contact with the client. Consider whether taking notes on a computer will create a physical barrier between the lawyer and client.

6. Use deliberate silence. Give the client time to gather his thoughts, proceed with his story at his pace, and answer your questions with appropriate time to reflect. Within reason, allow the client to proceed at an easy, comfortable pace—do not rush the client and the interview. A lawyer wants to convey that she wants the true facts, not the first words that pop into the client's mouth. Become comfortable with the sound of silence. Permit the client time to think and sort out ideas and feelings. This not only communicates that the lawyer is listening, but it also shows respect for the client's thought process and story. In addition, when necessary, the lawyer should remind the fast-talking client to slow down and think about his responses to the lawyer's questions so that

both the lawyer and the client can be assured that they are exchanging accurate information.

H. BARRIERS TO EFFECTIVE COMMUNICATION

As the client explains what brought him to see a lawyer, the lawyer should be mindful of whether she has perceived the client's message accurately, whether the client appears to be withholding information, or whether the communication has failed in some way. The lawyer must be able to analyze what might be impeding or inhibiting the client's communication.

There are many inhibitors or barriers to effective communication and these may occur at any stage in the interview. Inhibitors of communication are any social-psychological barrier which impedes the unconstrained flow of relevant information by making the client unable or unwilling to give it to the lawyer at the moment. Some common barriers are as follows:

1. Language differences and the difficulty in understanding unfamiliar accents;

2. The use of jargon: over-complicated, unfamiliar language and/or technical terms;

3. Emotional barriers and taboos: some people may find it difficult to express their emotions and topics may be completely "off limits" or taboo. Taboo or difficult topics may include, politics, religion, mental and physical disabilities, sexuality and sex, racism and any opinion that may be seen as unpopular.

4. Lack of attention, interest, distractions, or irrelevance to the receiver;

5. Differences in perception and viewpoint/perspective;

6. Physical disabilities such as hearing problems or speech difficulties;

7. Physical barriers to non-verbal communications: not being able to see the non-verbal cues, gestures, posture and body language can make communications less effective. Telephone calls, messages and other communication methods that rely on technology are often less effective than face-to-face communication;

8. Expectations and prejudices which may lead to false assumptions or stereotyping: people often hear what they expect to hear rather than what is actually said and jump to incorrect conclusions;

9. Cultural differences: the norms of social interaction can vary greatly in different cultures, as do the way in which emotions are expressed. For example, the concept of personal space varies between cultures and between different social settings.[12]

There are inhibitors internal to the interview and inhibitors external to the interview. The lawyer cannot fix external inhibitors like the client's memory failure, but being cognizant of it will be beneficial to the attorney-client communications. The lawyer does have control over internal inhibitors such as ego threat. A client will withhold information from the lawyer when the lawyer does not engage in active listening, when the lawyer appears judgmental of the client or the client's circumstances or when the lawyer is not culturally sensitive.

I.   CROSS-CULTURAL CONSIDERATIONS

Attorney Atticus Finch states to his daughter Scout in Harper Lee's 1960's novel, *To Kill a Mockingbird*, "You never really understand a person until you consider things from his point of view—until you climb inside of his skin and walk around in it."[13]

The lawyer needs to be aware that the client's values and sense of the world may differ, sometimes substantially, with her own background. Recognizing and understanding cultural differences between the lawyer and client is important to the success of a client interview. Seeing the world the way the client sees the world allows the lawyer to empathize and build rapport. The lawyer cannot connect with the client and put herself into the client's shoes if the lawyer does not even understand if the client wears shoes. As noted in the previous section and in Chapter 3 of this book, failure to recognize and understand the client's cultural perspective will create communication barriers in the interview.

Professors Jennifer Robbennolt and Jean Sternlight in their book, *Psychology for Lawyers: Understanding the Human Factors in Negotiation, Litigation and Decision-Making*[14] ask, "So what's a good attorney to do? Is it enough to say "I don't discriminate and I always act in good faith, so I don't need to worry about any of this?"" The professors respond that such an approach is not good enough. The lawyer, like many other people, is not always aware of her stereotypes and expectations[15]. The lawyer who is

---

[12] SKILLSYOUNEED, https://www.skillsyouneed.com/ips/barriers-communication.html (last visited December 19, 2017).

[13] HARPER LEE, TO KILL A MOCKINGBIRD, Chapter 3 (1960).

[14] Jennifer Robbennolt and Jean Sternlight, PSYCHOLOGY FOR LAWYERS: UNDERSTANDING THE HUMAN FACTORS IN NEGOTIATION, LITIGATION AND DECISION-MAKING 192 (American Bar Association 2013).

[15] Implicit bias refers to the attitudes or stereotypes that affect our understanding, actions, and decisions in an unconscious manner. These biases, which reside deep in the subconscious, are activated involuntarily and without an individual's awareness or intentional control. See, Kirwan

unaware of cultural differences between herself and the client will inevitably step on toes and miss cues.

Clearly, it is not practical for the lawyer to do cultural research on each potential client. Cultural competence "requires the lawyer to have some knowledge of the potential differences among cultures, a willingness to keep an open mind about how another person sees the world, and flexibility in responding to different and sometimes unexpected perspectives."[16]

Recognizing that each client is unique is the first step in developing cultural competence. Each client comes from a milieu of cultures that influence everything about the client including how the client sees the world, how the client communicates, and what values the client assigns to such legal concepts as justice, fairness, and equality. Chapter 3 discusses inter-cultural competence and the skills discussed there should be applied to client interviewing and counseling.

A lawyer demonstrates cultural competence when she "reads" the client and makes adjustments to be able to communicate better across cultural boundaries. Such a lawyer is cognizant of non-verbal and verbal messaging. She attempts to tailor her body language, facial expressions, and even the interview environment so as to meet the varying needs of each client. She does not assume that every client is like the lawyer. She tries to understand the client's silent messages and to respond to those messages. Thus, if it appears to the lawyer that the client is uncomfortable, the culturally competent lawyer will know whether the proper reaction is to silently make some adjustments in the interview or to openly explore with the client what is causing the discomfort.

Similarly, the culturally competent lawyer will tailor his verbal communications for each client, beginning with how the client wishes to be addressed. For instance, in some cultures it is a sign of respect to use the title and surname of the other party in conversation rather than to use that person's first name. If the lawyer does not know the cultural preference of the client, the lawyer will ask for clarification from the client. Moreover, the culturally competent lawyer will not assume that the meaning of the language in the client's message is the same as in the lawyer's culture. Thus, the culturally competent lawyer will openly acknowledge to the client that he does not know the client's perspective and will ask for an explanation to gain greater understanding or, if he knows something about the client's culture before the interview, he may do additional research to gain greater familiarity concerning the client's background.

Lastly, the culturally competent lawyer will be sensitive to invasive questions that may need an introduction before being posed to the client.

Institute for the Study of Race Ethnicity, Ohio State University, www.kirwaninstitute.osu.edu (last visited December 19, 2017).

[16] Robbennolt and Sternlight, *supra* note 14.

For example, the lawyer may need to make adjustments in the interview with a client in a divorce proceeding whose religion makes certain topics about the marriage undisclosable.

J. INTERVIEWING WITNESSES

Lawyers are often called upon to interview witnesses. Like clients, witnesses can vary from friendly to hostile or adverse witnesses and from eyewitnesses to expert witnesses. They also serve different purposes because they possess different information that the lawyer needs.

Interviews with prospective witnesses have much in common with interviews with clients, but major differences do exist. The lawyer must build a much closer relationship with the client than the witness. In addition, communications between the lawyer and the client are protected by the attorney-client confidentiality which can aid in the free flow of information. On the other hand, issues related to rapport, trust, perception, judgment and memory are just as important in witness interviews as they are in client interviews. Thus, much of this chapter can also be applied to witness interviews.

PRACTICE EXERCISE

Your professor will select a scenario for each of you to role play. Students will be assigned the role of the interviewing lawyer or the client. Then in a role reversal, the interviewing lawyer will become the client in the subsequent interview. The student who role plays the client will provide the interviewer with an oral critique of what was and was not effective in the interview.

WRITING EXERCISE

Memorialize your meeting with your client in a paired writing assignment, such as a Memo to File, an advice letter or an opinion letter which are discussed in Chapter 15.

CHAPTER 14

COUNSELING THE CLIENT

■ ■ ■

By Kathleen Friedrich

A. WHAT IS CLIENT COUNSELING?

Two clients can have the same legal problem, but a solution that satisfies one of the clients may be unthinkable to the other. Good lawyers not only help clients identify the available options; they also help clients find the right solution for their circumstances.

Lawyers make a distinction between advising and counseling a client. Advising a client is telling the client what options may be available for a particular set of circumstances. Counseling involves more than merely giving advice. Counseling is the process by which the lawyer helps the client reach a decision about which of the available options to undertake.

Counseling occurs throughout the progress of a case and it occurs on big and small issues, not just the ultimate outcome of a matter. In all decisions on consequential matters in the client's case, the lawyer should (1) set out the options; (2) explain the probable consequences, legal and practical, of each option; (3) fully answer the client's questions; and (4) provide suggestions and guidance if the client wants such help. However, since the client will be the one who ultimately lives with the consequences, the client should select from among the options, not the lawyer.

Counseling is about giving appropriate information to clients so that they can make informed decisions about what the best option is for them. Thus, in counseling, the lawyer weighs advantages, costs, risks, and chances of success of one option against the advantages, costs, risks, and chances of success of other options. Counseling is examining these variables with the client, explaining them to the client, and assisting the client to reach a decision about which of the options is best for the client.

B. DEVELOPING AN EFFECTIVE COUNSELING RELATIONSHIP

The modern view of counseling is that it is collaboration, a partnership of sorts between the lawyer, who shares her expertise on the law with the client, who shares his expertise on the facts and circumstances.

When client focus groups were asked to give their perception of what attributes a "good" attorney had in the area of counseling, clients responded that the "good" lawyer gives the "right kind" of advice.[1]

Here are some of the responses of some client focus groups:

- "Tells me what to expect";

- "Tells me what I don't know";

- "Points out issues, areas and consequences that I may not have thought about";

- Speaks in the language of "ordinary" people—not "like a lawyer";

- "Keeps me informed";

- "Doesn't badger clients, i.e., forcing the client to make decisions the way the attorney wants, rather than the way the client wants";

- "Answers my questions."

These responses also describe a good legal interviewer because the key characteristics of a good interviewer are the same for a good counselor. Being a good interviewer and a good counselor are not separate and distinct skill sets; rather they are a continuum of skills that make up the successful attorney-client relationship. Thus, the good counselor, like the good interviewer, among other qualities also needs to be an active listener, build and maintain rapport, show dignity and respect to the client, not be judgmental, be helpful and supportive of the client, and, as discussed in Chapter 3, not only be aware of cultural differences, but understand how the client's cultural perspective impacts his decision-making.

C. PREPARATION FOR COUNSELING SESSION

Effective counseling requires preparation for the actual counseling session. In most instances, the counseling session does not occur at the same time as the initial client interview. However, in circumstances where the client's matter involves an emergency or where a deadline is imminent, the lawyer may not have the luxury of breaking up the client interviewing and counseling sessions into separate meetings with the client.

1. IDENTIFYING THE CLIENT'S GOALS

The lawyer interviews the client to learn about the facts of the situation and to learn the client's underlying interests, needs, concerns, and feelings. The lawyer needs to explore the client's goals and objectives.

---

[1]   Excerpt from Earle Warner, *What Do Our Clients Want?: Findings From Focus Groups,* Kansas Legal Services Program (1989).

A goal or objective is what the client hires the lawyer to do on his behalf. In probing the client's goals or objectives, the lawyer can ask: "What are your goals?" "What do you want to happen?" "What do you want to do about this situation?" Answers to these questions can vary with each client from a vague response of "I don't know; what is available to me?" to the very particular response of "I want to sue Mr. X in court for $50,000 for all the pain and suffering he has caused me."

The lawyer needs to know how important each goal is to the client by learning how the client would rank them. To do so, the lawyer can ask such questions as: "Which of the things you mentioned is more important to you?" "How would you rank your concerns in the order of their importance?"

Sometimes it is necessary to sacrifice what the client wants to get for what the client needs. The lawyer cannot wisely counsel the client until she knows where the client would draw the line between his wants and needs. This requires the lawyer to distinguish between the client's goals and preferences. A preference is something the client would like the lawyer to do or not do while pursuing his goals. Client preferences are important because they will affect each potential solution's value to the client. Thus, the lawyer will not only need to identify the client's preferences, but will also need to know how intense the preferences are and why they exist.

2.   GATHERING AND EVALUATING INFORMATION

The lawyer may need to conduct a factual investigation or legal research. The lawyer may also need to gather videotapes, photographs, contracts, documents or other raw materials that can be used in resolving the problem.

3.   GENERATING ALTERNATIVE POTENTIAL SOLUTIONS

The lawyer should be creative and brainstorm all potential courses of action, legal and non-legal. The lawyer should not just itemize solutions that are obvious but should consider a spectrum of options that range from doing nothing to instigating litigation to exploring alternative dispute resolution. The lawyer should find ways to create solutions that without her imagination and strategic skills might not otherwise exist.

4.   IDENTIFYING THE PROS AND CONS OF EACH POTENTIAL SOLUTION

In assessing the pros and cons of these potential solutions, the lawyer should consider both legal and non-legal aspects and ramifications of decisions. What will work and what will not work for this client? What solution might be favored for this client over another solution and why?

For instance, when the lawyer considers whether a civil lawsuit will invade the client's privacy such that it may not be a tolerable solution for the client, the lawyer is exploring the downside to litigation. The lawyer is calculating the emotional costs to the client of this potential solution. Likewise, the lawyer should review the upsides or advantages to filing a civil lawsuit. The lawyer must evaluate what matters to the client. In some circumstances, business or financial factors are important, while in others, political factors may be important. In most circumstances, interpersonal or emotional factors are important even if not readily apparent.

5. COMPARING VARIOUS COURSES OF ACTION

After evaluating the pros and cons of each potential course of action, the lawyer should compare the various courses of action and the client's objectives in order to measure the advantages, costs, risks, and odds of success.

6. PLANNING HOW TO EXPLAIN OPTIONS

Lastly, the lawyer must plan how to explain the various courses of action to the client, recognizing that the lawyer should tailor her explanation of the law to the client.

D. COUNSELING MEETING

The lawyer should begin the counseling meeting by summarizing his understanding of the client's concerns and goals to verify that the lawyer heard the client correctly during the preceding interview and that the client has not changed her position in the interim. The lawyer can demonstrate alliance with the client by beginning the discussion of various options with an appropriate introduction such as "Let's brainstorm your situation together. . . ." or "Let's discuss/analyze these concerns together. . . ."

The lawyer should confirm his understanding of the priorities of the client's goals. Together with the client, the lawyer should sort the client's goals into short-term goals, (concerns that may be smaller tasks that need immediate attention), and long-term goals, (concerns that require more time and effort). In a situation where litigation is already ongoing, it may be that there are developments in the case that must be explained and those also become part of the short-term concerns that must be addressed.

Now the lawyer is ready to explain all of the courses of action to the client so that the client can choose the best potential solution for her circumstances. At this point, the lawyer shows his knowledge and expertise in the law as well as what the factual investigation has revealed thus far. The lawyer must advise the client about the relative benefits, risks, and costs of each proposed solution. The lawyer's task is to analyze with the client the legal and tactical consequences of each proposed solution and the chances of success. Perhaps the proposed solution has never been tried by the lawyer, by his firm or by any other lawyer. The client needs to be told how experimental the proposed solution is.

In addition, the lawyer needs to encourage the client to discuss the non-legal consequences of any proposed solutions. Non-legal consequences include

- **social consequences:** the effects on the client's relations with other people;

- **psychological consequences:** the internal feelings that clients personally experience as a result of the choices they make;

- **economic consequences:** the monetary effects of a particular course of action; and

- **moral, religious, or political consequences:** the effects on the client's underlying values.

In relative terms, legal consequences are often fairly predictable. In contrast, non-legal consequences are often difficult to predict. This exploration requires the participation of the client because only the client can inform the lawyer about how one option may impact her.

In some cases, the lawyer may need to provide further assistance to the client in the decision-making process. This assistance can be in the form of providing the client time and space to consider the options. It may be in the form of allowing the client to ask more questions. Or it may take the form of giving the client more information, such as how many prior clients have found one option more attractive than another and why. The lawyer needs to recognize that the decision-making abilities of each client are different. Rather than directing the outcome, as was the historical role of the lawyer, today's lawyer needs to support and respect the client's decision.

Once the client has reached her decision about which solution to choose, the lawyer then implements the chosen solution.

E. EFFECTIVE COUNSELING PRINCIPLES

Like any skill, lawyers become better at counseling with practice. New lawyers will become better as they develop an effective problem-solving style and approach. There are some principles that are universal to any counseling situation.

The first principle is involvement of both lawyer and client in the counseling session. Lawyers should involve the client in the counseling session so that there is a genuine conversation between the two. A practice that may be helpful to the lawyer is to view the conversation as though it were with a close friend or relative.

The second principle is respect. Lawyers should show the client respect that recognizes the client's autonomy and capacity to make his own decisions about which solution works best for him.

The third principle is the development of a common language. Lawyers should consider in advance how they will explain legal concepts and terminology to the client, particularly to the unsophisticated client who has had no prior introduction to the American legal system.

The fourth principle is selflessness. Lawyers should ignore their own emotional needs. If lawyers keep in mind that they are not at the center of the case, they can avoid being the kind of lawyer that clients find difficult to work with—lawyers who are dogmatic, paternalistic, judgmental, condescending, controlling, or overbearing.

The fifth principle is empathetic objectivity. Lawyers should explain the various solutions to the client as objectively and neutrally as possible. This detachment helps the lawyer to see the client's circumstances as they really are, without delusion. At the same time, the lawyer should give the client empathy. Empathy helps the lawyer to understand the client and his needs and goals. The effective counselor is one who is able to combine objectivity with empathy; the effective counselor is able to see the client's circumstances from within and yet, at the same time, from a distance. This gives the lawyer insight and perspective which allows her to counsel with compassion and without prejudice.

Finally, the sixth principle is realism. Lawyers need to face the harsh facts and help the client to do the same. Lawyers do not do any favors to the client by sugar-coating bad facts or bad circumstances. Lawyers need to remain realistic. Even very good cases with very good facts will sometimes have problems that were not revealed or evident at the time of the counseling session, so the lawyer must not guarantee success.

F. ETHICAL/MORAL ISSUES ARISING IN COUNSELING

The preceding text has focused on how the lawyer strikes a balance between the client's control over the representation and the lawyer's control over it. Questions arise concerning the extent to which the lawyer should assert power over the client to protect him from himself, or to protect others from him. For example, the family law client insists on waiving her right to spousal support, a course of action that the lawyer believes will seriously harm her personal and legal interests. To what extent should the lawyer try to intervene and prevent the harm?

Guidance in answering these types of questions is, in some circumstances, addressed by obligations imposed upon the lawyer by the rules of professional conduct in each jurisdiction. Below are some rules that control the boundaries of counseling a client.

Model Rules of Professional Conduct Rule 2.1 sets forth the aspirations of the legal profession regarding dispensing legal advice. The rule provides that the lawyer must "exercise independent professional judgment and render candid advice. In rendering advice, a lawyer may refer not only to law but to other considerations such as moral, economic, social and political factors that may be relevant to the client's situation."

According to Model Rules of Professional Conduct Rule 3.1, "[a] lawyer shall not bring or defend a proceeding, or assert or controvert an issue therein, unless there is a basis in law and fact for doing so that is not frivolous, which includes a good faith argument for an extension, modification or reversal of existing law." Moreover, some jurisdictions are strict about the nature of the advice that a lawyer can provide a client. For instance, in California, a lawyer cannot advise a client to violate the law or a ruling, unless there is a good faith belief that the law or ruling is invalid.[2]

The lawyer must also keep in mind that some of the client's goals may not be achievable. A client's goals must be ethically permissible. The Model Rules of Professional Conduct allow a lawyer to withdraw from representing a client if (1) "the client persists in a course of action involving the lawyer's services that the lawyer reasonably believes is criminal or fraudulent;" or (2) "the client has used the lawyer's services to perpetrate a crime or fraud."[3]

In circumstances where the client chooses a course of action that the lawyer considers immoral but it is not illegal, the lawyer would have grounds to withdraw from representing the client, especially where she cannot remain a zealous advocate for the client.[4] But the more effective course of action would be to appeal to the client's self-interest. The lawyer should try to counsel the client to "do the right thing" because such a course would more likely accomplish the client's goals.[5]

In some circumstances, the lawyer may learn that her client has impaired decision-making abilities such as in the instance of a minor or a person suffering from a mental disability. In these situations, the lawyer shall act as reasonably as possible to maintain a normal attorney-client relationship. There may be additional laws in the particular jurisdiction

---

[2]   CALIFORNIA RULES OF PROFESSIONAL CONDUCT 3–210 (2017).

[3]   MODEL RULES OF PROFESSIONAL CONDUCT, RULE 1.16 (2002).

[4]   *Id.*

[5]   While not dictated by the rules of professional responsibility, it is wise for the lawyer to confirm any advice in writing, especially where the advice is controversial, contrary to the client's goals, etc. Not only does a writing document the parties' communication, a writing elevates the importance of the lawyer's input and allows the parties to further reflect on that input.

where the lawyer practices that recommend that the lawyer seek appointment of a legal guardian who will make the decisions in the case on behalf of the client, or the rules may recommend other protective action.[6]

Returning to the example of the family law client who decides to waive her right to spousal support, the lawyer needs to be convinced that the client has made a deliberate, well-reasoned decision rather than one in the midst of emotional trauma arising out of the breakdown of her marriage. With most clients, the non-legal consequences often predominate over the legal consequences, so examining these non-legal consequences (such as the economic ramifications of waiving spousal support) with the client is essential.

G. CROSS-CULTURAL CONSIDERATIONS

As in interviewing, communications in the client counseling setting can be substantially affected by the lawyer's and the client's cultures and certain preconceived notions that each brings to the attorney-client relationship.

Clients have expectations about appropriate roles. Some clients may anticipate a relationship in which the lawyer will dominate. Lawyers' professionalism and expertise about the legal implications of the subject give them an elevated status. Clients, particularly if they perceive themselves to be of a lower professional status than the lawyer, will feel restrained by the lawyer's dominance and may even be submissive, even to the point of yielding decision-making to the lawyer.

Solid communication skills, empathy, open-ended questions, and explanation of the attorney-client relationship are the primary means for dealing with these problems. In effect, the lawyer must teach the client, through both explanation and through her conduct, that the attorney-client relationship is a cooperative, collaborative, equally participatory undertaking.

Culture and its concomitant social norms also restrict information flow through common conceptions of etiquette. Etiquette barriers affect individuals' comfort in discussing certain subjects with certain individuals and affect which course of action will be acceptable to the client. To deal with culture barriers, the lawyer must use active listening skills. The lawyer needs to evaluate the client's verbal and non-verbal messages.

If the client appears to be reluctant to discuss a particular subject, the lawyer must reflect on both the sensitivity of the subject, the rapport that has been established with the client, and the appropriate language to bridge the cultural differences. Exploration of the circumstances with empathy and candor can help to overcome some cultural barriers. However,

---

[6]   *See* MODEL RULES OF PROFESSIONAL CONDUCT RULE 1.14 (2002).

if the lawyer is so culture-blind that she fails to understand the perspective of her client, she will be unable to build an effective counseling relationship with the client.

Overall, the lawyer should take time to be sure that the client knows that the lawyer wants to understand the client's goals and priorities and the implications for the client of the options available. Remembering these basics will create an environment of mutual respect and encourage disclosure.

PRACTICE EXERCISE

Your professor will select a problem to be used in this telephone counseling exercise. Students will be assigned the role of the lawyer representing either the appellant or the appellee.

Students will telephone the person role-playing the appellant or appellee at an assigned time. The student's job will be to alert his/her client to the resolution of the trial court proceeding which leads to an appeal. Each student must understand who appealed and also explain to his/her client the appellate process. Student should be prepared to counsel the client about the next steps the client may pursue in the litigation, and explain the substance of the appeal.

Students will have 8–10 minutes to discuss the case with their client. If the student represents the appellant, the student will need to have authorization from the client to pursue the appeal by the end of the conversation. If the student represents the appellee, the student must notify the client of the appeal, prepare the client for the next steps in the case, and point out the strengths and weaknesses of the parties' positions on appeal.

After each student has completed his/her phone call, the student should receive brief feedback about the substance of his/her counseling, as well as his/her professional demeanor and his/her success at communicating information to the client.

WRITING EXERCISE

After the students have counseled their client about the resolution of the trial court proceeding and the appellate process on the telephone, the students will follow-up with an e-mail communication reiterating their counsel and confirming the next steps that they and the client have agreed to take.

The email communication should be no more than one page, single spaced, in length, and it should be presented in a professional tone free of spelling and grammatical errors. The header should appear as an email communication. Students should start and end the communication as a professional business correspondence.

The substantive paragraphs should be divided into at least two main topics: (1) a recap of the conversation the student had about the outcome of the trial court proceeding and the appellate process; and (2) a summary of the decisions that the student made with the client over the telephone about next steps for the case. Students may be assessed both on the substance of their descriptions of the litigation to date and the appellate process, as well as their use of professional format, language, and tone.

CHAPTER 15

PROFESSIONAL CORRESPONDENCE

■ ■ ■

By Jeffrey E. Proske

If the average attorney were to list all of the tasks she performed in the course of the average day, the bounty of that list would likely consist of professional correspondence, including e-mails, transmittal letters, advice letters, and demand letters. In some cases, the only contact a client, colleague, adversary or third party has with an attorney is through written correspondence.

Accordingly, an attorney's correspondence becomes the principal factor that clients, colleagues, courts, adversaries, and third parties have to evaluate the professionalism and credibility of the attorney and the positions she takes in a matter. An attorney's correspondence sets the tone for the relationship with the recipient and creates a standard of excellence to guide the conduct of the relationship. An attorney must take great care to ensure that she takes an appropriate amount of time to craft correspondence in a way that reflects a standard of personal and professional excellence that will command respect. A well-crafted letter telegraphs to the recipient that the attorney is credible, thorough and professional, and underscores the strength of the reasoning implicit in the words in the letter. Conversely, a letter with even one typographical error or a grammatical gaffe can undermine a flawlessly reasoned, well-supported position, and can ultimately undermine the attorney's credibility as an advocate.

This chapter will discuss the issues an attorney must bear in mind when crafting any piece of professional correspondence, from the simplest e-mail to the most complex demand letter, and will provide examples of well-crafted correspondence as well as some not-so-well-crafted correspondence.

A. THE LEGAL SIGNIFICANCE OF PROFESSIONAL CORRESPONDENCE

The correspondence generated by an attorney is fundamentally different from correspondence generated by other members of society because it is automatically subject to a framework of laws that have evolved to protect the sanctity of the attorney-client relationship. State and federal law provide strong confidentiality protections for correspondence between attorneys and their clients in order to encourage a relationship of absolute trust which ultimately serves the client's interest in obtaining the most effective representation.

Generally, attorney-client privilege laws forbid attorneys from disclosing their correspondence with clients to third parties or even to courts in most circumstances for any reason without the client's consent.[1] Without these protections, clients would be less inclined to be forthright in sharing sensitive and confidential information that could be useful in their legal representation.

Unlike correspondence generated by members of the general public, correspondence from attorneys is also subject to rules of professional responsibility that govern the legal profession and create standards of practice with which attorneys must comply. Accordingly, an attorney's correspondence must meet the requirements of professionalism, ethics, and competence required by Model Rules of Professional Conduct.

B. CREATING A RECORD THROUGH PROFESSIONAL CORRESPONDENCE

Every letter or e-mail an attorney writes to a client, a colleague, a court, an adversary, or a third party serves the dual purpose of transmitting the content of the correspondence and of creating a written record of services rendered by the attorney on behalf of the client. By having a written record of specific tasks that were performed, documents that were sent, services that were rendered, and discussions had, an attorney can prove that such actions actually happened if they later become the basis of a dispute. In the unfortunate event that a client is dissatisfied with an attorney's services and pursues an action for malpractice against the attorney, having a written record of specific actions taken can provide useful protection.

C. PERMANENT RECORDS IN THE DIGITAL AGE

The written history of an attorney's representation created through professional correspondence will, in many instances, become a permanent record of that history available for the general public to view long into the future. With the increasing reliance by courts, law firms, businesses, and individuals on the Internet, social networking, electronic filing, and digital information storage, professional correspondence can be widely disseminated throughout the world and become permanently on display for the world to see. An attorney is well-advised to take this permanence and accessibility into consideration when drafting correspondence. No self-

---

[1]   *See* CAL. EVID. CODE § 952 (2018).

respecting attorney wants her professional legacy to be a letter rife with typographical and grammatical errors or poor legal reasoning recorded for all posterity for anyone with an Internet connection to see.

D. DRAFTING PROFESSIONAL CORRESPONDENCE: IMPORTANT ELEMENTS

Before putting pen to pad, an attorney must consider the specific objectives shewants to achieve in writing a piece of professional correspondence. By focusing on the specific objectives, the attorney can eliminate irrelevant matters and create a clear and simple record of specific actions taken, advice given, and requests made.

Even the simplest correspondence must meet basic requirements. If the main goal is to send a copy of a document to a client, at least five specific points must be noted by the attorney in crafting the transmittal letter to accompany that document: (1) the name of the document being transmitted; (2) the significance of the document to the client; (3) the specific date the document was actually sent; (4) the manner in which it was sent, whether as an attachment to an e-mail or as an enclosure in an envelope sent via first class mail; and 5) the address it was sent to.

The last three of those points are especially important in the context of litigation, where failure to send certain documents by the statutorily mandated deadline can have grave consequences for the client. They are also important in the context of business and transactional work, where contracts frequently call for delivery of things in accordance with strict deadlines. Failure to deliver a contractually required document by a defined deadline can result in irrevocable financial penalties for the client.

These objectives can be achieved by including the information in the structure of the letter, as follows:

Law Offices of Oliver, Wendell & Holmes

June 20. 2013

ATTORNEY-CLIENT PRIVILEGED
<u>VIA FIRST CLASS MAIL</u>
Patricia Meagher
2222 Mockingbird Ln.
Los Angeles. CA 90016

      Re: Meagher v. Downs
             Los Angeles Superior Court Case No. LA 238906

Dear Ms. Meagher.

Enclosed is a copy of the medical report we received from our expert witness. Dr. Jasper John. in connection with his evaluation of your condition. Please do not hesitate to contact me if you would like to discuss Dr. John's report.

Very truly.

Gerry Oliver

Gerald F. Oliver

E. DRAFTING PROFESSIONAL CORRESPONDENCE: KNOWING THE AUDIENCE

The objectives, tone, and structure of an attorney's correspondence will be dictated in part by the intended audience, their level of sophistication, and the outcome sought.

An attorney should have a very good understanding of a client's level of sophistication with respect to the subject of the representation before sending the client a letter in the matter. Legal issues can be complex and incomprehensible to non-lawyers, even to sophisticated non-lawyers. Accordingly, the attorney must decide how to effectively convey the important information to the client using language the client will understand.

There are several easy ways to make otherwise complex legal concepts comprehensible to non-lawyers, such as eliminating legalese and technical jargon. For example, if an attorney is representing a client in a litigation matter and is sending the client a copy of a motion to dismiss, the attorney could include a simple transmittal letter that advises the client of the significance of the motion without discussing procedural subtleties that are ultimately meaningless to the client. Most clients will not understand what a motion is, let alone the procedural significance of the motion in the case.

The following is an example of a poorly drafted transmittal letter:

Law Offices of Oliver, Wendell & Holmes

June 20. 2013

VIA FIRST CLASS MAIL
Patricia Meagher
2222 Mockingbird Ln.
Los Angeles. CA 90016

      Re: Meagher v. Downs
             Los Angeles Superior Court Case No. LA 238906

Dear Patti.

Enclosed is a Motion to Dismiss filed by the Defendant in your law-suit. The motion states that your complaint fails to state a cause of action for which relief can be granted. While we don't believe the motion will succeed. we must respond to the motion in the time granted under the Code of Civil Procedure. Please review the motion papers and let me know if you have any questions.

Very truly.

Jerry

The following is an example of a well-drafted transmittal letter:

Law Offices of Oliver, Wendell & Holmes

June 20. 2013

ATTORNEY-CLIENT PRIVILEGED
VIA FIRST CLASS MAIL
Patricia Meagher
2222 Mockingbird Ln.
Los Angeles. CA 90016

      Re: Meagher v. Downs
              Los Angeles Superior Court Case No. LA 238906

Dear Ms. Meagher.

Mr. Downs. the defendant in your lawsuit. has filed a motion with the court asking it to dismiss your case. He claims that the facts we have included in your complaint do not provide the court with sufficient grounds for the compensation you are seeking.

We do not believe the motion will succeed. and we will file an appropriate response with the court. But we want you to understand that even if his motion does succeed. the court will likely allow us to resubmit your complaint with additional facts that do provide grounds for compensation.

I have included a copy of the motion papers for your records and would be happy to discuss them and their significance with you if you like. The court will hold a hearing on the motion on July 3. 2013. You are welcome to accompany me to the hearing. but your presence is not required. The court is not likely to announce its decision at the hearing. so I will inform you about the court's decision when I learn of it.

Very truly.

Jerry Oliver

F. TONE AND STYLE

The tone and style of a letter will depend considerably on who the recipient of the letter is, whether that is the client, opposing counsel, the court, or a third party involved as an expert, and it will depend on the relationship between the attorney and the recipient. A letter to a client will always be courteous, informative and professional, and should be conversational in tone. A comfortable conversational tone in a letter to a client reinforces the underlying notion of the special, confidential relationship between the attorney and the client. A letter to opposing counsel or to a party adverse to the client may take a more stern and forbidding tone. However, in any correspondence, irrespective of the recipient, the attorney should take great care to ensure that the tone is courteous and professional. Humor can be appropriate in legal correspondence where the attorney has established a relationship with the recipient and is confident that she will take the humor in the manner intended.

Legal representation frequently involves highly volatile circumstances wherein the parties have a lot at stake emotionally and financially. Clients hire attorneys to represent them in such situations in part because they need to rely on their attorney not to be as emotionally involved in the matter and to think clearly and strategically to resolve their problem. Nonetheless, every attorney is tempted at some point in her career to fire off an angry retort to someone who has said, done, or written something offensive in some way that deserves a response.

The important thing to do in such moments of anger is to step away from the offensive matter for some period of time in order to gather thoughts and craft a reply that comports with one's standards of courtesy, decorum, and professionalism. Just because the opposing counsel behaves badly, it is not an excuse for an attorney to breach standards of professionalism in responding to bad behavior.

Many examples exist of attorneys who lose their cool and send angry letters to respond to slights by opposing counsel only to find their letters later submitted into evidence to support motions for sanctions for unprofessional conduct. Good attorneys always keep in the forefront of their mind the knowledge that every word they write in any correspondence, whether on paper or electronic through e-mail or otherwise, is permanent and can come back to them—sometimes in unpleasant ways. A good rule of thumb is to get into the habit of waiting some period of time—an hour or even a day—to hit "send" on a piece of correspondence written in the heat of anger.

G. SPECIFIC TYPES OF PROFESSIONAL CORRESPONDENCE

There are many types of correspondence that an attorney will be called on to draft over the course of her career, including letters to clients providing advice about specific strategies and actions to take in a matter, letters to non-clients or opposing attorneys to perform or stop performing certain acts, and opinions of counsel that provide assurances to contracting parties that conditions required by a contract are being met, among others. This section will focus on two important forms of professional correspondence, the advice letter and the demand letter.

1. THE ADVICE LETTER

The term "advice letter" generally refers to correspondence the attorney sends to inform the client about the attorney's understanding of the scope and nature of the representation, to provide the client with specific legal findings based on research performed, and to advise the client on the various options available to achieve specific objectives. Advice letters also serve the purpose of creating a record of the specific advice given and the actions the attorney has taken in representing a client in the event such actions become the subject of dispute between the attorney and the client.

The following are the components that must be included in an advice letter:

- Date
- Name, address of recipient and manner of delivery
- Greeting
- "Re:" or subject line
- Summary of the issues addressed
- Statement of facts
- Discussion of the relevant law
- Discussion of the application of the law to the facts
- Caveat re: advice based on facts at the time of writing
- Conclusion and recommendation
- Request for authority to proceed
- Closing
- Attorney-client privilege notation

2.   THE DEMAND LETTER

The term "demand letter" generally refers to correspondence the attorney sends to parties who are adverse to their client to demand that those parties perform specific acts or desist from performing specific acts. For example, demand letters are used in the context of litigation during the discovery phase as part of the process of compelling the opposing party to produce discoverable material in response to discovery requests. Demand letters are also used to prevent others from violating clients' intellectual property rights that are protected under patent, trademark, or copyright laws. Demand letters also serve the purpose of creating a record of the specific actions taken by the attorney to resolve disputes, which may be a prerequisite to obtaining relief from a court.

The following are the components that must be included in a demand letter:

- Date

- Name, address of recipient and manner of delivery

- Greeting

- "Re:" or subject line

- Statement of representation and summary of nature of claim

- Persuasive statement of facts

- Persuasive discussion of the relevant law and the basis for prospective claims

- Demand and discussion of response

- Statement of further action to take

- Statement of a deadline for response

- Closing

The substance of both an advice and demand letter is legal analysis. The advice letter must set forth the rule of law and show the client how his facts apply to the rule using the objective CREAC paradigm discussed in Chapters 6, 9, and 10. The demand letter must persuade the opponent that the application of the law and facts favors your client, using the persuasive CRAC paradigm discussed in Chapters 6 and 16.

CHAPTER 16

PERSUASIVE LEGAL WRITING

■ ■ ■

By Mary-Beth Moylan and Adrienne Brungess

A. THE PURPOSE OF PERSUASIVE LEGAL WRITING

Persuasive writing is written advocacy. Your aim in persuasive writing is to support your client's legal position and convince your reader to agree with the legal conclusion that benefits your client. To be an effective persuasive writer, you must keep two primary principles in mind: perspective and audience.

Perspective requires you to reflect on how you view a problem or situation, and sometimes more importantly, how your client views her problem or situation. Perspective also requires evaluation of your opponent's viewpoint, so that you may anticipate potential arguments and evaluate all legally relevant facts and law. It is through assessing your perspective, and your opponent's, that you learn how or why you are focused on the view of the problem that you have. Once you have a solid command of your motivation, then you can turn to communicating that position to others.

Audience requires you to evaluate who you are trying to convince, and to coax that audience to see the problem or situation the way you do. Your audience for persuasive writing will be a judge, a mediator, an opposing attorney, or sometimes a legislative body.[1] The words you choose and the format of your writing should be determined after assessing your audience. While all legal audiences expect a professional tone, not all tools of persuasion are equally effective for each audience. Tailoring your writing to your particular audience is a crucial aspect of persuasion.

---

[1] *See* Chapter 8 on Knowing Your Audience.

B. TRANSITIONING FROM OBJECTIVE TO PERSUASIVE WRITING

1. OVERVIEW

Persuasive writing differs from objective writing in three fundamental ways. First, a persuasively written document has a new purpose—argument; objective writing seeks to evaluate and predict.[2] Second, persuasive writing focuses on a different audience—a court, mediator, or opposing counsel; objective writing is generally addressed to a supervising attorney or a client.[3] Third, information is presented differently in a persuasive document; rules are crafted favorably for the client and cases are assessed in the light most favorable to the client. Conversely, office memorandums, for example, should discuss the topic and the rules with a neutral eye and voice.

Objective analysis is fundamental to effective persuasive argument; you should consider objective analysis as the foundation for, rather than the alternative to, persuasive writing. A skilled advocate will first analyze the case objectively, gaining perspective on the opposing party's claims, then strategically craft a document that highlights her client's strengths and the opposing side's weaknesses. To accomplish this, you must analyze the law not as fixed and constant but as indeterminate and malleable.[4] Instead of searching for a single correct answer, look at the problem in different ways and consider different possible answers and interpretations. When you are aware of the different possibilities, you can more persuasively construct the best argument for your client.[5] Therefore, when organizing persuasive arguments, a skilled advocate will first predict the likely outcome based on the facts and available case law; then he will work backward from that outcome to construct the most persuasive analysis in support or opposition.[6]

---

[2] *See* Chapter 7 on the Process of Legal Writing.

[3] *See* Chapter 8 on Knowing Your Audience.

[4] Kathy Stanchi, *Teaching Students to Present Law Persuasively Using Techniques from Psychology*, 19 PERSPECTIVES: TEACHING LEGAL RES. & WRITING 142 (2011).

[5] Julie M. Spanbauer, *Teaching First-Semester Students that Objective Analysis Persuades*, 5 JOURNAL OF THE LEGAL WRITING INSTITUTE 167, 171 (1999), available at http://www.journallegal writinginstitute.org/archives/1999/spa.pdf (last visited Feb. 14, 2018).

[6] *Id.*

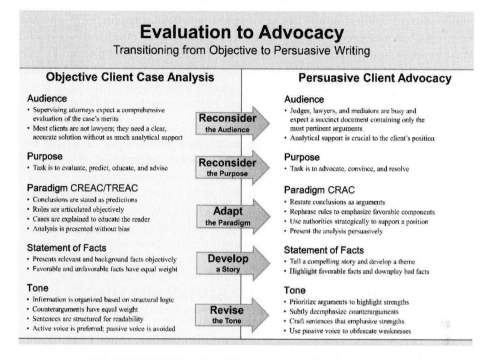

2. OBJECTIVE VS. PERSUASIVE PARADIGM

The large-scale organization of a persuasive document does not differ dramatically from that of an objective one. For example, an office memo discussion section is generally organized to reflect the formula the reader expects, such as a CREAC[7] approach. Similarly, a brief to a court has an argument section with a CRAC structure. The main substantive difference between the two paradigms is the omission of the "E" section—the explanation.

Consider here the different purposes of the documents—the objective memo explains the relevant law to educate the reader on the topic and support the writer's prediction. The purpose of the trial brief is to convince a busy reader to reach the conclusion asserted in the brief. In persuasive writing, the objective explanation is omitted or condensed substantially and thoughtfully to more effectively support the position that favors the client. In other words, the focus is on the favorable analysis, rather than the neutral explanation.

Some persuasive writing strategies are the same or similar to those employed in objective writing. For example, just as in objective writing, a persuasive brief should attack one topic at a time and use a single CRAC for each component of the argument. Also, all briefs, whether objective or persuasive, should include roadmaps and point headings to guide the

---

7   *See* Chapter 6 on Legal Reasoning and Analysis.

reader or to provide the necessary overview and background for the reader to understand the problem. However, when writing persuasively, consider strategy—present your best argument first and select issues thoughtfully based on the strength of the law. And, the best persuasive writing will anticipate and refute the opposing side's best arguments and make assertive conclusions.

Additionally, in a persuasive document, the ultimate conclusion about your topic should be stated assertively. In objective writing, a writer will phrase her prediction equivocally—"The court will probably find that. . . ." In persuasive writing, there should be a clear position of the best outcome for your client. For example: "The Court should grant the plaintiff's motion because. . . ." or "Defendants violated the law when they. . . ." In sum, the goal is to persuade, rather than to predict and inform. Keeping the different goal in mind will make the transition to this new writing paradigm painless.

C. CRAC—A PERSUASIVE PARADIGM

In Chapters 6 and 9, you were introduced to the objective writing paradigm CREAC—Conclusion, Rule, Explanation, Application, and Conclusion. The CRAC paradigm, which stands for Conclusion, Rule, Analysis, and Conclusion, is used for persuasive writing.[8] The persuasive paradigm amounts to (1) presenting a thesis, (2) stating and explaining the rule, (3) applying the rule, and (4) wrapping up the issue in a neat package for the decision maker. This paradigm should be used in the Argument section for each issue that the legal writer needs to discuss.

The order of the components of the CRAC paradigm is important and should be maintained. Legal audiences expect to encounter a proposition or thesis at the outset of any legal presentation—whether written or verbal. They then want to know the legal authority for the proposition or thesis. Once provided legal authority, the trained legal mind urgently wants to know whether and how the rule applies to the factual situation presented. Finally, the legal reader looks for a summary of how the legal analysis leads to a particular outcome. The CRAC formula satisifies the legally trained reader by providing the information expected and sought, without adding any unnecessary filler.

While the persuasive paradigm is the starting point, eventually the goal is to write formulaically without the formula being obvious to the reader. New persuasive writers should follow the formula closely. Each section of the CRAC should be clearly and separately identifiable. The initial and final conclusion may range from one sentence to a short paragraph, while the rule may require multiple paragraphs. The analysis

---

[8] Others might call the paradigm IRAC or TRAC, substituting the "Issue" or "Thesis" for the initial Conclusion, but the basic structure is the same.

section should be the longest section of the CRAC and is likely to be several paragraphs long. At the outset, it is important to understand the role of each part of the CRAC.

1. INITIAL CONCLUSION

Readers absorb information best if they understand its significance as soon as they receive it. The initial sentence or paragraph of the CRAC of each issue should state the conclusion you want the decision maker to reach on that issue and summarize the grounds for that conclusion. Ideally, the initial conclusion should combine the legal and factual basis for your conclusion and should persuade the reader through use of a theme. A more detailed discussion of theme is provided later in this chapter.

2. RULE—PERSUASIVELY ARTICULATED

As indicated above, legal readers seek a source of authority for the conclusion you wish them to reach. Providing a statement of the rule with statutory or case law support for the rule you advance is critically important. A legal argument without a legal rule is like an ice cream sandwich without the ice cream filling. In other words, it is not an ice cream sandwich at all.

Unlike the Rule in CREAC, which should be an objective and neutral statement of the rule drawn from a statute or case or a synthesis of those sources, the persuasive rule should present the rule in the light most favorable to your client or cause. The formulation of the rule can be an art in persuasive brief-writing.

Creating a persuasive rule starts at the same place as an objective rule—researching and evaluating the law governing your client's case. However, a skilled legal writer is strategic when crafting a favorable rule and phrases it thoughtfully. A favorable rule must still be accurate; however, it is crafted to best suit the needs of the analysis to follow. Although you cannot simply omit unfavorable information if it is binding and legally relevant, you can emphasize favorable points and deemphasize those that are unfavorable or harmful to your client.

There are a variety of techniques that will enhance the persuasive impact of a rule. The rule construction must be deliberate and strategic. For example, stating a rule narrowly restricts its perceived application; a broad rule statement has the opposite implication. Also, beginning the rule with the outcome you want for your client leads the reader toward that position. Further, including the favorable part of the rule at the beginning, while burying unfavorable components in the middle, will highlight the rule's more convincing elements. And, emphasizing the opposing side's burden of proof may shift the reader's focus to what the opposition cannot support. An even more simplistic strategy is to use active voice and concise sentence structure for favorable rule components and passive voice with more complicated sentence structure for contrary rule propositions.

To illustrate, compare the following three examples:

Example of an Objective Rule:

California Civil Code Section 3344(a) provides that the knowing use of another's photograph for commercial purposes without the person's prior consent is a violation of that person's right of publicity. Section 3344(d) provides an exception to the consent requirement contained in § 3344(a), which states that the use of a photograph in connection with "any news, public affairs, or sports broadcast or account, or any political campaign" does not require consent.

Example of a Persuasive Rule for Plaintiff:

The defendant's knowing use of another's photograph for commercial purposes, without the person's consent, violates California Civil Code Section 3344(a). The only exception to the statutory consent requirement is if the defendant can prove that the use of a photograph was in connection with a matter in the public interest. Cal. Civ. Code § 3344(d).

Example of a Persuasive Rule for Defendant:

The use of another's photograph does not violate California Civil Code Section 3344(a) unless the photograph is used knowingly and for commercial purposes without the person's consent. However, no consent is required when the defendant can show that the use of the photograph was in connection with a matter of public interest. Cal. Civ. Code § 3344(d).

To further illustrate, consider the following examples of persuasive rule phrasing:

Example of a Persuasive Rule for Moving Party:

Although judges and law clerks are afforded a presumption of impartiality in performance of their duties, disqualification is proper when a reasonable person with knowledge of the facts would conclude the judge or clerk acted with partiality. *First Interstate Bank of Ariz. v. Murphy*, 210 F.3d 983, 989 (9th Cir. 2000). Proof of a law clerk's relationship with one of the litigants is a pertinent factor to consider when assessing this presumption. *Barksdale v. Emerick*, 853 F.2d 1359, 1360 (6th Cir. 1988) (determining that the fact that one of the members of a judge's small staff chambers was the son of one of the litigants, although not dispositive, was relevant).

Example of a Persuasive Rule for Opposing Party:

A federal judge need not disqualify herself unless a reasonable person with knowledge of all the facts would conclude that the judge's impartiality might reasonably be questioned. 28 U.S.C. § 455 (2006); *Hamid v. Price Waterhouse*, 51 F.3d 1411, 1417 (9th Cir. 1995 (holding that even when a judge's clerk secured employment with a law firm representing one of the parties in a case before the judge, no reasonable person would conclude that the judge was partial where the clerk had minimal involvement with the case). Additionally, in a situation where a judge's clerk has a relationship an attorney, a judge fulfills her duty to avoid the appearance of partiality when she instructs her clerk not to do any work on the matter. *First Interstate Bank of Ariz. v. Murphy*, 210 F.3d 983, 989 (9th Cir. 2000) (holding that a judge's instruction to a clerk to refrain from any work on a case being litigated by a firm with which the clerk had secured employment was consistent with the judge's duty to avoid the appearance of partiality).

Similar to how selecting broad or narrow holdings can extend or restrict a rule, selecting favorable parts of the rule to introduce first can frame the rule broadly or narrowly and can enhance the persuasive value of the rule. In objective writing, the rule is frequently supported with a case illustration that discusses the details of the precedent case.[9] In persuasive writing, the rule is more often supported by only the most pertinent and client-friendly portions of the authority and not by a case illustration. Instead of case illustrations, the persuasive rule will frequently be supported by parenthetical explanations that provide succinct, focused information to support the rule.[10]

---

[9]   *See* Chapter 6 on Legal Reasoning and Analysis.

[10]   *See id.*

That is not to say that case illustrations are not useful in persuasive writing. But, your choice to include a case illustration should be deliberate. A case illustration may be effective if you are citing to a key governing case or if it is necessary to support analogical reasoning. However, even in these instances, you probably do not need to include every detail of the case you would include in a case illustration for an objective memo. Instead, you should focus on only the most pertinent information, such as the key facts, holding, and reasoning.

More frequently, however, advocates tend to use parenthetical explanations to support a statement of the rule. If you want to cite a case to support an argument but the relevance of the case is not apparent, a parenthetical explanation offers a quick way to include a bit of information about the case so it is clear why the case supports your position. You can also provide supplemental cites plus parentheticals to provide the reader with additional examples of how the rule has operated in prior cases.

3. ANALYSIS

Your goal in the analysis paragraphs is to show that applying the rule to the facts of your case compels the result that you seek. The most direct way to accomplish this is with deductive reasoning, if the rule supports this method. But when the facts are particularly important to the court's analysis, it is more effective to discuss the facts of comparable cases and analogize them to your case, demonstrating how your case is similar to those cases that reach the desired result.[11] The most common mistake that students make in the analysis portion of the CRAC is in failing to complete the analogy with a statement indicating the legal significance of the comparison. It is not enough to say that apples are similar to oranges because they are both round, healthy food. A complete comparison of the apple and the orange would need to indicate why the similarities between the two are legally relevant. In the case of the apple and the orange, a concluding sentence to the analysis paragraph may be something like "Therefore, because the apple and the orange are both fruits, they should make up a sizable portion of the average person's daily diet."

You can also demonstrate the applicability of a legal rule by distinguishing facts of adverse cases from your client's case. For example, assume that you have a very clear rule from a statute that prohibits littering in public parks. The rule has been applied in numerous cases to prohibit people from leaving garbage in the parks after picnics and parties. You have a client who has been cited under the anti-littering law for dumping compost in a flower bed in the public park. Your client was trying to beautify the park by adding his compost to the flower bed. You would distinguish the facts of your case from the facts of cases where litterers

---

[11] *See id.*

were successfully prosecuted. You might say something like the following in a brief to the court.[12]

> In *Brown* and in *Choi*, people left non-biodegradable garbage on the park surface, causing the park to diminish in appearance. *Brown v. Parks Dept.*, 458 Fict. Supp. 2d 749, 752 (E.D. Cal. 2010); *Choi v. Pufall*, 87 Fict.R.D. 915, 918 (N.D. Cal. 2000). Further in those two cases, park rangers were forced to clean up the messes that were left by the partygoers. *Brown*, 458 Fict. Supp. 2d at 753; *Choi*, 87 Fict.R.D. at 919. Here, Mr. D'Elia attempted to enhance the atmosphere in the park by leaving a biodegradable substance that would merge with the flower bed and create a more beautiful park. No park ranger was called upon to clean up his mess, and in fact, park rangers have stated that the flower beds where Mr. D'Elia laid the compost are thriving. *Decl. Ranger Jones* at ¶ 7 (Oct. 30, 2012). Therefore, the rationales for applying the littering laws articulated in *Brown* and *Choi,* namely, to control park appearance and to conserve park ranger time, do not apply to Mr. D'Elia's case.

Finally, analysis can and often should include a confrontation of the other side's argument. Anticipating and rebutting counter-arguments, if done in an affirmative way, can bolster your main legal point. Valid counter-arguments should not be left unaddressed. And yet, a positive and affirmative posture is important in persuasion. Many students struggle over how to rebut potential counter-arguments without taking on a defensive posture. The best way to strike the balance is to weave counter-points into your main argument without highlighting that you are doing so. For example, instead of starting a paragraph with a point you think that the opposing side will make, start your paragraph with your affirmative response to the point and then indicate that opposing counsel may take a contrary opinion but explain why that opinion is flawed and offer support.

4. FINAL CONCLUSION

In the final conclusion, it is the advocate's job to restate persuasively the conclusion forecast in your introductory paragraph. And, once the brief has recapped the main points that lead the reader to the desired conclusion, it should articulate to the court exactly what relief is sought, e.g., "Therefore, Count III of the Complaint should be dismissed for lack of subject matter jurisdiction."

---

[12] Note: The cases in this example are fictitious and therefore do not have real citations. Fictitious citations are provided to help give you context for proper citing practices.

D. TYPES OF PERSUASIVE WRITING

Other chapters discuss some of the specific types of persuasive writing that you will be required to draft, including pretrial motions, appellate briefs, client demand letters, and mediation briefs. For the purpose of this chapter, it is important to understand that while all those types of writing can use the basic CRAC paradigm to communicate persuasive legal analysis, the format and tone of each type of writing will vary depending on the audience.

For example, a pretrial memorandum of points and authorities in support of or in opposition to a motion to a trial court will use the CRAC formula in the argument section of a brief to advance the application of a particular legal rule to the facts in the first instance. An appellate brief will also employ CRAC in the argument section, and will aim to focus the court on perceived errors by the trial court in rule selection or rule application. So, the tone of those two types of court filings may be very different even though the same CRAC formula is used to structure the argument.

A demand letter may also use the CRAC formula to provide structure for the legal argument, but again the tone will be different in a document whose audience is the opposing attorney. In that type of persuasive writing, the articulation of the initial conclusion is unlikely to require as much introduction of the issue because presumably an opposing attorney will know the issue. In that case, the initial conclusion may become more of a purpose statement for the letter.

Regardless of the specific persuasive document you are writing, virtually all persuasive legal writing will include a persuasive statement of facts, a compelling theme, and a persuasive tone. It will also need to be mindful of cultural differences in communication, and target the recipient of the communication in a manner most appealing to that reader.

E. CRAFTING A PERSUASIVE STATEMENT OF FACTS

A statement of facts has standard components regardless of the type of document. For example, the reader will generally expect to find basic information about your client, the opposing party, and your client's problem or goal in the first paragraph of any statement of facts; the reader will also expect to find information about the time and location of events early in a statement of facts. And, the organization of the factual information should be thoughtful; facts are usually presented using a chronological or topical approach. Additionally, statements of facts in both objective and persuasive documents do not include legal conclusions or argument, and therefore should not include references to legal authority.

The primary difference between an objective and persuasive statement of facts is the tone. In an objective document, a skilled legal writer will present the relevant facts with a neutral tone and an objective perspective. Both favorable and unfavorable facts are presented with equal weight. Although even unfavorable facts must be included in a persuasive document if legally relevant, they are not presented with the same neutrality. The persuasive brief weaves a compelling story and attempts to deemphasize unfavorable facts.

When drafting a persuasive statement of facts, tell the factual story in a way that fits your favorable theory of the case. A skilled legal writer will be more deliberate with regard to the "lead" to the factual story—consider whether the first sentence draws the reader in and introduces your theme. Additionally, it should be clear to the reader from the very beginning of your story which side your story favors. The factual story should introduce your client in a positive and compelling way. A persuasive statement of facts may also contain emotionally significant factual information; this is less common in objective writing (unless those particular facts might affect the outcome of the case).

In fact, a skilled advocate will even consider story elements such as character and conflict when crafting a persuasive story. To tell a good story you must understand the basic components of a good story. For example, a good drama focuses on a compelling central character (your client—the protagonist); it develops the crisis faced by the protagonist, building to a climax—and then the resolution (what you hope to get for your client).[13] Also, the story benefits if the main character (your client) has a nemesis (the opposing side). So, a skilled advocate will tell a story that helps the audience identify with her client, understand the client's plight, determine the client's proposed resolution is the righteous one, and thereby attempt to defeat the villain (the opposition).

Be aware of your professional obligations when creating a story. A persuasive storyteller will likely tell a one-sided story when describing facts consistent with a theme and focused on a targeted audience. However, you should not distort or unfairly exaggerate facts. A skilled advocate will hide inconsistencies that might undermine the message. Ethical rules do not preclude you from crafting the story in a light most favorable to your client. However, the facts must be presented in a manner that you believe are true. You cannot make a false statement of fact to a tribunal or offer evidence you know to be false.[14] Even coming close to the line of veracity is dangerous, because if the reader has the sense that the facts are exaggerated to a point of falsity, the reliability of the entire persuasive piece may be compromised. Readers want to trust writers, but stories that

---

[13] Foley & Robbins, *Fiction 101: A Primer for Lawyers on How to Use Fiction Writing Techniques to Write Persuasive Facts Sections*, 32 RUTGERS LAW JOURNAL 459, 466 (2001).

[14] MODEL RULES OF PROFESSIONAL CONDUCT RULE. 3.3(a)(1), (3), R.3.3(b) (2002).

seem too one-sided can seem untrustworthy and contrived. Be creative and persuasive, but steer well clear of the fabrication line.

F. DEVELOPING A THEME

A skilled persuasive writer weaves a theme throughout the argument. The theme should be immediately obvious to the reader. It should act as a unifying thread throughout the document and the arguments made should relate in some way to the theme. Your theme should indicate your premise and your arguments should prove it.

The theme should not focus on your legal argument; because a dry message that the law does or does not support a position is not compelling. It takes more than logic to effectively persuade your reader. The theme should make your client's cause desirable and attractive to the reader for reasons other than legal support for the position. Consider the worldview, philosophy, message, or moral to your client's story. Often a theme will go beyond a single idea and instead put two ideas in conflict, such as "the defendant valued money more than safety."

To develop a theme, consider what moves you about the client's case and what might move a judge or jury. Think about what is compelling about your client's position—not just legally, but emotionally and personally. What makes someone care about your client's cause? If you were telling a non-lawyer friend or relative about the case, what would you say the case is about? The core principles that you would articulate to a non-lawyer about the case are likely to be the building blocks for your theme.

Try to develop your theme before you begin drafting your persuasive document. This will help guide you as to which facts to include to make a compelling story.

G. PERSUASIVE TONE

Persuasive tone does not invite the use of many adjectives, adverbs, and hyperbole. Very often, advocates confuse persuasive tone with rhetoric and over-emphasis. To achieve persuasive tone, there are subtle devices that you can use to provide emphasis and de-emphasis, as well as to direct the focus of your reader's attention to the points that are important to your client. Some examples of these tools are topic prioritization, sentence structure, and voice.

1. TOPIC PRIORITIZATION

An objective document is generally organized based on logic alone; it does not necessarily consider which legal issue most strongly favors the client. When writing a persuasive document, a skilled advocate will prioritize the legal issues so as to effectively highlight her strongest arguments; further, she will place weaker arguments or counter-arguments in a manner that will de-emphasize them. Therefore, you should select topics based on the strength of the law, equity, or judicial priority, and carefully consider where you place rebuttals to your opponent's strongest arguments so that they are not given unnecessary emphasis.

2. SENTENCE STRUCTURE

A skilled persuasive writer is thoughtful and deliberate about sentence structure. This begins with careful selection of the subject-verb unit. A reader will generally expect that a sentence will tell the story of whomever or whatever appears first in the sentence. To focus attention on a person or thing, make it the clear subject of your sentence and state it first; conversely, to deflect attention, focus on a different person or thing first. For example in a case about a murder: "Atkins and Jones, armed with handguns . . ." highlights the actors Atkins and Jones and the reader will expect the sentence to be about them. Conversely, "The complainant, Eric Nesbitt alleges that . . ." focuses on the victim and the allegations that he makes.[15]

Further, the reader will expect that the action is expressed by the verb used. So, if you want to draw attention to an action, express it clearly in the verb of the sentence; to downplay an action, express a different action in the verb. For example, in *Atkins v. Virginia*, the defendants brought the victim to an ATM machine to rob him before they killed him. The dissenting opinion wrote, "Cameras recorded their withdrawal of additional cash." The passive voice highlights the action of the camera recording; "withdraw" is not the action. But, "The victim was forced to withdraw $200" focuses on the forceful withdrawal as the action.[16] If your client was the defendant in the case, which characterization of the action would be more persuasive for his position?

Additionally, the reader will expect to find important information at the beginning and end of a sentence. Place the information you want to emphasize at the beginning or end of the sentence; conversely, place information you want to downplay in the middle. Consider carefully what information you provide as your sentence's lead or as the final clause and whether it emphasizes a favorable point for your client.

---

[15] These sentences come from the majority and dissent in the U.S. Supreme Court case, Atkins v. Virginia, 536 U.S. 304 (2002); *see* Raymond P. Ward, *Techniques for Emphasis and De-Emphasis*, FOR THE DEFENSE 35–37 (Nov. 2008) available at http://raymondpward.typepad.com/files/ftd-0811-ward.pdf (last visited Dec. 4, 2017).

[16] *See*, Ward, supra note 15, discussing majority and dissenting opinions in Atkins v. Virginia, 536 U.S. 304 (2002).

3.   ACTIVE VS. PASSIVE VOICE

Be thoughtful about whether to use active or passive voice. In objective writing, you may have been instructed to primarily use active voice. Active voice means your verb is active because the subject of the sentence is performing the action. Active voice tends to be preferred because it is more concise and uses more assertive verbs, which allows the reader to process the information more easily.[17]

However, in persuasive writing, the use of voice is more strategic. While active voice draws attention to the actor, passive voice deflects the action from the actor or omits the actor entirely. Use of a passive verb evades direct admission or responsibility. Again, using the *Atkins v. Virginia* example: "Atkins and Jones, armed with handguns, abducted the victim, robbed him of the cash he had, and drove him to an ATM, where cameras recorded their withdrawal of additional cash." This sentence uses strong active verbs to describe the facts. Alternatively, "The victim, Eric Nesbitt, alleges that he was driven to the ATM where he was forced to withdraw $200" uses passive voice to downplay the role the defendants played.[18]

Be cautious that your use of passive voice is not misleading and does not attempt to obfuscate the failure to complete a requirement in the case. For example, assume you are filing a motion to request that the court allow you to serve notice of an action by way of publication instead of personal service. To do so, assume the rule requires a sworn affidavit by the process server who attempted but failed to serve the defendant to "set forth with particularity" what actions she took to serve process on the defendant. You file an affidavit that does not identify the process server and instead states that "attempts were made" to serve the defendant. The court may determine that the service of the affidavit is insufficient and dismiss the action.[19]

H.   CROSS-CULTURAL CONSIDERATIONS

In many countries where the structure of the legal system is inquisitorial, rather than adversarial, the need for an attorney to engage in persuasive legal writing is diminished. Attorneys are expected to provide assistance to the court, and the written expression of the assistance comes in an objective analysis, rather than by advocating to the court on behalf of a client. Also, even in foreign nations with adversarial systems, certain persuasive techniques employed by advocates in the U.S. might not be embraced by the legal community. For example, a U.S. advocate might integrate creative imagery, alliteration, or use of metaphor in written or

---

[17]   ENQUIST & OATES, JUST WRITING (3d ed. 2009).

[18]   Ward, *supra* note 15.

[19]   *See* Deutsche Bank Natl. Trust Co. v. Brewer, 974 N.E. 2d 224 (Ill. App. 1st Dist. 2012).

oral argument; U.S. judges are generally receptive to advanced persuasive techniques when used effectively. But similar techniques might be perceived as unprofessional or inappropriately informal in a foreign court environment.

It is also the case that in international tribunals, the sources of persuasive law are more far reaching than in U.S. courts. For example, the International Court of Justice Statute (ICJ Statute), which governs practice in the International Court of Justice (ICJ), gives a list of authorities that the ICJ can consider.[20] The list includes not only international cases, international conventions, international treaties, and the ICJ Statute itself, but also domestic cases, treatises, and other works of learned scholars.[21] Because no authority is binding on international courts, when writing persuasively to an international tribunal a writer has a great deal of freedom in terms of what authorities to rely on. This freedom makes persuasive writing at the public international level more creative, but also, in many ways, more difficult. The task of identifying the audience and finding the correct authorities and analysis to sway the audience to your client's position is more challenging.

PRACTICE EXERCISE

Turn the following objectively written rule into a persuasive rule, and then apply the facts provided to the rule in a persuasive analysis paragraph in support of your client, Goldilocks.

Rule: No person or animal is permitted to sleep in the bed of another person or animal without express permission. Fairytale Stat. Ann. § 123.45 (2007). An exception to this rule has been found in the case of exigency, including situations where young princesses have been left in the forest to die. *Snow White v. Seven Dwarves*, 357 FT.2d 468 (1986).

Facts: An eight-year-old girl named Goldilocks was frolicking in the forest one day and found herself hungry, tired, and lost. After looking around for a path home for over an hour, she came upon the house of the three bears. Finding no one at home, she entered the house, ate the food on the table, and fell asleep in baby bear's bed. The door to the house was closed, but not locked. There was no sign on the door forbidding trespassing, and baby bear's bed was left unmade.

You may infer other facts about the Goldilocks case and the Snow White case that comport with traditional renditions of these fairy tales as needed to write your persuasive analysis.

---

[20] Statute of the International Court of Justice art. 38, Jun. 26, 1945, 59 Stat. 1055.

[21] *Id.*

CHAPTER 17

PRE-TRIAL MOTIONS

■ ■ ■

By Gretchen Franz

A. PRE-TRIAL MOTIONS GENERALLY

The purpose of a pre-trial motion is to persuade the court to rule a certain way on a legal issue and to issue an order regarding that ruling. While most pre-trial motions are made in writing, they can be made orally in open court—i.e. during trial or a hearing. It is more beneficial, however, to present the motion in writing because it gives the parties the opportunity to submit a Memorandum of Points and Authorities that details the arguments in support of the motion and to submit documentation such as affidavits or other evidence in support of the motion. In addition, oral argument can still be presented at the hearing on the written motion.

There are a wide variety of pre-trial motions that can be filed depending on the particular aspects of the case and what is allowed by controlling statutes, procedural rules, and case authority. The statutes, rules, and case authority will vary depending on whether the subject matter of the case is civil or criminal and whether the case has been filed in state or federal court.

Prior to filing a motion, it is always important to check the applicable Federal Rules of Civil or Criminal Procedure, if in federal court, or the controlling rules regarding civil or criminal procedure, if the case is filed in state court. Likewise, it is always important to check the applicable statutes and case authority. There are numerous practice guides and other secondary sources that can be consulted to determine the types of pre-trial motions applicable to a particular case. Determining what motion to file depends upon the nature of the case and the necessity for requesting relief from the court. At this point, your research skills will prove invaluable.

Common Pre-Trial Civil Motions Include:

- Motions to Dismiss for Lack of Subject Matter Jurisdiction
- Motions to Dismiss for Lack of Personal Jurisdiction
- Motions to Dismiss for Failure to State a Claim

- Motions for Partial or Full Summary Judgment
- Discovery Motions

Common Pre-Trial Criminal Motions Include:

- Motions to Dismiss Charges
- Discovery Motions
- Motions to Obtain Evidence
- Motions to Suppress Evidence
- Motions to Exclude a Witness

B. PRELIMINARY CONSIDERATIONS

Prior to filing a motion, think carefully about whether the motion is the best course of action for the client. Considerations to weigh include the strategy of how the motion may affect the case, the time and cost involved in preparing and arguing the motion, the client's opinion about the motion, whether a meet-and-confer with opposing attorneys is required by law or would be helpful, and whether sanctions could be imposed for filing a frivolous motion.

Strategy. Carefully consider what motions to file. File only those motions that will significantly help the client's case overall. Winning certain motions may influence the opposition to re-evaluate the strength of his client's case and may provide an impetus to early settlement. Be sure to also consider how losing the motion may affect the client's case and ability to negotiate a settlement. Remember the time, cost, and emotional and physical energy involved with a trial may not be in the client's best interest or, at a minimum, may not outweigh the benefits of the motion.

Time/Cost. As the client's advocate, consider the time involved and cost of preparing the motion and supporting documentation. Determine whether this is the best way to spend time and money on the case. Preparing a motion and arguing it in court can be time-consuming and costly. Carefully consider whether winning the motion will significantly help the client's position. If so, the time and cost involved may be justified. Also, consider the merits of the motion. If winning the motion will be an uphill battle, it may not be worth the time and cost—unless winning the motion is essential to the case or may initiate or further settlement discussions.

Client Counseling. Prior to filing any motion, discuss strategy, time, cost, and the chance of success on the merits with the client. Also, discuss the possible ramifications if the motion is denied. Let the client know how denial of the motion may affect the posture of the case, strategy moving forward, and settlement negotiations. Remember to always provide objective advice. It is ultimately the client who provides the authority to file the motion. Never guarantee that the court will rule a certain way. The client must understand that there is no certainty that the court will decide the motion in her favor.

Meeting and Conferring with the Opposing Attorney(s). Certain rules require that the attorneys meet-and-confer for particular motions. In a meet-and-confer session, the attorneys attempt to agree to the outcome of the motion to avoid the time and cost involved with filing the paperwork and appearing at the court hearing. Additionally, even if not required by law, the result sought by filing the motion might be obtained by a voluntary discussion between opposing attorneys. Sometimes the opposing attorney will stipulate to an issue—if it is one that must be resolved but is not crucial to the opposition's case. This step, if successful, will save time and money. Again, make sure to check with the applicable procedural rules.

Sanctions. Never file a frivolous motion. A frivolous motion is one that has little or no chance of being won primarily because the motion has no legal merit. The absence of legal merit may be due to the lack of an underlying justification for the motion based in either fact or law. The court can assess sanctions against an attorney who files a frivolous motion.[1]

Audience. The primary readers of the motion and supporting documentation are the trial judge and opposing counsel. The judge will make the decision regarding the motion. Therefore, it is important to conduct research on the judge who will hear the motion. The judge's background or prior decisions may provide insight as to how best to present the arguments in support of the motion. Common places to find information about a particular judge are (1) Martindale-Hubbell, (2) court websites that contain judicial profiles, (3) prior opinions issued by the judge, (4) discussions with other attorneys who have appeared before the judge, (5) discussions with former law clerks, (6) articles written by the judge, and (7) speeches given by the judge.

Do not assume that the judge is familiar with the overall case or the particular law that supports the motion. Most often, judges become familiar with a case in stages based upon court filings and hearings on various issues. Judges rely on the attorneys' written submissions for an accurate version of the facts and explanation of the law. Judges will often hear multiple motions in one day. Therefore, as with all legal writing, make your points clearly and succinctly.

---

[1] Fed. R. Civ. P. 11 is the rule that permits the imposition of sanctions for frivolous motions in the federal system. Similar rules exist in the state court systems as well.

C. FORMAT AND FILING INSTRUCTIONS

The applicable procedural rules will include the formatting and substantive requirements for a particular motion. Always make sure to check the Local Rules for the court that will hear the motion to ensure compliance with all procedural and substantive requirements of that court.

Generally, pre-trial motions must be in writing and the original copy of the motion and any supporting documentation must be filed with the main clerk's office of the court in which the case is being heard. Many courts now accept electronic filings. A copy of the motion and any supporting documentation must also be served upon the opposing attorney(s). Prior to filing the motion, request a hearing date from the clerk of the court. At the hearing, the attorneys present arguments and evidence to the judge. The judge may issue a ruling at that time, or she may take the matter under submission and issue her ruling at a later date.

D. PRE-TRIAL MOTION DOCUMENTS[2]

The party filing the motion will prepare a (1) Notice of Motion, (2) Memorandum of Points and Authorities in Support of the Motion, (3) any documentary evidence needed to support the motion, such as declarations, and (4) a Proposed Order.

As set forth by the applicable procedural rules, the opposing party will have a certain amount of time to file (1) Opposition to the Memorandum of Points and Authorities, (2) any documentary evidence needed to support the opposition to the motion, such as declarations, and (3) a Proposed Order supporting the opposing party's position.

The moving party will then have a short period of time, set by the procedural rules, to file a Reply to the Opposition Memorandum of Points and Authorities. Most courts disfavor a sur-reply (a reply to the reply).

A Proof or Certificate of Service, which certifies to the court that the opposing party has received notice that the documents have been filed and has received a copy of the filed documents, must be included with each set of documents each party files with the court.

E. COMPONENTS OF PRE-TRIAL MOTION DOCUMENTS

Caption. Each separate document filed with the court should begin with a Caption. The Caption provides the basic technical information concerning the case, including the following:

---

[2]   Prior to preparing any motion, check the local rules for the court in which the motion will be filed. Different jurisdictions may have different requirements for each motion.

- The name, address, telephone number, and bar license number of the attorney filing the motion, and the name and party designation on whose behalf the motion is filed.

- The name of the court where the motion is filed.

- The docket number assigned to the case.

- The initials of the judge who will hear the motion.

- The title of the motion.

- The names of the parties to the action and designation of their position in the action—e.g., Plaintiff and Defendant.

Notice of Motion or Motion. The terms Notice of Motion and Motion are sometimes interchanged. However, they serve separate functions. The Notice of Motion informs the court and opposing attorneys that a motion will be made at a certain time and place. This provides the opposition the opportunity to respond in writing and to appear at the hearing on the motion. The Motion itself sets forth the grounds (authority) for the motion and the relief requested. Many times, the Notice of Motion and Motion are set forth in one document that reasonably furnishes information about the motion itself such as:

- The date, time, and location of the hearing.

- The name of the judge that will be hearing the motion.

- The relief (result, order) sought.

- The basis of the motion—i.e. the statutory or other authority for requesting the relief sought.

- A list of any supporting documentation—e.g., Memorandum of Points and Authorities and declarations.

- Signature Block.

The following is an example of a Notice of Motion and Motion with caption and signature block:

Ellen Maxwell, State Bar Number 123456
Pacific McGeorge and Associates
3200 5th Ave.
Sacramento, CA 95817
916-123-4567

Attorneys for the Defendant
LESTER QUICKDRAW

SUPERIOR COURT OF THE STATE OF CALIFORNIA
COUNTY OF SACRAMENTO

THE PEOPLE OF THE STATE OF CALIFORNIA
 	
      Plaintiff,
 	
vs.
 	
LESTER QUICKDRAW,
 	
      Defendant.
	Criminal Action No. 2013-01 GF
	
	DEFENDANT QUICKDRAW'S NOTICE OF MOTION AND MOTION TO SUPPRESS CONFESSION

TO THE DISTRICT ATTORNEY OF THE COUNTY OF SACRAMENTO:

PLEASE TAKE NOTICE that on [insert date], Defendant Lester Quickdraw will move for an Order under California Penal Code § 1538.5 suppressing Mr. Quickdraw's involuntary, coerced confession. This Motion is made on the grounds that the confession was obtained in violation of Mr. Quickdraw's Fifth Amendment rights under the United States Constitution.

This Motion is made on the basis of this Notice, the attached Memorandum of Points and Authorities, Declaration of Brenda Golddigger, any evidence introduced at the hearing on this Motion, and the entire record and proceedings on file in this action.

Dated: [insert date]

Respectfully submitted,
Ellen Maxwell

Ellen Maxwell
Pacific McGeorge and Associates
3200 5th Avenue
Sacramento, CA 95817
916-123-4567

Attorneys for Defendant
LESTER QUICKDRAW

Memorandum of Points and Authorities. The Memorandum of Points and Authorities sets forth the arguments that support the relief requested by the motion. It is often called a "Brief." This is the crux of the motion. It sets forth the law and facts that support the court's ruling in the client's favor. The Memorandum of Points and Authorities is persuasively written to convince the court to decide the motion in the client's favor.

A Memorandum of Points and Authorities includes: (1) an Introduction, (2) Statement of Facts, (3) Argument, (4) Conclusion, and (5) a Signature Block.

The following is an example outline of a Memorandum of Points and Authorities:

Ellen Maxwell, State Bar Number 123456
Pacific McGeorge and Associates
3200 5th Ave.
Sacramento, CA 95817
916-123-4567

Attorneys for the Defendant
LESTER QUICKDRAW

SUPERIOR COURT OF THE STATE OF CALIFORNIA
COUNTY OF SACRAMENTO

THE PEOPLE OF THE STATE OF CALIFORNIA	)	
Plaintiff,	)	Criminal Action No. 2013-01 GF
vs.	)	MEMORANDUM OF POINTS AND AUTHORITIES IN SUPPORT OF LESTER QUICKDRAW'S MOTION TO SUPPRESS CONFESSION
LESTER QUICKDRAW,	)	
Defendant.	)	
_____	)	

INTRODUCTION

STATEMENT OF FACTS

ARGUMENT

CONCLUSION

Dated: [insert date]

                         Respectfully submitted,

                         Ellen Maxwell

                         Ellen Maxwell
                         Pacific McGeorge and Associates
                         3200 5th Avenue
                         Sacramento, CA 95817
                         916-123-4567

                         Attorneys for Defendant
                         LESTER QUICKDRAW

F. COMPONENTS OF A MEMORANDUM OF POINTS AND AUTHORITIES

Introduction. This section of the document provides the first opportunity to persuade the reader of the merits of the argument in support of the motion. It should include a short theme that captures the essence of the argument by intertwining law and facts. It should set the stage for the reader by introducing the story that supports the granting of the motion.

The Introduction should also explain the nature of the case, the parties, the procedural event that led to the filing of the motion, the relief requested by the motion, and the primary legal points that support why the motion should be granted.

The Introduction should include:

- A persuasive theme that supports the argument set forth in the motion.

- The rule(s) that supports the filing of the motion including the technical standard by which the court judges the motion—i.e. the standard of review.

- A summary of the case.

- A summary of the best reasons why the motion should be granted (or denied if filing an opposition brief).

- A statement of the relief requested.

Statement of Facts. This section sets out the relevant facts and the necessary background facts. The Statement of Facts for a Memorandum of Points and Authorities is similar in structure to the Facts section of the formal memorandum. However, unlike the Facts of a formal memorandum, which are objective in nature, the Statement of Facts in a Memorandum of Points and Authorities needs to be persuasively written.

Your presentation of the facts of the case is extremely important. Since the court follows precedent, the facts are determinative of whether the court should reach the same or a different result than that of previous cases. You should include the legally relevant facts and those facts that provide context to the story of what happened. (See Chapter 16 on Persuasive Legal Writing for a discussion of how to craft a persuasive statement of facts and Chapter 10 on the Formal Memorandum for a discussion of the types of facts that should be included in the Statement of Facts section and how the facts may be organized).

The goal of the Statement of Facts is to emphasize facts that support the client's argument. However, "bad" facts, or those facts which are not the best for the client, must also be included. It is better to address the "bad" facts and explain why they do not defeat the client's argument, than to have the opposition raise those facts for the first time. By not including "bad" facts, the argument loses credibility with the judge. While it is important to emphasize the client's version of the facts, the "bad" facts can be presented so as to minimize their impact. One strategy is to surround the "bad" facts by "good" facts so that the writer focuses on the facts that support the client's position.

Additionally, all of the facts in the Statement of Facts must be supported by a citation to where the information was derived. If a civil case, the facts may have been obtained through discovery. For criminal cases, the facts may have been obtained from police or eyewitness reports. For both civil and criminal cases, citations to the documents submitted in the court record are required in the Statement of Facts.

Argument. The purpose of the Memorandum of Points and Authorities is to persuade the judge (and opposing parties) that the law and facts of the case support the relief requested in the motion. Think carefully about how to present the arguments. Which arguments are the most important? How can these arguments be most effectively presented? (See Chapter 16 on Persuasive Legal Writing for a discussion of how to present arguments persuasively).

1. UMBRELLA PARAGRAPH

The umbrella paragraph provides an overview of the argument and its organization. If there is more than one main argument, or an argument with sub-parts, that support the motion, an umbrella paragraph should be provided for each.

2. PERSUASIVE POINT HEADINGS

Persuasive point headings must be provided for each main argument and for all sub-arguments. Unlike predictive point headings for formal memoranda that are objectively written, the point heading in a Memorandum of Points and Authorities is a persuasive statement of the disposition of the particular argument. The persuasive point heading should include the result sought, it should identify the part of the rule that supports that result, and it should include the key facts that support the result.

3. CRAC

Each argument or sub-argument identified in the persuasive point heading should be presented in CRAC format. (See Chapter 16 on Persuasive Legal Writing for a discussion of the persuasive paradigm.)

<u>C</u>onclusion: Begin each argument or sub-argument with a persuasive thesis sentence that concludes this argument or sub-argument favorably for the client and that succinctly states why the court should reach this conclusion.

<u>R</u>ule: A statement of the rule(s) or a synthesis of the applicable rules.

<u>A</u>rgument: This is your analysis of the legal issue. Apply the legal authority to the facts of the case. Explain how the law supports your client's position. Your argument may be based on deductive reasoning, analogical reasoning, or policy based reasoning. (See Chapter 6: Legal Reasoning and Analysis Toolkit for a discussion of the different types of legal reasoning).

In your argument, it is important to acknowledge and distinguish adverse authority for three reasons: (1) to honor your ethical duty to alert the court to adverse legal authority; (2) to take the "punch" out of the opponent's argument by citing the case first and explaining why it does not alter the outcome of the motion; and (3) to avoid losing credibility with the court.

Citations must be provided for all legal authority relied upon in the Argument. The citation format will depend on the citation manual required by the court in which the motion is filed.

<u>C</u>onclusion: Restate the factual conclusion and, if necessary, based on the complexity or length of the argument, summarize the key points supporting the conclusion.

Conclusion. This section of the brief should consist of a statement of the decision the client wants the judge to reach on the overall motion. It should wrap the motion up with a bow by concisely, but persuasively, summarizing all of the arguments made in the Argument section. Complete the brief by respectfully requesting that the court grant the relief sought, or if opposing a motion, denying the relief sought.

Signature Block. End the Memorandum of Points and Authorities with a Signature Block. Include the date, the phrase "Respectfully submitted," and a signature line with the attorney's name, the law firm's name, address and telephone number, and the party represented. Be sure to include a signature on the signature line.

Proposed Order. A Proposed Order should be included with the motion papers. The Proposed Order should include the decision you wish the court to make. The sample provided below is an example of a basic Proposed Order. Many times, however, the attorney will include the facts supporting the motion and include an opinion for the court's convenience or at the court's request.

The following is an example of a basic Proposed Order:

IN THE
SUPERIOR COURT OF THE STATE OF CALIFORNIA
COUNTY OF SACRAMENTO

THE PEOPLE OF THE STATE OF CALIFORNIA)	
)	Criminal Action No. 2013-01 GF
)	
Plaintiff,)	
)	[Proposed] ORDER GRANTING
)	DEFENDANT QUICKDRAW'S MOTION TO
vs.)	SUPPRESS CONFESSION
)	
LESTER QUICKDRAW,)	
)	
Defendant.)	
_____)	

DEFENDANT QUICKDRAW'S MOTION TO SUPPRESS CONFESSION came on for hearing before this Court on [insert date]. After considering the Memorandum of Points and Authorities in Support of the Motion, the Opposition Brief, and Reply Brief, all documents on file, and the arguments of counsel, the Court finds that the confession was obtained in violation of Defendant's Fifth Amendment rights under the United States Constitution.

IT IS THEREFORE ORDERED that Defendant's Motion to Suppress Confession is GRANTED.

Dated: [insert date]

_____

GRACE FREDERICK

JUDGE, SUPERIOR COURT OF CALIFORNIA, COUNTY OF SACRAMENTO

Memorandum of Points and Authorities in Opposition. As mentioned earlier, the party opposing the motion is provided the opportunity to respond to the arguments made in the moving party's motion, and to present arguments as to why the motion should be denied. The format of the Memorandum of Points and Authorities in Opposition to the Motion follows the same format as the Memorandum in Support of the Motion.

Reply Memorandum of Points and Authorities. Also, as mentioned previously, after the opposition party files a Memorandum of Points and Authorities in Opposition to the Motion, the moving party is provided the opportunity to respond to that opposition in a short Reply, usually no more than five pages. The moving party is not entitled to raise new arguments in the Reply but, instead, can only respond to the arguments raised in the Memorandum of Points and Authorities in Opposition to the Motion. The Reply also follows the same format as the Memorandum in Support of the Motion.

Proof or Certificate of Service. The Proof or Certificate of Service is a separate page attached to the end of the documents being filed with the court. The Proof or Certificate of Service certifies to the court that all documents have been successfully served on all parties to the action, the manner in which service was made, and the identity of the person who served the documents, if personal service was made.

The following is an example of a Proof of Service:

Ellen Maxwell, State Bar Number 123456

Pacific McGeorge and Associates

3200 5th Ave.

Sacramento, CA 95817

916-123-4567

Attorneys for the Defendant

LESTER QUICKDRAW

SUPERIOR COURT OF THE STATE OF CALIFORNIA
COUNTY OF SACRAMENTO

THE PEOPLE OF THE STATE OF	)	
CALIFORNIA	)	Criminal Action No. 2013-01 GF
	)	
Plaintiff,	)	PROOF OF SERVICE
	)	
vs.	)	
	)	
LESTER QUICKDRAW,	)	
	)	
Defendant.	)	
_____	)	

I certify that on this __ day of [month], [year], I served the attached NOTICE OF MOTION AND MOTION TO SUPPRESS CONFESSION, and MEMORANDUM OF POINTS AND AUTHORITIES IN SUPPORT OF THE MOTION upon Plaintiff by causing a copy thereof to be mailed, first class postage prepaid, to the attorney for Plaintiff, District Attorney Stephanie Kate, Office of the District Attorney, Criminal Division, 123 Courthouse Way, Sacramento, California, 95817.

Dated: [insert date]

Respectfully submitted,

Ellen Maxwell

Ellen Maxwell

Pacific McGeorge and Associates

3200 5th Avenue

Sacramento, CA 95817

916-123-4567

Attorneys for Defendant

LESTER QUICKDRAW

G. CROSS-CULTURAL CONSIDERATIONS

The United States is a common law system. In this system, courts are bound by the concept of stare decisis—in Latin this means "let the decision stand." Stare decisis is the doctrine by which judges are bound by precedent. To be specific judges must follow decisions rendered by higher courts in their jurisdiction. Persuasive arguments in support of pre-trial motions are crafted based upon precedent for the court in which the motion is filed.

Judges in civil law countries, however, are not bound by stare decisis or precedent. In those countries, the law is derived from enacted codes. Unlike common law countries where judges make law, civil law judges do not. Therefore, decisions by judges in civil law countries are not binding on future cases.

Unlike the common law system, which has a developed system of rules regarding discovery, no formal discovery process exists in a civil law system:

> The civil process tends to be conducted primarily in writing, and the concept of a highly concentrated and dramatic "trial" in the common-law sense is not emphasized. The judge supervises the collection of evidence and preparation of a summary of the record on which a decision will be based. Since there is no "pretrial" phase of the proceeding, the evidence is not "discovered" in the sense understood by common-law lawyers. Instead, the parties submit proposed evidence to the judge in writing or at oral hearings, and the judge delivers rulings concerning the relevance and admissibility of evidence. Admissible evidence is presented, for the first and only time, in the final hearing that constitutes the trial.[3]

Thus, if seeking an order from a judge in a system that is not a common law one, the presentation of the arguments in support of the order will not follow the traditional persuasive paradigm or the pre-trial motion practice described in this book.

---

[3] JAMES G. APPLE AND ROBERT P. DEYLING, A PRIMER ON THE CIVIL-LAW SYSTEM 27 (Federal Judicial Center 1995).

CHAPTER 18

THE APPELLATE PROCESS AND STANDARD OF REVIEW

■ ■ ■

By Jennifer A. Gibson

A. THE APPELLATE PROCESS

The purpose of this chapter is to provide a basic introduction to the appellate court systems in the United States and to the appellate process in general. The information contained in this chapter will help you understand the basic principles of appellate litigation by providing practical information that must be considered and used when deciding whether to file an appeal and how to prosecute that appeal once it is initiated.

Every appellate lawyer can recall an initial consultation with a potential client who was absolutely convinced that the appellate court would reverse the decision in the lower court because the appellate judges would wisely adopt the client's version of the facts. For the client, the appeal may appear to present the final opportunity to retry the facts of the case, this time with three judges instead of one.

The client must understand that the very role of the appellate court prevents that kind of rehearing of the case. An appellate court is a court of law that corrects legal errors. Thus, its power to right a wrong done in lower court is very limited. Once the lower court has reached a decision, presumptions are triggered that prevent the appellate court from altering the result on appeal, even if it were moved by the facts of the client's case. The statistics for reversals on appeal bear out that these presumptions are very effective.

B. OVERVIEW OF THE APPELLATE COURT SYSTEMS

As presented in Chapter 2, most states have a three-tiered court system with trial courts, intermediate courts of appeal, and the state's Supreme Court or high court.[1] Only nine states do not have intermediate

---

[1] New York's trial court is the Supreme Court and its highest court is the Court of Appeals.

courts of appeal.[2] Instead, the Supreme Courts or the high courts in those states handle all appeals from the trial courts. At the trial court level, matters are heard and decided by a single judge. At the intermediate appellate court level, a panel of three judges usually decides the appeal. These decisions do not need to be unanimous. Only a majority of the panel is required to agree to a decision. At the state's highest court, cases are decided by the entire court, which can be anywhere from five to nine judges. In California, for example, there are seven justices on the state's high court.

Each state has rules of appellate procedure that govern practice before its courts of appeal. In addition to these statewide appellate rules of procedure, some individual appellate courts have local rules that apply to that specific appellate court or even to just one division in that court. For example, Division 2 in California's Fourth Appellate District has a local practice of issuing tentative opinions one week before oral argument. No other appellate district in California has adopted this practice.

The federal court system is also a three-tiered system: district courts, circuit courts of appeals, and the United States Supreme Court, which is the highest court in the land on federal issues. The trial courts in the federal system are called district courts, and each state (and the District of Columbia) has at least one.[3] In California, for example, there are four federal district courts: northern, eastern, central, and southern. In the District of Columbia, there is one district court.

The intermediate courts of appeal in the federal system are divided into thirteen circuits. The fifty states are divided into eleven circuit courts of appeals, beginning with the United States Court of Appeals for the First Circuit through the United States Court of Appeals for the Eleventh Circuit. The other two circuit courts are the United States Court of Appeals for the Federal Circuit and the United States Court of Appeals for the District of Columbia. The Federal Circuit has nationwide jurisdiction over cases arising from a variety of subject areas, including patents, trademarks, international trade, government contracts, certain money claims against the United States government, veterans' benefits, and public safety officers' benefits claims. The Court of Appeals for the District of Columbia has jurisdiction over appeals from the district court for the District of Columbia.

As in the state court system, a single judge decides matters at the district court level. In the circuit courts, three-judge panels decide appeals. That three-judge panel decision can be reversed, however, if a party petitions for a rehearing en banc. An en banc decision is one issued by all

---

[2]   Those states are Delaware, Maine, Montana, New Hampshire, Rhode Island, South Dakota, Vermont, West Virginia and Wyoming. Nevada used to be included on this list. However, on November 4, 2014, Nevada voters approved the creation of a Court of Appeals.

[3]   Because the federal system refers to its trial courts as district courts, this chapter uses the term lower court to refer to both state trial courts and federal district courts.

the active sitting judges within the circuit. While en banc reversals are not typical, they do occur. At the Supreme Court level, all nine justices on the United States Supreme Court decide matters, unless one or more of the justices decide that they have a conflict and should not hear the matter.

The United States Code Annotated publishes the Federal Rules of Appellate Procedure, which govern appellate practice in all thirteen United States courts of appeals. These forty-eight rules govern a number of issues, including the right to appeal, a party's right to oral argument, and the number of briefs a party should file. The Supreme Court has its own rules that govern appellate practice before that Court called the Rules of the Supreme Court. The rules are also published by United States Code Annotated and can be found on the United States Supreme Court's website.

1.   STARE DECISIS

As discussed in Chapters 2 and 17, *stare decisis* is a doctrine that promotes political and social stability by encouraging public confidence in the legal system. It fosters the belief that the law does not change simply because, as the years pass, different judges have replaced other judges on an appellate court. The doctrine strongly influences judges to apply the same legal reasoning to cases that are similar to prior cases. The significance of *stare decisis* is highlighted during the appellate process because the doctrine dictates what appellate decisions are binding on the issues being considered in an appeal.

Decisions of the appellate court can be published or unpublished. A published decision is reported in the state's official case reporter, and it may be cited as authority in later unrelated cases. Published decisions of intermediate courts of appeal are binding on lower courts. In most instances, in states in which the intermediate appellate court is divided into multiple districts or divisions, the published decision of one division is generally not binding on another. In most states, where there are conflicting court of appeals decisions, and the high court has not resolved the conflict, the lower courts can generally decide which decision to follow. Once the state's highest court resolves the conflict, however, all courts within the state must follow that decision. Raising issues that have been authoritatively decided by a state's high court can result in sanctions for filing a frivolous appeal.[4]

In most states, unpublished decisions, decisions not published in the state's official reporter, may not be cited as authority in any subsequent unrelated case. Thus, even if an unpublished decision can be found online, it may not be cited as authority in another unrelated case. Although this is

---

[4]   An appeal is frivolous if filed in a case where the judgment below was plainly correct and the legal authority contrary to appellant's position is so clear that there really is no appealable issue. Romala Corp. v. U.S., 927 F.2d 1219, 1222 (Fed. Cir. 1991). Note that even if it has objective merit, an appeal is frivolous if it is pursued for an improper purpose.

the general rule, practitioners should consult each jurisdiction's local rules on citing to unpublished decisions.

The federal system is a lot more hierarchical than most state court systems. *Stare decisis* operates to bind subsequent panels of judges to published decisions issued by the first panel of judges to decide an issue within that circuit. Thus, the decision binds not only district courts within the circuit but also subsequent appellate court panels within the circuit as well.[5] Only when a circuit court's full panel of judges (sitting en banc) decides to consider a specific case, may an appellate court overrule a decision previously issued by a three-judge panel from that circuit.[6]

Stare decisis has become murkier in the federal court system since Federal Rules of Appellate Procedure Rule 32.1 was implemented. That rule permits litigants to cite to unpublished appellate court decisions issued on or after January 1, 2007. While the rule does not make those decisions binding on subsequent decisions, they are persuasive. Each of the circuit courts has issued local rules that implement Rule 32.1. Consult the local rules for each circuit court of appeals in which you will be filing appellate briefs to determine the precedential value of unpublished decisions in that circuit.

2. STARE DECISIS ACROSS SYSTEMS

Because each state has two court systems, one state and one federal, *stare decisis* has implications across court systems. Generally, federal courts must follow the decision of the highest state court on an issue of state law.[7] For example, if the intermediate appellate court's decision is the highest decision on a state issue, the federal court must follow that decision, unless it is persuaded that the state's high court would decide the issue otherwise.[8] However, federal courts are not required to follow a state court's decision on federal issues.[9] State courts are only required to follow decisions of the United States Supreme Court on federal and constitutional issues.[10]

---

[5]   Oneida Indian Nation of New York v. County of Oneida, 617 F.3d 114, 122 (2d Cir. 2010).

[6]   *Id.*

[7]   The highest state court is the final authority on state law. Fid. Union Trust Co. v. Field, 311 U.S. 169, 177 (1940) (citing Erie Railroad Co. v. Tompkins, 304 U.S. 64, 78 (1938)).

[8]   C.I.R. v. Bosch's Estate, 387 U.S. 456, 465 (1967) (internal quotations and citations omitted).

[9]   "Although state courts have the authority to decide issues of federal constitutional law, state court decisions are not binding upon the federal courts." Sys. Contractors Corp. v. Orleans Parish Sch. Bd., 148 F.3d 571, 575 (5th Cir. 1998).

[10]   "We are not bound by decisions of the lower federal courts, even on federal questions, they are persuasive and entitled to great weight." Barrett v. Rosenthal, 146 P.3d 510, 526 (Cal. 2006).

C. TAKING THE APPEAL: GENERAL CONSIDERATIONS

Who gets to appeal, and what can they appeal? Appellate courts are courts of limited jurisdiction. That means that the jurisdiction of those courts is defined by statute. Thus, for an appeal to be valid, it must fall within the appellate court's statutory jurisdiction.

The client's decision to file an appeal requires consideration of a number of issues, specifically, whether the judgment or order is appealable, whether there is an active or justiciable issue for the appellate court to resolve, and whether the appeal was filed timely and properly. These preliminary considerations are critical because the negative consequences for filing an appeal that is frivolous or that lacks merit may fall on the attorney, the client, or both.[11]

1. IS IT APPEALABLE?

Perhaps the most important of these considerations is whether the order or ruling being challenged is in fact appealable. An order that is a final judgment, meaning it ends the controversy among the litigants and leaves nothing for the lower court to do other than to enforce the judgment, is appealable. It is for this reason that an order granting summary judgment is not appealable. Rather, it is the final judgment entered based on the order granting summary judgment that is appealable.

This final judgment requirement is often referred to as the "one-judgment rule." The one-judgment rule prevents piece-meal appellate review by ensuring that in most cases an appeal can be filed only after the lower court has completely resolved the matter between the parties, deciding which party has won and which one has lost. Because appeals can take up to two years, from the date the notice of appeal is filed, to be resolved, permitting a litigant to appeal each order of the lower court before a final judgment is entered can bring the litigation to a grinding halt. Thus, the one-judgment rule avoids "piecemeal, prejudgment appeals" that undermine "efficient judicial administration."[12]

But as with most rules, there are exceptions. For instance, the one-judgment rule does not apply to post-judgment orders, which are usually immediately and separately appealable. An example of a post-judgment order that is separately and immediately appealable is an order on a motion for attorney fees. Furthermore, both state and federal statutes allow appeals of other orders that are not final judgments. For example, an order granting a new trial may be appealed. Orders for temporary spousal

---

[11]   FED. R. APP. P. 38 (West 2018).

[12]   Firestone Tire & Rubber Co. v. Risjord, 449 U.S. 368, 374 (1981).

or child support may be as well. Orders appointing a receiver are generally also appealable even though those orders are not final judgments.

Further, most jurisdictions have a certification process that permits parties to appeal orders that are not expressly made appealable by statute or that are not final judgments. In the federal system, for example, the district court can certify an interlocutory order for appeal if the court is of the opinion that the order involves a controlling question of law that is not easily determined and immediate appellate review may materially advance the termination of the litigation.[13]

On the issue of appealable orders, one caveat for appellate practitioners is to beware of the collateral order, which is an order that does not end the litigation but resolves an important question separate from the merits of the case. Orders of that nature are immediately appealable and are not reviewable from the final judgment in the case. Both state and federal court systems have this exception. Collateral orders can be traps for the novice practitioner because if an appeal is not filed timely, appellate review is forever lost.

A collateral order that is immediately appealable has three primary characteristics: (1) it conclusively decides a contested issue, (2) the issue is separate from the merits of the action, and (3) the order would be "effectively unreviewable later in the litigation."[14] The classic collateral order is one granting a motion to disqualify retained counsel.

A specific category of collateral orders that are referred to as "death knell" orders also exists. If the order effectively terminates the litigation between the parties by delivering a "death knell" to the litigation and thereby making it impossible for one party to obtain effective relief, it is a collateral order and is immediately appealable. An example of a "death knell" order is an order denying certification of a class in a class action lawsuit. In that case, the order effectively ends the class action and requires the plaintiffs to bring individual actions.[15] Another example is an order determining that a state official is entitled to qualified immunity from a lawsuit. In that case, again, unless the order is appealed, the plaintiff's ability to obtain relief against that state official, and likely the state, is lost.

2. DOES THE PARTY HAVE THE RIGHT TO APPEAL?

The next factor in deciding whether to file an appeal is justiciability, which refers to whether the court is being asked to decide an actual controversy between actual parties aggrieved by the lower court's decision.

---

[13]   28 U.S.C. § 1292 (2006).

[14]   Osborn v. Haley, 549 U.S. 225, 238 (2007)

[15]   Safaie v. Jacuzzi Whirlpool Bath, Inc., 122 Cal. Rptr.3d 344, 349 (4th App. Dist. 2011).

This justiciability requirement exists to prevent appellate courts from rendering advisory opinions that do not affect actual parties.

Three considerations determine whether an appeal presents a justiciable issue. First, the party bringing the appeal must have standing, meaning the party must be a party of record and must be aggrieved by the trial court's order or have a stake in the controversy. Second, the issue must not be moot, meaning subsequent events must not have rendered it impossible for the appellate court to provide effective relief on appeal. An appeal challenging conduct that is capable of repetition against the same party yet evading review is not considered moot, however.[16] Third, the issue must be ripe, meaning that a wrong must have occurred and a present need for the appellate court to act exists. Unless these three criteria are met, the issue is not justiciable, and the appellate court will decline to address the appeal on the merits.

3. WAS THE APPEAL TIMELY FILED IN THE RIGHT COURT?

Perfecting the appeal means timely filing the notice of appeal in the lower court along with the appropriate filing fee. Filing the notice of appeal timely is critical because a timely filed notice of appeal is a jurisdictional requirement that cannot be waived or overlooked by the appellate court. The appellate court must dismiss any appeal in which the notice of appeal was not filed timely. For this reason, the failure to file it timely can be grounds for malpractice.

In both federal and state courts of appeal, the time limit for filing the notice of appeal is triggered by the entry of the final judgment. In federal court, the appellant has thirty days from entry of the judgment or order being appealed.[17] In cases where the United States is a party, the time limit to appeal is sixty days.[18] Sometimes, the respondent, the party who did not initiate the original appeal, may decide to file a cross-appeal of an issue in the case. In the federal courts, the time for filing the notice of the cross-appeal is either the time remaining after the first party filed the initial notice of appeal or fourteen days after the first notice of appeal was filed, whichever is later.[19]

Most states have time limits ranging from thirty days to 180 days from the entry of judgment. In Colorado, for example, the notice of appeal must be filed within forty-nine days after the entry of the final judgment appealed.[20] In Alabama, the notice of appeal must be filed within forty-two

---

[16] Sosna v. State of Iowa, 419 U.S. 393, 399–402 (1975).

[17] FED. R. APP. P. 4.

[18] *Id.*

[19] *Id.*

[20] COLO. SUP. CT. R. 4.

days of the date of the entry of the judgment or order appealed.[21] In California, a party must file the notice of appeal within sixty days from the service of notice of entry of judgment or within 180 days from entry of the judgment, whichever date is earlier.[22]

Given the enormous risk of dismissal because of a late notice of appeal, practitioners often choose to file the notice of appeal before going through what could be time-consuming preliminary considerations in assessing the merits of the appeal. If the appeal is later determined to be imprudent, the practitioner can always dismiss it voluntarily.

4. WRIT IT?

Even if an interlocutory order is not appealable by statute, permission, or certification, practitioners may seek review in the appellate court using a petition for a writ of mandate, prohibition, or certiorari. A reviewing court issues a writ of mandate to correct an abuse of discretion or compel the performance of a ministerial duty. Appellate courts issue writs of prohibition to prevent a judicial act that exceeds the jurisdiction or power of the particular judge or court. Writs of certiorari are issued to correct a judicial act that has already been completed, and which is in excess of the court or judge's jurisdiction or power. While not encouraged as a substitute for an appeal, the writ petition is one means by which appellate courts can exercise their reviewing power expeditiously.

Because writ relief is by definition extraordinary relief, the requirements for obtaining writ review are stringent. Those threshold requirements are the following: (1) an abuse of discretion or erroneous ruling; (2) the threat of irreparable or substantial injury absent the writ; and (3) the lack of an adequate legal remedy. Even when these requirements are met, however, writ review is not guaranteed.

Writ petitions are further segregated into statutory writs and common law writs. Statutory writs apply to specific circumstances, and in some instances, a statutory writ petition is the *exclusive* method of obtaining review. For example, challenges to an order denying a motion to quash service[23] or a ruling on a motion to disqualify a judge[24] are reviewed exclusively by statutory writ. The time limits for filing a statutory writ are also stringent, with some writs having to be filed in as little as ten days of the challenged action.

The right to bring a common law writ is not created by statute, but as the label suggests, the remedy arises out of English common law. Even though common law writs do not have time limits, as a rule, a common law

---

[21] ALA. R. APP. P. 4.

[22] CAL. R. CT. R. 8.104.

[23] McCorkle v. City of Los Angeles, 70 Cal. 2d 252, 257 (1969).

[24] Curle v. Super.Ct. (Gleason), 24 Cal. 4th 1057, 1063 (2001).

writ petition should be filed as soon as possible following written notice of the ruling or order the petitioner wishes to challenge. By its very nature, a common law writ petition is a request for emergency or extraordinary relief. Expeditious filing is particularly important if the argument is that the threat of harm is great. In a case of that type, an unreasonable delay in filing the petition will undercut the party's claim to such extraordinary relief.

5. STAYING ENFORCEMENT OF THE JUDGMENT WHILE THE APPEAL IS PENDING

In many cases, filing an appeal automatically stays the enforcement of the judgment entered in the lower court. In other cases, however, it does not. In particular, perfecting or filing an appeal does not automatically stay enforcement of a money judgment, an order transferring real property, or a custody order. Thus, an appellate practitioner must always consider the issue of obtaining a stay of enforcement while the appeal is pending if a stay is not automatic.

There are three traditional ways of obtaining a stay of enforcement until an appeal can be decided. For money judgments or appeals involving possession of real property, the appellant can obtain a stay of enforcement by posting a bond or undertaking backed by a personal or corporate surety, or by depositing cash or negotiable securities with the court.[25] If posting a bond or undertaking is not possible or appropriate, the appellant can file a request with the lower court for a discretionary stay. This request for a discretionary stay should be made to the same court that entered the judgment. If the request for a discretionary stay is denied, the appellant can also seek a stay by filing a petition for a writ of supersedeas or stay in the appellate court. A request for a discretionary stay in the lower court is a prerequisite to requesting a stay in the appellate court, however. In addition, the appellant requesting a stay from the appellate court must demonstrate a risk of irreparable harm to the remedy sought in the appeal if a stay is not granted.

D. TAKING THE APPEAL: SPECIFIC CONSIDERATIONS

Even if the order is one that is appealable, the appellate practitioner must still assess whether the appeal is right for the client. Four further considerations affect that determination. The first consideration is the standard of review that applies to the issue, that is, whether the issue is one that allows the appellate court to exercise its independent judgment instead of deferring to the lower court's decision. Second, was the issue

---

[25] C. Athena Roussos, *Staying a Judgment While an Appeal is Pending*, THE DAILY RECORDER (August 2009).

adequately preserved in the lower court? Third, was the appellant prejudiced by the error in the lower court? Finally, assuming the issue has merit and has been properly preserved, is the appeal appropriate for the client?

1. STANDARD OF REVIEW

Standard of review is the "keystone" [26] of appellate decision-making for it is the lens through which an appellate court will review a lower court's decision and decide "the extent to which its own independent judgment should control the outcome on appeal." [27] Standards of review are rooted in the traditional functions of the lower and the appellate courts. In its proper role, the appellate court provides predictability for litigants by ensuring that the legal principles governing trials are sound, uniform, and correct.[28]

Lower courts are charged with determining the facts of the particular case at hand and applying the correct law to those facts. It is the "first-hand observer" of the happenings at a trial and serves as the fact-finder and litigation manager who is familiar with the litigants and their counsel.[29] Because of the lower court's position, its decisions about factual issues and credibility determinations are accorded great deference on appeal. Without that deference, decisions made in the heat of battle based on the totality of circumstances before the lower court could be reversed routinely by appellate courts reviewing the cold record of the proceedings and arriving at different conclusions.[30]

Ultimately, standards of review serve the critical function of maintaining the proper roles of the lower court and the appellate court. Given that critical function, the rules that govern briefing requirements in both state and federal appellate courts require parties to identify explicitly the standard of review applicable to each issue raised in the appeal before the parties address the merits of the issue.[31]

In both the state and federal system, there are five primary standards that apply to issues on appeal: (1) de novo, (2) abuse of discretion, (3) clear error, (4) substantial evidence, and (5) mixed question. These five standards span the spectrum from no deference to the lower court's decision to great deference to the lower court's decision.

---

[26] Amanda Peters, *The Meaning, Measure, and Misuse of Standards of Review*, 13 LEWIS & CLARK L. REV. 233, 234 (2009).

[27] MICHAEL R. FONTHAM, MICHAEL VITIELLO & DAVID W. MILLER, PERSUASIVE WRITTEN AND ORAL ADVOCACY IN TRIAL AND APPELLATE COURTS 287, section 10.2. (2d ed. 2007).

[28] *Id.*

[29] Peters, *supra* note 26, at 239.

[30] *Id.*

[31] *See e.g.*, FED. R. APP. P. 28 (a) (9) (B).

a. De Novo

De novo is Latin for "anew." When an issue is reviewed de novo or "anew," the appellate court reviews the issue without affording any deference to the lower court's decision.[32] De novo review applies only to purely legal issues or questions of law, ones that do not require an appellate court to resolve factual disputes or exercise discretion based on facts in the record. De novo review of legal issues stems from the recognition that appellate courts, which are comprised of deliberative panels of judges, are more suited to articulate rules of law that should apply to issues within a jurisdiction than a single judge.[33] Thus, for issues subject to de novo review, the appellant stands a better chance of prevailing on appeal because the appellate court can reach a different decision from the lower court.

Examples of legal issues appellate courts review de novo are decisions on motions for summary judgment, interpretations of statutes, determinations of the correct law applicable to the facts of a case, determinations regarding constitutionality of laws or state actions, and interpretations of contract terms where the lower court did not use conflicting evidence to aid in the interpretation. Whenever the issue involves correcting legal errors or articulating the correct rule that should be applied to settled facts, the standard is likely de novo.

b. Substantial Evidence

Substantial evidence applies to factual determinations by juries in federal proceedings and to factual determinations by both juries and the lower courts in the state systems. Under the substantial evidence standard, the appellate court must affirm the lower court's judgment or decision when the record as a whole demonstrates that the decision is supported by substantial evidence. Thus, even if the reviewing justices would have ruled differently or drawn different inferences from the facts if there is evidence to support the lower court's decision, the appellate court is without power to reverse. Substantial evidence is not the same as any evidence. Rather substantial evidence is evidence of "ponderable legal significance," which is "reasonable," "credible," and of "solid value."[34] It is not about quantity, but quality. Therefore, the testimony of a single witness could constitute substantial evidence to support a factual finding.

Factual issues the appellate court reviews for substantial evidence are distinct from factual issues that turn on a failure of proof in the lower court. For issues that turn on the respondent's failure of proof at trial, the question for a reviewing court is whether the evidence compels a finding in favor of the appellant as a matter of law. The issue is not reviewed for

---

[32] FONTHAM ET AL., *supra* note 27, at 288–289.

[33] *Id.* at 288.

[34] Union Pac. R. Co. v. Munoz, 326 F.2d 248, 250 (9th Cir. 1964).

substantial evidence. Rather, in deciding whether the appellant is entitled to reversal, the appellate court must decide whether the appellant's evidence was (1) uncontradicted and unimpeached and (2) of such a character and weight as to leave no room for a judicial determination that it was insufficient to support a finding.[35]

PRACTICE EXERCISE

Consider the following hypothetical: A plaintiff sued the defendant for injuries sustained in a car accident. The plaintiff's theory of the case states that the accident occurred because the defendant ran a red light while the plaintiff had the green light. Four witnesses—the Pope, Nelson Mandela, Warren Buffet, and Oprah Winfrey—all testify that at the time of the accident the plaintiff had a red light. Another witness, James Frey,[36] testifies he had a clear view of the intersection and the plaintiff had the green light and the defendant's light was red. If the jury finds the defendant's light was red and the plaintiff's light was green, what standard of review applies? Would the appellate court be able to reverse that finding?

c.   Clearly Erroneous

The clearly erroneous standard applies to factual findings by district courts in the federal system.[37] Thus, whenever the district court's decision is based on a determination of the facts, including ultimate facts, the appellate court reviews the decision for clear error. This standard also applies to credibility determinations by the district court. A finding is clearly erroneous if the finding is against the clear weight of the evidence, or even if evidence exists to support it, if the "reviewing court is left with the definite and firm conviction that a mistake has been committed."[38] As long as the district court's decision is plausible in light of the entire record, the appellate court may not reverse it even if it would have reached a different result.[39] Moreover, even if the district court's historical factual findings were based on undisputed evidence, the federal appellate courts still review those findings for clear error, not de novo.[40]

The clearly erroneous standard respects the distinct role of the appellate court in correcting legal errors and the fact-finding role of the lower court. Given the lower court's unique position to observe the proceedings in real-time and its traditional role as the fact-finder, its

---

[35]   Sonic Mfg. Technologies, Inc. v. AAE Systems, Inc., 196 Cal. App. 4th 456, 466 (6th Dist. 2011).

[36]   James Frey is the author of the best-selling book, A MILLION LITTLE PIECES (2003). He offered the book as a memoir of his life. He later admitted that parts of the book were fiction.

[37]   Concrete Pipe & Products of Calif., Inc. v. Construction Laborers Pension Trust for So. Calif., 508 U.S. 602, 622 (1993).

[38]   *Id.*

[39]   Hovey v. Ayers, 458 F.3d 892, 900 (9th Cir. 2006).

[40]   See Anderson v. City of Bessemer City, N. C., 470 U.S. 564, 574–575 (1985).

factual determinations should be accorded more weight than an appellate court reviewing a cold record. And the clear error standard ensures that deference is granted.

PRACTICE EXERCISE

In the previous practice exercise, the plaintiff sued the defendant for injuries sustained in a car accident. Recall that the plaintiff's theory of the case is that the accident occurred because the defendant ran a red light while the plaintiff had the green light. This time, five witnesses, the Pope, Nelson Mandela, Warren Buffet, Queen Elizabeth of England, and Oprah Winfrey testify that at the time of the accident the plaintiff had a green light. The defense produces an authenticated traffic camera photo showing that at the exact time the plaintiff entered the intersection he was speeding and the light was red. If the court finds the plaintiff had a green light and the defendant had a red light, what standard of review applies? And what is the likely result on appeal?

d. Mixed Question

At times, the standard of review that applies is unclear because the issue presents a mixed question of law and fact. Essentially these are issues that require the lower court or jury to first make findings of historical or ultimate facts and then apply a legal standard to those factual determinations to arrive at a conclusion. Whether an independent standard of review or a more deferential one applies to the appeal, is determined by whether the legal issues or the factual issues predominate. In essence, the selection of the appropriate standard of review in these cases depends on which judicial actor is better positioned to decide a particular issue.[41] If the process of deciding the issue primarily requires the lower court's fact-finding expertise, then the factual nature of the inquiry predominates and the appellate court reviews the issue for clear error or under the substantial evidence standard. If the issue requires "the exercise of judgment about legal principles," de novo review applies.[42]

Some examples of common mixed questions of law and fact are findings that a party was negligent, whether there was probable cause to conduct a search or whether a defendant was in custody when interrogated. Courts review the issue of negligence for clear error or substantial evidence because the factual determinations predominate and because the lower court's fact-finding function is better suited to determine whether the defendant acted as a reasonable person under those particular circumstances.

---

[41] Randall H. Warner, *All Mixed Up About Mixed Questions*, 7 J. APP. PRAC. & PROCESS 101, 130 (2005).

[42] Tolbert v. Page, 182 F. 3d 677, 682 (9th Cir. 1999).

By contrast, with issues such as whether a police officer had probable cause and whether a defendant was interrogated while in custody there is a need to "unify precedent" and ensure consistent application of a constitutional requirement. Therefore, even though a decision on both issues involves some factual determination, they are reviewed de novo.[43] One positive in raising mixed questions on appeal is that the lack of a clear decisive standard provides the parties some flexibility to argue for a more deferential or less deferential standard of review.

e.   Abuse of Discretion

Farthest along the standard of review spectrum is abuse of discretion. There is no consensus on what it means to say that a lower court has abused its discretion. At times, courts have defined this standard as permitting reversal only if the appellate court has determined that the lower court's decision "lies beyond the pale of reasonable justification under the circumstances."[44] Therefore, unless the lower court's decision was considered "irrational," the appellate court will not reverse. In light of that frequently cited definition, practitioners generally viewed an issue subject to the abuse of discretion standard as one that an appellate court, in actuality, would never reverse.

But it is possible to obtain a reversal of a decision subject to abuse of discretion because courts can abuse their discretion even if their decisions are not "irrational" or "wacky." If the lower court's decision falls outside the legal principles granting the court its discretion, the appellate court may reverse. "The discretion of a lower court judge is not a whimsical, uncontrolled power, but a legal discretion, which is subject to the limitations of legal principles governing the subject of its action, and to reversal on appeal where no reasonable basis for the action is shown."[45] An appellate court will also find an abuse of discretion if the lower court failed to exercise its discretion or erroneously believed it lacked discretion to act. Nevertheless, an appellate court may not reverse a lower court's ruling that is subject to an abuse of discretion standard of review if the reviewing court merely disagrees with the ruling.[46] If the lower court's action falls within the permissible range of options set by the governing legal criteria, then the appellate court cannot reverse.[47]

---

[43]   Ornelas v. U.S., 517 U.S. 690, 697 (1996) ("We think independent appellate review of these ultimate determinations of reasonable suspicion and probable cause is consistent with the position we have taken in past cases. We have never, when reviewing a probable-cause or reasonable-suspicion determination ourselves, expressly deferred to the trial court's determination.")

[44]   Harman v. Apfel, 211 F.3d 1172, 1175 (9th Cir. 2000).

[45]   In re Sims, 534 F.3d 117, 132 (2d Cir. 2008); City of Sacramento v. Drew, 207 Cal. App. 3d 1287, 1297 (1989).

[46]   Debra Lyn Bassett, *"I Lost at Trial-in the Court of Appeals!": The Expanding Power of the Federal Appellate Courts to Reexamine Facts*, 38 HOUS. L. REV. 1129, 1152 (2001).

[47]   Myers v. Hertz Corp., 624 F.3d 537, 547 (2d Cir. 2010), *cert. denied,* 132 S.Ct. 368 (2011).

Many different issues fall within the lower court's discretion. These are largely "ad-hoc" and situation-specific types of issues. Typically, these issues require the lower court to survey the specific circumstances of the case and make a judgment about what is appropriate under the specific circumstances. On appeal, those decisions will be reviewed for an abuse of discretion.

Such matters include trial management issues, discovery orders,[48] evidentiary rulings,[49] sanctions, and family law decisions like custody and visitation. Because the lower court is on the sidelines of the litigation battlefield and is intimately familiar with the trial or proceedings, it has a better sense regarding those issues than an appellate court reviewing a cold record. Therefore, the appellate court is reluctant to substitute its judgment for that of the trial court.

In sum, having familiarity with the standards of review allows the appellate practitioner to select the arguments or issues to be raised in the appeal by weeding out weaker issues in favor of those subject to the appellate court's independent review. Even if the issue is one that could be reviewed under a deferential standard, the appellate practitioner should consider ways to transform the issue into one of law so that the court will apply an independent standard of review. Because the standard of review is the lens through which the appellate court will decide the client's appeal, identifying the standard of review is the key step in assessing whether an appeal is or is not within a client's best interest.

2.   WAS THE ISSUE PRESERVED?

Another key consideration in deciding whether to file an appeal is whether the errors that are being challenged were preserved in the record. Often, the appellate practitioner was not the trial attorney. In those cases, appellate counsel must review the actual record of the proceedings to make sure that the error being challenged was not only raised before the lower court but was actually considered and decided by the lower court. Moreover, it must be clear that the party did not concede or later withdraw its objection to the lower court's actions. If an issue is not adequately preserved, it is forfeited or waived.

Whereas a "waiver is a positive act the defendant makes—the intentional relinquishment of a known right, a forfeiture is an act of omission—the failure to make the timely assertion of a right."[50] Both can foreclose an appeal of the issue. The waiver rule prevents litigants from

---

[48]   Ingham v. United States, 167 F.3d 1240, 1246 (9th Cir. 1999).

[49]   The standard of review applicable to the evidentiary rulings of the district court is abuse of discretion. Old Chief v. U.S., 519 U.S. 172, 174 (1997).

[50]   MICHAEL E. TIGAR & JANE B. TIGAR, FEDERAL APPEALS JURISDICTION AND PRACTICE § 5:3 (3d ed. 2012).

acquiescing to the lower court's ruling and later seeking relief in the appellate court for an error that could have been prevented or cured below.

Waiver and forfeiture are not jurisdictional, however.[51] Thus, even if the issue was waived or forfeited, the appellate court has discretion to consider the issue on appeal if the issue is one that concerns a substantial interest and presents an issue of law. But the issue must be one that is not dependent on the development of a factual record.

An appellate court may address plain errors on appeal even if the errors were not preserved.[52] A plain error is an error "so obvious and substantial that failure to notice and correct it would affect the fairness, integrity, or public reputation of judicial proceedings."[53] This exception for plain errors is particularly important on the issue of jury instructions in federal courts. In federal courts, the rules do not allow review of jury instructions if the party failed to object to the instruction given or failed to object to the court's failure to give a particular instruction on the record. [54] Under those circumstances, review may only be had if the issue is one of plain error.[55]

3.   WAS THE ERROR PREJUDICIAL?

Even if the appeal presents a legal error that was properly preserved, the appellate court will not reverse unless the error constitutes prejudicial or reversible error. That is, the appellate court will not reverse unless it has determined that the error affected the outcome of the proceedings. In California, an appellate court cannot reverse unless the court concludes that the error complained of has resulted in "a miscarriage of justice."[56]

Whether an error constitutes prejudicial error depends on the type of error that is alleged. Where the error violates a basic guarantee of procedural fairness, appellate courts will always regard it as harmful and reversible even if no specific prejudice can be shown. Such errors are termed "structural," in the sense that they are presumed to infect the proceedings so deeply that they cannot be deemed harmless. Further, these structural errors cannot be waived and will be reversed irrespective of whether an objection was made in the lower court. Some examples are the failure to provide notice of a hearing, the erroneous denial of the right to counsel, or the denial of right to trial by an impartial tribunal.[57]

---

[51]   Oklahoma City v. Tuttle, 471 U.S. 808, 815–816 (1985).

[52]   FED. R. CRIM. P. 52.

[53]   U.S. v. Lopez, 923 F.2d 47, 50 (1991).

[54]   FED. RULE CIV. P. 51.

[55]   *Id.*

[56]   Cal. Const. art. VI, § 13.

[57]   See Neder v. U.S., 527 U.S. 1, 8 (1999).

The next most favorable prejudicial error standard is the *Chapman* standard.[58] The standard applies to violations of most federal constitutional rights, particularly those in the criminal context. Under the *Chapman* standard, the appellate court must reverse unless the prosecution can prove beyond a reasonable doubt that the violation did not affect the result.[59]

Non-constitutional issues are subject to the least favorable standard for appellants. In those cases, the appellate court must affirm unless there is a *reasonable chance* the error affected the result in the lower court. In other words, is it reasonably probable that a result more favorable to the appealing party would have been reached in the absence of the error?[60] Unless the evidence is very close, the answer is usually no.

4.   IS THE APPEAL RIGHT FOR THE CLIENT?

Even if the issue is appealable, can be reviewed de novo, and raises prejudicial error, it still may not be in the client's best interest to pursue the appeal. In some cases, potential adverse consequences may militate against filing an appeal, even if prejudicial error occurred. What are those circumstances?

Many arise in the criminal context. For example, even if prejudicial error occurred, a successful appeal may subject the defendant to additional charges on retrial. If that risk is more than theoretical for the client, pursuing the appeal could be harmful to the client's interests, and the practitioner must advise the client of that risk.

In the civil context, one major potential adverse consequence is the payment of attorney fees and costs for the respondent if the appeal is unsuccessful. In some cases, that could amount to tens of thousands or even hundreds of thousands of dollars. The appellate practitioner also has a duty to advise the client of this risk.

In addition to potential adverse consequences, other considerations may make an appeal unattractive. For one thing, appeals are very expensive. Not only must the client pay an attorney to handle the appeal, the client must also pay for the record of the proceedings, which could cost thousands of dollars. Second, appeals take a long time and the landscape of the litigation can change over the course of that time to the benefit of the client. In those cases, an appeal may not be the most effective way to resolve the issue for your client. Finally, an appeal can take an emotional toll on the client and the relationships impacted by the litigation. The

---

[58]   Chapman v. California, 386 U.S. 18, 24 (1967).

[59]   *Id.*

[60]   People v. Watson, 46 Cal.2d 818, 836 (1956).

appellate practitioner must bring these issues to the forefront so that the client can make an informed decision about whether to pursue the appeal.

E. THE APPELLATE PROCESS

1. THE RECORD

Once the notice of appeal is filed, the appellant has to designate the record and request that the record is prepared. The record is the universe of the appeal and consists of the reporter's transcript and clerk's transcript. Matters that were not before the lower court are outside the record and, therefore, outside the scope of the appeal. It is the appellant's duty to provide the appellate court with an adequate record of the proceedings so that the appellate court can determine whether prejudicial error occurred in the proceedings. Thus, failure to provide an adequate record can result in dismissal of the appeal or other sanctions.

The reporter's transcript is the transcript of the oral proceedings before the trial court. In requesting the reporter's transcript, the appellant must pay for the transcript to be prepared. If a reporter was not present at the proceedings, the parties may file an agreed or settled statement that accurately summarizes the testimony at the trial or hearing. The costs for a transcript can be substantial, especially if the lower court proceedings were lengthy. As mentioned above, cost is one reason a client might decide not to proceed with an appeal.

The clerk's transcript consists of the original pleadings, exhibits, and other papers filed with the lower court clerk. The appellant requests the clerk's record or transcript and the clerk prepares it and files it with the appellate court.

There are substitutes for the clerk's transcript as well. Instead of the clerk's record, the appellant may choose to proceed by appellant's appendix in state courts. In federal court, the appellant also has the option of preparing an appendix, but in some circuits, excerpts of the record are required.[61] Regardless of the form the record takes, ultimately, it is the appellant's duty to ensure that the appellate court has an adequate record to assess whether the error complained of in fact occurred.

2. THE BRIEFS

There are primarily three briefs filed over the course of an appeal. The first brief is the appellant's opening brief. Next is the respondent's brief. Finally, the appellant has the option of filing a reply brief, which addresses arguments raised in the respondent's brief.

---

[61] CHRISTOPHER A. GOELZ AND MEREDITH J. WATTS, CALIFORNIA PRACTICE GUIDE: FEDERAL NINTH CIRCUIT CIVIL APPELLATE PRACTICE 4:240 (2012).

Of the three, the appellant's opening brief is considered the most important because it defines which issues the appellate court will review. Thus, if the opening brief fails to raise an issue and the respondent's brief does not raise the issue, the appellant cannot raise it in the reply brief. Sometimes the appellate court may ask the parties to file a supplemental brief on an issue not raised in any of the briefs. The request for supplemental briefing is usually a signal to the parties regarding the issue the appellate court considers determinative in the appeal.

3. ORAL ARGUMENT

Once the briefing is complete, the court may schedule oral argument. In the federal courts, the parties do not have a right to oral argument.[62] Rather, if the panel that has examined the briefs unanimously decides that oral argument is unnecessary, oral argument will not be granted.

Even so, in most cases, the appellant should request oral argument and explain in the opening brief why oral argument should be provided. Usually, the appellate court will grant oral argument unless the appeal is considered frivolous, the dispositive issue was decided recently and authoritatively, or the brief adequately presents the issues to be decided and oral argument would not aid that process.[63]

Some state appellate courts do not limit the right to oral argument; instead, they send notices advising the parties that they are ready to make a decision and consider oral argument unnecessary. Because oral argument provides clues about the court's likely decision and is the client's final opportunity to influence that decision, in most cases, it is in the client's interest to go forward with oral argument. Yet, it is still the client's decision whether to request oral argument.

4. THE DECISION

In the federal system, outright reversal of the district court's decision is rare.[64] Partial reversals are more common. When the district court's decision is reversed, the reversal effectively annuls or sets aside the lower court's decision for all purposes. If a decision is reversed, both state and federal courts of appeal usually remand the case for further proceedings or with instructions for the lower court. Sometimes, the appellate court remands with instructions for the lower court or district court to enter a different judgment than the original one.

---

[62] FED. R. APP. P. 34.

[63] FED. R. APP. P. 34 (A)(2).

[64] See Appendix Table B-5.

U.S. Courts of Appeals—Appeals Terminated on the Merits, by Circuit and Nature of Proceeding, During the 12-Month Period Ending Mar. 31, 2017, available at http://www.uscourts. gov/sites/default/files/data_tables/fjcs_b5_0331.2017.pdf (last visited Nov. 2017).

In the federal system, if the lower court's decision is affirmed, the appellant must consider whether to seek en banc review of the decision.[65] The respondent may also petition the entire circuit court for en banc review if the lower court's decision is reversed.[66] A simple majority of the active judges on the circuit can grant en banc review.[67]

Another option is to seek review in the United States Supreme Court. Any party to any case in the federal courts of appeals can petition the Supreme Court to review the case via a writ of certiorari before or after the federal appellate court has rendered a decision.[68] Chances of obtaining review in the Supreme Court are minuscule because the Supreme Court will only exercise its discretion to grant certiorari for compelling reasons. Those compelling reasons include conflicts among circuit courts of appeals on an important federal question, conflicts among state high courts on important federal questions, and important federal questions decided by a state court or a circuit court of appeals that the Supreme Court has not previously addressed, but should.[69]

In state court systems, if the lower court's decision is affirmed, the appellant must consider whether to file a petition for rehearing. If that petition is unsuccessful, the appellant can seek discretionary review in the state's highest court. But the chances of obtaining review from a state's high court are slim because the grounds for granting discretionary review are limited. Generally, a state's high court grants review for issues that are necessary to secure uniformity of decision or to settle an important question of law.[70] That the appellate court or the lower court's decision was wrong is not sufficient reason to grant review.

---

[65] FED. R. APP. P. 35 (B).

[66] FED. R. APP. P. 35 (B).

[67] FED. R. APP. P. 35 (A).

[68] 28 U.S.C. § 1254 (1) (2006).

[69] ROBERT L. STERN, EUGENE GRESSMAN, STEPHEN M. SHAPIRO & KENNETH S. GELLAR, SUPREME COURT PRACTICE 222 (8th ed. 2002).

[70] See California, for example, CAL. R. CT. R. 8.500.

CHAPTER 19

THE APPELLATE BRIEF

■ ■ ■

By Mary-Beth Moylan

In Chapter 18, you considered the appellate process, the standard of review on appeal, and the differences in the role of appellate judges and those of the trial courts. This chapter focuses on the nuts and bolts of drafting an appellate brief. Crafting an effective appellate brief requires mastery of both the general components of an appellate brief, as well as knowledge of your goals when writing an appellate brief.

A. GOALS IN DRAFTING AN APPELLATE BRIEF

Knowing your goals in writing your appellate brief is critical, as they should be reflected throughout each component of your brief. One of the most important, and often overlooked, goals in drafting an appellate brief is to explain to the appellate court why your client should prevail on appeal, as distinguished from why they should have won in the first instance. Additionally, every appeal has a theme. Your goal should be to have your reader know and appreciate your theme by the time she is done reading your appellate brief. Themes are challenging to write as we tend to think that themes mean something cute or sympathetic, or containing artful or profound prose. Some themes may be profound, but more often your theme will be a simple compelling statement about why an error was made or a result is unjust.

As discussed in Chapter 16, a theme should project the human element of the case and ideally should be weaved throughout all aspects of the written brief. Of course, on appeal, the theme must often shift from the very factually specific emotional tone that it may have taken at the trial court level. Humanizing the record is important, but, ultimately, the appellate court is bound to correct legal errors, and so the theme here should reflect that role. Give the court a legal and an emotionally compelling reason to favor your side when approaching a theme in an appellate brief.

An additional goal to keep in mind through the appellate process is amicable resolution. Many cases settle during the appellate process. If you craft a compelling appellate brief that causes your opponent to feel insecure in the decision of the lower court, you have positioned your client well for any post-trial court mediation or settlement discussions. Many appellate courts require mediation in some cases before full briefings and hearings are conducted at the appellate level.[1] Filing a strong appellate brief and then requesting mediation might result in a favorable resolution of the dispute. Your goal for appeal should be to prevail, either through alternative dispute resolution or through the courts. A good outcome for your client is the ultimate goal.

B. APPELLATE BRIEF COMPONENTS

The components of an appellate brief may vary slightly from jurisdiction to jurisdiction, and the ordering of sections may also fluctuate by court. Most appellate jurisdictions require that an appellate brief contain the following substantive sections:

1. Jurisdictional Statement

2. Statement of Oral Argument

3. Issue Question

4. Statement of the Case and Facts[2]

5. Summary of Argument

6. Argument

7. Conclusion

In addition to these substantive sections, appellate briefs also must contain certain technical sections. Most appellate jurisdictions require that an appellate brief contain the following technical sections:

1. Table of Contents

2. Table of Authorities

3. Signature block for counsel

4. An addendum

5. A certificate of service

6. Front and back cover[3]

---

[1]   *See e.g.* Ninth Circuit Mediation Office, http://www.ca9.uscourts.gov/mediation (last visited Feb. 14, 2018).

[2]   Some jurisdictions may require a separate Statement of the Case and Statement of Facts. Recent revisions to the Federal Rules require a single section detailing the procedural and factual history relevant to a dispute. FED.R.APP.P. 28(a)(6).

[3]   While some jurisdictions are moving to electronic filing for all briefs and supporting documents, some appellate courts still also require that the brief be bound with a front and back cover.

1.   JURISDICTIONAL STATEMENT

The jurisdictional statement needs to establish for the appellate court that jurisdiction to hear the appeal is proper. In federal court, proper jurisdiction requires 1) that the federal district court had proper subject matter jurisdiction, 2) that the appellate court is permitted to hear the appeal (because there was a final judgment or other appealable order), and 3) that the appeal has met the procedural requirement of timeliness. While the jurisdictional statement may seem like a technical requirement, it is an opportunity to persuade the court by providing some information about the claims that were alleged below, thereby demonstrating that the litigation has been properly and vigorously pursued.

a.   District Court's Subject Matter Jurisdiction

The jurisdictional statement must demonstrate that the lower court exercised proper subject matter jurisdiction over the case. In the federal system, proper jurisdiction in civil cases requires the subject matter of the case to be federal in nature[4] or the parties to the litigation to be citizens of different states with an amount in controversy in excess of $75,000.[5]

To demonstrate the propriety of the jurisdiction, the advocate should include a reference to the applicable jurisdictional statute and facts to show that the provisions of the statute were satisfied in the case. For example, in a case that was heard in the lower court based on federal subject matter jurisdiction, the facts would include a reference to the statute or federal common law theory under which the plaintiff originally brought suit. For a case heard based on diversity jurisdiction, the facts would include the citizenship of each party to the litigation and the facts establishing the amount in controversy.

b.   Court of Appeal's Ability to Hear the Appeal

In addition to proper jurisdiction in the lower court, the jurisdictional statement must also demonstrate that the case is properly submitted to the Court of Appeal. Under federal statute, appeals to the circuit courts are limited to those cases in which a final judgment has been entered or another appealable order has been issued by the federal district court.[6] Chapter 18 describes some of the types of interlocutory orders that are appealable prior to the entry of a final judgment such as orders relating to attorney's fees, the denial of a class action, and the appointment of a receiver. The jurisdictional statement must indicate which type of order or judgment is being appealed.

---

4   28 U.S.C.A. § 1331 (2006).
5   28 U.S.C.A. § 1332 (2006 and Supp. 2014).
6   28 U.S.C.A. § 1291(2006).

Further, to establish that the case is properly submitted for an appeal, the advocate must indicate that a final judgment or other appealable order has been issued. The date of the final judgment should be included. If the appeal is taken from an order other than a final judgment, a statutory provision or court rule permitting the appeal from such an order should be referenced and cited.

c. Timeliness

The federal rules and state court procedural rules require that in addition to lower court subject matter jurisdiction, and an appealable judgment or order, an appeal must meet a timeliness requirement to be properly presented to the appellate court.[7] To show that the appeal has been timely filed, the advocate should indicate both the date of the judgment or order appealed from and the date that the notice of appeal was filed and served on the appellee.

2. STATEMENT OF ORAL ARGUMENT

Oral argument is not guaranteed for appeals in the federal system. Many state appellate courts also do not guarantee oral argument. Increasingly, courts are willing to decide appeals on the briefs and the record, primarily because the volume of cases prohibits oral arguments for all appeals. The statement of oral argument section of the appellate brief provides an opportunity to convince the appellate court that the case is one that merits an oral presentation.

Federal Rule of Appellate Procedure 34 provides the standard for the granting of oral argument in the federal circuit courts. It provides that oral argument should be granted where novel and complex issues are presented by the appeal.

Since full dockets mean that more cases will be decided without the benefit of a hearing, it is critically important for an advocate to put forth reasons why her case meets the novel and complex standard. The advocate should be specific about why the case would benefit from a hearing, and should convince the court that the oral argument would present an opportunity for further development of the complex legal issues.

Very often the appellee, as well as the appellant, will want the opportunity to be heard before the appellate court reaches a decision. This is particularly true where the outcome in the lower court favored the appellee, but the reasoning adopted by the court was not advanced by the appellee's advocate. If the appellee thinks the reasoning was not sound, an

---

[7] In the federal system, FED. R. APP. P. 4 provides for 30 days from the judgment, unless the United States is a party, in which case, 60 days are allowed. As indicated in Chapter 18, state court times for appeal vary from 30 to 180 days.

opportunity to once again promote stronger reasoning may be important to the ultimate success on appeal.

3.   ISSUE QUESTION

The issue question is also sometimes referred to as an issue statement. Depending on the court or the local practice, some appellate courts will expect to see the issues presented as questions, and others will expect to see the issues presented as statements beginning with the word "whether."

Written either as a question or a "whether" statement, the issue should be presented with a reference to relevant law and a reference to legally significant facts. From reading the issue question or statement, the appellate judges should have a solid understanding of the question that must be answered on appeal. And if the issue question or statement is well drafted, the judges should intuitively understand the answer that the party writing the brief seeks.

When crafted as a question, the issue should be presented as a question that can be answered "yes" or "no." Ideally, the advocate will formulate her question so that the answer the judges are led to is a "yes" answer. Affirmative answers are generally better than "no" answers because they place a positive spin on the case.

Take the example of an appeal of a decision of a lower court holding that dismissal of a challenge to a California initiative was proper because the initiative did not violate California's single subject rule. The California Constitution has a very straightforward provision that does not permit initiatives "embracing more than one subject" to be voted on by the electorate.[8]

The following example shows a "whether" statement that frames the issue on appeal for the appellate court:

> Whether Article II, section 8(d) of the California Constitution prohibits the placement of the People's Choice Initiative on the Ballot in November 2008 when the measure embraces more than one subject.

Notice that the relevant law, the California Constitution, is referenced, and there is also a reference to the specific ballot measure, the People's Choice Initiative, which is purported to violate the single subject rule. However, this example could use more facts about that initiative to persuade the court to intuit the desired result.

---

[8]   CAL. CONST. ART. II, § 8 (d).

Now consider, the same issue presented in the form of a question designed to elicit a "yes" or "no" answer. In this example, additional facts are also provided to help the reader glean the desired result.

> Does the People's Choice Initiative, which proposes to change the method of redistricting in the State of California and proposes to change the process for electing judges in the State of California, embrace more than one subject in violation of Article II, section 8(d) of the California Constitution?

In this issue question, the legal source and standard is once again referenced, as is the title of the initiative. However, this question adds details about the People's Choice Initiative and tells the reader that the initiative proposes to change the method for redistricting in the State of California and the process for electing judges. The detailed description of the two substantive changes to the law that the initiative seeks to effectuate strongly suggests to the reader that the answer to the question about whether the law embraces more than one subject should be "yes." This makes for a persuasive issue question and leads the reader to intuitively want to answer "yes" to the question posed.

Of course, the above issue question would be a cleverly crafted question for the appellant in the case. If you represented the appellee in this case, the first construction of the issue as a more general issue statement using "whether" might be preferable.

Regardless of your side of the appellate case, the need to present the law and facts in a manner that favors your client and leads the reader to have a solid understanding of the question to be resolved is critical. The issue question or statement is the place for you to first advocate for your desired result.

4. STATEMENT OF THE CASE

The Statement of the Case is the section of the appellate brief that recounts the procedural history of the proceedings in the lower court. Sometimes this section is part of the Statement of Facts, and sometimes it is its own separate section. Check your local rules to learn which structure is preferred.

Whether contained within the Statement of Facts or as a freestanding section, the Statement of the Case should present all relevant procedural history and give the court a clear picture of the procedural life of the case prior to the appeal. The court will want to understand the history of the motions filed and their resolution, any evidentiary hearings or important discovery decisions, and the outcome of a trial, if one occurred.

5.   STATEMENT OF FACTS

The Statement of Facts in an appellate brief serves the same function as the Statement of Facts in a persuasive brief to the trial court. As in any persuasive memorandum or brief, the Statement of Facts should include all facts applied in the Argument section of the brief. It should also provide background facts that give the reader context and help the reader to understand a more complete picture of the story. The best crafted Statement of Facts weaves the legally relevant facts and the background facts in such a way as to create a compelling story of the party for which the brief is written.

To ensure that all legally relevant facts are introduced in the Statement of Facts, many brief writers write the Argument section first and then go back to draft the Statement of Facts. Alternatively, if writing the Statement of Facts first, the writer should return to the facts section to edit and amend it after the Argument section is written.

Substantively, the Statement of Facts should contain only facts. Legal argument should be saved for the Argument section. The presentation of the facts should appear to be neutral, even though subtle persuasion tactics should be used so that the story is told in a favorable light for the client.

One way to be subtly persuasive is to use selective detail or quotes to emphasize facts that support your case. Another way is to use punctuation to slow the reader in places where you want to draw emphasis. Rhetorical devices like repetition, parallel construction, and cadence can build momentum through strong facts. Overdoing these writing techniques has potential drawbacks, though. Remember to make thoughtful use of quotations, punctuation, and rhetorical devices. If you use too many, or the same ones repeatedly, the reader can become focused on the writing technique rather than the story. A reader who is conscious of your writing technique is not often one who is being subtly persuaded.

6.   SUMMARY OF ARGUMENT

There are two main purposes for the Summary of Argument section: (1) to provide a roadmap for the argument; and (2) to give a broad view of the legal arguments. The Summary of Argument is useful to the reader if it gives an abbreviated version of the main points of the argument. Sometimes it is used by judges and law clerks as a refresher before oral argument, or as a warm up to the legal issues before the reader needs to tackle the minutiae of the legal problem.

In its role as a roadmap to the Argument section, the Summary of Argument should succinctly state all major arguments. It should also provide the reader with context and order for the section that follows. For example, if the Summary of Argument discusses point A and then point B, the Argument section needs to be structured in the same order.

The broad view that should be provided by the Summary of Argument is akin to a focus on the forest, rather than the individual trees. In the Argument section, the brief writer should hone in on each tree that makes up the forest of the argument. In the Summary of Argument section, the brief writer should paint a picture of the entire forest including policy insights into the law and how the spirit of the law is met by a ruling in favor of her side.

7. ARGUMENT

The Argument section of the brief is the longest and most important section of the appellate brief. This is where the legal standards and rules should be applied to the facts of your case, and the most persuasive application of the rules should be presented. As with other forms of persuasive writing, the CRAC paradigm should be used for each issue. Point headings should be used to signal and separate main issues, and sub-headings should be used to signal and separate each sub-point within the main issue.

The two main differences between the persuasive trial court Argument section and the persuasive appellate court Argument section are the audience and the existence of a prior holding concerning the specific legal issue on appeal. The appellate audience is one that is looking for legal error on a cold record. Appellate justices and judges are generally focused on the legal standard, and so the persuasively written brief needs to acknowledge and address the importance of the standard of review, which is addressed in Chapter 18. The existence of a prior opinion is also a unique aspect of the appellate brief. Advocates on both sides need to address the prior opinion with respect and a certain amount of deference. Even if the appellant thinks the lower court wrote a terrible opinion or reached an untenable decision, saying so directly in an appellate brief is generally not considered persuasive to an appellate court. Instead, the artful advocate will subtly and respectfully point out the flaws in the analysis of the prior opinion or decision by referencing legal and factual authorities.

Substance wins appellate arguments, not superlatives or vitriol. Too often students and attorneys think that hyperbole will win the day, but, in fact, overstatements or unprofessional references to the lower court opinion more often than not alienate appellate courts. The soundness of the legal position is judged by the application of the factual record to a legal standard. Advocates can prevail on appeal by convincing the court that the wrong rule of law was applied, or that the rule of law was applied incorrectly to the facts of the case.

Very often issues on appeal will be complex, and they may involve multiple substantive and procedural considerations. The single issue CRAC paradigm is rarely sufficient to organize the myriad of issues that may need to be addressed. Variations on the CRAC paradigm can be used, and inclusion of the Standard of Review within the initial Conclusion paragraph is not uncommon. A couple of examples of possible variations on the traditional CRAC structure are included below, but these are certainly not the only variations that can be employed when structuring a persuasive argument in an appellate brief.

The following is one possible Argument outline:

ARGUMENT

Umbrella paragraph setting up the order of the issues

I.   Point Heading Issue #1

- Thesis/Conclusion/What You Will Show
- Standard of Review
- Substantive Rule

         A.   Sub-heading #1

- Application
- Conclusion

         B.   Sub-heading #2

- Application
- Conclusion

II.   Point Heading Issue #2

- REPEAT if sub-headings or CRAC if no sub-headings

III.   Point Heading Issue #3

- REPEAT if sub-headings or CRAC if no sub-headings

The following is another possible Argument outline:

ARGUMENT

- Umbrella paragraph

- Standard of Review

I. Point Heading #1

- Umbrella

- Sub-heading #1CRAC

- Sub-heading #2 CRAC

II. Point Heading #2

- REPEAT or just CRAC if no sub-headings

---

8. CONCLUSION

The Conclusion of an appellate brief should summarize the main points that have been presented and restate the relief requested. It does not differ significantly from the Conclusion section of any other persuasive document, except that the relief requested should relate to the lower court's decision or judgment.

In some ways, the Conclusion and the Summary of Argument serve a similar purpose. Both summarize main points, and both give the reader a broad-brush look at the legal problem. However, they are not the same section and should not use the same wording. The conclusion is generally shorter than the Summary of Argument, and it should focus much more on the relief requested than the Summary of Argument does.

A common mistake that students make in crafting the Conclusion of the appellate brief is to forget that the audience has changed. An appellate court is not usually in a position to provide relief in the first instance. So, asking an appellate court to "grant a preliminary injunction" is not an appropriate request. Rather, the appellate court should be asked to "reverse the decision of the court below and remand the case for further proceedings."

C. FINISHING WITH FLOURISH

Finally, appellate courts all require different components and have different requirements in terms of word count or page length, binding, number of copies, and other formatting specifications. You should always consult the local rules of the court in which you are practicing to find out what sections are required and what formatting practices must be followed. Most clerks of court are very particular about the captions on the cover, and the content of the appellate briefs. It is a common practice for clerk's offices to reject non-conforming briefs at the window. To avoid missing a filing deadline or finding yourself with sanctions from the court because of a non-conforming appellate brief, make sure you have followed the local rules with precision.

The appellate process is a vital part of the legal system, and provides recourse to litigants when mistakes are made by judges or lawyers in lower courts. Many lawyers do not regularly practice in appellate courts, which is why it is all the more important to know the rules and requirements when you do have the responsibility of appearing in a court of appeal. The stakes are high for the client and for the attorney in the appellate process. Prepare your appellate brief with the greatest of care, including a very thorough "White-Glove Inspection" as described in Chapter 28. Your appellate brief and your appellate argument are often your client's last opportunity to convince a decision maker of the validity of a righteous position. Make sure you have done everything you can to conform with the rules and present a persuasive and professional appeal.

CHAPTER 20

ORAL ARGUMENT

■ ■ ■

By Mary-Beth Moylan

A. THE PURPOSE OF ORAL ARGUMENT

The purpose of oral argument is different for each of the participants in the process. The advocates and the court have different goals to achieve, but they share a common interest in a productive conversation about the legal problem involved in the case.

Most new oral advocates feel nervous at the prospect of presenting in front of more seasoned lawyers, judges, and clients. Remembering the purpose of oral argument for each of the participants can help to focus the advocate and make the experience more successful, as well as less nerve-wracking.

While the purposes of the participants may vary depending on the level of court, the stage in litigation, or the local practice of the court, this chapter gives a general sense of the purposes of each of the participants in an oral argument—including the advocates, the court, and the clients. Where the purpose might diverge based on level, stage, or local practice, examples of divergence are noted.

1. THE ADVOCATE'S PURPOSE

The advocate's purpose is to convince the court that her client's position is the correct one. The advocate is present at the argument to orally support the persuasive brief that she has already presented to the court. The advocate should be focused throughout the conversation on persuading the court of the correctness of her client's position.

The advocate's other purpose is not to lose any ground that has been gained in the writing of a well-crafted brief and to identify areas that require additional briefing. The advocate must be consistent in the message presented and avoid any presentation that would undercut the effectiveness of her written product. In situations where a full briefing has not been requested or permitted, it might be the advocate's goal to convince the court that further research and briefing on a particular point is necessary. It is not uncommon for an oral argument to conclude with a request by the court for further briefing on a point of law, or further development of the factual record to support a contention made during the argument. Awareness by the advocate that the court may be seeking more written support is an important skill for the advocate to develop. If an advocate can encourage the court to accept supplemental briefing, she may gain an opportunity to respond fully to the concerns that she hears the court expressing during the oral argument. Many cases are won based on the initial written briefing, but some are won after supplemental briefing after an oral argument by an advocate who really listened to the questions of the court and responded to them fully in the subsequent writing.

Additionally, the advocate should aim to put a human face to the legal claims that have been presented. Oral argument is an opportunity for the advocate to humanize her client and encourage the court to see that not only is the client's position legally correct, but that a decision in the client's favor is the "right" decision to make.

2. THE COURT'S PURPOSE

The court's ultimate purpose in deciding a case, motion, or petition, is to decide the matter correctly and consistent with the rule of law. Oral argument is one tool that the court can use to understand the legal and factual issues that are relevant to the legal problem and to assist in coming to a just and proper decision.

Courts, whether a single judge in a trial court deciding a motion to dismiss, or a three judge panel in an appellate court deciding on the correct interpretation of a new statute, or the nine Justices on the Supreme Court deciding a matter of constitutional law, often have already tentatively made a decision before they hear oral argument from the advocates. In cases where a decision has already been tentatively made, some courts even publish the "tentative opinion" to the advocates before the hearing and ask advocates to respond to the tentatively planned resolution of the issue. In other courts where tentative opinions are not released, some judges nonetheless use oral argument as a time to test out their hypothesis on the advocates. They ask questions that demonstrate to the advocates the way the judges are leaning and give the advocates an opportunity to try to change the judges' minds.

In trial court settings, where there is usually a single judge making the decision, oral argument can be an opportunity for a true dialogue between the court and the advocates for each side as the judge tries to understand the relevance of legal authority to the particular facts of the case that the advocates are presenting. Very often on a motion hearing in the trial court, the judge will jump in immediately with questions about the case and the advocate is asked to do more answering than presenting so that the judge can have her questions and concerns satisfied expeditiously. Trial court judges usually have substantial caseloads, and many hearings are set for the same law and motion calendar. For this reason, one of the court's goals is usually to gain a complete understanding of the matter quickly. Thus, direct targeted responses by the advocates are most appreciated.

In appellate court settings, where there are usually three or more judges hearing oral argument on an appeal or petition, the goal of oral argument can be a bit different. In many circuit courts and state appellate courts, the opinion drafter has already been designated before the oral argument takes place. The goal then may be different for the different judges sitting on the panel. The judge designated to write the opinion may have a goal of ensuring that she has all the facts and key points of law correct before she writes the opinion. The judge who is in the minority may be looking to find additional ways to bolster his dissent. More important though, the judges may have a goal of trying to convince their colleague or colleagues to change a vote. Often in a multi-judge oral argument hearing, the judges will speak directly to one another or will ask the advocate leading questions with the intention of eliciting a response that will prove a point to a colleague on the bench. In these settings, the court's purpose may intersect with the advocate's purpose as both try to persuade a decision maker to vote in favor of the client.

3.   THE CLIENT'S PURPOSE

The client's purpose in oral argument is generally consistent with the advocate's purpose. The client wants his advocate to convince the court to rule in his favor. While clients are often not present at the oral argument, they sometimes do attend to see the process at work and to experience their "day in court."

Depending on the nature of the proceeding and the type of client, the client's goal for oral argument may be more or less pronounced. Sometimes the client is an individual with a personal stake in the claim being argued. Sometimes the client is an agency or organization that is represented by in-house counsel. The client who is an individual with a personal claim is more likely to want to see and hear his advocate making passionate arguments to advance his position in the eyes of the court and the courtroom. The in-house counsel client is likely to be assessing the performance of the advocate differently. The in-house counsel client may attend oral argument to make sure that the correct arguments are raised and to assess the tone of the bench in an effort to anticipate a ruling and help the advocate gauge the receptivity of the other side to settlement discussions.

All clients want to see advocates making the most cogent arguments possible to advance their positions. Clients want decisions in their favor.

Their ultimate goal in oral argument is to have advocates who are well-prepared and effectively articulate their cause.

B. PREPARATION FOR ORAL ARGUMENT

Once an oral argument has been set, it is the job of the advocate to prepare fully for the hearing or appellate argument. Preparation will vary depending on the nature of the hearing and the level of court, but these basic steps can be used across all court levels and hearing types.

1. INITIAL STEPS TO TAKE

The first step in preparation for oral argument is to learn the rules of court in the jurisdiction of your hearing. In all likelihood, you will have researched the rules for requesting and setting oral argument in the process of drafting your motion or brief. In many trial level courts, the motion must be noticed on a law and motion calendar, which is preset by the judge's clerk.[1] In many appellate courts, oral argument must be requested in the brief, and there are criteria that apply to determine whether an oral argument is appropriate.[2] In some courts, a hearing must be requested by a party after the "tentative ruling" is issued.[3] Knowing the criteria applied to set an oral argument, and knowing whether a formal request for oral argument must be made is critical to securing the opportunity to present oral argument. Therefore, the first step in preparation is to know the rules that you will play by in your jurisdiction. Remember to look at the large scale rules—federal or state rules of court— as well as the local rules for the particular court or judge to whom your matter is assigned.

Once your oral argument has been set and you have reviewed the rules of court relating to the procedure of oral argument, the second step in preparing for oral argument is to study the record and law relevant to your case so that you are fully versed in the substance of your case. By the time you walk into court to present your argument to the court, you should know every relevant fact and legal authority inside and out.

Your goal is to be an expert on your client's case. To be an expert, you should know the facts that are evidenced in the record and where each fact is established. You should know the facts and legal rules of each case that supports your conclusion about how the motion or case should be resolved. Reading and re-reading the factual record, pleadings, and supporting

---

[1] *See e.g.* Local Rule 230(b), United States District Court for the Eastern District of California, http://www.caed.uscourts.gov/caednew/assets/File/EDCA%20Local%20Rules%20Effective%204-1-2017.pdf (last visited Feb. 14, 2018).

[2] *See* FED. R. APP. P. 34(a) (2012).

[3] *See e.g.* Sacramento Superior Court Local Rule 2.02(D) (explaining that tentative rulings will issue by 2:00 p.m. on the day before a scheduled law and motion hearing), https://www.saccourt.ca.gov/civil/motions-hearings-tentative.aspx (last visited Feb. 14, 2018).

declarations, as well as the case authority and relevant statutory provisions, are essential steps in your preparations.

This phase of preparation can be thought of as the information loading phase, and it can be time consuming. The process is similar to studying for a final examination where you must cram as much information as possible into your brain since you cannot be sure what questions the professor will ask. Many attorneys create outlines or charts during this phase of oral argument preparation so they can review the information more easily or identify connections between various aspects of the case. No matter what preparation technique you employ, the end result should be a commanding knowledge of the facts and law.

After you have filled your head with all of the relevant facts and legal authorities, the third step to prepare for oral argument is to narrow your focus and hone in on a few key points. This process is where you get to exercise your skills as a lawyer. Focusing in on the key points of your argument requires strategic thinking and planning. As you embark on the focusing process, you must keep in mind your theory of the case[4] and the interests of the court charged with resolving your motion or case. Also keep in mind the time limitations you will have for presenting your argument. Most courts permit no more than thirty minutes of oral argument for each side on a regular motion or an appeal.

With limited time, you will not be able to fully brief the court on all the knowledge you have about the case, so in this phase of preparation you must decide which points are the most important to convey to the court and which arguments have the strongest likelihood to ensure success for your side. Sometimes the key points you identify will be threshold issues that must be resolved in your favor in order for the case to proceed. Sometimes your key point may be one based on policy or notions of fairness—particularly in a case where your client's position has great emotional appeal. In a case where your client's position is not emotionally appealing, your key point may be focused on the importance to the system of applying the black letter law. Strategic thinking about both procedural and substantive issues will help you to sort through the points you want to highlight and the order in which you wish to present your points to the court.

2. AN EFFECTIVE MOOT

One of the best ways to prepare for an oral argument is by enlisting friends or colleagues to provide you with a moot court experience. A moot court is a practice argument before a panel of pretend judges in which you test out your presentation and practice responding to questions that arise in the course of your argument. Ideally, the moot court experience should

---

[4]   Discussed more fully below and in Chapter 16 on Persuasive Legal Writing.

take place somewhat close in time to the argument so that you have had ample time to prepare for it, but also far enough away from the argument date that you have time after the moot court to make changes and do further research as needed.

a. Select a Diverse Audience of "Moot Judges"

An effective moot starts with selecting the right people to act as judges for you. It is helpful to have both "judges" who are very familiar with the legal area involved in your case and "judges" who have more limited background in the area of law. Those who are experts in the area of law will necessarily ask different questions than those with a more basic understanding. The judge or judges you appear before in court could fall anywhere in the spectrum from basic understanding to expert, so hearing and preparing for a wide range of questions is best.

Asking younger colleagues and older colleagues to help you prepare is also wise. Sometimes a law student who has been an extern for a judge you will appear in front of will have the best understanding of the types of questions that you might be asked. On the other hand, a lawyer with years of practice in your jurisdiction is invaluable for giving guidance and insight. Solicit help across the spectrum of experience levels and remember that while most judges are likely contemporaries of your more seasoned colleagues, many have law clerks helping them to decide cases who are very recent law school graduates. You will be best prepared if you get a variety of experience levels and viewpoints during your practice argument.

b. Anticipate Difficult Questions

Ideally a moot court experience should enable you to anticipate the most difficult questions you might be asked in the hearing or appellate argument and give you an opportunity to try out some answers to those questions. It is a great idea to have someone writing down all the questions that are asked during the moot court so that you can revisit those questions and other possible answers after the moot court experience is over.

After you present your arguments to your panel of moot judges, you can ask your colleagues to help you to brainstorm any other difficult questions that might be asked but did not arise during the moot presentation. It can be helpful to also think about what prompts by you might trigger these difficult questions in the mind of a judge, so that you can try to avoid heading down that path in the actual argument.

Your moot judges should take notes during the moot court experience so that they can provide you feedback on the effectiveness of your structure and the substantive responses that you have presented. Collect all the notes that your colleagues provide so that you may use them in the next phase of your preparation.

3. UPDATE LEGAL RESEARCH

Armed with a list of questions that arose in your moot court, and the notes that your colleagues provided about your practice argument, you can return to your preparations by making sure that your research is all updated and that no new law has been decided that would alter your argument. The process of updating research should be on-going. If a case that impacts your argument is decided one day before the hearing on your motion or appeal, the court will expect you to know about it.

Mooting the argument can help you organize key cases. After you have experienced the most difficult of the questions you may receive during the moot court preparation process, you can reassure yourself that authorities you plan to use to support your point are still good law. An annotated list of hard questions and corresponding authorities that provide good answers is very useful and makes updating the key authorities a little easier to organize. By crafting, keeping, and updating a list that includes authorities you plan to use to respond to hard questions, you will ensure maximum preparation for the oral argument.

4. MOOT THE ARGUMENT IN A MODIFIED WAY

As a lawyer, you will have a chance to enlist colleagues to give you the kind of moot court discussed above, but as a law student you can do your own form of modified moot court even if you cannot gather a group of experienced practitioners to help you. First, you can write down all the questions you anticipate receiving and draft answers to those questions. Second, you can run through your argument uninterrupted in front of a mirror or to your pet. Third, you can ask friends or relatives to listen to you present the argument and ask questions that occur to them even if they do not have a background in law. Any questions that will allow you to practice being interrupted and working your way back into your main points in a fluid manner are helpful to your preparation.

5. RESEARCH YOUR AUDIENCE

As outlined above, practicing with colleagues and trying to prepare for any type of question that might come your way through a moot court experience is very helpful, but perhaps the best way to feel prepared for an argument is to know your audience. This means both researching the profile of the judge or judges who will hear your argument and going to the courtroom ahead of your argument time to listen to other attorneys present their arguments to the court. Getting a feel not only for the kinds of questions, but also the tone of the discourse, is extremely helpful in making you feel calm and ready to put your best foot forward.

There are a number of ways to go about researching judges. The first is to ask around your office. In most legal communities judges are well known and have reputations for their demeanor on the bench and the types of questions they ask. If no one in your office is familiar with a judge, or even if they are and you want more information, the second resource is the internet. You can find biographical information about federal court and state court judges on a number of websites and in hard copy publications.[5] Additionally, some local bar associations publish handbooks or indexes that provide attorney commentary about members of the bench in their jurisdiction.[6] The third way to learn about federal district court judges and appellate level judges in the state and federal systems is to read their opinions.[7] You can learn quite a bit about a judge by reading the opinions she writes and the types of arguments that she finds persuasive.

C. STRUCTURING THE ARGUMENT

The structure or outline of your oral argument is important for several reasons. First, a well-structured oral argument is easy to follow. Courts appreciate advocates who make difficult arguments easy to understand. Second, a well-structured oral argument promotes self-confidence. If you have done the work to outline and structure a solid argument, you will feel more comfortable discussing the case and returning to your structure than if you "wing it." Third, your substantive arguments will make more sense if they are presented in a structured and logical way. The following section takes you step by step through the structuring of your argument.

1. INTRODUCTION

Every oral argument, regardless of level of court, should start with an introduction. In the U.S. Supreme Court and some other appellate level courts, the practice is to begin your argument with the words "May it please the Court," but in most courts that formalistic introduction is not required. However, some salutary greeting is expected and appropriate, and your first line should always demonstrate deference to the court and provide a personal introduction. The introduction is your first opportunity to make a good impression with the court. It is also an opportunity to get past any initial nervousness and steady yourself for the substance of your presentation. For these reasons, you should memorize this portion of your argument.

---

[5]   *See e.g.* ALMANAC OF THE FEDERAL JUDICIARY (2012); Federal Judicial Center, http://www.fjc.gov/public/home.nsf/hisj (last visited Feb. 15, 2018); New York Unified Court System, http://www.nycourts.gov/judges/directory.shtml (last visited Feb. 5, 2018).

[6]   *See e.g.* Federal Bar Association Judicial Profile Index, http://www.fedbar.org/Membership/Member-Resources/Index-of-Judicial-Profiles.aspx (last visited Feb. 15, 2018) (note membership login is required to access this database); Dallas Bar Association, Judicial Profiles, https://www.dallasbar.org/node/110 (last visited Feb. 15, 2018); Salt Lake City Bar Association, Judicial Profiles, http://slcba.net/category/judicial_profiles/ (last visited Feb. 15, 2018).

[7]   Trial level judges in state courts do not publish their opinions, so those are harder to find.

In terms of substance, the introduction should provide the following information to the court: (1) your name, (2) the party you represent, and (3) your position relative to the matter on the calendar. For an appeal of a motion for summary judgment scheduled for 2 p.m., the following would be an appropriate introduction:

> Good Afternoon, your Honors, may it please the Court, my name is Kristina Roszowksy, and I am counsel for Defendants—Appellees in this matter. The trial court grant of summary judgment should be affirmed for three reasons.

This introductory material should be presented clearly and succinctly. If you have a difficult last name to pronounce, it is particularly important for you to speak slowly and clearly so that the judges have an opportunity to hear your name and make note of the pronunciation.

2. THEME

Theme is a concept that gives beginning oral advocates some amount of angst. Crafting an effective and persuasive theme is a challenge. Many first efforts at a theme result in overly dramatic mantras about justice and fair play. Many second efforts result in over simplified quips or jingles. Using a theme effectively means introducing a theme to the court at the outset of the argument and revisiting the theme in subtle ways throughout the presentation.

The theme for an oral argument should be a statement of the overriding message you want the judges to take away with them. Ordinarily, the theme is introduced either in between the introduction and the roadmap or immediately following the roadmap. It should be a short statement—not more than one or two sentences—encapsulating what your argument is about. Ideally, the theme should encompass all the issues you will be discussing so that when the judges think back about your argument they will remember your theme and it will trigger a recollection of all your best points. A theme can be based on lofty, justice-based ideals, or it can be highly technical, but it should never overstate your case or personally attack the other side.

An example of a theme in a case involving the recognition of a foreign adoption of a child may be something like the following:

> This case is about protection of the expectations of a child and her parents in a global society. The plaintiffs in this case formed their family in one country and moved to another as a family with the justifiable expectation that the judicial decision of their home country would be afforded respect and their family would be recognized everywhere in the world. A refusal to recognize the adoption of the child in this case will violate principles of comity between nations, but more importantly, it will leave a little girl without a legally recognized family.

Sometimes a theme will not be this dramatic, or this long. A theme can be based in law or fact, but usually it is some combination of the two. When in doubt about how to articulate a theme, consider the human element of the problem. What feels unfair or unjust? When representing a government agency or a large institution, sometimes the best themes are policy-based themes about the necessity of bright line rules or the importance of institutional fairness.

3.   OUTLINING

An outline is essential to a good oral argument. In the same way that you need to build the foundation of a good written product with an outline, you should build a structure for your oral argument with an outline that you will have with you throughout the presentation. Like a written product where your audience sees your structure through the use of headings and sub-headings, you want to share the structure of your oral argument with your audience as well. Since you will not be handing the judges your written outline for your oral argument, the way to share your structure in oral advocacy is through the use of verbal roadmaps and transitions.

a.   Roadmap

After you greet the court, make your introduction, and tell the court what the case is about with your theme, you should tell the court what your major points will be in a way that indicates the outcome you want the court to reach. The roadmap of your major points should be presented in a way that incorporates the facts of the case and the major legal rules. In other words, you want to present the major points in your roadmap as legal conclusions that apply to the specific facts of your case, not as general or descriptive topic headings.

For example, in a case involving the ability of parents to be reimbursed for costs of educating their disabled child at a private school under the federal Individuals with Disabilities in Education Act (IDEA), the roadmap of the issues might read as follows:

> In this case, the summary judgment order against Plaintiffs' IDEA claims for reimbursement for their daughter's education was incorrectly granted for two reasons:
>
> First, the child in this case could only receive an appropriate education, which is guaranteed by the IDEA, by attending a private school that met her specific needs.
>
> Second, the cost of the private school selected by her parents was reasonable under the standard set forth by relevant case law.

The integration of the facts and the legal standard that leads to the desired conclusion is far more compelling than a roadmap that is descriptive in nature like the one that follows.

> The lower court incorrectly granted Defendants' Motion for Summary Judgment.
>
> My first point today will relate to the IDEA and the standards it establishes.
>
> My second point will relate to the costs of education at private school.

In addition to failing to integrate legal standards and a factual basis for the claims, this second sample roadmap illustrates two other deficiencies. First, it focuses the attention on the advocate by use of the first person. Second, it focuses the attention on the success of the opposing side by opening with a reference to the defendants' motion. The roadmap should focus on the application of the law to your client's facts and be presented in a light most favorable to your client.

b.   Order of Arguments

When crafting the roadmap for your oral argument, you need to make sure that you present your main issues in the order that you wish to discuss them in the body of your argument. While the court may, of course, decide to ask you questions about your third point before you even embark on a discussion of your first point, you should structure your presentation in a way that you think best reflects the strength of your arguments and the logical flow of your legal points. If you are thrown off your structure, the organization that you presented in your roadmap is often a way to move smoothly back to your best arguments. You can always say "Moving back now to the second point," and regain your structure.

Deciding the order in which to present your arguments can be difficult. You should strive to present the issues in the order that makes the most sense strategically. Generally, this means you want to present your strongest points first. If you have an issue on which you have strong legal and factual support, and resolution of the issue in your favor will result in a complete resolution of the case, that issue should be the first one you argue on behalf of your client.

Sometimes though, you may have strong legal and factual support on an issue that is not dispositive to the motion or appeal, or you may have threshold issues that must be resolved before the court can determine the merits of the case. In those circumstances, leading with the strongest legal and factual issue might not be appropriate. If you suspect that a judicial audience would want to discuss jurisdiction before the merits or would want to explore the possibility of the case being completely resolved prior to discussing the possibility of it being partially resolved, elect to order your argument to accommodate those concerns.

Finally, points that are collateral to winning your argument should be omitted from oral argument altogether. An example of a collateral point might be an alternative argument, which is in your brief as a back-up to the main argument. You do not need the court to decide in your favor on the alternative argument if the main argument is accepted. Similarly, you could have a separate count that has not been challenged on the motion before the court. Inclusion of either your alternative arguments or arguments relevant to the separate unchallenged count would be inappropriate to include in the main body of your oral argument. In the case of the alternative argument, however, it is appropriate to be prepared to discuss such a back-up argument if the court or opposing counsel raises it during the course of the argument.

No matter which order you discuss your argument points, you should present the points consistently in the roadmap and in the main body of the argument, and you should be willing to stray from your established order if the court asks you to discuss a later argument point first.

4. RECITATION OF FACTS AND USE OF THE RECORD

Oral argument is a wonderful opportunity to present sympathetic facts and to bring a dry record to life by pointing out the most crucial favorable facts for your side. It is also a chance to show how the facts contained in the record should be properly applied to legal rules to lead to a favorable result for your side even when those facts may not be sympathetic. Rarely though is an argument based on simply reciting the facts of the case effective in terms of persuading the court to rule in your favor.

As a well-prepared oral advocate, you should be ready to discuss the specific facts that are relevant to each portion of your argument. One way to ensure you will not forget key facts is to annotate an outline of your oral argument with citations to the factual record and short quotations from key documents that you suspect you will want to highlight. Be selective about which facts to focus on in your argument, but do not omit facts that may favor your opponent's argument, as the judges are likely to question you about such omissions. It is far better to have a chance to discuss and mitigate a perceived bad fact than to appear to be evading a negative fact.

5.   USE OF LEGAL AUTHORITIES

The use of legal authority in your oral argument is necessary both in your main argument and in responding to questions from the court. For each major point you plan to make, you should have some legal authority to cite in support. The heart of your argument should be a discussion of how the legal authority relevant to your issue applies favorably to the facts of your case. Understanding how all relevant legal authority supports or detracts from your argument is critical to your ability to fulfill this task.

Stylistically, and from court to court, there is variance in the proper manner for referring to authorities. Some courts expect advocates to provide full citations for all cases cited. Others are satisfied with a reference to a case name alone as long as the case is referenced in the written filing. A good rule to follow is to have full citations, including the date and the jurisdiction of any case you plan to rely on, annotated into your oral argument outline. This way you can quickly retrieve the information and provide it to a judge if asked.

6.   TRANSITIONS

By their very nature, transitions are difficult to plan for and structure since you do not know precisely where the discussion with the court will take you. However, a strong initial roadmap and the use of signposting can help you build in natural pathways back to your main structure. These pathways can make transitions back from an answer to a question and into your main argument smoother. They can also provide opportunities to weave your theme back into your argument and leave a lasting impression on the court that is favorable to your client.

While in your initial roadmap you may say something like: "the decision of the lower court should be affirmed for the following three reasons," your signposts are then the signals that you are moving from one point to another. For example, after you finish your introduction, roadmap, and theme, you might say "Turning to my first point." At the conclusion of the discussion of the first main argument, you can then say "Turning to my second point." If in the middle of the discussion of your second point, a judge asks a question that implicates arguments you planned to discuss in your third point, you can say "that brings me to the third point and yes, your Honor, the case of *Jones v. Smith* does support a finding for my client." After you fully respond to questions on the third point, and time permitting, you can again use your signposts to return to the place where you left off in the second point by indicating that you are returning to point two.

Transitioning smoothly can be an even greater challenge when there is a panel of judges, rather than a single judge. Having clear signposts and even outlining your argument with mini-roadmaps within each main argument section can be helpful to keep you and your audience focused when multiple judges are asking questions on different aspects of the case.

Extremely well prepared advocates will give mini-outlines of their answers before launching into the discussion of a complex legal authority so that they can find their way back to a particularly important aspect of the case from which they might otherwise be derailed. Such an answer could look something like this.

> No, your Honor, *Jones v. Smith* is distinguishable from this case for two reasons: First, as a factual matter because the plaintiff in *Jones* had not been offered a public education and second, as a legal matter because *Jones* was decided before the most recent amendments to the IDEA were passed. The factual distinction is important because . . . [several points about the factual difference].
>
> Now turning to the legal matter, the amendments changed the way that Congress defined a free and appropriate public education. . . .

The use of the mini-outline or roadmap serves as a way for the oral advocate to organize her thoughts and provides a transition back to the second important point that she wanted to make relating to the applicability of a legal authority to her client's problem.

7. CONCESSIONS

No moment can feel worse in an oral argument than when a judge asks "Counsel, do you concede that point?" The exercise this chapter addresses is "Oral ARGUMENT." No one wants to make a concession in an argument, right? Conceding means losing, does it not? Well, sometimes it does.

The key for an oral advocate is to know what can be conceded and what cannot. There are probably many points in any given case that can be conceded without consequence. In fact, attorneys can win points for being reasonable and cooperative if they appear willing to concede certain non-essential points. It can even make a case look stronger if the attorney is able to say "even if my client concedes that the plaintiff was an excellent worker, the termination was still within the letter and the spirit of the law." However, there are always a few concessions that can throw the entire case. Those are the concessions not to make. To tell the difference between the concessions that have horrible consequences and those that do not, you need to have thought long and hard about the elements of the claims involved in the case and the ultimate legal issue that the court must decide.

Crafting a list of concessions that can and cannot be made before the oral argument is a useful thing to do. Most detrimental concessions occur when an attorney has not thought through the implications of his answer. When in doubt, it is best not to concede a point. A better solution is the honest one: "Your Honor, I have not thought about the implications that a concession like that would have on this case. I am not prepared to concede that point at this time."

8. CONCLUSION

The conclusion to your argument is the last thing the court will hear you say. Your goal should be to finish the last minute of argument in a position of strength by summarizing again the points you have made and asking the court for the specific relief you want granted in this proceeding.

Similar to the introduction, this is a portion of the argument that should be committed to memory. Many advocates try to have a one minute conclusion and a one sentence conclusion both memorized so that if they find themselves with a very quiet bench of judges, they can recap their arguments and ask for their relief with the one minute closing. And, if they have been peppered with questions from the judges and time is running out, they can summarize their requested relief with the one sentence version.

D. REBUTTAL

In appellate arguments in particular, the party who brought the petition or appeal often is offered a possibility to reserve time for rebuttal argument. This is time that can be saved from the main argument time to use after the other attorney has presented his arguments. Where reserving time for rebuttal is an option, a good advocate will always try to preserve a short time to "have the last word." Make sure to request the reservation of time expressly at the outset of the argument.[8]

To successfully use rebuttal time, you should listen carefully to the opposing counsel's argument and limit the scope of your presentation to one or two short and critical points. The best rebuttals are directed strikes that do not reiterate the points that the advocate made in his main presentation. An advocate who can return to the podium, correct an

---

[8] The California Supreme Court website makes clear that even self-represented people will be held to this requirement. If rebuttal time is not reserved, it is waived. California Courts: the Judicial Branch of California, *At Oral Argument*, http://www.courts.ca.gov/12421.htm (last visited Feb. 15, 2018).

erroneous statement of fact that is critical to the analysis, clarify a point of law that the opposing attorney was confused about, and then sit back down after thanking the court, has perfected the art of rebuttal.

Similar to the presentation of the main argument, the rebuttal should be tightly structured. The use of a roadmap at the beginning of the rebuttal time can help both the court and you focus on the key points you want to make. Even more importantly, if you have selected two points to rebut and a judge is more interested in your second point, she can direct you immediately to that second point without wasting precious time on an issue that is not important to the decision maker. A rebuttal roadmap in a case to a single trial court level judge deciding a motion for summary judgment might look something like this:

> Your Honor, I have two points on rebuttal. First, I will characterize the holding in the recent case *Jones v. Smith* differently than Plaintiff did, and second, the declaration filed by Plaintiff in opposition to this motion does not establish the basis for a claim under the statute in question.

After this type of roadmap, the advocate would then turn to a discussion of the first point about the characterization of the holding unless the judge asked a question relating to the second point concerning the declaration. Regardless, the good advocate would have presented two direct points in rebuttal to the plaintiff's argument and would have offered a clear and understandable structure for the short presentation.

E. VERBAL AND NONVERBAL PERSUASION

The dialogue between the court and the advocate are the essence of oral argument. The legal analysis and relevant application of the facts to the law in response to questioning by the judge or judges is the most important aspect of the exercise. However, as in all forms of human communication, both verbal and nonverbal cues can contribute to the overall experience by all parties involved. The Tenth Circuit, in its Practitioner's Guide, stresses the importance of flexibility in answering questions at oral argument, but also provides the following tips for attorneys appearing before that court: (1) act natural, (2) make eye contact, (3) use your normal voice, (4) avoid exaggerated and unnecessary gestures or movements, (5) dress conservatively, and (6) avoid unnecessary noise.[9]

---

[9] The United States Court of Appeal for the Tenth Circuit, *Practitioner's Guide*, https://www .ca10.uscourts.gov/sites/default/files/clerk/UPDATED-Practioner%27s%20Guide%2007-06-2017. pdf (last visited Feb. 14, 2018).

1. MAKE AN IMPRESSION

Oral argument presents a unique opportunity to humanize the case for the judge or judges who will be deciding the dispute. From the moment you enter the courtroom, your presence will be observed and associated with your client's cause. This means you must pay attention not only to the verbal portion of your presentation, but also the non-verbal portion, starting from the way you conduct yourself when other advocates are speaking. Your professionalism and civility will be noticed, and you should strive to conduct yourself with the utmost propriety throughout the proceedings.

When it is your turn to present, there are some nonverbal mannerisms that can help you to make a good impression. Maintaining good posture and making eye contact with the judges are important to your overall appearance as confident and reliable. Whether we like it or not, we are judged and we judge others every day by initial impressions. A person who appears confident and commanding is more likely to convince the listener that the substance of what she says is sound and correct. Someone who does not make and hold eye contact may be viewed as evasive or disengaged. To present the best possible face for your client's cause, you must present yourself in a confident and straight forward manner.

2. A FORMAL CONVERSATION

Oral argument is a very formal conversation. Questions should be answered as you would respectfully answer royalty. "Yes or No, your Honor" are appropriate responses to a question from a judge. It is generally not enough to stop at "Yes or No, your Honor," but you also need to add legal and factual support to each response. And, all responses must be delivered in a respectful tone.

The key to engaging in a formal conversation is to remember that it still is a conversation. There should be a dialogue between you, as the advocate, and the judge, as the decision maker. Some advocates become intimidated by the formality of the proceeding, and then they forget to engage in the give and take of conversation. Responding to questions and discussing the case in a courteous and professional way is the main objective for the oral argument. The advocate who tries to recite a soliloquy or engages in a fist pounding, impassioned speech will not win points for his client's cause. The single worst thing that an advocate can do in the course of the oral argument is to forget that the judge is the decision maker and needs to be engaged in the conversation. Advocates who speak when the judge is trying to talk or interrupt a question by the judge are missing the point of the exercise and usually losing considerable points for their side.

3. ACTIVE LISTENING

One way to guard against falling into a stilted over-formality or an overly dramatic monologue is to engage in active listening. Active listening is variously defined as "attentive listening to avoid misunderstanding: the practice of paying close attention to a speaker and asking questions to ensure full comprehension"[10] or "a way of listening and responding to another person that improves mutual understanding."[11]

Sometimes active listening is characterized by repeating the question back to the person who asked it or restating what you heard someone say. Repeating too many questions that a judge asks you would not be looked on favorably, but occasionally repeating a question to make sure you understand what is being asked is an acceptable way to ensure engagement in the conversation.

Additionally, focusing in on the questions and maintaining eye contact throughout the question being asked are critical active listening skills that are very important to a successful oral argument. When eye contact is maintained, an advocate has the advantage of seeing an expression on a judge's face that may signal a quandary. If a judge exhibits a questioning glance, the advocate can (and should) pause to allow for the judge to interject the question. Remember, the judge is the decision maker. If he has a question about the facts or law, the job of the advocate is to answer that question in the best light for her client. If the judge does not get to ask the question, the advocate may lose the case because of that one never-asked, and therefore never-answered, question. Only by fully engaging in conversation, can the advocate work with the judge to cover all the issues and concerns that the judge may have.

4. USE OF NOTES

Some advocates stand up to present oral argument completely note-free. Those advocates are usually the ones engaged in moot court competitions in law school. Very few practicing lawyers bring nothing up to the podium with them when making an oral argument. The trick is to bring some notes but not to be tied down to reading those notes during the argument. Eye contact is very important both as a nonverbal persuasive technique and as an active listening device, so notes that pull your eyes down to the page and away from eye contact with the judge are necessarily a detriment. That said, bringing up an outline that is annotated with

---

[10] Bing.com Dictionary, http://www.bing.com/Dictionary/search?q=define+active+listening & qpvt=Definition+of+Active+Listening & FORM=DTPDIA (last visited Feb. 15, 2018).

[11] International Online Training in Intractable Conflict, Conflict Research Consortium, University of Colorado, http://www.colorado.edu/conflict/peace/treatment/activel.htm (last visited Feb. 15, 2018).

citations to legal authority and the factual record can be very helpful if you are asked for some particular information.

5. CIVILITY AND PROFESSIONALISM

Civility, professionalism, and ethical practice are critical in all aspects of lawyering, and oral argument is no exception. Especially in the very public forum of a courtroom, it is vital that parties from both sides demonstrate respect for one another, the court, the staff, and the public.

As discussed above, an advocate is judged on his professional demeanor from the time he enters the courtroom. Not only is the judge observing the behavior of all counsel, but the judge's staff including the clerk or bailiff, the court reporter, and the law clerks also observe oral argument and often take note of attorney conduct. Moreover, other attorneys in the community and clients who are watching oral argument also fill the seats in the courtroom and form judgments about the professional conduct of those presenting in court.

An unpleasant remark to opposing counsel or rude treatment of the court reporter or clerk can quickly land an attorney in disfavor with the court and the legal community. In contrast, civil and professional conduct can also be noticed and remembered. In a legal community where you are likely to appear more than once before the same judge or judges and where you will interface with the same attorneys again, professional courtesy in one case today may translate into the granting of an extension of time in a different case tomorrow. And, more importantly, it makes everyone's work day better and more pleasant.

F. CROSS-CULTURAL CONSIDERATIONS

The tone and culture of oral argument in an adversary system can be quite different than the tone and culture of oral argument in a legal system based on civil law and an inquisitorial system. Even within the United States, the expectations of formality and style vary across court levels and jurisdictions. Understanding the expectations in the court in which you will appear can mean the difference between success and failure at oral argument. The single best way to understand the approach to oral argument taken in your jurisdiction is to go to the court where you are scheduled to appear and watch the proceedings.

1. THE ROLE OF ORAL ARGUMENT INTERNATIONALLY AND IN FOREIGN JURISDICTIONS

In many cultures, the practice of oral argument is not intended to be a formal conversation. Instead, the purpose is for the advocate to read the presentation into the record and for the court to absorb the information orally as well as in writing. In systems that have more formal presentations, judges are hesitant to interrupt an advocate, and it would seem rude to have a presentation style that includes smiling and constant eye contact. Joking is rarely appropriate in oral argument in any jurisdiction, but international tribunals and many foreign jurisdictions would find joking particularly inappropriate.

International courts and international tribunals are created by international organizations and they usually have their own set of rules of practice. For example, the International Court of Justice (ICJ) is the judicial organ of the United Nations and practice in that court is governed by the Statute of the ICJ.[12] Nation-states, which are referred to as States in international law, are allowed to bring disputes with other signatory States before the ICJ. The practice in international tribunals like the ICJ is to have States represented by counsel from their own country and to have arguments presented to a panel of judges made up of judicial officers from various countries. Procedurally, the applicant State presents first, followed by the respondent State, but both sides are provided an opportunity to respond to one another in rebuttal and sur-rebuttal. Oral arguments in international forums therefore tend to last longer than oral arguments in domestic courts.

In systems where the role of the advocate is to assist the court in its investigation of the matter, rather than to advocate zealously on behalf of a side in an adversary proceeding, the nature and tone of oral argument is necessarily different. If you find yourself practicing in a civil law system where the role of counsel is different than it is in the United States, you must adjust your preparation and presentation consistent with your audience and your role. Note that in many systems, lawyers function in different categories and not all lawyers go to court. For example, in France and Japan, there are various exams that can be taken depending on the type of legal work that the attorney wishes to perform. Only the very small percent of lawyers that take and pass the Bar exam in those countries can appear before the court. In contrast, in the United States almost all lawyers pass a Bar exam irrespective of whether they want to present arguments in court.

2. CULTURAL EXPECTATIONS IN DIFFERENT U.S. JURISDICTIONS

Even within United States jurisdictions, the expectations of oral argument practice vary from jurisdiction to jurisdiction and from state court to federal court. All courts have local rules that outline the particulars of practice in those jurisdictions. For example, a large city court

---

[12] The Statute of the International Court of Justice can be accessed on the ICJ website. International Court of Justice, http://www.icj-cij.org/en/statute (last visited Feb. 15, 2018).

is likely to have a much more sophisticated system of filing papers and setting arguments than a small town court with a single judge. Federal courts tend to be more formal in their proceedings and rules than state courts, and by their nature, federal courts are generally situated in the largest cities in any state. So, you are unlikely to find a federal court that has a small town culture. Wherever you find yourself presenting arguments, the first step is to find and follow local rules.

Sometimes the written local rules will not give you the complete picture of the local culture or practices. To get a full understanding of the tone and formality of a proceeding in any jurisdiction, you should observe local practices and talk to local members of the Bar who appear regularly in local courts. Even across federal courts, the procedures for presenting oral argument to a district court may vary widely from the Southern District of New York to the Eastern District of California. An attorney coming from New York to appear *pro hac vice*[13] in Sacramento is well-advised to research the practices in the Eastern District of California before presenting an argument in a style favored by a New York City judge.

3. LEVEL OF COURT DIFFERENTIATIONS

Even within the same geographic areas, the cultural expectations and level of formality may be quite different depending on the level of court. Generally, proceedings in the trial court are less formal. Advocates in a pretrial motion setting may not be expected to prepare a formal presentation. Sometimes motions may even be made and argued without formal briefing first. State and federal appellate courts tend to be more formal than the trial level courts in both systems. Attorneys are expected to make a formal presentation, answer questions, and direct the court to the factual record for all citations. Finally, the highest courts of most States, and certainly the Supreme Court of the United States, are the most formal venues for delivering oral argument. Few advocates enter into a high court without being fully prepared, having had a moot court experience, and having fully researched their audience.

PRACTICE EXERCISES

PRACTICE EXERCISE 1

The best way to perfect the skill of oral advocacy is to make oral arguments. Standing up in front of people and answering questions is a skill that everyone, regardless of speaking style or personality, can practice and improve. The following exercise offers one opportunity to practice.

---

[13] A status that permits an attorney admitted and living in one state to appear for a limited time in a federal court in another state.

The purpose of this exercise is to get you on your feet and to provide you with an opportunity to practice an introduction, roadmap, and theme.

Start with Federal Rule of Evidence 803, which creates an exception to the hearsay rule and gives federal district courts the power to accept certain evidence that would otherwise be considered out of court statements offered to prove truth. Rule 803 provides an exception to the hearsay rule for factual findings resulting from an investigation set forth by public records and reports. These include records, reports, statements, or data compilations, in any form, of public offices or agencies. Fed. R. Evid. 803(8).

One case, *Zeus Enters. Inc. v. Alphin Aircraft, Inc.*, 190 F.3d 238, 241 (4th Cir. 1999), provides: "The admissibility of a public record is assumed as a matter of course, unless there are sufficient negative factors to indicate a lack of trustworthiness."

Another case, *Amica Life Ins. v. Barbor*, 488 F. Supp. 2d 750 (N.D. Ill. 2007), provides: Administrative proceedings that are not adversarial in nature and judicial findings of fact are not covered under Rule 803(8).

Imagine that your clients seek to introduce a report from a foreign agency that found them to be appropriate parents for an adopted child. They want to prove that they are the child's parents in a U.S. Court and that they were qualified to be appointed as parents for the child. The report that you wish to introduce was compiled and produced by the Dutch Council for the Protection of Children in the ordinary course of its duties to investigate the propriety of placement of adoptable children in appropriate homes. You want to argue to the court that the Dutch Council's report falls within the meaning of Rule 803, that it is a trustworthy report, and that it does not fall within the judicial finding of fact or administrative proceeding definition. Prepare an introduction for the plaintiffs, a roadmap of your argument, and try to include a theme.

PRACTICE EXERCISE 2

Students can also learn from watching others give oral arguments. A number of state Supreme Court and federal appellate court websites have links to oral arguments that are valuable teaching tools. A few of the links are provided below. Your professor may suggest links to see oral arguments in a local jurisdiction or may assign you to attend a live court hearing so that you can observe the local rules of practice.

Links to Oral Argument Videos

- Iowa Judicial Branch: Video Arguments of the Iowa Supreme Court: https://www.iowacourts.gov/iowa-courts/supreme-court/oral-argument-videos/ (last visited Feb. 14, 2018)

- Illinois Courts: Video Arguments of the Illinois Supreme Court: http://www.illinoiscourts.gov/Media/On_Demand.asp (last visited Feb. 14, 2018)

- Minnesota Judicial Branch: Video Arguments of the Minnesota Supreme Court: http://mncourts.gov/SupremeCourt/OralArgument Webcasts.aspx (last visited Feb. 15, 2018)

- United States Courts for the Ninth Circuit: Audio and Video Arguments of the Ninth Circuit Court of Appeals: http://www. ca9.uscourts.gov/media/ (last visited Feb. 15, 2018)

CHAPTER 21

JUDICIAL WRITING

■ ■ ■

By Lindsey D. Blanchard and Richard Schickele

A. WHAT IS JUDICIAL WRITING, AND WHY IS IT IMPORTANT TO UNDERSTAND JUDICIAL WRITING?

Our use of the term judicial writing covers two distinct categories: (1) bench briefs (or bench memos), which are written by law clerks and are not intended for circulation beyond the court; and (2) orders and opinions, which are designed to inform litigants and the public of the court's decisions.[1] Some appreciation of these distinct types of judicial writing is valuable for all law students. If you are planning to sign up for a judicial externship as part of your coursework, or to apply for a post-graduation judicial clerkship, then the importance of understanding how bench briefs and judicial opinions are written is clear. Even if you never work in a court, however, you should understand as a practicing attorney how the persuasive brief that you submit to court is used by the court in the process of reaching and writing its decision. You will also benefit from understanding the reasons behind the court's filing of an order, an unpublished opinion, or a full opinion. Finally, in learning how your briefs are analyzed and evaluated, you will more fully appreciate many of the concepts that have been discussed in previous chapters on persuasive writing—i.e., the importance of clear organization, theme, accuracy in recounting the facts, thorough research and correct citations, candor, and professionalism.

---

[1] Other types of documents produced by the court include findings of fact and conclusions of law (i.e., a statement issued at the conclusion of a bench trial of the judge's determination of the facts that were supported by the evidence presented and her final decision on the legal points raised) and jury instructions (i.e., the directions the judge gives to the jury, at the conclusion of a jury trial, regarding the law of the case). *See* BLACK'S LAW DICTIONARY (10th ed. 2014) (defining "conclusion of law," "finding of fact," and "jury instruction"). Those topics are beyond the scope of this textbook.

B. BENCH BRIEFS

As noted in Chapter 9, bench briefs are a form of objective writing very similar to a formal or short-form memorandum. A judge's law clerk[2] reads the parties' briefs associated with a motion pending before the court, identifies the issue or issues raised by the motion, summarizes the relevant facts, summarizes the parties' contentions, and—based on his or her research—provides an objective legal analysis of the issues along with a recommended outcome. Because Chapters 10 and 11 provide a general framework for objective memoranda, this chapter will focus on the unique features of bench briefs.

Bench briefs are prepared in both trial and appellate courts. The primary difference between them is that in the trial court, a bench brief is generally prepared only for one judge, whereas in an appellate court, the bench brief may be shared by several judges. Accordingly, bench briefs in the trial court vary considerably depending on the preferences of the recipient judge. Some judges tell their law clerks to dispense with the facts, some don't want a summary of the parties' positions, and others may want the law clerk to propose questions to be asked of the attorneys at the hearing or argument. Therefore, one of the first things you should do when serving as a judicial extern or a law clerk is to ascertain what your judge wants in a bench brief. The following are the most common components of bench briefs.

1. ISSUES PRESENTED

The first task facing a judicial extern or law clerk is to decipher the filings to determine what is really at issue. The filings typically consist of a motion, a brief in support of that motion, a brief by the responding party in opposition to that motion, and a reply brief by the moving party. When both sides are well represented, each filing likely will be carefully constructed to convince the reader to decide the matter one way. On the other hand, where the parties are poorly represented or represent themselves, the filings may be less illuminating. In either instance, one of the first lessons a law clerk or an extern must learn is not to rely on the parties' representations of the record, but to read the record documents for himself. Ultimately, the court must independently determine what issue or issues need to be decided. The attorneys' filings may be helpful, but they are not necessarily controlling. Thus, just ascertaining what is at issue will require critical reading.

---

[2]   Traditionally, a law clerk was hired by a particular judge and worked only for that judge. Now, many courts have staff attorneys and pro se law clerks who may be assigned to work for different judges on different matters.

2.   LEGAL STANDARD OR STANDARD OF REVIEW

As discussed in more detail below, each motion at the trial level will be governed by a particular legal standard, and each issue on appeal will be governed by a particular standard of review.[3] Although the parties should include the applicable standard in their briefing, the law clerk should conduct her own independent research to determine the correct standard. That—rather than the parties' briefs—should be the compass for the bench brief. When in doubt, asking the judge, a long-serving law clerk, or an attorney in the clerk's office for guidance on the applicable standards may save you considerable time.

3.   FACTS

The facts in a bench brief should be tailored to the motion at issue. For example, a bench brief on a motion to dismiss for lack of jurisdiction need not recite the entire history of the controversy, but should focus on the facts relevant to jurisdiction. That said, a certain amount of context is desirable, even if strictly speaking, not necessary. For example, a brief summary of the claims at issue and the relief sought may be of interest to the trial judge considering a motion to dismiss, even if they do not bear on the court's jurisdiction. Also, appellate judges often want to know the identity of the trial judge, even though this arguably should not affect their treatment of the appeal.

4.   THE PARTIES' ARGUMENTS

If you are preparing a bench brief prior to argument on a motion or an appeal—in particular on a motion or an appeal that involves voluminous and obtuse filings—this section is particularly important. A bench brief that summarizes the parties' positions regarding each issue in an intelligible manner or that explains why a particular filing is unclear, will help to prepare the judge or judges for oral argument.

5.   ANALYSIS

Once a bench brief sets forth the issues, the applicable legal standard or standard of review, the relevant facts, and the parties' positions, the analysis and the result may be fairly straightforward. Where the issue is in doubt, however, the legal analysis is the heart of the bench brief. Either way, the legal analysis should present a fair application of the standard

---

[3]   Although some cases go to trial before a jury or a judge, many more are resolved short of trial by motion, such as motions to dismiss or motions for summary judgment. As discussed in more detail below, trial courts are bound to apply certain legal standards in resolving those motions. Those standards are different than appellate standards of review, which dictate the lens through which the appellate court reviews the trial court's findings and rulings.

and rules to the particular facts in the case. Only then can the bench brief assist the judge in evaluating the parties' competing contentions.

6. RECOMMENDATION

Sound legal analysis, not the law clerk's recommendation, is the hallmark of a good bench brief. However, the law clerk should still set forth the disposition of the legal issues that the law clerk recommends based on his or her legal analysis. Although the judge may not agree with the recommendation, especially in a close case, the judge will appreciate an objectively fair analysis because it will allow the judge to better evaluate the parties' arguments. In fact, some judges find it more important for them to understand the arguments that a bench brief rejects, than to agree with all the reasons that the bench brief finds persuasive. Thus, a recommendation based on what the law clerk thinks the judge wants is ultimately a disservice to the judge and the law clerk—the judge will not be adequately prepared for the parties' arguments and will learn that she cannot trust the law clerk's work.

C. OPINIONS AND ORDERS

While bench briefs contribute to judicial decision making, opinions and orders are how courts present their decisions to the outside world. The terms "order" and "opinion" are sometimes used interchangeably when referring to a court's decision, but those words have separate meanings. An "order" is a court's "written direction or command."[4] Orders are used to state the court's ruling on a particular motion (e.g., granting a plaintiff's motion for default judgment or denying a defendant's motion for summary judgment), and if the ruling disposes of a case in its entirety, to direct the clerk of court to enter judgment. However, a court also may enter an order to direct a party to take some action (e.g., an order to show cause requiring a party to appear in court), to prohibit a party from engaging in certain behavior (e.g., a restraining order or injunction), or to provide filing deadlines for the life of a case on its docket (e.g., a scheduling order).[5]

---

[4]   *Order*, BLACK'S LAW DICTIONARY (10th ed. 2014).

[5]   Many orders consist of only one or two sentences or a paragraph. However, some types of orders are required by court rules to include certain content and, accordingly, may be several pages long. For example, Rule 16 of the Federal Rules of Civil Procedure requires the district court to establish, in every federal civil case, deadlines by which the parties must "join other parties, amend the pleadings, complete discovery, and file motions." FED. R. CIV. P. 16(b)(3)(A) (2017). And, Rule 65 requires a restraining order or an order granting an injunction to: "(A) state the reasons why it issued; (B) state its terms specifically; and (C) describe in reasonable detail—and not by referring to the complaint or other document—the act or acts restrained or required." FED. R. CIV. P. 65(d)(1). Many state court systems have similar rules. *See, e.g.*, IDAHO R. CIV. P. 16(a)(2) (2016) (listing the required components of a pretrial scheduling order in Idaho courts); MINN. R. CIV. P. 65.04 (2018) (governing the form and scope of injunctions and restraining orders in Minnesota courts).

When a court issues an order ruling on a party's motion (particularly a dispositive motion such as a motion for summary judgment) or on an appeal, the order often is accompanied by a lengthy "opinion" that explains the ruling. Although the presentation of a court's opinion may vary slightly by judge, the content is largely consistent and includes a description of the issues and arguments raised by the parties, the relevant facts, the governing law, and the court's conclusion and reasoning.[6] In other words, in most cases, the opinion—and not the order—contains the legal analysis. This chapter, therefore, discusses judicial opinions at both the trial court and appellate court levels.

1. IMPORTANT LIMITATIONS

As a preliminary matter, certain limitations that apply to opinion-writing must be addressed. You will recall, from Chapter 2, that both the federal and state court systems have a hierarchical structure. At the base of that structure in the federal system and in each state court system are trial courts, where a case is initiated and litigated through pre-trial motion practice (as discussed in Chapter 17) and—if the claims survive—eventually decided by a judge or a jury usually through presentation of evidence and witnesses. The losing litigant then has the right to appeal the adverse decision.

This hierarchical structure is important for two reasons. First, under the doctrine of precedent, courts must apply the law as dictated by the courts above them. Second, the role of each court in the hierarchy dictates the type of analysis in which the court can engage. Each of these limitations tends to manifest itself differently in trial and appellate court opinion-writing.

Also, each court may have local rules and practices which should be respected. While this chapter will discuss the common components of judicial opinions, individual courts or judges may have their own preferences regarding the content, organization, and tone of a judicial opinion. Therefore, if you work for a judge and are tasked with drafting an opinion, it is important to review her prior opinions and consult with her or her other law clerks before you begin writing.

2. PUBLISHED VS. UNPUBLISHED

Judicial opinions may be designated as "published" or "unpublished." Many, if not most, trial court decisions are not published. Accordingly, their audience is for the most part limited to the parties to the case. Such "unpublished" opinions need only set forth those findings of fact and

---

[6] *Opinion*, BLACK'S LAW DICTIONARY (10th ed. 2014) (defining "opinion" as "[a] court's written statement explaining its decision in a given case, [usually] including the statement of facts, points of law, rationale, and dicta").

conclusions of law necessary to explain the court's resolution of the case. On occasion, however, a trial court may determine that its opinion will have some effect beyond directing the parties to the case, and will have the opinion published. In those instances, the law clerk in preparing the opinion should consider the suggestions for published dispositions set forth in the following sections.

Published opinions are judicially-created law—arguably, the most important type of judicial writing. Courts, and certainly appellate courts, mostly publish opinions in order to establish law.[7] They publish their decisions not just to decide the controversy before them, but to provide guidance to the bench and the bar as to how the issue should be handled the next time it arises. Accordingly, while deciding the matter and clarifying the law for all concerned, the court should attempt to anticipate the various ways the ruling may be applied.

D. TRIAL COURT OPINIONS

Trial court opinions usually contain the following components: (1) an introduction; (2) a background section that describes the facts and procedural history relevant to the pending motion, as well as the issues and arguments raised by the parties; (3) a discussion of the legal standard governing the motion; (4) the court's analysis of the issues; and (5) the court's conclusion, or ruling, on the motion.

1. INTRODUCTION

Most court opinions include a short paragraph at the beginning of the opinion that identifies the matter before the court (i.e., the name of the motion) and the names of the parties involved. Sometimes, the introductory comments also will state the court's ruling and briefly preview the court's reasoning. While these introductory remarks may be included under an "Introduction" title, they often simply follow the case caption and name of the judge.

2. BACKGROUND

The "Background" section of a court's opinion is the explanation of the factual and procedural history relevant to the matter pending before the court—i.e., the "who," "what," "when," "where," "why," and "how" of the motion. This section typically presents the facts and procedural history in chronological order, although the court may use separate sections and

---

[7]   At one time, all dispositions were published. However, the workload of many appellate courts substantially reduced the amount of time that the judges could spend on each case. Thus, a number of courts have opted for issuing unpublished decisions (usually in the most straightforward cases) as a means of allowing the judges to spend more time on their precedent-setting, published opinions.

labels for those components.[8] Depending on the type of motion, the "facts" may be derived solely from the complaint (e.g., a motion to dismiss for failure to state a claim)[9] or from the parties' submissions of declarations and exhibits (e.g., a motion for summary judgment).[10] In the latter case, the court's knowledge of the relevant facts is based not only on the parties' descriptions of the facts in their briefs, but also on the court's independent review of the facts in the parties' supporting submissions. Thus, although the description of the facts and procedural history in the court's opinion may not include citations to the record (depending on the judge's preference), it is important that the parties' briefs contain substantively and technically accurate citations to the documents that support their factual assertions for purposes of maintaining credibility and ensuring that the court can locate the relevant materials.

3. LEGAL STANDARD

After explaining the factual and procedural background of the motion, the court typically sets forth—in its own section or in the "Analysis" section (discussed below)—the legal standard that governs the particular motion. For example, which party bears the burden, what documents or evidence can the court rely on, and how should the court view the evidence? The answers to these questions will greatly impact the court's analysis.

The difference between the standards governing two common civil motions—a motion to dismiss for failure to state a claim and a motion for summary judgment—highlights the important role the legal standard plays in the resolution of the motion. When evaluating a motion to dismiss for failure to state a claim, the court ordinarily does not consider matters outside the pleadings, must assume the facts in the complaint to be true, and must construe all reasonable inferences from those facts in the light most favorable to the plaintiff.[11] However, a court evaluating a motion for summary judgment does go beyond the pleadings. The court will grant a motion for summary judgment only if, after analyzing the evidence presented by the parties, it concludes there is no genuine issue of material fact and the moving party is entitled to judgment as a matter of law.[12] While the record is to be viewed in the light most favorable to the non-

---

[8] Because a chronological presentation is both the most common approach, as well as the default approach, any deviation should be explicitly noted.

[9] *See* FED. R. CIV. P. 12(b)(6); FED. R. CIV. P. 12(d).

[10] *See* FED. R. CIV. P. 56(c).

[11] *See, e.g.*, FED. R. CIV. P. 12(b)(6); FED. R. CIV. P. 12(d); Knievel v. ESPN, 393 F.3d 1068, 1072 (9th Cir. 2005). However, "[a] court may consider evidence on which the complaint 'necessarily relies.'" Marder v. Lopez, 450 F.3d 445, 448 (9th Cir. 2006). To satisfy this standard, the document must be referred to in the complaint, must be central to a claim, and must not be questioned by any party as to its authenticity. *Id.*

[12] *See e.g.*, FED. R. CIV. P. 56(a); Celotex Corp. v. Catrett, 477 U.S. 317, 322–23 (1986); Anderson v. Liberty Lobby, Inc., 477 U.S. 242, 249–50 (1986).

moving party, that party must set forth facts showing there is a genuine issue for trial.[13]

In addition to regular motion practice, federal trial courts also have an appeal system that requires application of certain standards of review. In federal court, a magistrate judge in addition to a district judge may be assigned to a case. Certain motions may be assigned to the magistrate judge, and the parties are permitted to file objections to the magistrate judge's decisions on those motions with the district judge. In these instances, the district judge must apply the appropriate standard of review, as the appellate courts do in reviewing the district courts' rulings. For example, magistrate judges rule on non-dispositive discovery motions in civil cases, and the district judge may set aside the magistrate judge's ruling only if it "is clearly erroneous or is contrary to law."[14] But, magistrate judges also decide petitions by prisoners who are challenging the conditions of their confinement, and objections to the district judge on those rulings are governed by a de novo standard of review.[15] Thus, in a similar fashion to the legal standards governing particular motions, the standard of review on appeal of a magistrate judge's decision greatly impacts the district judge's analysis.

4. ANALYSIS

The substance of the court's opinion is found in its analysis of the issues—in other words, its application of the relevant law to the facts. Much like in an office memo or bench brief, this portion of the opinion often is labeled as the "Analysis" or "Discussion" and, depending on the number of issues before the court and the complexity of those issues, this section may be further subdivided. For example, if a defendant moves for summary judgment on three claims in the plaintiff's complaint, the court's analysis likely will be divided into three parts (possibly with additional subparts).

At the trial court level, the court's analysis is subject to certain constraints. First, except in limited circumstances, the court will only analyze the issues and arguments raised by the parties.[16] Second, unless there is no mandatory authority on point, the court is bound to apply the mandatory authorities in its jurisdiction. Accordingly, it is important that the parties have clearly set forth the issues, their arguments, and the relevant authorities that support their positions.

---

[13]   Anderson, 477 U.S. at 256–57.

[14]   FED. R. CIV. P. 72(a).

[15]   FED. R. CIV. P. 72(b).

[16]   One such limited circumstance in federal court is when the court perceives there to be a lack of standing or other impediment to its jurisdiction over the case; in such instances, the court may examine that issue sua sponte. See FED. R. CIV. P. 12(h)(3) ("If the court determines at any time that it lacks subject-matter jurisdiction, the court must dismiss the action.").

Although each judge will have a unique tone and writing style, the typical format of a judge's analysis for each issue raised in a motion follows the objective writing paradigm discussed in this book: CREAC.[17] Thus, after identifying the issue before the court (and often the conclusion the court has reached), the judge will set forth the governing rule; explain how the rule has been applied to similar situations in past cases through case illustrations or parentheticals; apply the rule to the present facts, comparing and contrasting those facts to the facts in the precedent and applying policy as necessary to show his reasoning; and state his conclusion.

5.   CONCLUSION OR DISPOSITION

Like the introduction, the court's overall conclusion may or may not be labeled as such. It typically is very brief and simply summarizes the court's rulings. However, it also may state the consequences of the ruling. In addition, some judges include the "order" and instructions to the clerk of court in this portion of the opinion, rather than drafting and filing a separate "order" document.

E.   APPELLATE COURT OPINIONS

Published appellate court opinions take on various formats, but most contain several common features, including: (1) an introduction; (2) a statement of the case; (3) the court's statement of the issues presented; (4) the applicable standard of review; (5) the court's explanation for its resolution of the issues; and (6) a statement of disposition. In addition, these opinions may contain another feature unique to appellate opinions—a concurrence or dissent.

1.   INTRODUCTION

The introduction should identify the matter before the court, the issues presented, and the court's resolution of those issues. It prepares the reader for what is contained in the opinion. A comprehensive introduction is also a boon to legal researchers as it informs them of whether the opinion is relevant to the issue they are researching.[18]

---

[17] *See* Chapter 9 on Objective Legal Writing. Common variants depending on the judge or issue include IRAC (Issue, Rule, Analysis, Conclusion) and CRAC (Conclusion, Rule, Analysis, Conclusion).

[18] For example, Chief Justice Roberts' opening paragraph in Trinity Lutheran Church of Columbia, Inc. v. Comer reads:

> The Missouri Department of Natural Resources offers state grants to help public and private schools, nonprofit daycare centers, and other nonprofit entities purchase rubber playground surfaces made from recycled tires. Trinity Lutheran Church applied for such a grant for its preschool and daycare center and would have received one, but for the fact that Trinity Lutheran is a church. The Department had a policy of categorically disqualifying churches and other religious organizations from receiving grants under its playground resurfacing program. The question presented is whether the Department's

2. STATEMENT OF THE CASE

Context matters. The statement of the case tells the reader how the court saw the case—in other words, which facts the appellate court considered important as the basis for its legal opinion. This may or may not be how the parties, or the lower court, saw the case, but the statement will inform the application of the opinion's legal holding to future cases.

3. STATEMENT OF THE ISSUES

The parties must present the issues in their appellate briefs, and they should do so fairly, but in a manner that favors their clients. Accordingly, a better appellate opinion defines the issues as the court sees them and does not rely on the parties' statements of the issues.[19] How the court defines the issues, just like its statement of the facts, helps define the opinion's application to future controversies.

4. STANDARD OF REVIEW

Arguably, the applicable standard of review ought to be a matter of statutory or case law. Nonetheless, the parties have strong reasons for advocating for different standards. What appellant does not want the appellate court to apply a de novo standard of review? Also, some standards of review seem malleable. For example, the grant of an injunction may be reviewed de novo, but the trial court's underlying findings may be reviewed for clear error. Whatever standard the court chooses to employ, it becomes part of the case's precedential value and will inform the opinion's application to future controversies.[20]

5. REASONING

The opinion then decides the issues, setting forth the court's reasoning. Normally, an appellate court will reason based on the applicable precedent. Indeed, even U.S. Supreme Court Justices, although not bound by precedent, tend to base their opinions on precedent. Of course, there may not be any direct precedent, or the existing precedents may be ambiguous or conflicting, or they may not account for later developments in the law. The opinion should explain why, starting with the existing precedents, the court reaches its resolution of the case. It should clearly explain the legal and factual judgments that guide the court to its conclusion. Often, the unfolding of the court's reasoning will in itself respond to the parties'

---

policy violated the rights of Trinity Lutheran under the Free Exercise Clause of the First Amendment.

137 S. Ct. 2012, 2017 (2017).

[19] In fact, occasionally the U.S. Supreme Court when granting certiorari, or even later, revises or refines the issues presented.

[20] See Chapter 18 for more information about the appellate process and applicable standards of review.

contentions. However, if certain of the parties' arguments are not adequately covered by the court's explanation of its ruling, then the opinion should address those particular arguments as necessary to fully explain its reasoning.

An opinion's reasoning is its most personal aspect, and any law clerk who assists a judge in drafting her opinion should appreciate and defer to the judge's particular preferences. The collection of a judge's opinions constitutes her judicial philosophy or jurisprudence. These are the writings that the judge will have to defend long after her law clerk has moved on. Accordingly, despite the heavy workload in some busy appellate courts, the law clerk should be careful to defer to the judge's perspectives and the judge should take the time to ensure that a proposed opinion not only reaches the correct result, but does so through a line of reasoning that is consistent with the judge's jurisprudence.

6. STATEMENT OF DISPOSITION

An appellate opinion will ordinarily conclude with a statement that the lower court's opinion is affirmed or reversed (and remanded). On occasion, however, the appellate court may provide further directions for the parties and the lower court.

7. CONCURRENCES AND DISSENTS

For appellate courts, a distinguishing feature of opinions is that they are inherently the product of more than one judge. Accordingly, on most appellate courts, the process of creating a published opinion involves several drafts between judges. A non-authoring judge may have suggestions as to wording or style, but not infrequently, a non-authoring judge may have concerns with substantive portions of a proposed opinion. This may require some negotiation, as a particular judge's perspective does not become the opinion of the court unless and until it is adopted by a majority of the panel. These negotiations may place a law clerk in an interesting, but delicate, situation. On the one hand, the law clerk should fully support her judge's position; on the other hand, she should also be on the lookout for possible options that might reconcile the differing positions.

If a consensus is not reached, and a judge on an appellate panel does not agree with the authoring judge's perspective, he or she may write either a "concurrence" or a "dissent." A concurrence is an opinion written by a judge who agrees with the outcome reached by the authoring judge, but on different grounds.[21] A dissent is an opinion written by a judge who

---

[21] *Concurrence*, BLACK'S LAW DICTIONARY (10th ed. 2014) (defining "concurrence" as "[a] vote cast by a judge in favor of the judgment reached, often on grounds differing from those expressed in the opinion or opinions explaining the judgment").

disagrees with the outcome reached by the authoring judge.[22] Concurrences and dissents may range from a short, one-paragraph statement, to a full explanation of the disagreement and how the law ought to develop.

There are five types of dissents that a judge may want to write: the friendly dissent, the simple dissent, the petitioning dissent, the futuristic dissent, or the disabling dissent. The friendly dissent accepts that the majority is bound by precedent, which the judge thinks is wrong and should be reconsidered, even though the panel may not be able to do so. In other words, the judge understands that her colleagues were required to decide the appeal in a certain way, but she thinks the law should be changed or reconsidered. Sometimes, a friendly dissent may be written as a concurrence. The simple dissent is a statement that the majority simply got it wrong or goes beyond where the judge can go. There is no ulterior motive; the judge does not expect anyone to agree with her, she simply doesn't agree with the majority. The petitioning dissent is a plea to a higher court, or perhaps to the judge's colleagues, to take the case en banc. A petitioning dissent explains in some detail why the majority's approach is bad for the law and inconsistent with Supreme Court precedent. The dissent may extensively cite prior opinions by current Justices in an attempt to attract their attention. The futuristic dissent differs from a petitioning dissent in that the judge does not expect her colleagues or a higher court to take up the case. Rather, the judge seeks to plant an idea or a different approach that might germinate and grow to influence the development of the law. Such a dissent will generally stress policy reasons for why the law ought to develop in a certain way. Finally, the disabling dissent is designed to tell the attorneys and the lower court how to get around the majority's opinion. Disabling dissents usually issue in cases where the appellate court remands the case to a lower court, and the dissent may explain how a party can avoid the consequences of the majority's opinion or that the matter remains within the trial court's discretion and the majority's opinion does not compel the exercise of that discretion in a particular way.

One consideration relevant to the nature of a dissent may be whether the dissent would enhance the weight of the majority's opinion. Thus, for example, if the majority opinion is vague or perhaps tied closely to the particular facts of the case, the dissenting judge might want to simply note her dissent and leave the opinion ambiguous or fact-specific so it can be distinguished by future panels. A fuller dissent runs the risk of solidifying the opinion as precedent.

---

[22] *Dissenting opinion*, BLACK'S LAW DICTIONARY (10th ed. 2014) (defining "dissenting opinion" as "[a]n opinion by one or more judges who disagree with the decision reached by the majority").

The type of dissent written by a judge will impact collegiality. Even a disabling dissent will be more palatable to the judge's colleagues if it focuses on such generally accepted themes as a trial judge's inherent discretion or a party's right to amend its complaint or answer. Therefore, because the judge will continue to sit with her colleagues for some time, a dissent should be as respectful of the majority as is consistent with its substantive point. Likewise, although the judge authoring the opinion of the majority of the court may challenge a concurrence or dissent, he or she should treat those opinions with respect.

PRACTICE EXERCISE

The opinions included in your law school casebooks usually are excerpts of full opinions. Accordingly, it may be difficult to identify some of the components discussed above within those opinions. Online commercial databases, however, include copies of the full court opinions. In fact, the publishers of those databases often *add* information to the opinions, such as headnotes for research purposes or a brief synopsis of the opinion right under the caption. For example, most U.S. Supreme Court opinions are preceded by a "syllabus," which is prepared by the Supreme Court's Reporter of Decisions and is not part of the opinion. (That content, while helpful for research purposes, is not technically part of the court's opinion and should not be cited as such.)

Using an online database, locate a district court opinion or appellate court opinion in your jurisdiction. Identify each of the abovementioned components in the opinion, noting where all of the information is included and whether and how the court labels that information.

CHAPTER 22

ALTERNATIVE DISPUTE RESOLUTION

■ ■ ■

By Ederlina Co, Mary-Beth Moylan, and
Stephanie J. Thompson

A. TYPES OF ALTERNATIVE DISPUTE RESOLUTION

There are many forms of Alternative Dispute Resolution (ADR). Most forms are variations on three generally recognized ADR processes: Negotiation, Mediation, and Arbitration.[1] The art of negotiation and the process of negotiating settlements are discussed in detail in Chapter 23. This chapter will introduce you to the processes of mediation and arbitration, and the role of practicing attorneys in these processes. There are many books and entire law school courses that are devoted entirely to these forms of ADR, and if this introductory chapter whets your appetite for more information, please consider reading more from other sources and enrolling in your school's course offerings on these subjects.[2]

Increasingly, negotiated settlements, mediation, and arbitration are the tools that practicing attorneys use to resolve disputes. Most litigated cases go through some form of ADR, and most contracts now include a provision requiring that the parties participate in some form of ADR to attempt to resolve the dispute before they have a right to file a complaint in court. Many contracts even require binding arbitration and abandon court adjudication altogether. If you have a brokerage account or have a credit card you have almost assuredly agreed to binding arbitration to resolve any disputes that arise out of those contractual relationships.

The fundamental differences between mediation and arbitration are important to note before exploring these processes and the role of practicing attorneys in them.

Mediation "is a process where the parties to a dispute are assisted by someone external to the dispute, the mediator, who aids their decision-

---

[1] For a more complete list of the types of Alternative Dispute Resolution that can be employed to resolve disputes, see Center for Public Resources, *The ABC's of ADR: A Dispute Resolution Glossary*, 13 (11) ALTERNATIVES (TO THE HIGH COST OF LITIGATION) 1 (1995).

[2] For one comprehensive book on Mediation, see LAURENCE J. BOULLE, MICHAEL T. COLATRELLA JR., & ANTHONY P. PICCHIONI, MEDIATION SKILLS AND TECHNIQUES (2008).

making about the dispute in various ways."[3] Mediators take an active role in the settlement process and attempt to help guide the parties to a mutual agreement. In mediation, however, the parties, and not the mediator, decide whether and how to settle a dispute. Mediation procedures are more flexible than court adjudicatory or arbitration proceedings, and if a party decides not to settle the dispute, the party may pursue other remedies.

Arbitration is an adjudicatory process presided over by a private neutral, the arbitrator, who, like a judge, rules on the merits of the dispute. Unlike a mediator, an arbitrator decides how to settle a dispute. There are many similarities between arbitration and a court trial, with attorneys presenting arguments, filing briefs, calling witnesses, and presenting other forms of evidence. Arbitration procedures are more informal than court trials, however.

In the course of a single legal dispute, the parties may attempt to come to resolution through negotiation (without the involvement of a third party), mediation (with the assistance of a neutral mediator), and arbitration (with a decision maker in a private setting).

B. MEDIATION

Mediation is a non-binding process where the parties and a mediator work together in a confidential setting to generate a mutually agreeable solution to a dispute. It is a forward-looking process that is designed to find a solution, not to produce a prevailing party. Unlike other types of dispute resolution, mediation is designed to promote communication and a better understanding of the dispute among the parties. In this regard, the mediator's job is to facilitate communication and help the parties prioritize their needs and concerns. A mediator allows the parties to explore their own potential solutions to the dispute and aids them in gaining a better understanding of their opponent's potential solutions to the dispute.

The mediator has no authority to impose a solution on parties to a dispute but will sometimes offer his opinion regarding what a fair settlement might be. The parties, with the assistance of their counsel, are the ones empowered to settle the dispute. There is no formal witness testimony or cross-examination or other common trappings of trials. Instead, there is a lot of talking, thinking, negotiating, and problem-solving. The mediator is only there to help the parties informally work toward developing their own agreement.

1. WHY MEDIATION

Any party to a dispute or conflict may decide to enter mediation. In addition, parties may be legally obligated to participate in mediation by

---

[3] *Id.*

contract, law, or court order. Regardless of how parties enter mediation, the benefits of mediation are many.

First, mediation is an alternative to the adversarial process. The focus in mediation is on finding a mutually acceptable solution, not to declare a winner. The parties are encouraged to clarify their problems and attempt to find a workable solution that is acceptable to all. By using a non-adversarial-process, the parties have a greater opportunity to continue or transform their relationship to serve their long-term interests. For example, businesses may be able to preserve their associations, employers and employees may be able to repair their working relationship, and divorced couples may be able to co-parent more effectively if they can resolve their disputes based on their complementary interests. Additionally, because the mediator is there to guide the parties to finding their own solution instead of imposing one, the mediation process has the added benefit of offering the parties personal satisfaction. Parties are shown to have greater satisfaction and acceptance of a resolution when they solve the problem themselves. This process can be therapeutic for many parties.

Second, mediation is significantly less expensive and faster than other forms of dispute resolution. Most cases filed with a court can take more than a year to resolve. With mediation, a dispute can be resolved as soon as the parties meet and agree to the terms of a settlement, thereby saving the parties the expense of litigation, including costs associated with discovery, motion practice, and trial. Most mediations, even in moderately complex matters like employment discrimination cases, can be mediated in a matter of hours or days.

Third, the parties to a mediation have complete control over whether they enter a mediated agreement. A mediator will not issue a binding decision on the dispute. Even if a party is required by contract, law, or court order to participate in a mediation, the party's decision to settle the dispute is voluntary. Mediation offers a no-risk opportunity to settle the case; if the mediation fails, the parties are free to continue their dispute and seek resolution through another form of ADR or in court.

Finally, mediation offers parties a flexible process and access to creative solutions for their disputes. The mediator and parties can shape the ground rules for their session. Although a mediator will guide the proceeding, neither the mediator nor the parties are bound by formal rules of evidence or procedure. There are also no set rules on how long a mediation session will last or the type of settlement that the parties may reach. In fact, in mediation, parties may not always resolve their dispute based on their legal rights and entitlements. Instead, their mediated agreement may reflect their views of what is right and wrong or because practical considerations help the parties move to end the dispute. For example, in contract disputes, the parties often ignore legal rights and simply rewrite the contract in the mediation so they can continue a once profitable business partnership instead of fighting over unclear contract language for years while both businesses suffer. The solutions that evolve from mediation are completely customized, allowing the parties to craft a solution suitable for their needs.[4]

There are drawbacks to mediation or circumstances that may weigh against pursuing mediation. For example, if a party wishes to establish legal precedent with a case, a mediated agreement will not serve this interest. Likewise, if a party is likely to prevail on a motion to dismiss or motion for summary judgment early in the case, the party may decide to pursue litigation. If other parties to the dispute have not yet joined the proceeding or have not yet been identified, the existing parties may not be able to properly resolve the dispute. Finally, if budget restrictions or the parties' attitude towards settlement will not allow serious negotiations, such circumstances may caution against participation in mediation.[5]

2. THE MEDIATION PROCESS

Mediations and mediator styles vary widely, but a mediation generally contains at least five stages: (1) the opening mediation session, (2) the parties' statements about the problem, (3) defining of the problem and the parties' interests, (4) problem solving and negotiation, and (5) the final mediated agreement and closure of proceedings.[6]

First, after the parties arrive at the neutral pre-determined location, the mediator makes introductory remarks explaining the mediation process, her particular way of working, and any ground rules that will govern the discussion. These common ground rules include instructions that only one person speaks at a time, no yelling, no interrupting, and questions need to be directed to each other, not to the mediator. During the mediator's opening remarks, the mediator usually describes her role as a neutral and impartial facilitator, the mediation objectives, the roles of the parties in the mediation, and emphasizes the confidential nature of the meeting. The mediator, at this time, also will likely ask the parties to state their commitment to the process and that they are willing participants in the mediation.

After the mediator's opening remarks, the parties then have an opportunity to describe the problem that brings them to the mediation. The mediator will likely ask both parties to explain their concerns, frustrations,

---

[4]   MEDIATION SKILLS AND TECHNIQUES, *supra* note 2, at 4–5.

[5]   BENNETT G. PICKER, MEDIATION PRACTICE GUIDE: A HANDBOOK FOR RESOLVING BUSINESS DISPUTES § 2.2.3 (2d ed. 2003).

[6]   MEDIATION SKILLS AND TECHNIQUES, *supra* note 2, at 61.

goals for the mediation, proposed outcomes, and anything else the parties feel they need to express at the outset.

Next, the mediator will gather more detailed information. The mediator will try to collect as much information as possible from the parties by asking questions and looking at documents, if documents have been provided. This information-gathering stage may occur in joint sessions with both parties present to promote the exchange of information between the parties or in private or separate caucuses to gather additional information that a party may not have felt comfortable sharing in a group setting.[7]

After the mediator has gathered information, the mediator will restate what she sees as the problems, the barriers to resolution, and synthesize the parties' concerns into a workable list of issues to be resolved. Frequently, hearing the dispute described from the perspective of a neutral facilitator is all it takes for the parties to start to arrive at a solution. The mediation is often the first time the parties have taken the time to think about the other side's perspective on the matter or even had a serious settlement discussion.

At this point, the parties will have an opportunity to discuss the issues that divide them. The mediator's involvement in these discussions varies and depends on the mediator's style. Some mediators employ a more facilitative style that is designed to help the parties generate ideas on how to resolve their dispute for themselves. Common facilitative techniques are asking the parties questions that help them see the dispute from the other side's perspective or help them question their own assumptions about their needs in the dispute. For example, the mediator might ask a party to explain how they arrived at a particular damage figure, hoping that the party might have insight into the weakness of their damage demand.

Other mediators employ a more evaluative mediation style. In evaluative mediation, the mediator takes a more directive approach in the discussion that is designed to advise the parties, to a lesser or greater degree, how the dispute should be fairly resolved. A common evaluative technique is to provide an opinion as to the merits of particular issue or position. In the example above concerning damages, the evaluative mediator, instead of asking questions to help the party to discover for itself a potential weakness with its damage demand, will simply explain why she thinks the party's damage demand is unreasonable. Evaluative mediators often employ a kind of shuttle diplomacy, alternately meeting separately

---

[7]   Shuttle mediations take place with each party in separate physical locations. In a shuttle mediation, the mediator shuttles messages to and from each party and serves as the sole avenue of communication between the parties. Shuttle mediations usually take place when legal or safety reasons require the parties be kept apart, when there is a gross imbalance of power between the parties, or when better communication would take place in separate meetings because of linguistic or cultural factors. MEDIATION SKILLS AND TECHNIQUES, *supra* note 2, at 244–45.

with each participant and privately explaining the weaknesses in their case and emphasizing the strengths of the other party's case. In this way the parties are often brought to agreement.

Although there is debate over whether a more facilitative style or a more evaluative style is preferable, most mediators employ some combination of facilitative and evaluative techniques. Both facilitative and evaluative mediation styles have proven effective in resolving disputes.

Finally, if the mediation goes well, the parties may reach an agreement. The parties may reach their agreement at any point during the proceeding. The mediator will ask the parties to put the terms of their agreement in writing, including any releases of liability. If the participants are parties to litigation, the parties may also agree to terminate the litigation and ask the court to enter judgment based on the parties' settlement agreement.

3. THE ATTORNEY ROLE IN MEDIATION

Practicing attorneys have several roles in the mediation process. Attorneys help clients decide whether to use mediation in the first place and must persuade opponents or other parties to participate in mediation. In addition, attorneys help clients identify their goals for the mediation, choose a mediator, and establish ground rules for the mediation. Attorneys also serve as advocates during mediation, or if the client will appear at the mediation without the attorney, attorneys must prepare the client to negotiate on his own behalf. Finally, attorneys must review mediated agreements and, in some instances, engage in post-mediation activities.[8]

The first question an attorney must advise a client on is whether to enter mediation at all, assuming it is not already court-ordered or required by statute. An attorney should consider whether the client has a reasonable chance of achieving a more valuable outcome by mediating the dispute rather than litigating it. Attorneys should pay close attention to the risks and costs of continuing the dispute. An attorney also needs to consider whether the parties will be able to negotiate with each other in a productive manner. Finally, an attorney should consider whether the parties can overcome typical obstacles that frustrate parties during the negotiating process. If mediation is appropriate, the attorney must then convince the opposing party or other parties to mediate. Attorneys are often concerned that their willingness to enter mediation will be viewed as a sign that the client does not have a strong legal case.[9] Familiarity with mediation and its benefits is usually the most compelling persuader for a reluctant

---

[8]   SARAH R. COLE ET AL., MEDIATION: LAW, POLICY, AND PRACTICE ch. 13 (2016–2017 ed.); DWIGHT GOLANN & JAY FOLBERG, MEDIATION THE ROLES OF ADVOCATE AND NEUTRAL 233–34 (2d ed. 2011).

[9]   MEDIATION: LAW, POLICY, AND PRACTICE, *supra* note 8, at § 13:2; MEDIATION THE ROLES OF ADVOCATE AND NEUTRAL, *supra* note 8, at 233, 241–44.

participant whether it is an opponent, other party, or the attorney's client.[10]

If the client agrees to mediate, attorneys must help clients identify their goals for the mediation, choose a mediator if one is not already designated, and establish the ground rules for the mediation. A client's goals can range from solving a problem to repairing a relationship to obtaining the best monetary outcome. A client's goals will help determine the type of mediator to select and the ground rules for the mediation. Who the mediator is, what style the mediator uses, and the ground rules of a mediation can drastically affect how a mediation proceeds.[11]

To select a mediator, an attorney should consider the mediator's qualifications, background, and experience, and importantly, whether the mediator will be able to establish trust and confidence with both parties and use a mediation style that fits both the parties and the pending dispute. Depending on the dispute, a facilitative mediator or evaluative mediator may be most appropriate. A mediator who focuses on broad issues or narrow issues may also prove to be the better choice.[12]

Regardless of who the mediator is, an attorney should also be prepared to "customize" the mediation to the client's needs by establishing ground rules for the mediation. Before the mediation, attorneys and clients should decide on the scope of the mediation, the style the mediator may use, and the extent of each party's participation or involvement in the mediation. Other ground rules attorneys should consider before mediation govern who is allowed or required to attend the mediation, whether discovery must be finished before mediation, and the confidentiality terms of the mediation and any settlement agreement.[13]

Once a mediation date has been set, attorneys must prepare for the session so that the mediation is productive. An attorney should prepare the arguments that will persuade the other side of the client's likelihood of success on the merits of a claim and a range of settlement possibilities that are acceptable to the client. An attorney should also have an understanding of a client's needs and interests, and a mediation strategy. Professor Lela Love's helpful acronym "CALLTHELAW" summarizes the primary contributions the attorney can make during mediation:

'Courtesy, cooperation, and candor;

Articulate client's interest, issues and proposals;

---

[10] MEDIATION: LAW, POLICY, AND PRACTICE, *supra* note 8, at § 13:2; STEPHEN J. WARE, PRINCIPLES OF ALTERNATIVE DISPUTE RESOLUTION § 4.24 (2d ed. 2007).

[11] MEDIATION THE ROLES OF ADVOCATE AND NEUTRAL, *supra* note 8, at 233–34.

[12] MEDIATION: LAW, POLICY, AND PRACTICE, *supra* note 8, at § 13:3; PRINCIPLES OF ALTERNATIVE DISPUTE RESOLUTION, *supra* note 10, at § 4.24; MEDIATION THE ROLES OF ADVOCATE AND NEUTRAL, *supra* note 8, at 233, 246–47.

[13] MEDIATION: LAW, POLICY, AND PRACTICE, *supra* note 8, at §§ 13:3–13.4.

Listen to own client and reframe for other side when helpful;

Level with the client regarding BATNA,[14] particularly the litigation alternative;

Tell a compelling, moving story, using simple clear language;

Highlight common interest;

Elicit and offer proposals responsive to interest of both parties;

Link objective criteria to support proposals;

Articulate the strengths of your litigation case; and

Win-win result.'[15]

Attorneys must be able to adapt their typical preparation techniques and strategies. In mediation, attorneys may spend more time on issues that have little legal significance because they are important to the parties. Attorneys may also spend as much time negotiating with their client as the opponent or other party.[16]

Integral to any mediation plan is a determination of the role of the client. An attorney should consider whether giving the client an active role would advance his interests and whether the client is someone who needs attorney protection. If the client will have a central role during mediation, attorneys must advise him of the mediation procedure and on how to conduct himself during mediation. This is especially true if the attorney will not be present. Finally, attorneys need to inform their clients about any confidentiality terms and what type of information is of strategic importance. The more prepared a client is, the more likely the client will settle and feel as though the mediation process was fair.[17]

Not all mediators will request a mediation brief or pre-mediation statement from the parties prior to the mediation, but most do. Attorneys should prepare their briefs or statements only after their mediator informs them about what he wants. A mediation brief is usually written in a persuasive tone. Professor Harold Abramson explains that a comprehensive pre-mediation submission should include: (a) a factual summary, including a description of important disputed and undisputed facts, (b) identification of the key legal issues in dispute and the party's view on each of the issues, (c) the relief sought, (d) any motions filed to date

---

[14] BATNA refers to the a party's Best Alternative To a Negotiated Agreement. Parties often enter mediation because they believe they may be able to achieve a better outcome to a dispute than they would without entering mediation. To make an informed decision about entering a mutual agreement during mediation, a party must know what his alternatives are to the agreement. His best alternative to the mutual agreement is his "BATNA." MEDIATION SKILLS AND TECHNIQUES, *supra* note 2, at 187–88.

[15] MEDIATION: LAW, POLICY, AND PRACTICE, *supra* note 8, at § 13:7.

[16] *Id.*§§ 13:6–13:7.

[17] *Id.*

and their status, (e) discovery and its status, including what the parties need to complete before trial, (f) the client's interests, (g) any prior settlement discussions, (h) why the case has not settled, including any obstacles the parties have encountered in prior settlement discussions, and (i) what the client wants from the mediator in terms of the mediator's style and level of involvement. Attorneys should attach to the brief key documentary evidence and should indicate who will attend the mediation. Attorneys may also need to prepare for a pre-mediation meeting with the mediator, which sometimes occurs in person or by telephone.[18]

Finally, if the parties reach a settlement agreement during mediation, the parties must draft and execute a settlement agreement preferably before leaving the mediation. Attorneys should pay special attention to any release of liability, including whether there is a "full and complete" release of any party and whether the mutual agreement is subject to a condition precedent or dependent on a subsequent event taking place, such as additional approval of the agreement by a board, agency, or others.[19]

If, on the other hand, the parties do not reach a settlement agreement despite best efforts, attorneys should pay attention to the necessities involved in terminating the mediation. For example, some parties may be required by law or contract to terminate the mediation with formal written notice to the other party.[20] Attorneys should also make clear to their clients that they may pursue mediation any time along the litigation timeline. Leaving a mediation on a good note with the opposing attorney and client, as well as the mediator, is the best approach, even if the parties could not reach a mutual agreement in the allotted time.

4. CROSS-CULTURAL CONSIDERATIONS IN MEDIATION

As parties increasingly turn to mediation to resolve their disputes, scholars have begun examining the effect race, prejudice, and bias play in mediation. Some scholars have expressed concern that traditionally disadvantaged groups, particularly people of color, experience unfair results in mediation. Empirical data supports these concerns. The University of New Mexico Schools of Law and Sociology performed a study of small claims court mediations in Albuquerque, New Mexico. In the study, hundreds of civil cases were randomly assigned to court adjudication or mediation. The results showed that participants of color fared less favorably in monetary outcomes in court-adjudicated cases and even worse in mediated cases compared to white participants. A claimant of color was likely to obtain fifteen percent less than a white claimant during mediation,

---

[18] *Id.* § 13:6.

[19] *Id.* §§ 7:4 & 13.8.

[20] *Id.* § 13.8.

and a respondent of color was likely to pay eighteen percent more than than a white respondent. In cases where co-mediators of color mediated the dispute, however, there was no disparity in mediated outcomes.[21]

Scholars have also begun examining the role of implicit bias in mediation. Within the mediation community, mediator neutrality is seen as vitally important because it helps give legitimacy to the mediation process. Whether a mediator is neutral is usually based on demonstrable criteria, including whether the mediator has a conflict of interest in the proceeding, whether the mediator conducts the proceeding even-handedly, and whether the mediator favors of one party over the other. Implicit bias, however, refers to the attitudes and stereotypes people unconsciously hold. Implicit bias can affect how we interact with others and can predict behavior. Using the Implicit Association Test, social scientists have found that most Americans (88%) have an implicit bias that favors white individuals over African American individuals. Moreover, social scientists have found that an individual's implicit biases, and not explicit cognitions, more accurately predict behavior. Although mediators do not have the authority to decide disputes and bind parties to a judgment, they do have significant influence on the mediation process and on the outcome of the proceedings.[22]

Cultural competence requires that mediators, as well as practicing attorneys who represent clients in mediation, remain vigilant about addressing bias, conscious or unconscious, to ensure fair mediation processes and outcomes. Mediators and participants alike must be aware of the tendency to stereotype, should challenge their working assumptions, and take time to inquire in a respectful manner how cultural differences affect how people view issues and processes.[23]

C. ARBITRATION

Arbitration is most commonly initiated when the parties to a contract have agreed to resolve their disputes outside of court through a private procedure. Arbitration is a creation of contract, which means that contracting parties may design an arbitration process that is formal (more like a trial) or informal (more like a discussion) as suits their needs and the complexity of the dispute. One of the most important arbitration design decisions that parties make is whether the arbitration will be binding or non-binding (or advisory). Binding arbitrations produce an "arbitration award" that is similar to a court judgment. Most states have laws that make arbitral awards almost as easy to execute as court judgments. In non-binding arbitrations, the parties do not need to adhere to the arbitrator's

---

[21] MARK D BENNETT & SCOTT HUGHES, THE ART OF MEDIATION 121–22 (2d ed. 2005).

[22] Carol Izumi, *Implicit Bias and the Illusion of Mediator Neutrality*, 34 WASH. U. J.L. & POL'Y 74–76, 79–96, 99–109 (2010).

[23] THE ART OF MEDIATION, *supra* note 21, at 123.

decision. The decision is merely advice as to how a neutral party believes that matter would be fairly resolved.

1. WHY ARBITRATION

There are a number of reasons why parties might prefer to have a private judge hear their dispute, but the most common reason is expediency. Private arbitration moves more quickly than most court procedures, especially in the age of tight court budgets. In courts all over the country, civil cases are postponed so that criminal cases can be heard. Since criminal defendants are constitutionally entitled to a speedy trial, the brunt of delays and limited judicial resources are frequently felt by civil litigants. There is no competition with criminal cases in the arbitration arena, which is entirely civil.

An additional benefit to arbitration includes the parties having significantly more control over the costs of resolving a dispute. The process can be tailored to directives of the private parties. The parties can also select who the "decider" of the dispute will be. Unlike trial courts, where a judge is usually assigned to a case through a random selection process, the parties to an arbitration can agree on a method for selecting their decision-maker and can select someone who has expertise in the particular field at issue.[24] Very often a list of arbitrators is presented to both parties, and a striking out process begins until an arbitrator is selected. Alternatively, under some arrangements, each party selects an arbitrator from an arbitration service and those arbitrators together select a third arbitrator who will hear the dispute.

In arbitration, the parties may also have more control over the timing and privacy of significant actions in the process, including discovery and the "trial." Subject to the arbitration agreement, the expansiveness of discovery and its timing are in the control of the litigants. And, since arbitration proceedings are not public, there is no concern about disclosure of private information through the public record of a court proceeding. While it is possible for the parties to agree to more limited discovery in court proceedings and to seal off certain filings, ultimately, the timing and scope of public disclosures in court are up to the judge. Hearings on discovery and pretrial motions in court are governed by the court's schedule, not the litigants. In arbitration, however, the parties and the parameters of their arbitration agreement are in charge.

There are some drawbacks to the arbitration process. First, the process can favor one party over another. If one party has considerably greater resources and can afford to engage in more discovery or research, there is

---

[24] Jarrod Wong, *Court or Arbitrator—Who Decides Whether Res Judicata Bars Subsequent Arbitrating Under the Federal Arbitration Act?,* 46 SANTA CLARA L. REV. 49 (2005) (articulating some advantages of arbitration as ease of procedure, speed and privacy, and drawing on expert knowledge).

little to equalize the playing field in an arbitration setting. In fact, if a contract provides for binding arbitration and one party cannot afford counsel to advise her in the proceeding, no panel of pro bono attorneys is likely to be available to assist her through a private litigation. Second, there is no jury and, hence, possibly less fairness. A single arbitrator usually hears the case, unless the contract or arbitration rules provide for a panel. Third, there may be no right of appeal from an unfavorable decision. Although usually an arbitration award can be enforced in court, the losing party to an arbitration may find herself without recourse through the courts. Some agreements to arbitrate provide for an appeal process, either in an arbitration setting or through an appeal to the courts. Many agreements, however, do not include an appellate process. Because arbitration is governed by private agreement, an omission of an appeal may result in a single erroneous ruling resolving the dispute.

2.   THE ARBITRATION PROCESS

An arbitration generally contains at least six stages: (1) initiation of the arbitration proceeding, (2) preparation for the arbitration, including appointment of the arbitrator or panel of arbitrators (3) prehearing or preliminary conferences to set a timetable and establish governing procedures and the scope of the arbitration, (4) the arbitration hearing, (5) the arbitrator's decision-making, and (6) the award.[25]

A party may initiate arbitration proceedings in three ways. First, if there is no prior agreement to arbitrate, parties to a dispute can initiate arbitration through a submission agreement or voluntary participation. Second, and more commonly, a party will initiate arbitration proceedings because the parties are bound by a contract clause to arbitrate disputes. The complaining party, the claimant, serves a demand to arbitrate on the responding party, the respondent. In contrast to a court proceeding, the respondent does not have to file an answer to the demand or notice. If the respondent does not file an answer, the arbitrator considers the claims denied. Finally, some courts will order parties to enter arbitration. Although the arbitration is mandatory, it is usually nonbinding.[26]

Once parties have initiated an arbitration, the parties must prepare for the proceeding. During the preparation stage, which can take weeks or months, the parties will select an arbitrator or a panel of arbitrators. The arbitrator or panel will then address the scope of pre-arbitration discovery. Similar to other aspects of arbitration, the arbitration agreement usually determines the extent of the parties' discovery. Some agreements will allow for discovery in accordance with the Federal Rules of Civil Procedure.

---

[25]   JOHN W. COLLEY & STEVEN LUBET, ARBITRATION ADVOCACY §§ 2.1.1–2.1.6 (2d ed. 2003).

[26]   *Id.* § 2.1.1; ABRAHAM P. ORDOVER & ANDREA DONEFF, ALTERNATIVES TO LITIGATION: MEDIATION, ARBITRATION, AND THE ART OF DISPUTE RESOLUTION 147 (2d ed. 2003); PRINCIPLES OF ALTERNATIVE DISPUTE RESOLUTION, *supra* note 10, at § 2.36(b).

Others incorporate rules from organizations like the American Arbitration Association, which typically limits discovery but also provides the arbitrator with wide discretion with respect to discovery. Although the general goals behind arbitration weigh against the parties conducting extensive discovery, the arbitrator's preference may be the strongest factor determining the extent of pre-arbitration discovery.[27]

In complex disputes, the arbitrator will conduct a prehearing or preliminary conference for purposes of defining the issues and the scope of the arbitrator's decision. In addition, the parties can address scheduling and any procedural, discovery, or evidentiary matters. During the prehearing, the parties can submit necessary motions or objections, which the arbitrator will rule on at the arbitration hearing assuming no further briefing is necessary. The parties can conduct any necessary communications with the arbitrator at the hearing because once the arbitration begins, the arbitrator cannot conduct ex parte conversations with the parties or the parties' attorneys.[28]

In almost all cases, an arbitrator then conducts an evidentiary-type hearing. An arbitrator will conduct the hearing in similar fashion to a court trial. Both parties make opening statements, introduce evidence and conduct direct examination of their witnesses, cross-examine the opposing party's witnesses, and make closing statements and arguments. The arbitrator often questions the witnesses during the proceeding. Usually, the parties do not adhere to strict rules of evidence, but the parties are subject to procedural, fairness, relevance, and materiality objections. Although parties may waive an oral hearing and submit the dispute on the papers, parties rarely do this. [29]

If the issues in the arbitration are not complex, the arbitrator may state her decision as soon as the hearing is closed. If the issues are complex, or there are multiple arbitrators involved, more typically, arbitrators will take the matter under submission and meet later to reach their final decision. Sometimes, the parties will submit post-hearing memoranda or briefs. Usually, arbitrators will issue their decision within thirty days.[30]

Finally, after a necessary deliberation, the arbitrator will render a decision in the form of an award. The arbitrator may give it orally, but usually, it is written and signed by the arbitrator or arbitrators. Unlike a

---

[27] ALTERNATIVES TO LITIGATION: MEDIATION, ARBITRATION, AND THE ART OF DISPUTE RESOLUTION, *supra* note 26, at 148; PRINCIPLES OF ALTERNATIVE DISPUTE RESOLUTION, *supra* note 10, at § 2.36; ARBITRATION ADVOCACY, *supra* note 25, at § 2.1.2.

[28] ARBITRATION ADVOCACY, *supra* note 25, at § 2.1.3; ALTERNATIVES TO LITIGATION: MEDIATION, ARBITRATION, AND THE ART OF DISPUTE RESOLUTION, *supra* note 26, at 150.

[29] PRINCIPLES OF ALTERNATIVE DISPUTE RESOLUTION, *supra* note 10, at § 2.37; ALTERNATIVES TO LITIGATION: MEDIATION, ARBITRATION, AND THE ART OF DISPUTE RESOLUTION, *supra* note 26, at 151–52; ARBITRATION ADVOCACY, *supra* note 25, at § 2.1.4.

[30] ALTERNATIVES TO LITIGATION: MEDIATION, ARBITRATION, AND THE ART OF DISPUTE RESOLUTION, *supra* note 26, at 152–53; ARBITRATION ADVOCACY, *supra* note 25, at § 2.1.5.

court decision, oftentimes the arbitrator does not include reasoning with the award. In larger cases, however, arbitrators will provide a statement of reasons in support of their decision if the parties request or require it. As noted above, depending on the arbitration agreement, the arbitrator's award may be binding or nonbinding. If nonbinding, a party can reject the award and proceed to trial in court.[31]

Courts generally do not like to upset arbitral awards, and federal courts are required to stay proceedings in cases that are filed where the issue presented should have been referred to arbitration through an agreement of the parties.[32]

3. THE ATTORNEY ROLE IN ARBITRATION

Practicing attorneys contribute at each stage of the arbitration process, and their contribution is similar in many ways to their role in court litigation. Attorneys must help clients draft an arbitration demand on behalf of a claimant, or an answer to a demand on behalf of the respondent. In addition, attorneys must prepare and represent clients at any prehearing or preliminary hearing. Next, attorneys must represent their clients at the arbitration hearing. Finally, attorneys must review the arbitration award and, in some cases, engage in post-arbitration advocacy.[33]

First, attorneys must help clients draft an arbitration demand or response to the demand. A demand is the client's notice to the other party of his intent to commence the arbitration process. Although there is no set content or format for a demand, an attorney should include the names of all of the parties, a statement of facts in chronological order, a quote with the precise language of the arbitration clause, a statement of the party's claim or claims and how the claims relate to the contract arbitration clause, and the relief the party seeks. The attorney should ensure that the demand is timely served on the other party. If, on the other hand, the client receives a demand, the respondent is not required to respond or answer the demand. An arbitrator will consider a failure to respond as a denial of the claims. As a practical matter, however, if the client has a choice to respond to the demand, the best interest of the client is to respond with any defenses, denials, contentions, and counter-claims.[34]

Attorneys must prepare to represent their clients at the prehearing or preliminary hearing. During this hearing, an arbitrator can address the arbitrability of any or all of the pending issues and any disputes about

---

[31] ALTERNATIVES TO LITIGATION: MEDIATION, ARBITRATION, AND THE ART OF DISPUTE RESOLUTION, *supra* note 26, at 153; ARBITRATION ADVOCACY, *supra* note 25, at § 2.1.6; JAY FOLBERG ET AL. RESOLVING DISPUTES: THEORY, PRACTICE, AND LAW 585 (2d ed. 2010).

[32] 9 U.S.C. § 3 (2006).

[33] ARBITRATION ADVOCACY, *supra* note 25, chs. 3–6.

[34] *Id.* §§ 3.1–3.2.3.

discovery. The parties can also exchange documents and lists of witnesses, enter stipulations of fact, address scheduling matters, and explore settlement possibilities outside of the arbitrator's presence. The preliminary hearing is usually a party's first chance to make an impression on the arbitrator, so an attorney should present as cooperative and collaborative. In most cases, an arbitrator will ask for the parties to submit a prehearing position statement or opening brief, which informs the arbitrator of the relevant facts, claims, supporting law, and relief sought. Typically, the brief is a five to ten-page memorandum.[35]

Next, attorneys must represent their clients at the arbitration hearing. Similar to preparing for a trial, an attorney must prepare the client, witnesses, and exhibits for arbitration. Attorneys should have a persuasive story that includes a logical theory and theme with moral force to tell the arbitrators. Attorneys must prepare their clients by explaining the arbitration process and how it is different from litigation. Attorneys must also build their case in chief around the legal elements of each claim. They must prepare their clients and witnesses to testify on direct examination and plan their cross-examination of the opponent party and opponent witnesses. Finally, attorneys must prepare their exhibits before arbitration.[36]

The procedural rules at a court trial, including the Federal Rules of Civil Procedure and the Federal Rules of Evidence, will not necessarily apply to an arbitration hearing. Attorneys should check the arbitration clause for specific rules that may apply during the hearing and consult with the individual arbitrators well before the hearing. Once the arbitrator calls the hearing to order, the claimant and respondent may present their opening statements. Attorneys for the claimant and respondent then have an opportunity to present their case in chief or defense through direct examination and cross-examination. Finally, the attorneys usually have an opportunity to present their final argument, although sometimes an arbitrator will ask the attorneys to submit post-hearing briefs instead of, or in addition to, the final argument.[37]

Finally, the arbitrator will fashion a written award based on the facts and applicable law of the case. The arbitrator's award usually does not include reasoning like a judge's written opinion, but the award should include a ruling on all of the pending claims and damages requests. In this regard, a typical arbitration award resembles a jury verdict form. As noted

---

[35] *Id.* §§ 3.5–3.5.14.

[36] *Id.* at ch. 4; PRINCIPLES OF ALTERNATIVE DISPUTE RESOLUTION, *supra* note 10, at § 2.37.

[37] ARBITRATION ADVOCACY, *supra* note 25, at ch. 5 & § 6.1; PRINCIPLES OF ALTERNATIVE DISPUTE RESOLUTION, *supra* note 10, at § 2.37.

above, the award may be binding or nonbinding depending on the parties' initial arbitration agreement.[38]

4.   CROSS-CULTURAL CONSIDERATIONS IN ARBITRATION

In the context of international business agreements, international commercial arbitration is the preferred method of dispute resolution. Starting in 1976, the United Nations Commission on International Trade Law (UNCITRAL) developed rules for international arbitration that have been widely adopted and revised repeatedly throughout the years.[39] The most recent major version was produced in 2010, and there was a slight addition in 2013.[40] The new rules include provisions that address multiple-party arbitration, and objections to expert witnesses. There are a number of international arbitration associations and services that provide arbitrators well-versed in international commercial business laws.

The expectation in the arena of international commercial law is that parties will submit to arbitration in their contracts. To be well-versed in this area of law is to also understand the UNCITRAL rules and the procedures for enforcing judgments across borders when an arbitral award has issued. While a detailed discussion of those procedures is best left for a course in international commercial arbitration, it is important for all lawyers to understand the expectations of conducting business in a global setting. When confronted with a problem involving the Convention on the International Sale of Goods, or any other cross-border legal transaction, attorneys need to look for and plan for international arbitration provisions in the agreements that they draft and review for clients.

PRACTICE EXERCISE

Take an assignment you are working on in your course. Divide into groups of five. One student should take on the role of the mediator. Two should act as the clients, and two should act as the advocates, one for each side of the dispute.

The goal for each group is to explore the possibility of negotiated settlement with the help of a neutral mediator.

The mediator will need to decide the following: (1) whether to meet with the parties together or in separate sessions, (2) whether to adopt a facilitative or evaluative approach, or some combination of both, and (3) whether to

---

[38] ARBITRATION ADVOCACY, *supra* note 25, at § 6.6; PRINCIPLES OF ALTERNATIVE DISPUTE RESOLUTION, *supra* note 10, at § 2.37.

[39] United Nations Commission on International Trade law, UNCITRAL Texts and Status, http://www.uncitral.org/uncitral/en/uncitral_texts/arbitration/2010Arbitration_rules.html (last visited Dec. 3, 2017).

[40] *Id.*

encourage a settlement that may impact constitutional principles or public policies.

The advocates will need to decide the following: (1) whether to allow your clients to talk to each other or the mediator without you present, (2) whether to encourage a settlement, and (3) whether to take a conciliatory or aggressive position in the negotiation.

The clients will need to decide the following: (1) whether to take a conciliatory or aggressive approach in the negotiation, and (2) whether to consider settlement.

Act out the mediation. At the end of the mediation, discuss any agreements that were reached, consider which processes worked best and why, and explain why you made the decisions you did based on your role in the mediation.

CHAPTER 23

NEGOTIATION AND SETTLEMENT

■ ■ ■

By Adrienne Brungess

A. THE ROLE OF NEGOTIATION IN LAWYERING

Virtually all careers in law will include work that requires lawyers to employ negotiation skills. For example, transactional attorneys negotiate contracts or policies while shepherding the process and coordinating the moving parts of the transaction; litigators must attempt to resolve pre-trial issues such as discovery or calendaring disagreements through negotiation. Negotiation may be necessary at various stages of a case from its inception through final resolution in court, mediation, arbitration, or by way of the parties reaching a full agreement on all matters.

Additionally, litigators are generally expected to make efforts to resolve disputes by way of settlement and avoid the need for court appearances whenever possible. In fact, attorneys or clients can be sanctioned by the court for failing to do so.[1] This is true at every stage of litigation, from pre-trial motions to appellate proceedings. Settlement gives attorneys and parties an element of control in the process that they lose when handing the case to a judge or arbitrator to decide. Further, parties are more likely to accept and abide by terms they helped create as opposed to terms that have been imposed upon them without their consent. Negotiated settlement reduces costs for the parties and the court. And, negotiated settlement relieves the courts from congested calendars and allows courts to focus on matters that are more appropriate for judicial review and intervention.

Frequently, cases will resolve by way of assisted negotiation, where a mediator, evaluator, or arbitrator participates in the negotiation to facilitate progress. Parties may choose to participate in mediation, for example, and elicit the help of an experienced, objective third party to facilitate the process. Or, parties may be required to participate in mediation or arbitration during the course of litigation or appeal.[2]

---

[1]   *See* CAL. FAM. CODE § 271; CAL. CIV. PROC. CODE § 2023.010(i).

[2]   *See* Chapter 22 on Alternative Dispute Resolution.

For all these reasons, negotiation skills are important to the successful practice of law.

B. THE IMPORTANCE OF PREPARATION

A skilled negotiator prepares her case diligently. Success at the negotiation table comes from a clear understanding of both parties' goals and motivations, the case facts, the governing law, and a thorough evaluation of the strengths and weaknesses of both parties' positions. Attempting to negotiate when unprepared will fail to serve the client; moreover, when opposing counsel is prepared, it will ultimately put the unprepared attorney and her client at a serious disadvantage in the negotiation. Thus, preparation is a source of power and confidence in the process.

A skilled negotiator is also creative. Negotiation is most successful when all participants are not only willing but eager to participate in the process and create the best possible options and terms for everyone. Keen understanding of the facts of the case and relevant objective criteria allow the negotiator to brainstorm more offers and compromises, thus generating more options for potential resolution. Further, the negotiator must have all the relevant information. A good attorney-client relationship is crucial to this goal. If the client does not fully trust her lawyer, she may not fully disclose relevant facts, which could impair the successful resolution of the case.[3]

1. CONSIDERING GENDER AND MULTI-CULTURAL CONCERNS

A skilled negotiator is aware of differences in communication styles between genders and among cultures. Culture creates rules for how disagreements should be resolved and provides part of the framework for interpreting behavior and motives.[4] Further, culture plays a significant role in how individuals exchange and process information.

> Cultures are like underground rivers that run through our lives and relationships, giving us messages that shape our perceptions, attributions, judgments, and ideas of self and other. Though cultures are powerful, they are often unconscious, influencing conflict and attempts to resolve conflict in imperceptible ways. Cultures are more than language, dress, and food customs. Cultural groups may share race, ethnicity, or nationality, but they

---

[3]   *See* Chapters 13 on Interviewing the Client, 14 on Counseling the Client.

[4]   Kevin Avruch, *Culture as Context, Culture as Communication: Considerations for Humanitarian Negotiators,* 9 HARV. L REV. 391, 395–396 (Spring 2004) (citing MARC HOWARD ROSS, CULTURE AND IDENTITY IN COMPARATIVE POLITICAL ANALYSIS, IN COMPARATIVE POLITICS: RATIONALITY, CULTURE, AND STRUCTURE 42 [Mark Irving Lichbach & Alan S. Zuckerman eds., 1997]).

also arise from cleavages of generation, socioeconomic class, sexual orientation, ability and disability, political and religious affiliation, language, and gender to name only a few.[5]

Cultural and gender stereotyping can affect a party's or negotiator's behavior and performance. Overcoming the impact of stereotypes is difficult. Thus, a skilled negotiator will consider how stereotypes might affect both the behavior of the parties, as well as her own, before communicating with counterparts. Although the extent to which stereotypes affect self-confidence or perceived power is unclear, evidence shows that altering a perceived stereotype can positively affect performance in the negotiation context.[6]

When assessing how culture will affect the process, consider whether the events involved in the case are viewed differently by people from different cultures. For example, assume local police officers arrest a suspect in a public area. Witnesses may perceive the event differently depending on each person's prior experience with law enforcement; a witness with a negative experience with police may give a different account than one with only positive experiences.

To assess how culture might affect the negotiation process, consider the following:

a.   The Role of Conflict

How is conflict viewed in each party's culture?[7] If the parties do not agree that conflict can play a useful role in the negotiation process, they will respond differently. Conflict brings about the exchange of ideas; conflict challenges beliefs and methods and often is the catalyst for change. For example, conflict is socially acceptable and sometimes even encouraged in the United States. Citizens are given countless forums in which they may voice and discuss their complaints. However, other cultures consider public conflict dishonorable and shameful.[8]

b.   The Role of Formality and Emotion

Is formality valued? Americans are generally informal compared to other cultures. Some cultures view addressing another informally in the business context as disrespectful, where informality with contemporaries

---

[5]   Michelle LeBaron. *"Culture and Conflict." Beyond Intractability*, Conflict Information Consortium, University of Colorado, Boulder, posted: July 2003 available at https://www.beyond intractability.org/essay/culture_conflict (last visited Dec. 20, 2017).

[6]   Kray, Galinsky, & Thompson, *Reversing the Gender Gap in Negotiations: An Exploration of Stereotype Regeneration,* Vol. 87, No. 2 ORGANIZATIONAL BEHAVIOR & HUMAN DECISION PROCESSES 386, 407 (March 2002).

[7]   STEFAN H. KRIEGER & RICHARD K. NEUMANN, JR., ESSENTIAL LAWYERING SKILLS 60 (4th ed. 2011).

[8]   *Id.*

is common in the United States. Consider whether informality on your part might imply lack of preparedness or an inappropriate demonstration of respect.[9] Evaluate also whether it is culturally acceptable to show or discuss emotions. Some cultures find emotional matters personal and private, and members do not readily express themselves emotionally.[10] Thus, it is important to consider the emotional context and how to elicit trust and candor.

c. Body Language

What does body language communicate among the different cultures represented? Nonverbal communication is a significant part of how people communicate and it varies among cultures. An American might pat a child on the head as a sign of affection; however, many Asian cultures consider it inappropriate to touch the head, which is a sacred body part. Thus, "touching may convey closeness in some contexts and create offense in others."[11] In the Middle East, the left hand is used for bodily hygiene and should not be used to touch another. And, in Muslim cultures, it is considered inappropriate to touch someone of the opposite gender.

Further, in mainstream Western culture, eye contact is perceived as signifying honesty and respect; Westerners may question credibility when a counterpart does not maintain eye contact.[12] However, in some Hispanic, Asian, Middle Eastern, and Native American cultures, eye contact is considered rude or lacking appropriate deference.

As part of preparing a case, be aware of cultural issues and stereotypes that may affect the process. But be realistic. When preparing a case, you cannot anticipate every cultural detail that may arise. Instead, try to "develop an instinct for situations where another person's cultural assumptions may be very different from yours."[13] A skilled negotiator will look for signs of cultural differences and try to determine appropriate responses.[14] Awareness and flexibility are crucial to this end.

> "A generous frame of mind on your part and a genuine liking for other people—and their differences—go a long way. . . . So do flexibility, empathy, patience, and a reluctance to see things in judgmental terms. It helps, also, to understand how your own culture 'shapes [your] attitudes, values, biases, and assumptions about lawyering' and about social interaction and life generally."[15]

---

[9] *Id.*

[10] *Id.*

[11] LeBaron, *supra* note 5.

[12] KRIEGER & NEUMANN, *supra* note 7, at 62.

[13] *Id.* at 64 (emphasis omitted).

[14] *Id.*

[15] *Id.* (citing Carwina Weng, *Multicultural Lawyering: Teaching Psychology to Develop Cultural Self-Awareness*, 11 CLINICAL L. REV. 369, 398 (2005)).

A skilled negotiator is tolerant of differences and able to suspend judgment.[16] Differences in the way people interpret information can lead to or escalate conflict. Try to understand something about the other person's cultural foundation and values to better interpret emotions expressed in cross-cultural negotiations.[17]

2. FACT INVESTIGATION AND ANALYSIS

In preparing your case, you will invariably have to investigate facts to fully understand all relevant aspects of the matter. As the attorney on the case, you must determine if the information you have is complete. When speaking with the client, did you establish a relationship of trust that will ensure your client has been completely forthcoming?[18] Are there other witnesses you need to speak to? Are you able to elicit reliable information from witnesses? Do documents exist that would support your client's position? Evaluate your factual sources thoroughly.

A skilled negotiator will consider her professional obligations when investigating facts. When contacting witnesses, for example, you cannot falsely represent yourself or your role. You also cannot communicate about the case with a person you know to be represented by counsel without authorization, or use methods to obtain evidence that violate the witness's legal rights.[19]

The negotiator is generally more reliant upon facts than law in the negotiation context; thus, you may spend more time investigating facts than researching law. Further, effective organization of facts will educate the negotiator about the case and help him determine where more investigation may be necessary. Good fact organization and analysis is crucial to the negotiator's understanding of the strengths and weaknesses of the case.

a. Story Model

When evaluating your facts, consider whether they logically lend themselves to a chronological organization scheme. The "story" is generally how cases are presented to a fact-finder—telling a compelling story from beginning to end. Further, a particular fact may have more significance when viewed in the sequential context of other facts. Therefore, organizing the facts chronologically can help the negotiator locate inconsistencies in the evidence and thereby assess the reliability of particular factual sources. It can also help the negotiator locate and fill in gaps in the story provided by the client or another witness. A chart that details the evidentiary source,

---

[16] Avruch, *supra* note 4, at 406.

[17] LeBaron, *supra* note 5.

[18] *See* Chapter 13 on Interviewing the Client.

[19] KRIEGER & NEUMANN, *supra* note 7, at 222–223 (*citing* MODEL RULES 4.1(a); 4.2; 4.4(a)).

the account given, and any gaps or inconsistencies can be useful to chronological organization and understanding of your client's story.[20]

b. Elements

Alternatively, if the case involves a dispute over a rule that has multiple legal elements, it may be most effective to organize the facts topically by element rather than chronologically. To organize the facts by the governing rule, determine what is required to support the cause of action (or refute it). Once identified, state the elements as a factual proposition, in the context of the facts of the case, and identify what evidence is required to show that particular element (or what a decision-maker must ultimately find for the plaintiff to prevail).[21] Then, organize the facts discovered under each proposition—will the element be supported by documentary evidence or witness testimony? What evidence would you use in court to make an argument that the element is or is not met? A chart that includes the elements, factual propositions, and supporting evidence is a useful way to organize this information and access it quickly later.[22]

3. THOROUGH RESEARCH

The skilled negotiator has a complete understanding of the law governing the case; but, the law is generally not used as a "hammer" in negotiations. The entire point of a negotiated settlement is to resolve the problem outside the strict parameters of the law, allowing more creative solutions. However, you must understand the legal basis of the underlying claims and defenses and what the law allows or prohibits.

When preparing for a negotiation, you should create a research plan as you would when assessing any new case. You will identify the specific legal issues that may be relevant to the terms being negotiated, educate yourself (if necessary) with secondary sources, locate applicable primary authority, update all your findings,[23] and ultimately determine the strengths and weaknesses of your legal case.

4. BATNAs AND BOTTOM LINES

A skilled negotiator understands that where parties' interests cannot be mutually satisfied, the negotiation could fail. As you prepare, consider what your client's "bottom line" is—the point where you will walk away from the bargaining table.

Additionally, determine your client's **B**est **A**lternative **T**o a **N**egotiated **A**greement (BATNA) and speculate as to the other parties' BATNAs. The

---

[20]   *Id.* at 160.

[21]   *Id.* at 149–150.

[22]   *Id.* at 150.

[23]   *See* Chapter 25 on Research Strategies.

BATNA represents the standard against which any proposed agreement will be measured.[24] What is your client's best-case scenario if the negotiation fails? What are the potential alternatives to a negotiated settlement? Will one of the parties pursue a lawsuit? Is the alternative better than what is currently being offered? "Good planning involves imagining the other party's BATNA as well. Unless you have a good idea of the other side's alternatives to settling with you, you really do not know how strong or weak you are in the negotiation."[25]

A skilled negotiator will first determine her BATNA before assessing the client's bottom line. The BATNA will assist you in planning ranges of offers that might be acceptable along the way to a final agreement. Use this information to create options and alternatives that would be acceptable to the client and provide all parties some benefit. Be wary of focusing too much on the bottom line; early focus on the bottom line can inhibit problem-solving and exploration of options. Bottom lines also lead to positional approaches (see below) rather than collaboration.

5. PRE-NEGOTIATION COMMUNICATION

In most situations, you will have had some form of communication with the other relevant people participating in the negotiation (opposing counsel, or party, or, perhaps, both) before sitting down at the negotiation table; you probably spoke on the phone or exchanged e-mails. Frequently, formal correspondence about the case may have been exchanged or the case may already be in litigation.

Always be thoughtful about the content and tone of your correspondence about a case. Your writing may be establishing the first impression about you; the reader will begin to assess your credibility and preparedness at this stage. It will also reflect your willingness to engage in meaningful discussions about resolving the case or particular pertinent issues.[26]

A skilled negotiator will consider the effect a statement or position may have on later efforts to resolve the matter. An unreasonable position taken early in the case may undermine your credibility later when you ultimately accept a more reasonable solution that would have been acceptable to your client from the beginning.

---

[24] KRIEGER & NEUMANN, *supra* note 7, at 304.

[25] *Id.*

[26] *See* Chapter 15 on Professional Correspondence.

C. AT THE TABLE—OVERVIEW OF NEGOTIATION STYLES AND METHODS

The negotiation process itself has four main stages: (1) the opening, (2) the information stage, (3) the value-exchange stage, and (4) the closing.[27] During the opening stage, participants establish rapport with one another, assess each other's trustworthiness, establish tone, and determine the issues to be negotiated.[28]

In the second stage, the information stage, participants ask questions and exchange relevant information necessary to the foundation of the agreement. During this stage, the parties should affirm facts, gather missing information, and cautiously share concerns and needs. A skilled negotiator will not gloss over the second stage and will ensure that pertinent information has been exchanged; it can be detrimental to begin dealing before all relevant information has been explored. Information provides a greater opportunity to create value for both parties; additionally, offers that follow will have greater credibility because they follow an investment of time and discussion.

In the third stage, the value-exchange stage, the parties make offers and concessions. This stage of give-and-take is known as the negotiation dance.[29] This is the distributive stage, where the value created in the information stage is divided. Parties will make proposals and also concessions. Here, the negotiator tries to advance the interests of her own client and maximize her client's outcome. The negotiator should focus on the best outcome for the client overall and how to create a deal the client will be pleased with.[30]

Finally, the negotiation will close—hopefully with a full or partial agreement. In the case of agreement, the parties will obtain an appropriate level of commitment, usually by way of a verbal promise to be confirmed in writing later.

Negotiators are people with individual styles and varying personality traits. There is no single way to approach a negotiation, and you should be sincere. However, there are strategies and methods that are considered more effective in reaching the best resolution for all parties involved. A skilled negotiator will assess the case and select different techniques to fit the unique situation. Thus, you should be aware of strategies from both the problem-solving and adversarial models.

---

[27] *See* LEIGH L. THOMPSON, THE MIND AND HEART OF THE NEGOTIATOR (4th Ed. 2009); CHARLES B. CRAVER, EFFECTIVE LEGAL NEGOTIATION & SETTLEMENT (7th Ed.2012).

[28] *See* CRAVER, *supra* note 27, at 78–80.

[29] HOWARD RAIFFA, THE ART AND SCIENCE OF NEGOTIATION (1985).

[30] *See* CRAVER, *supra* note 27, at 118–119.

Sometimes parties mistakenly argue for positions that are irreconcilable with their underlying interests. The following example illustrates the difference between the positional-adversarial and problem-solving approaches: Two sisters each want the very last orange. They argue—who will get the one remaining orange? Neither one wants to budge and give the orange to the other. Their mother comes, takes the orange, and cuts it in half and gives each one-half. Both sisters are unhappy. Then, their mother asks them each what they want the orange for. The first sister answers that the recipe she is making calls for the zest of one orange. The second sister answers that the recipe she is using calls for the juice of one orange. Now neither has what she needs because no one inquired about the other's interests.[31]

1. PROBLEM-SOLVING MODEL—INTEREST-BASED APPROACH

The most popular model of negotiation that is currently taught is generally known as integrative or problem-solving negotiation.[32] In this model, negotiators focus on the underlying interests and goals of the parties, not their positions. Counsel will work together to create options for resolution that will substantially satisfy each party's fundamental interests and thus ultimately benefit everyone. This method can work in both dispute and transactional contexts.

Integrative bargaining seeks to "expand the pie." Skilled negotiators focus on the value that each side brings to the deal and explores the various options for mutual benefit. The theory is that positional bargaining fails to generate useful agreements. Negotiators that hold fast to a position generally disregard their clients' real concerns.[33] To expand the pie, consider viewing the matter from the other party's perspective. Those who can take the counterpart's perspective are likely to discover hidden agreements and areas for mutual gain.[34]

Crucial to this method is the use of objective criteria to help resolve disputed terms. A skilled negotiator will use reliable objective sources to support the fairness of a proposal.[35] Look for independent standards and customs, market rates and trends, local economic statistics, and other similar sources of information. In this regard, a Google search can be productive. For example, are you negotiating a salary? You can research local salaries for similarly-situated individuals by locating statistics or employment

---

[31] FISHER & URY, GETTING TO YES: NEGOTIATING AGREEMENT WITHOUT GIVING IN (2011).

[32] *See* FISHER & URY, *supra* note 31; MENKEL-MEADOW, SCHNEIDER, LOVE, NEGOTIATION PROCESSES FOR PROBLEM SOLVING 89 (2006); CRAVER, *supra* note 27, at 133; KRIEGER & NEUMANN, *supra* note 7, at 302.

[33] FISHER & URY, *supra* note 31, at 4–5.

[34] THOMPSON, *supra* note 27, at 81–82.

[35] FISHER & URY, *supra* note 31, at 83.

advertisements. Reliable objective sources are usually more useful than legal authority when trying to reach an understanding about a disputed term.

Summary of Problem Solving Model Process

- Identify both/all parties' interests.

- Research relevant legal authority.

- Locate applicable objective sources.

- Assess BATNA and ways to improve it.

- Set clear and reasonable goals; identify common goals.

- Consider alternative solutions and possible options.

- Plan starting points, bottom lines, and concessions.

2. ADVERSARIAL APPROACH

This approach is more traditional and is also known as positional or distributive bargaining.[36] This method envisions a pie of limited resources that must be divided, which is where value is claimed rather than generated. This type of bargaining is also called "zero-sum" negotiation—for one side to gain the other must lose.[37] This approach is more frequently employed in the dispute-resolution context. Here, the negotiator focuses on how to maximize her client's gain and minimize the loss. Counsel will trade offers and counteroffers, ultimately reaching agreement or impasse, attempting to persuade the other to concede based on argument, or sometimes threat.[38]

The negotiator who takes an adversarial approach to an issue will probably consider, or even chart out, her own client's goals and bottom lines and try to estimate those of the other party. The goal in the negotiation will be to convince the other side to concede as close to her bottom line as possible, while holding as closely as possible your client's goal or target.[39]

Summary of Adversarial Model Process

- Assess BATNA and how to improve it.

- Determine client's bottom line without revealing it. That does not mean you should lie about it; however, this approach works only if it is kept hidden from the opposing side.[40]

---

[36] *See* CRAVER, *supra* note 27, at 133; KRIEGER & NEUMANN, *supra* note 7, at 302.

[37] KRIEGER & NEUMANN, *supra* note 7, at 301.

[38] *Id.* at 332.

[39] *Id.* at 333, 335.

[40] THOMPSON, *supra* note 27, at 45–46.

- Set realistic but optimistic goals. Your target points define the upper limit of what you can get in the deal. First offers represent an important "anchor point." Negotiators who set high goals generally claim more value in the negotiation.[41]

- Plan your concessions.[42] Most negotiators plan to make concessions during the course of the dance. Consider how you will justify the concessions you make so you retain credibility and how you will time them during the course of the process.

D. E-NEGOTIATIONS

Technological advances and the widespread internet have dramatically impacted the way lawyers negotiate. Consider how easy it is to use digital media to communicate with clients or counsel in another state or country. Therefore, negotiations are more commonly taking place via digital channels rather than in-person meetings. Attorneys can discuss and resolve matters via email, online chat, text, videoconference, or some combination of all methods. Although the ability to reach across the world instantaneously has benefits, e-channels are not always conducive to a productive settlement discussion.

Videoconferencing and other online communication methods allow for instantaneous contact and response with almost anyone, almost anywhere in the world. If a matter is of some urgency, it can be addressed more quickly via internet resources than it would be if the participants all had to arrange to meet in person, or wait for traditional mail channels. Further, research demonstrates that email negotiators, for example, rely more heavily on logic and facts to support arguments and less on emotional appeals.[43] This might be advantageous when emotions are impeding progress and resolution in a case. Email communication facilitates a depersonalized, task-oriented approach. Further, email negotiators might also feel less inhibited without face-to-face contact, which may lead to more shared information. Email negotiations also allow time for research and reflection, as well as collaboration with the client or colleagues, which in-person meetings do not provide.

However, there are drawbacks to negotiating over digital media that the skilled negotiator must consider when strategizing the negotiation channel and presentation. For example, video-chat technology can break down or experience delays during the process and this can become frustrating and undermine momentum. Also, the ability to observe non-

---

[41] *Id.* at 47.

[42] *Id.* at 50.

[43] Simon Hazeldine, *Negotiating by Telephone & Email—The Challenges and Practical Solutions.* October 5, 2015, https://www.linkedin.com/pulse/negotiating-telephone-email-challenges-practical-simon-hazeldine (last visited December 7, 2017).

verbal cues during the negotiation can be critical to its success; even when communicating over video camera, body language and emotional responses cannot be clearly interpreted. Therefore, the negotiator may miss important facial expressions, mannerisms, and efforts to create distance and fail to make appropriate adjustments in presentation and strategy.[44] Similarly, the negotiator cannot demonstrate empathy, acknowledgement, or validation as easily using e-channels as she would be able to in person.

Negotiators using internet-based e-communication methods do not establish the kinds of interpersonal relationships with other participants that in-person meetings facilitate. As a result, it is more difficult to establish trust, and trust is critical to a successful negotiation. "Mutual invisibility in e-negotiations can facilitate adversarial, contentious, and trust-breaking behavior. Denial is stronger when damaging a faceless other, particularly when we feel protected by a shield of anonymity and physical distance."[45] E-negotiators are more likely to be contentious and feel less bound by social norms than they do when negotiating in person.[46] Further, research shows that email negotiations have fewer creative and integrative outcomes than face-to-face negotiations and result in impasse more frequently.[47]

Negotiators should consider techniques that might improve the efficacy of e-negotiating. If negotiating via video chat, the negotiator might nod affirmatively with greater frequency, and attempt to maintain eye contact to demonstrate active listening and engagement more deliberately than she would in person. Also, the negotiator might take more opportunities to reflect and paraphrase what she heard to ensure accuracy and show commitment. Further, the negotiator might ask more questions to show interest and concern in the context of an e-negotiation and summarize more frequently.

In the context of email negotiation, the negotiator should engage in some exchange of pleasantries, as she would when greeting in person, as this is generally expected (in the U.S.) and is part of establishing rapport and building trust. Written negotiation correspondence should include clear language that illustrates both parties' interests and goals for mutual gain by both sides. It might also be important to add more detail in email negotiations regarding feelings and assumptions than the lawyer would probably communicate in person.[48]

---

[44] NICHOLAS HARKIOLAKIS, DAPHNE HALKIAS, E-NEGOTIATIONS: NETWORKING & CROSS-CULTURAL BUSINESS TRANSACTIONS 78 (2016).

[45] Id. at 76.

[46] Noam Ebner, *Trust-Building in E-Negotiation.* COMPUTER-MEDIATED RELATIONSHIPS AND TRUST: MANAGERIAL AND ORGANIZATIONAL EFFECTS 7 (L. Brennan & V. Johnson eds.2007)

[47] Noam Ebner, *Negotiating via Email, supra* note 46, at 8. Also available at: https://ssrn.com/abstract=2348111 (last visited December 7, 2017).

[48] Hazeldine, *supra* note 43.

Finally, the skilled negotiator should consider different channels at different stages of the process when e-communication is necessary. Less complex issues might more readily resolved via email, where more complex issues might be addressed in person or via video-chat.[49] If collaboration and integrative bargaining seem critical to the case at issue, consider face-to-face, or phone or video chat in the alternative. In any case, lawyers should make deliberate choices and strategize appropriately for each different communication channel and should not expect the same process and results from each method.

E. ETHICAL CONSIDERATIONS

A skilled negotiator considers her role on behalf of her client as well as her ethical and legal obligations to all parties. Ethical guidelines are not limited to litigation, and attorneys are expected to adhere to professional standards when representing clients in a negotiation.[50]

Although exaggeration may be common in the negotiation context, you should not misrepresent the facts of your client's case.[51] The line is not always clear and you should be cautious. Consider whether you would verify the accuracy of the factual information to the court if the case proceeded in that context; if a judge might consider your representation inaccurate, you should not present the facts that way in negotiation.

PRACTICE EXERCISE

Cross the Line[52]

Break into pairs. Students should stand on either side of a line (taped to floor) and face each other or sit across from each other and envision the line. The only rule is this: The student that persuades the other to cross the line in five minutes wins $1000 (not really).

---

[49] *See* Ebner, *supra* note 47, at 11; *see also* Hazeldine, *supra* note 43.

[50] KRIEGER & NEUMANN, *supra* note 7, at 305 (*quoting* http://www.abanet.org/litigation/ ethics/settlementnegotiations.pdf (visited Oct. 7, 2010): "[R]ecently, the ABA's Section of Litigation adopted Ethical Guidelines for Settlement Negotiations. Although these guidelines are not binding authority, they provide more detailed guidance than the Rules in regard to a lawyer's responsibility to clients and opposing parties during settlement talks.").

[51] *See* MODEL RULES OF PROFESSIONAL CONDUCT RULE 4.1(a) (stating: "[i]n the course of representing a client, a lawyer shall not knowingly . . . make a false statement of material fact or law to a third person. . . ."); MODEL RULE 4.1, Comm. 2 (stating: "Under generally accepted conventions in negotiation, certain types of statements ordinarily are not taken as statements of material fact. Estimates of price or value placed on the subject of a transaction and a party's intentions as to an acceptable settlement of a claim are in this category. . . .").

[52] Although this exercise is not original, its origin is unknown.

CHAPTER 24

CONTRACT DRAFTING

■ ■ ■

By Jeffrey E. Proske

A. WHY IS CONTRACT DRAFTING AN ESSENTIAL LAWYERING SKILL?

Contract drafting is a practical skill attorneys employ in the course of their careers for many types of clients in various contexts from drafting residential leases for individuals, to purchase and sale agreements, licensing agreements, employment agreements, real estate purchase agreements, loan agreements, and stock and asset purchase agreements. Contract drafting refers to the memorialization of the specific points of an agreement between parties who each wish to obtain specific objectives through a legally enforceable contract in exchange for something from the other party or parties. The drafting process precedes the parties' execution of the contract and culminates in the execution and performance of the contract.

Contract drafting is a skill that requires the attorney to envision a proposed relationship between two or more parties from its inception to its end, and to map out how that relationship is going to work; who is obligated to do what, where, when and how; and what rights the parties have to require the other party or parties to the contract to perform actions during the course of the contract.

Well-drafted contracts provide individuals, businesses, and governments with a measure of predictability and trust that the objectives they have contracted to achieve will actually happen. Well-drafted contracts encourage parties to engage in transactions by minimizing their fear that they are putting their interests and money at risk. In this way, good contract drafting helps fuel the engine of commerce and economic growth by inspiring economic actors to engage in commerce and have faith that they will achieve their objectives in a predictable and reliable manner.

Federal, state, and international law has evolved to support and encourage confidence and predictability in contracts by giving parties who suffer losses from another party's breach to go to court to recover damages for breach of contract. The prospect of expensive and corrosive litigation for breach of contract is usually an effective disincentive to ensure that parties perform the obligations they have agreed to.

A well-drafted contract creates an effective roadmap to help the client understand what specific actions they are required to perform, how they are required to perform them, and when they are required to do so. By employing effective contract drafting skills, an attorney helps clients plan their performance under their contracts day by day, month by month, and year by year, and provides them assurance that they can predict how the other party or parties to their contracts will perform as well.

B. OVERVIEW OF CHAPTER

This chapter will demonstrate how the essential elements of contract you learn about through your contracts class are applied in the real world of legal practice where an attorney's principal goal is to help the client achieve specific outcomes through a contractual relationship and to do so without landing in court.

The following sections will review the essential elements of an enforceable contract; provide guidance on preparing for the drafting process and ethical considerations in contract drafting; and provide a list of many of the essential components to include in a well-drafted contract with application in a wide variety of contexts with samples of well-drafted provisions, as well as some not so well-drafted provisions.

C. COMPETENCY, LEGAL AND ETHICAL REQUIREMENTS IN CONTRACT DRAFTING

Unlike various fields of legal practice where there are clear rules about how parties and their attorneys must interact with timelines and deadlines, contract drafting is relatively free of such requirements. While there are legal parameters that govern most contractual relationships, attorneys have great freedom to define how a specific contractual relationship will be conducted within those parameters. For example, California Civil Code Section 1550 provides the basic elements required to form an enforceable contract:

- Parties capable of contracting
- Their consent
- A lawful object
- A sufficient cause or consideration

In addition to these basic elements, there are federal, state and local laws and regulations, such as the Uniform Commercial Code, laws governing real estate transactions, labor and employment matters, environmental matters and a host of other laws, which must be adhered to in the drafting process which impact the parties' freedom to contract.

Of course, having such a great measure of freedom to contract has great benefits for clients and their attorneys, but it also places a burden on the attorney to be prepared to address the full range of risks the client will be exposed to during the course of the contract and to deal with them effectively in the drafting process. This requires the attorney to be competent to provide the services.

The California Rules of Professional Conduct, which are consistent with the Model Rules, provide contract drafters with some guidance on how to conduct themselves in their representation of clients in contractual matters with competence. Rule 3–110 states that competence means to apply the "1) diligence, 2) learning and skill, and 3) mental, emotional, and physical ability reasonably necessary for the performance of such service." Rule 3–110 further provides where a lawyer does not have sufficient experience to act competently, the member may become competent by "1) associating with or, where appropriate, professionally consulting another lawyer reasonably believed to be competent, or 2) by acquiring sufficient learning and skill before performance is required."[1]

In the context of contract drafting this usually means understanding the client's objectives and knowing their tolerance for risk. It also means knowing enough about your client's life, business, and industry to be able to contemplate how the performance of duties under the contract will impact that life, business, and industry. It is the attorney's responsibility to ensure the client understands exactly what the contract requires the client to do, when, where, and how, and to receive sufficient assurance from the client that the client is ready, willing, and able to perform the actions required.

D. GETTING SMART ABOUT YOUR CLIENT'S OBJECTIVES AND THE RISKS INVOLVED IN OBTAINING THEM

The contract drafting process is driven by one principal goal—ensuring your client obtains the very specific objectives he wants from the contract. Even the most sophisticated clients often fail to contemplate all of the risks associated with a project. Business clients may only have their eye on the impact of the project on their bottom line without fully understanding the risks involved in achieving that bottom line result. They rely on their attorney to approach the project from a more objective perspective to spot potential problems in advance.

---

[1]   CAL. RULES OF PROFESSIONAL CONDUCT 3–110 (2017).

For an attorney to be able to understand as many of the risks involved in a transaction as possible, the attorney must have a thorough understanding of the client, his expectations of the transaction, his specific goals in entering the contractual relationship, his vulnerabilities, and his capacity to perform the obligations required in the proposed contract. Attorneys obtain this understanding through the client interview process.

If a client approaches his attorney with a project to purchase a business, the attorney should learn through the client interview process how the client expects to pay the purchase price, how the client expects to run the business once he has purchased it, any changes he would like to make to it, and when he would like to have the purchase completed among many other things.

E. THE BEGINNING, MIDDLE AND END OF THE CONTRACT

In order for an attorney to effectively contemplate all of the rights and duties that will need to be addressed in a contract, it is crucial that the attorney understand the life-cycle of the contract. Every contract has a beginning, a middle, and an end. That is to say there is a specific date when the client becomes obligated to perform duties under the contract and has a right to receive benefits under it (the beginning), a period of performance (the middle), and a specific date when those duties and rights terminate (the end). For example, in the context of an employment agreement, there is a date when the employee must report to work and commence the duties outlined in the contract; a period of time during which the employee performs services in accordance with the terms of the contract; and a date when those services terminate. Similarly, in this employment agreement example, there is a date when the employer is required to commence payment of salary and provide benefits, a period during which those obligations continue, and a date when they terminate.

Accordingly, before commencing the contract drafting process, the attorney must create a timeline reflecting the life-cycle of the contractual relationship. By creating the time-line, the attorney can begin to visualize the scope of the contractual relationship and how the various duties and rights fit into that life-cycle and how they terminate. Creating a timeline is helpful in many contractual contexts, but most especially for contracts that are expected to be in effect for days, weeks, months or years, such as leases, purchase and sale contracts, licensing contracts, manufacturing contracts, and employment contracts.

F. THE ESSENTIAL COMPONENTS OF THE CONTRACT

Contracts generally share a number of common components that provide a useful framework for the attorney during the drafting process. The following sections discuss each of these common components individually in the sequence they typically appear in contracts, and provide examples of well-crafted components, as well as some common problems that occur in the drafting process.

1. THE TITLE

Every contract should have a title that provides a sufficient amount of information to convey to the reader the ultimate object of the contract. The ultimate object of the contract refers to the basic objectives of the parties in entering into the contract. Titles provide a very fast and easy way for the parties and their attorneys to identify specific documents. This is particularly important for busy clients and attorneys who have stacks of documents on their desks or in their digital files at any given time and need quick access to them.

A well-drafted title will identify a specific contract in a way that distinguishes it from the others in a stack. So, in the context of the employer and employee example above, the ultimate objective is to establish the rules governing a proposed employment relationship between the employer and the employee. The following would be appropriate titles for such a contract:

Example satisfactory title:	"Employment Agreement."
Example excellent title:	"Employment Agreement Between Alpha Systems, LLC and Dorothy Mae Trix"

Similarly, if the ultimate object of the contract is to provide the rules governing the transfer of ownership of a business from one party to another, an appropriate title would be as follows:

Example satisfactory title:	"Contract for the Purchase and Sale of a Business."
Example excellent title:	"Contract for the Sale of Alpha Systems, LLC by Alpha Parent, LLC to Beta Systems, Inc."

2. THE PREAMBLE

The Preamble to a contract refers to the first paragraph of the contract below the title, which provides the following information to the reader in a simple sentence:

- The type of contract [e.g., Employment Agreement]
- The names of the parties [Alpha Systems, LLC and Dorothy Mae Trix]
- The "Effective Date" [the specific date when the rights and duties of the parties under the contract commence]

Example Preamble in Context:

Employment Agreement Between Alpha Systems, LLC and Dorothy Mae Trix

Preamble

This Employment Agreement ("Agreement") is entered into by Alpha Systems, LLC ("Employer") and Dorothy Mae Trix ("Employee") and is effective on June 1, 2017. ("Effective Date").

---

3. THE RECITALS

The term "recitals" refers to the set of sentences appearing after the Preamble that provide the reader with general information about why the parties have entered into the agreement. Recitals are not enforceable provisions of the contract and should not contain any specific information about the rights and duties of the parties, but they serve the purpose of informing third parties, such as judges, of the motivations of the parties and their ultimate objectives in forming a contract together. Recitals thereby serve roughly the same general purpose as the legislative history for a statute.

In the context of the employment agreement between Alpha Systems, LLC and Dorothy Mae Trix, an appropriate set of recitals in context may look like the following:

Employment Agreement Between Alpha Systems, LLC and Dorothy Mae Trix

Preamble

This Employment Agreement ("Agreement") is entered into by Alpha Systems, LLC ("Employer") and Dorothy Mae Trix ("Employee") and is effective on June 1, 2017. ("Effective Date").

Recitals

1. Employer wishes to hire Employee for a senior management position with the Employer.

2. Employee wishes to work for Employer to provide services in a senior management position.

3. Employer and Employee have engaged in discussions with respect to Employee's suitability for the senior management position.

---

4. WORDS OF AGREEMENT

For a contract to be enforceable there must be sufficient consideration for each party to be obligated to perform under the contract. In contemporary drafting, it is sufficient to state simply "the parties agree as follows" just after the final recital to memorialize the existence and sufficiency of the consideration for each party's promise to perform. In addition to evidencing that there has been an exchange of promises as consideration, these words "the parties agree as follows" signify to the reader that all of the provisions that follow constitute the enforceable rules of the contractual relationship between the parties.

Example Words of Agreement in Context:

Employment Agreement Between Alpha Systems, LLC and Dorothy Mae Trix

Preamble

This Employment Agreement ("Agreement") is entered into by Alpha Systems, LLC ("Employer") and Dorothy Mae Trix ("Employee") and is effective on June 1, 2017. ("Effective Date").

Recitals

1. Employer wishes to hire Employee for a senior management position with the Employer.

2. Employee wishes to work for Employer to provide services in a senior management position.

3. Employer and Employee have engaged in discussions with respect to Employee's suitability for the senior management position.

The parties agree as follows:

---

5. DEFINITIONS: PROPER NAMES, COMPLEX CONCEPTS AND LISTS

Contract drafters often define long proper names, complex concepts, and terms that contain a list of items that are used throughout the contract for easy reference. Using defined terms for proper names and complex concepts ensures that each time the name or concept is referred to in the contract the reader will not be confused about who the provision in question refers to or what the concept means.

Defined terms in contracts always appear with the first letter of each word in the definition capitalized so the reader will distinguish the defined terms which have legal significance from those that do not. An employment agreement may refer at times to the party who has been defined as "Employee," but may also refer to "employee" in a general sense that is intended to refer to all employees, and not just the party defined as "Employee." The initial capitalized "E" signals to the reader that the reference to Employee is a defined term that has legal significance that the undefined term does not.

As a general rule, definitions should simply describe names, concepts and lists, and should not contain language that is intended to obligate a party to perform an action or to grant a party an entitlement to the benefit of another party's obligation. For example, a definition of the employee's duties should not contain a statement that the "employee shall perform the following duties." The appropriate place for language that compels a party to act is in the covenants section which will be discussed below.

a. Proper Names

Defining proper names serves the purpose of creating a single word or phrase to identify a party or third party which avoids the confusion that could result from referring to the same party in multiple ways. If our employment contract were to refer to "Alpha Systems, LLC" in one paragraph, and then refer to "Alpha" in another, and "Employer" in yet another, it could get quite confusing for the reader to identify who is referred to from section to section. Accordingly, the attorney could simply define "Alpha Systems, LLC" as "Alpha" and refer to "Alpha" throughout the contract. This is a particularly helpful tool where there are many parties to a contract and where the parties' names are long and complicated and there is a great likelihood that the reader could confuse who is who.

Defining parties by their role in the contractual relationship is also a useful tool to make it abundantly clear to whom the contract is referring. For example, in the employment agreement, the contract drafter could define "Alpha Systems, LLC" by its role in the contract as the "Employer" and "Dorothy Mae Trix" by her role in the contract as "Employee." These terms serve the purpose of simplifying the references to each party, while also creating a helpful reminder to the reader of the roles of each of the parties in the contract.

b. Complex Concepts and Lists

The same method of creating definitions for proper names can also be applied to defining complex concepts or lists. For example, in the employment contract, if the contract refers in numerous sections to the Employee's duties that include "preparing and sending monthly sales reports to the CEO, attending weekly marketing meetings, attending the annual conference of XYZ Professional Association, using Employee's best efforts to achieve monthly marketing goals, preparing annual marketing surveys for each year of the contract, and conducting annual reviews of all employees under Employee's immediate supervision," it would be tedious and distracting for the reader to have to read this entire list each time the duties are referred to in the contract. A simpler method would be to simply define "Duties" to mean all of the items in the list so each time the word "Duties" appears in the contract it serves as a shorthand term for the entire long list of duties. Defining complex concepts or lists in this way serves the additional purpose of ensuring that there are not competing or conflicting versions of the same complex concept or list in the various sections of the contract that could open the door to misinterpretation or unnecessary confusion.

Example Contract Using Defined Terms:

Employment Agreement Between Alpha Systems, LLC and Dorothy Mae Trix

Preamble

This Employment Agreement ("Agreement") is entered into by Alpha Systems, LLC ("Employer") and Dorothy Mae Trix ("Employee") and is effective on June 1, 2017. ("Effective Date").

Recitals

1. Employer wishes to hire Employee for a senior management position with the Employer.

2. Employee wishes to work for Employer to provide services in a senior management position.

3. Employer and Employee have engaged in discussions with respect to Employee's suitability for the senior management position.

The parties agree as follows:

Definitions

"Employee Duties" means preparing and sending monthly sales reports to the CEO, attending weekly marketing meetings, attending the annual conference of X Professional Association, using Employee's best efforts to achieve monthly marketing goals, preparing annual marketing surveys for each year of the Agreement, and conducting annual reviews of all employees under Employee's immediate supervision.

---

6. PRINCIPAL EXCHANGE PROVISIONS

The principal exchange provisions are the provisions of the contract that set forth the fundamental exchange between the parties. They are sometimes referred to as "action items" or "deliverables" in the contract. In the employment contract context, the principal exchange provisions would be the employee's agreement to perform the specified duties for the term of the contract and the employer's agreement to pay the employee a salary in exchange for her performance of the specified duties. In a contract for the sale of an object, the principal exchange provisions would state the seller's agreement to sell the object and the buyer's agreement to buy the object, the purchase price for it and the time, place and manner for payment and for the delivery of the object to the buyer. The principal exchange provisions should spell out with great specificity how, when, and where the parties are to perform their duties.

7. REPRESENTATIONS AND WARRANTIES

Representations and warranties are essential tools contract drafters use to manage the expectations of the parties with respect to all sorts of issues, including, the legal status and capacity of the parties, their right to enter into the contract, and their ability to perform under it.

A party can only make representations and warranties with respect to matters about itself and matters under its own control and not about other parties. It is essential to view every representation and warranty from the viewpoint of the individual party that is making the representation and warranty. In the employment contract example, it would be inappropriate for the employee to represent and warrant that the "employer is a Delaware limited liability company in good standing" because the employee has no independent understanding if that is the case and has no appropriate means of ensuring that that representation is true. It is the responsibility of the employer to ensure such a representation is true.

Representations and warranties can cover a large spectrum of issues in a contract, such as a party's financial condition, the absence of tax, environmental, or other governmental claims or pending litigation, statements about business operations, and insurance matters. For instance, in contracts for the sale of an object there are usually representations about the condition of the object on the date of execution of the contract coupled with the seller's warranty promising that that condition will be the same on the day the contract closes and the object passes to the buyer.

In contracts between corporations, partnerships, limited liability companies or other fictitious entities, there are usually representations and warranties stating that the entity has been duly granted the authority by its board of directors or other governing entity or officer to enter the contract and perform the obligations required of it. Representations and warranties may also address other contextual matters that are important to the parties such as representations and warranties in employment agreements about matters related to the office atmosphere, available support, equipment, and parking.

a. Representations

It is important for contract drafters to understand the distinction between a "representation" and a "warranty." "Representations" are statements of fact about a party or a specific condition that have significance in the contract that the party making the representation asserts to be true as of the commencement date of the contract and every day thereafter until the termination date.

For example, in the employment agreement, the employer may consider it a critical part of the employment contract that the employee has a certain credential, such as membership in a professional or trade association, and that this credential be current through the term of the contract. Accordingly, the employer may request that a representation be inserted in the contract stating that the employee does in fact have this credential. By agreeing to include this representation, the employee is agreeing that the representation that she has the credential is true at every moment from the commencement date of the contract through the termination date.

A representation on its own does not require the party to do anything, but it provides the other party assurance that a certain baseline condition exists at the start of the contract and will continue to be true until the contract terminates. However, the employer cannot rely on a representation alone for legal recourse if during the term of the agreement it turns out the employee has let the credential lapse. The way to create the legal obligation that the employee ensures the credential is current over the entire term is by coupling the representation with a warranty.

b. Warranties

A "warranty" is a promise a party makes to stand by a specific representation and ensure that it remains true and correct from the commencement of the contract through the termination date. Warranties create legally enforceable promises in a contract that parties can rely on. When a representation accompanied by a warranty is breached, a fundamental ground rule that the parties relied on in entering the contract no longer exists. Accordingly, if it turns out that a specific representation has become untrue over the course of the contract term, where that representation is accompanied by a warranty, the party who relied on the representation would have a claim for breach of contract.

In the employment contract example, if the employee has both represented and warranted that she has a credential in good standing with XYZ Professional Organization and will maintain it through the term of the contract, and it turns out that during the term of the contract the credential has been suspended for failure to take certain actions, the employer will have grounds for an action for breach if the employee fails to stand by her warranty and reinstate the credential.

8.   COVENANTS

While representations and warranties are effective tools contract drafters use to establish a set of understandings about the context in which the parties will perform under the contract, covenants create the actual obligations for the parties to do certain things during the term of the contract.

A covenant is a promise of a party to perform a specific act during the term of the agreement. Contract drafters usually create a section of the contract that sets forth every single action each party is required to perform over the term of the contract. For example, in the employment contract the employer may covenant to provide the employee with a company car, an expense allowance, reimbursements for professional outlays, travel, and a range of specified benefits. Without having a clearly stated covenant by the employer to provide each of these things, the employer cannot be bound to provide them and the employee cannot sue for breach if they are not provided.

A covenant is distinguished from a representation and warranty, because a covenant requires the party making the covenant to take specific actions during the term of the contract, while representations and warranties relate to statements of fact regarding static conditions that must exist during the term of the contract. No action is required of the party making the representation and warranty—unless action is necessary to ensure the representation remains true through the term of the contract.

9. CONDITIONS

A party to a contract has the right to rely on the representations and warranties and covenants made by the other party and is relieved of its own duty to fulfill its covenants when the other party fails to perform theirs. The obligation of one party to perform the acts required of it under a contract are, therefore, conditioned on the performance of covenants by the other party, and on the truth of the representations and warranties made by the other party.

Contract drafters make this quid pro quo clear in contracts by creating a section in the contract for such "conditions" that spells out specifically which representations and warranties and which covenants will constitute conditions to the other party's performance. Usually, contract drafters make their client's obligations to perform their covenants under a contract conditional on the satisfaction of all of the representations and warranties and covenants of the other party. However, it is usually wise to build in some wiggle room in the event that a minor failing by a party to satisfy a covenant or to ensure the continuing truth and correctness of a representation and warranty allow the parties to cease performance.

For example, in the context of the employment contract, if the employee's obligation to provide the services required under the contract is conditioned on the continued truthfulness of the representation that the employer is in good standing in its state of establishment, and the employer fails to provide a required filing with the state causing the employer's good standing status to be suspended, the employee could cease the performance of her services until the employer stood by its warranty and reinstated its good standing. If the employee were to continue performing despite the failure of the representation and warranty, the employee may be said to have waived the fulfillment of that representation and warranty as a condition to her performance. The way this issue is addressed is usually by giving the party who has the right to rely on the covenant or representation the right to waive compliance when necessary so as not to terminate the contractual relationship when it is otherwise functioning as intended.

10. TERMINATION PROVISIONS

As stated above, every contract has a beginning, a middle, and an end. An employment contract starts on a specific date, remains in effect for a period of time, and then ends on a specific date. The attorney drafting the employment contract has to consider the risks inherent in the contractual relationship and build provisions into the contract that address issues of early termination, extension, and renewal in a way the parties can predict and rely on when such circumstances emerge.

For instance, what happens if the parties find after a month or a year that the benefits they were receiving under their contract are no longer sufficient? What if economic circumstances have changed after a few months making performance under the contract impossible? What if a party's performance fails to meet the other party's expectations and the disappointed party wants the ability to end the relationship prior to the stated termination date? What if the contract has an initial term of one year and the parties are so happy with the advantages they have under the contract that they want it to go on for another year, or many more?

Effective termination provisions deal not only with the question of when a contract ends, but also with what happens to the rights and duties of the parties under each scenario when termination occurs. For instance, in the employment contract context, if the contract allows the employer to terminate the employee's contract at any time for any reason, and the employer terminates the agreement the day before the employer is required under the contract to pay an installment of the employee's salary, and contributions to her benefit plans, what happens to the employee's accrued pay and benefits contributions? Unless the termination provision spells out what the employee is owed at the time the employer elects to terminate under that provision, the employee may have no recourse to obtain money and benefits owed to her. The attorney drafting the contract for the employee would want to make sure that, if the employer decided to exercise this right of termination, the employee would receive pay through the date of her contract termination together with any benefits contributions owed. The appropriate place to include that requirement in the contract would be in the termination provisions section.

Termination provisions should also contemplate what happens to each of the duties and rights of the parties when the contract terminates, including when representations and warranties are to expire. There are circumstances when parties may want representations and warranties to remain in effect longer than other rights and duties.

For example, in a contract for the sale of a car, if the seller represents and warrants that "the car is in good operating condition," would the buyer want that representation and warranty to terminate when the sale of the car was completed? Or would the buyer prefer to have the seller's representation and warranty survive the closing of the sale to provide some period of protection and recourse to the buyer in the event the car stopped operating the day after the sale closed or a week later? Unless the contract states that the representations and warranties with respect to the condition of the car survive the transfer of the car and the closing of the transaction, the buyer would not have any such protection.

11. GENERAL PROVISIONS

"General provisions" refer to the terms typically found at the end of the contract which relate to foundational understandings about the contractual relationship that apply to each party equally. For instance, provisions relating to which state's laws will govern the contract, whether the parties can assign their rights to benefits or delegate their duties under the contract, whether the contract is integrated, and which court will be the venue for litigating disputes under the contract are all "general provisions" that lay the ground rules for the contractual relationship.

General Provisions are sometimes referred to as "boilerplate," referring to the fact that they resemble standard, uniform provisions from agreement to agreement. However, an attorney must be knowledgeable about the effect of such provisions to avoid adverse consequences.

The provisions discussed below are typically included among the "General Provisions" in most contracts.

a. Assignment and Delegation

Assignment and delegation provisions prevent parties from assigning their right to receive a benefit under a contract, such as payments of money, or the benefit of the other party's services, and prevent the parties from delegating their obligation to perform their covenants under the contract. This type of provision is particularly important in contracts for personal services, such as acting or musical performance contracts, where it would be unacceptable to the employer to have anyone other than the person with whom they contracted provide the services.

Example Assignment and Delegation Provision:

> Neither party has the right to assign or delegate any rights or duties under this Agreement. Any purported assignment or delegation under this Agreement is void.

b. Successors and Assigns

Successors and Assigns provisions address issues that emerge when a party to a contract dies, becomes incapacitated, or, in the context of fictitious entities, gets sold or dissolved. The successors and assigns provision assures each party that in the event of death, or transfer of ownership, whoever takes the ownership interest of the deceased or defunct party will be bound to the contract as though they had entered it themselves.

Example Successors and Assigns Provision:

> This Agreement binds and benefits the parties and their respective successors and assigns.

c. Governing Law

The Governing Law provision provides the agreement between the parties about which state's jurisdiction and laws will apply to the interpretation and enforcement of the contract and provides the forum the parties agree to for the resolution of disputes under the contract.

Example Governing Law Provision:

> The laws of the state of California shall govern this Agreement, and any disputes that arise during the Term of the Agreement shall be filed in the U.S. District Court for the Central District of California.

d. Notice Provisions

Notice provisions serve the very useful function of telling the parties, their advisors, and third parties reading the contract who must be contacted with any notifications required by the contract, the agreed upon manner for such contact, and the address for each person to be contacted. Where parties to a transaction are represented, the notice provision usually includes the names, addresses, e-mail addresses, fax numbers, and phone numbers for the parties' attorneys in addition to the parties themselves.

Example Notice Provision:

All notices required under this Agreement shall be given in writing and delivered by fax, e-mail, U.S. postal service, or overnight courier to the parties at the addresses below:

Party A	Attorney for Party A
Name:	Name:
Address:	Address:
E-mail:	E-mail:
Phone No.:	Phone No.:
Fax No.	Fax No.:
Party B	Attorney for Party B
Name:	Name:
Address:	Address:
E-mail:	E-mail:
Phone No.:	Phone No.:
Fax No.:	Fax No.:

---

e. Severability

The severability provision ensures that, in the event one or more provisions of the contract become unenforceable for any reason, the remaining provisions of the contract will remain in full force and effect. If the contract drafter fails to include this provision, the parties, a court, and third parties may conclude that the parties intended that the entire agreement be invalidated if any one provision turned out to be illegal or unenforceable.

Example Severability Provision:

If any provision of this Agreement is illegal or unenforceable, that provision is severed from this Agreement and the other provisions remain in force.

---

f. Amendments and Modifications

Contract drafters will usually include an "amendments and modifications" provision in their contracts to ensure that the parties understand that the contract can be amended or modified as needed, and to ensure that a clear procedure is in place to effectively create such amendments or modifications. When contracts provide no clear guidance on whether the parties agree that amendments and modifications are allowed and include no clear procedure for creating them, there is a great risk of disruption and disputes about how to make changes to the contract.

Example Amendment and Modification Provision:

> This Agreement may be amended or modified only by an agreement in writing signed by both Parties.

g.   Merger and Integration

Merger and integration provisions state the parties' understanding that the contract they have executed is the final and exclusive agreement between the parties which supersedes any prior versions of the contract and any negotiations or discussions that preceded the execution. Parties and their attorneys spend a great deal of time negotiating points of agreement in a deal and often share numerous versions of a deal before arriving at a final, comprehensive contract that contains all the provisions agreed to. Unless the contract contains a merger and integration provision, doubts would be raised in the minds of judges and the parties as to which terms and provisions are to be considered the final, definitive, enforceable provisions.

Example Merger and Integration Provision:

> This Agreement is the final and exclusive agreement between the parties and supersedes all prior negotiations and agreements.

h.   Counterparts

Every party to a contract needs to have an executed original of the contract in order to enforce its provisions. To avoid confusion about which copy of the original is "the contract," attorneys will make it abundantly clear in the contract that there are multiple counterparts of the contract, each of which is to be treated as an original. They achieve this clarity with a "counterparts" provision which states that the contract may be executed in one or more counterparts, each of which is an original and all of which constitute only one contract between the parties.

Example Counterparts Provision:

> This Agreement may be executed in one or more counterparts, each of which is an original, and all of which constitute only one agreement between the parties.

12. THE SIGNATURE BLOCK

A well-drafted contract is only effective and enforceable when the parties have signed it. Good contract drafting requires special attention to the signature block to ensure that the parties are correctly identified and their capacity to execute the contract has been verified. Signature blocks can be complicated when one or more of the parties to the contract are fictitious entities such as corporations, limited liability companies, partnerships, or governmental entities.

When a party is a fictitious entity, the contract drafter must correctly identify the individual or individuals in the signature block who are duly authorized in accordance with the bylaws of the entity to execute contracts on behalf of the fictitious entity, and their role within the entity. To say that an individual is "duly authorized" is to say that they have produced the appropriate documentation whether in the form of shareholder consents or resolutions of the board of directors authorizing them to execute the contract on behalf of that entity. Without such documentation, the drafting attorney has no way to ensure the contract will be enforceable against the fictitious entity.

13. EXAMPLE COMPLETE EMPLOYMENT AGREEMENT

Employment Agreement Between Alpha Systems, LLC and Dorothy Mae Trix

This Employment Agreement ("Agreement") is entered into by Alpha Systems, LLC ("Employer") and Dorothy Mae Trix ("Employee") and is effective on June 1, 2017. ("Effective Date").

Recitals

- Employer wishes to hire Employee for a senior management position with the Employer.

- Employee wishes to work for Employer to provide services in a senior management position.

- Employer and Employee have engaged in discussions with respect to Employee's suitability for the senior management position.

The parties agree as follows:

Definitions

"Employee Duties" means preparing and sending monthly sales reports to the CEO, attending weekly marketing meetings, attending the annual conference of X Professional Association, using Employee's best efforts to achieve monthly marketing goals, preparing annual marketing surveys for each year of the Agreement, and conducting annual reviews of all employees under Employee's immediate supervision.

1. Deliverables

    1.1 Term

    This Agreement shall commence on the Effective Date and shall terminate on May 31, 2018 (the "Term").

    1.2 Employee's Duties

    Employee shall perform the Employee Duties during the Term in accordance with standard best practices in Employer's industry.

    1.3 Employer's Duties

    Employer shall pay Employee a salary of $50,000 during the Term in twelve equal installments of $4,166.66 with each installment to be deposited directly into an account designated by Employee on the first business day of each month during the Term.

2. Representations and Warranties

    2.1 Representations and Warranties of Employer

    The following representation and warranty is true as of the Effective Date and shall remain true during the Term of the Agreement.

    Employer is a Delaware limited liability company in good standing with its principal place of business in Sacramento, California.

    2.2 Representations and Warranties of Employee

    The following representation and warranty is true as of the Effective Date and shall remain true during the Term of the Agreement.

    Employee is a member in good standing with the Marketing Association of California.

3. Covenants

    3.1 Employer's Covenants

    In addition to Employer's obligations contained in Section 1.3, Employer shall provide the employee with the following during the Term:

    - A mid-size car;
    - An expense allowance of $1200 per month for meals while traveling on Employer's business;
    - Reimbursement for reasonable professional outlays for travel and entertainment

- Membership in the Employer's health plan;

- Participation in Employer's 401K plan

3.2 Employee's Covenants

In addition to Employee's obligations contained in Section 1.2, Employee shall do the following during the Term:

- Provide Employer with a monthly statement on the first business day of each month during the Term of travel and entertainment expenses, together with receipts for each item on the statement.

4. Conditions to Performance

4.1 Conditions to the Employer's Obligations

All of Employer's obligations under the Agreement are subject to the fulfillment of each of the following conditions. Employer may waive any failure to satisfy any one or more of the following conditions:

4.1.1   Employee's Representations and Warranties

The representations and warranties of Employee set forth in section 2.2 of the Agreement shall be true on the Effective Date and throughout the Term of the Agreement.

4.1.2   Employee shall have performed all of its obligations and agreements and complied with all of Employee's covenants set forth in section 3.2 of the Agreement.

4.2 Conditions to the Employee's Obligations

All of Employee's obligations under the Agreement are subject to the fulfillment of each of the following conditions. Employee may waive any failure to satisfy any one or more of the following conditions

4.2.1   Employer's Representations and Warranties

The representations and warranties of Employer set forth in section 2.1 of the Agreement shall be true on the Effective Date and throughout the Term of the Agreement.

4.2.2   Employer shall have performed all of its obligations and agreements and complied with all of Employee's covenants set forth in section 3.2 of the Agreement.

5. Termination

5.1 Termination on Termination Date

The Agreement shall terminate on the Termination Date, unless extended by Employer and Employee in an amendment to the Agreement signed by both Employer and Employee.

All rights and duties of the Employer and Employee in the Agreement shall terminate on the Termination Date unless modified pursuant to this section.

5.2   Employer's Right to Terminate

Employer may terminate the Agreement at any time prior to the Termination Date for any reason.

5.3   Employee's Right to Terminate

Employee may terminate the Agreement at any time prior to the Termination Date if Employer breaches a covenant contained in section 1.2 or section 3.1 of the Agreement.

5.4   Termination on Employee's Death or Disability

If the Employee dies or becomes unable to perform the Employee's Duties under the Agreement ("Disability"), the Agreement terminates as of the date of Employee's death or Disability.

5.5   Payment of Salary and Benefits on Termination

Employer shall pay any accrued salary and benefit contributions owed to Employee as of the effective date of termination under sections 5.1, 5.2 or 5.3 of the Agreement on the next pay date following the effective date of termination.

6.   General Provisions

6.1   Assignment and Delegation

Neither party has the right to assign or delegate any rights or duties under this Agreement. Any purported assignment or delegation under this Agreement is void.

6.2   Successors and Assigns

This Agreement binds and benefits the parties and their respective successors and assigns.

6.3   Governing Law

The laws of the state of California shall govern this Agreement, and any disputes that arise during the Term of the Agreement shall be filed in the U.S. District Court for the Central District of California.

6.4   Notice

All notices required under this Agreement shall be given in writing and delivered by fax, e-mail, U.S. postal service, or overnight courier to the parties at the addresses below:

Party A	Attorney for Party A
Name:	Name:
Address:	Address:
E-mail:	E-mail:
Phone No.:	Phone No.:
Fax No.:	Fax No.:

Party B	Attorney for Party B
Name:	Name:
Address:	Address:
E-mail:	E-mail:
Phone No.:	Phone No.:
Fax No.:	Fax No.:

6.5 Severability

If any provision of this Agreement is illegal or unenforceable, that provision is severed from this Agreement and the other provisions remain in force.

6.6 Amendment and Modification

This Agreement may be amended or modified only by an agreement in writing signed by both Parties.

6.7 Merger and Integration

This Agreement is the final and exclusive agreement between the parties and supersedes all prior negotiations and agreements.

6.8 Counterparts

This Agreement may be executed in one or more counterparts, each of which is an original, and all of which constitute only one agreement between the parties.

To evidence their agreement to the terms of this Agreement, Employer and Employee have executed and delivered it on the Effective Date.

Employer: Alpha Systems, LLC

By: _____

Jimmy Diamond

Its: _____

President & CEO

Employee: Dorothy Mae Trix

By: _____

Dorothy Mae Trix, an Individual

CHAPTER 25

RESEARCH STRATEGIES

■ ■ ■

By Maureen Moran

A. WHO NEEDS A RESEARCH PLAN?

It is 3 a.m. and you are up, prepping for class. Again. You have reading to do for Torts, Contracts, and Civil Procedure, and if you fall behind even one day, you will be spending hours late at night for the next few days trying to catch up. Or, worse, you will be unprepared and that will be the day your professor will call on you. And to add to your stress, you have a research project for your legal writing class due in less than two days, and you have not even started. Your professor told you to draft a research plan before you set foot in the library or signed onto your legal research database. But with so much going on in your other classes—not to mention how very strung-out you feel from the late nights and intense workload of a first-year law student—you do not see why you should spend the time on a research plan when that research plan will not be turned in, and you will not even be graded on it.

So, you decide to skip the research plan and just dive in. You get results. But there seem to be a lot of them, and they don't seem to be what you want. You try again, but you still aren't finding what you are looking for. This research project seems overwhelming now, and the clock is ticking. Over the next couple of days, you find yourself having to put off reading for your other classes. Your level of panic starts rising. Why is this taking so long? Why can't you find what you're looking for? Are you just not cut out for law school? Maybe you don't really want to do this after all.

Ultimately, you turn in your research project after burning the midnight oil several nights in a row. You are not confident in your results, and you are pretty sure you hate your life—and law school. You spend the next few days catching up with your reading for your other classes, and soon enough, it's time to do the next research project, which, of course, is a more complex one.

So, how did skipping the research plan on that last assignment work out for you? Not so great, right? Since you want to sleep again sometime, you need to change your strategy for the next assignment. You need a good research plan.

While it seems tempting to skip a research plan you do not have to turn in, you will save yourself a lot of time and effort and agony if you take the time to plan your research before you jump in, especially if you have a complex issue to research (and you will, eventually, have to research complex issues). A research plan can help you:

- Keep your research focused and organized;

- Save time;

- Prevent duplication of effort;

- Prevent frustration; and

- Save money

This chapter will discuss these benefits of a good research plan, explain why a research plan saves you time, and help you formulate a research plan that can help you get through any research project without tearing your hair out.

B. RESEARCH COSTS MONEY, AND RESEARCH TAKES TIME: A GOOD PLAN CAN HELP YOU SAVE BOTH

It probably seems strange to hear that research costs money, because you have probably heard that research is free while you are in law school. But it is not free—someone has paid for all those books in the library and the subscription databases you use. And guess what? *That someone is you.* Your tuition is what covers the cost of legal research while you are in school. The cost is hidden from you now, but soon enough, you will be in practice and you will have to start thinking about how much your research costs because the connection between the cost of research and who has to pay for it will be more direct, and might be coming out of the pocket of someone who can make decisions about your future employment. And if there's one thing you should learn while you are in law school, it is this: Legal research is very expensive.

An anecdote: when I was a first-year associate in a litigation firm, I spent a weekend at the office with several other attorneys finalizing an important appellate brief. While the other attorneys made revisions, I was tasked with doing last-minute research and checking the citations to be sure that the cases we cited were still good law. The problem I had was that my preferred legal research database had recently been dropped by the firm as a cost-cutting measure, so I had to use the other database, which I had never developed great fluency with because I had simply defaulted to the other one when both had been available. I finished my cite-checking, we filed the brief, and I never thought about my research on that brief again.

Well, not until the next month, when the managing partner of my firm came into my office, shut the door, and showed me the bill from the database I had used. I had managed to rack up *four thousand dollars* in charges because of the way I had done the cite-checking (the bill should have been a couple hundred at most). I did not realize—and had not asked my colleagues—how this database was priced; I had simply assumed it was on a timed basis, like the database I usually used. And I was really good at searching quickly! But this database was billed on a per-search basis, and because I had retrieved each case prior to using the citator rather than just putting the citations directly into the citator, each retrieval was charged as a new search, and then an additional charge was incurred for the citator. The managing partner, as you might imagine, was not happy with me because he could not pass those charges on to the client, but the bill had to be paid—and it was coming out of his pocket and the pockets of the other partners in my firm.

While I never made that mistake again—and, really, it is the kind of mistake you can make *once* but is better not to make *at all* if you would like to keep your job—I learned a few lessons from that experience about being aware of how much research costs and how it is priced. I learned a lesson about relying on one resource and letting my skills in others go slack. And I also learned a lesson about planning my research.

There are two main things that make legal research very expensive: The cost of the materials and the cost of the researcher's time. Legal research materials are usually very pricey. You probably already got a shock when you had to buy your casebooks. Print resources can be quite expensive, and they have to be updated frequently, which not only involves paying for the pocket parts and supplements and updated volumes, but also the staff time to get all of those materials into the books.

Subscription databases are also quite expensive, though many law firms, law schools, government agencies, law libraries, and courts work out pricing arrangements tailored to their usage patterns and needs. However, there are three basic pricing models in use: (1) flat monthly fees, (2) pricing by the hour, and (3) pricing per search. These basic models may vary from database to database, so you should be familiar with all three pricing models and be prepared to tailor your research plan to the pricing model of the database you are using.

Even when you are using free or low-cost materials (and there are many available, from government resources to collections maintained by public law libraries), you need to understand that the researcher's time costs money as well. This is true even when you are not billing your time directly to a client (who may not be willing to pay for the cost of using a database on top of the cost of your billable rate to use that database). Just spending time on research means that you cannot spend your time on other tasks that need to get done. The more efficient and effective you can become at performing legal research, the more you will be able to control your time and manage your workload, thus controlling your costs.

You also need to know that not every employer will have the range of research options available to you in law school for your use in practice. Your employer may require you to use print resources or free resources to get started, or you may have to use a subscription database you do not prefer because your employer has decided to only pay for one. You may be sent off to a public, law school, or court law library to use a resource that your employer needs only occasionally. You may have a client who balks at being presented with a legal research bill showing a database charge or a fee the client thinks is excessive, and if that client will not pay, the partners in your law firm will have to eat the cost. If you work in-house, or for a court or government agency, any time you spend flailing around on ineffective research is time you do not have to devote to the other hundred things you need to take care of, and you will be stuck at the office late into the night. And if you have your own practice, you will be the one seeing diminishing returns in both time and money if you do not learn to research efficiently and effectively.

So how can you save time and money doing legal research? Have a research plan.

C. HOW TO BUILD A RESEARCH PLAN: ESSENTIALS

Now that you know why you should have a research plan, the question becomes how to build one. First, consider in greater depth the goals of a research plan, as outlined briefly above. Any research plan should help you:

- **Keep your research focused and organized**—By plotting out your issues, research terms, sources, and strategies in advance, you can keep your research on track and on task, especially as your research gets more complex.

- **Save time**—Putting in the time to plan your research will save you time down the road, by keeping your efforts focused and providing a means of checking your progress.

- **Prevent duplication of effort**—Having a research plan can help you avoid the problem of going over the same ground more than once because you have forgotten where you have already been.

- **Prevent frustration**—A research plan that builds in alternatives and variations can help you avoid the frustration of a too-narrow or too-broad search, or one that yields no results at all.

- **Save money**—Learning how to develop a research plan that can be adapted for a variety of pricing models can help you avoid costly errors in the "real world."

So, what are the essential components of a good research plan?

- Identifying the issue(s)
  - o Creating search terms
  - o Choosing your approach
- Choosing materials
  - o Secondary or primary sources?
  - o Print or electronic?
  - o Using finding aids
- Updating your research
- Closing the loop: how and when to stop

Each of these are discussed in more detail below.

1. IDENTIFYING ISSUES

The first thing you have to do in any research project is figure out what, exactly, you have to research. In order to do that, you need to figure out the legal issue or issues presented by your facts. Identifying the issue you want to research is the foundation for all that comes after, so you want to take your time and do a thorough job here.

To identify the issues, read your fact pattern and the call of the question carefully. Pick it apart in whatever way works for you—highlighting, cutting and pasting words, creating flash cards, using a whiteboard. It may help to use the "five W's and an H" method used by journalists to report the news and ask yourself a few related questions:

Who—Who are the players? People? Entities? What are their relationships? Does the conflict arise out of these relationships, or does it come from outside? Who has been harmed, and who might be responsible for the harm? Who is your client? Who benefits by what happened?

What—What is the nature of the dispute? What kind of action is this—tort, contract, criminal, civil rights? What happened? What is the nature of the harm? What does your client want to accomplish? What is the relief sought?

Where—Where did the events giving rise to the dispute occur? Where is the case filed? Which state's law will govern? What is the jurisdiction? Where did the money (or goods, or papers, etc.) go?

When—When did the events giving rise to the dispute occur? When was the case filed? When does the statute of limitations run out?

Why—Why did this happen?

How—How did this happen? How would your client like for things to be fixed?

You might consider, as well, a catchall "W"—"What else?" This will help you capture any ideas from your brainstorming that do not fit any of the above categories.

Once you have identified your issue, you can begin generating search terms.

a. Creating Search Terms

Now that you have identified your issue or issues, you need to figure out how you are going to find legal authority that will help you analyze the issues. Since you will be using some kind of finding aid—whether electronic or paper-based—to find your legal authority, you will need to create search terms to locate the law relevant to your issue. Here are some guidelines for creating search terms.

Brainstorm—Use your fact pattern, the call of the question, and the answers to your issue-identification questions to come up with as many potential search terms and variations as you can think of. Do not limit yourself to legal issues—be sure to include factual terms as well, since the law is always applied to facts and the outcome of a case often turns on factual questions.

Be Flexible—The law is vast, and the language used to describe and find it varies over time and from authority to authority. If you take a rigid approach, you may miss entire swaths of the law. You may have noticed that legal terms of art are not necessarily based on common sense or even the English language. The terms used in statutes or cases are selected by the legislators who drafted the laws, the judges who wrote the opinions, or even by the attorneys who wrote the briefs on appeal and whose terminology was adopted by the court. Moreover, sometimes the terminology used may not reflect the subject matter of a case but may reflect a controlling statute or rule. So, for example, a case involving text messages may not refer to "texting" but may refer to "electronic communications" instead if the statute at issue deals with electronic communications. "Wiretapping" may be used even if the device at issue had no wires.

Use Synonyms and Alternate Terms—Terminology may vary from source to source, even if the issue is the same. If you are using a keyword search rather than a subject search, you may miss good law on your issue if you cling too tightly to the exact wording in your problem.

Example: You want to research an issue regarding the theft of items from a motel room. The events giving rise to the suit occurred at a motel, but the issue of responsibility for theft applies to other types of lodging.

- If you limit your search terms to "motel," you will miss out on any source that does not use that term, but that might be relevant to your issue, because a database using a keyword search will only return hits on the specific term it is asked to look for.

- If you expand your search to include synonyms, such as "lodging," "motor inn," "motor lodge," "hotel," "inn," and "accommodation," you will pick up many more results.

Use Both Broad Categories and Narrow Terms to Capture Legal Significance—When generating search terms, ask yourself what is legally significant about the facts you have been presented with. When you have determined that, broaden your search terms to capture facts which may be legally related to your issue; or, if you feel that your search may be too broad and capture too many results, use narrower categories to refine your search.

Example: You have a fact pattern involving a horse bite.

If you focus only on horse bites, you may miss authority that discusses the issue of animal bites of some broader category than horses. Broaden your authority in steps in order to sweep in legally relevant authority involving other animals. In this case, the fact that *an animal* bit someone is more legally significant than the fact that it was a *horse*. However, the particular category of animal you use that is broader than "horse" but narrower than "animal" may affect the results you get. What categories of animals do horses belong to?

- Farm animals: This will sweep in results relating to all farm animals, but what if the bite took place in an urban area or the horse was a racehorse or family pet?

- Domesticated animals: This will bring in the family pet, but the category of "domesticated animal" also brings in dogs, which may be considered more dangerous than horses and thus have different rules applied.

- Working animals: This may include therapy animals, police horses, racehorses, draft horses, or even horse actors and show ponies. It may also include working dogs.

- Circus animals: If a circus horse bites an audience member or performer, are there different rules than when a police horse bites a member of the public? Similarly, are all bites from circus animals treated the same, or are tiger bites considered different from (and more serious than) horse bites?

- Wild animals: How is the bite of a wild horse legally different than the bite from a farm horse?

- Animals: This is a very broad category, and is best when discussing animal bites in general rather than that of a particular species or category of animal, or when you are having a hard time finding authority at all with a narrower approach.

Use Boolean Syntax to Maximize Results—While many databases allow for natural language searching that will pick up significant terms from what you type into the search box (similar to a Google-style search), Boolean syntax is a powerful tool for finding what you want in a database and eliminating what you do not. Many databases use some form of Boolean syntax (and there are variations from database to database) to search for specified terms in a certain order, within a certain proximity to another term, only with another search term, in all potential variations, or by eliminating results containing a specified term. Boolean connectors can be combined.

Since each database has its own variations, you should be sure to check the search term glossary (usually found on the Search page or an Advanced Search page) for any rules or idiosyncrasies of your database's Boolean syntax. For example, HeinOnline requires Boolean terms to be in all caps, while many other databases, such as Lexis, Westlaw, and Bloomberg Law, do not. Westlaw, Lexis, and Bloomberg use slightly different forms of syntax on certain commands, and some databases allow the substitution of symbols for words ("&" for "and"; a space for "or"; "%" for "but not"). Even on a simplified searching system such as Westlaw or Lexis Advance, Boolean syntax may be used (generally from the Advanced Search page).

Here are some examples of Boolean syntax.

Connectors: and, or, but not

Example: *sexual AND abuse BUT NOT assault* will find results which contain both the terms "sexual" and "abuse" but eliminate any results which also contain the term "assault."

Proximity Limiters: /n, w/n (where "n" is a number); /s, w/s; /p, w/p

Example: *"voting rights" /s enforcement* will only return results which contain the phrase "voting rights" within the same sentence as the word "enforcement."

Example: *assumption /3 risk /p liability* will find results which contain the term "assumption" within three words of the term "risk" AND will only return results which ALSO contain the term "liability" within the same paragraph of any result which contains the term "assumption" within three words of the term "risk."

Root Expanders and Universal Characters: ! and *

Root expanders will find all variations of a term past a truncated point; this search method is especially helpful when a relevant term may differ depending on whether it is used as a verb, noun, adjective or adverb; in the singular or plural; and which verb tense is being used. Universal characters substitute for a character in the middle of a word and can pick up irregular plurals, misspellings, or variations.

Example: *statut!* = statute, statutes, statutory

Example: *wom*n* = woman, women, womyn

Quotation Marks: Enclose an Exact Phrase

Example: *"assumption of the risk"* will return results where the exact phrase "assumption of the risk" is used.

When using quotation marks to enclose an exact phrase, keep in mind the following tips:

Tip #1: If you are not sure that the phrase will always be phrased exactly the same way, if a change in verb tense allows for a variation, or if your database ignores common words such as "the," use a proximity limiter and/or a root expander or universal character to capture variations. So while *"assumption of the risk"* will return only those results in which the exact phrase "assumption of the risk" appears, *assum! /3 risk* will pick up "assumption of the risk" as well as "assumed the risk," "assumes a risk," "risk assumed," and other variations which might be relevant.

Tip #2: Some of the newer search platforms, such as Westlaw, allow you to use different types of searching, either a Boolean search or a "Google-esque" search. Be aware that, at least on Westlaw as of this writing, quotation marks can be used to find an exact phrase ONLY when using Boolean syntax (usually from the Advanced Search page). The "Google-esque" search from the main search bar will interpret quotation marks around a phrase as a proximity limiter, so *"res ipsa loquitur"* will be interpreted as *res /3 ipsa /3 loquitur*.

Field Searching allows you to limit your search to certain fields in the document, such as subject, caption, title, text, author, judge, and attorneys. Appearances of your search term in other parts of the document will be ignored. Some databases use drop-down menus, and some use abbreviations. Check your database's glossary or advanced search menu.

Example: A classic example of why field searching can be a good idea is the term "copyright." In some databases, if you do a search containing the term "copyright," and you do not restrict your search to fields, you are likely to get results in which the only occurrence of the term "copyright" is in the copyright notice of the document. Using field searching to restrict your search to only the title, subject, and/or text of a document will eliminate this problem.

Tip #3: Experiment with your search terms. Be creative. String together different queries and try to guess which will yield many results, and which will yield a more focused selection. Write them down somewhere in your research plan and leave a space where you can track how many results you get when you try them out. Now is the time to learn how to build your search terms and search queries to best fit your approach, which will be discussed in the next section. Keeping track of which strategies worked well and which needed work—as well as noting any changes or adjustments you made as your research progressed—will not only help keep your current research project organized, it will also help you learn how to research more efficiently as you develop your skills.

Even the most experienced legal researchers strike out frequently; it is perfectly normal to have to run through multiple variations on a search before you get the results you need. Part of the learning process is learning patience and not getting discouraged when your query does not yield the results you had hoped for.

The most important thing you can learn about generating search terms, though, is that you should generate them *before* you sign on to any subscription database or pick up any print resource. You will find additional search terms (and eliminate others) as you research, but unless you have worked them out before you have signed on, you are wasting time—and since you may be getting charged by the hour, that wasted time can be costly.

b.   Choosing Your Approach

Now that you have generated your search terms, you should give some thought to your approach. Probably the approach with the greatest applicability across research platforms is the inverted pyramid: in other words, starting with a broad search and using filters to narrow down to particular issues. This approach encompasses both materials and search terms: start both with broad, general sources (such as secondary authority, which will be discussed in the next section) and broad, general search terms. A too-narrow search risks missing something crucial on a related issue or similar issue that does not use your particular search term; however, a too-broad search can be unwieldy. For example, if you are interested in finding law related to parental-consent laws for abortion, you should make your search narrower than "abortion" but broader than "parental consent," because you may be interested in parental notification or other restrictions on minors seeking an abortion that do not involve parental consent.

Keep in mind that many electronic databases allow you to narrow your search from the search results page without incurring an additional charge, using a feature such as Edit, Focus, or Locate. You can use this feature more than once, so you can search different permutations or combinations of search terms without any additional charges. So, to use the abortion example above, if your initial search is for abortion restrictions generally, you could search within those results for parental consent, spousal notification, parental notification, and waiting periods, all without incurring an additional charge. In addition, editing a search allows you to use restrictors such as jurisdiction, topic, or other parameters to get precisely what you want.

2. CHOOSING YOUR MATERIALS

Now that you have identified your issues, you need to consider where you intend to start looking for answers. In other words, it is time to choose your materials.

a. Know Your Materials

It is important to know your materials. Do you want to use an electronic source, or one in print? What are secondary sources, anyway? What are primary sources?

i. *Print vs. Electronic*

Print, despite what you may hear, is not yet dead. It is also, surprisingly enough, sometimes easier to use and more current than the electronic version of the same resource. A lot will depend on the demand for one particular source over another (and so, the version that is in greater demand will be the one the publisher will pay more attention to in terms of updating), and which resources are in demand depends a lot on the topic. Real estate lawyers may prefer print, but tax lawyers may prefer electronic. Follow the money to find the most-current version of a resource—or, alternatively, check the currency information in the individual database or print resource.

While most people have their strong preferences for print vs. electronic, there are advantages and disadvantages to both, and those relative advantages may change by publisher, by resource, and by form. For example, indexing might be better in print, but while you can search only one title at a time in a print source, you can select multiple databases on most subscription legal research platforms. To find out which sources you like in print and which in electronic format, try running the same search across platforms to get a feel for which you prefer. This strategy has a side benefit: since you can never predict once you leave law school which resources will be available to you, learning how to use both print and electronic resources now will help you down the road.

ii. Secondary Sources

Secondary sources can be described as any source that is not "the law." Primary sources are "the law." Secondary sources explain, locate, analyze, index, and otherwise make "the law" intelligible and findable. Examples of secondary sources include these reference materials:

- **Law reviews and journals:** Provide in-depth, often scholarly, analyses of current issues in the law and arguments for the creation of new laws or the extension of existing laws to new situations;

- **Treatises:** Provide in-depth treatment of the state of the law as it currently exists, with citations to leading cases and statutes. May be single-volume or multi-volume. Often referred to by publisher name or author name, even if the original author has long since passed away;

- **Legal encyclopedias:** Provide short articles summarizing the current state of the law and usually include leading cases, legislation and rules;

- **Practice guides:** Provide practical, how-to-do-it advice for practicing attorneys, including procedural steps, forms, and judges' commentary. Assumes a level of knowledge of the material that a student may not have; and

- **Legal dictionaries:** Provide definitions and citations for terms of art used in law.

As you will see, secondary sources are your first stop for most legal research questions. Familiarize yourself with the secondary sources available to you, whether online or in print, and ask law librarians, professors, and attorneys which are the leading authorities in the practice areas most of interest to you.

iii. Primary Sources

As noted above, primary sources are "the law." As discussed below, your best course of action is to resist the temptation to simply dive right into a primary-authority database and start searching; instead, use a secondary source to lead you to the leading primary authority on the topic you are interested in. In other words, let someone else get your research started for you.

- **Constitutions:** Usually published as part of a collection of statutes or codes.

- **Statutes**

  - **Annotated Codes:** Usually published by a private publisher and unofficial (though sometimes designated as the "official" version of a code; check your jurisdiction to be sure), these contain research aids such as case annotations, cross-references, legislative history, research topics, references to secondary sources, and other helpful resources for finding additional authority. The text of the statute will be the same as the official version, but the finding aids will vary from publisher to publisher.

- o **Unannotated Codes:** This is the version that is put out by the state or federal government as codified. There are no finding aids included. Some state governments use a private publisher for their official codes, and some issue only an electronic version on a state website.

- **Case Reporters**
    - o **Official and unofficial:** Some jurisdictions have an official version of their case reporter and an unofficial version. Some have only one version. There are often differences between publishers' versions, particularly when it comes to finding aids, cross references and annotations; the text should be the same. Check your jurisdiction for the official reporter.

    - o **Regional reporters:** Regional reporters collect the reported cases from a group of states' highest courts and publish them together in one of several regional reporters: Atlantic Reports, Pacific Reports, North Eastern Reports, North Western Reports, South Eastern Reports, and Southern Reports.

    - o **Unreported cases:** Back when case reporters only existed in paper, only certain cases were selected for publication. Now, unreported cases are routinely put into online databases, though without headnotes or other references. Check your jurisdiction for special rules regarding the use of unreported cases; some forbid it entirely, while others allow the cases to be used as persuasive authority. In any event, unreported cases can be a very useful research tool, even in jurisdictions which forbid the citation of unreported cases, because they can lead you to reported cases related to your issue.

- **Administrative Materials:** These are laws created by an executive-branch agency of the government which is tasked with carrying out the legislature's statutory directives.

- o **Rules and Regulations:** Agencies create rules and regulations to enforce their authority. Both the authority and the ability to promulgate rules and regulations are granted by statute, usually known as an enabling statute.

- o **Administrative Decisions:** These are decisions by administrative tribunals which interpret administrative rules and regulations, operating in much the same way as case law.

- o **Attorney General/Legal Counsel Opinions:** These are advisory opinions from administrative lawyers; they are not binding, but they give an indication of the agency counsel's interpretation of the law.

- **Legislative Materials**

  - o **Bills and Drafts:** Valuable for compiling legislative history.

  - o **Committee Reports and Hearings:** Often used to assist in statutory interpretation and in legislative history.

So now that you know what materials are out there, how will you decide which of them to use? The answer will depend on how much you know about the law before you start, and whether you have any primary authority to get you started. Remember that the purpose of this chapter is not to teach you how to use the sources you select; rather, it is to help you build a strategy that you can use with any legal research resources you have available. Consult your legal research text, your lawyering skills professor, or a law librarian for instruction on using and evaluating individual resources.

b. Starting with Secondary Sources

Unless you have a leading statute or case identified, your best bet is to start with secondary sources, such as law reviews and journals, legal encyclopedias, legal dictionaries, treatises, Restatements, practice guides, and other materials that explain the law in varying levels of detail. You undoubtedly are eager to get right into your research and pull up primary authority—after all, you have spent so much time getting ready, identifying your issues, choosing your search terms, and determining your approach—but consider the following benefits of starting off with secondary sources when you do not know the law:

- You *don't* know the law. So let someone who does—and has done all the work for you—give you the big picture;

- Secondary sources can give you an overview of your legal issue as well as identify the leading statutes, cases, and primary authority;

- Secondary sources can give you additional search terms in the form of terms of art used in that particular area of the law that you might not have thought of because your fact pattern did not raise them;

- Secondary sources can save you time and money by helping you understand the legal issue and taking you straight to the leading primary authority on that issue rather than trying to figure out if the cases and statutes you find are the most-cited or most-followed.

There are two caveats to using secondary sources, however.

- When using electronic resources, you can search more databases at once than you can with print sources. However, the more databases you include (and the broader the scope of those databases), the more you will be charged. Make sure you keep this in mind when you choose your database(s);

- ALWAYS UPDATE. Secondary sources are not updated as frequently as primary authority and may be out of date. Check currency information in your print materials or electronic database. You may be surprised—often, print materials are more current than the electronic versions of the same resource.

Once you have located a good secondary authority for your issue, you can begin looking for primary authority. There are two alternative ways to begin.

- You can start with a *case, statute, or other primary authority* mentioned in the secondary source. In that case, you can follow the "One Good Case" or "One Good Statute" approach outlined below, which is the same you would use if you had to find law on one case or statute that, for example, appeared in a complaint or indictment;

- You can use a *finding aid*, discussed further below, to find primary authority on a particular topic (or by using keywords). You may find this approach most useful if the cases or statutes found in your secondary source are all very old, or if there are none in your jurisdiction.

Before you go any further, however, it is time to check back in with your research plan. Are there any terms you need to add or delete from your list of search terms based on what you found in the secondary sources? How are your strategies working for you? Be sure to make notes so that you do not go over the same ground again.

c.   Starting with a Case or Statute

If you have a leading case or a statute to get you started, this is an easy step for you; you can start with a citator to find authority that mentions your case or statute. This is sometimes called the "One Good Case" or "One Good Statute" approach. However, you should not rely solely on your case or statute to help you find results; at some point, you will need to think about how to create an additional search to find other materials as you continue your research, or to narrow your search should your leading case or statute have been cited thousands upon thousands of times. That's when you should circle back to a secondary authority—which you can find through a citator or a topic search—to see if there are other issues or other developments which you might have missed by just looking at primary authority.

To get you started, though, here are some strategies for researching using One Good Statute and One Good Case:

One Good Statute:

- Run the citation through a citator to find additional authority (primary or secondary) that mentions your statute (you can use the restrictors on a citator to limit your results to a particular subsection);

- Use the notes of decision in an annotated code to find cases and other authority, such as statutes, administrative rules and decisions, and secondary authority;

- Use the table of contents, index, browsing features, tables, Key Numbers, and other finding aids in the annotated code to find additional, related authority; and

- If you have the name of an act but not the citation, you can find a cite through the popular name table.

One Good Case:

- Run the citation through a citator to find additional authority that relies on or mentions your case (you can use restrictors to limit your results by jurisdiction, level of court, depth of treatment, or topic);

- Use a Table of Authorities feature to get a list of the cases and other authorities that your case cites within it;

- Use headnotes and Key Numbers/Topics to find additional authority that may not cite your case directly but that addresses the same legal issues;

- Many databases have suggestions for related sources in their sidebars from the results page—it may be worth looking at those suggestions;

- Many systems will also suggest additional search terms or topics which may help either broaden or narrow your search query, as needed.

Remember, these tips are just to get you started. Once you have some results, you will need to return to your research plan to see what your next steps will be. You may, for example, have to use some finding aids to find further results.

d. Finding Aids

If you have spent any time in your law school's library, you will be aware that the resources available for researching the law are impressively (or perhaps intimidatingly) vast—and that is just what you can see out on the shelves. Law libraries typically have hundreds of thousands of volumes and volume-equivalents available for use. So how do you find your way around the law?

Finding aids are just what the name suggests—tools to help you find what you are looking for. If you look at an annotated code section, you will see that it is much, much longer and contains more information than the same section from an unannotated code. Indeed, the text of the statute itself may be only a few words or a sentence, but the annotations may go on for pages. All of the information in that annotated code is designed to help you conduct research—to find the law.

The beginning of this chapter discussed the cost of legal research. What you may be wondering is why it costs so much when the cases and statutes and rules and regulations and other government information is made available free of charge. Why wouldn't law schools and lawyers simply use the government-issued, free versions? The short answer is, again, finding aids. People pay a lot of money to legal publishers not for the content of the law—which they could get for free—but for the finding aids that the publishers add to allow users to find the right case, the right statute, on the right topic, from the right jurisdiction, from the right time frame. Finding aids are the value-add that makes it worth paying a lot for legal research resources. They're also going to make your job much, much easier.

You might be tempted to ignore finding aids, and simply type in a few keywords to get started. After all, it works on Google, doesn't it? But keyword searching can only find what you type in; while some algorithms will suggest related topics, you should not rely on them to think for you. Finding aids are typically topic-or subject-based, and will thus help you find the right subject or topic areas before you start trying to use keyword searching. In other words, they help narrow the search for you. Finding aids are distinct from keyword searching, using a search engine, and Boolean search syntax, discussed above; they include West's Key Number and Digest system, Headnotes, Indexes, Tables of Contents and other tables, and Annotated Codes.

e. West's Key Number and Digest System

For many years, West Publishing was the dominant publisher of case reporters and codes in the United States. One of the reasons West became so popular was its Digest and Key Number system, which breaks down the law into topics and subtopics, assigns a topic name and number to them (a Key Number), then collects all the references to Key Numbers in an extensive index known as a Digest. There are currently over 450 main topics, and thousands of subtopics and sub-subtopics. This system has been used for years by attorneys and other legal researchers to find case law on specific topics quickly and accurately.

West employs reference attorneys who read each new published case it receives, assign a Key Number or Key Numbers to each paragraph where a point or points of law are discussed, and write a headnote, or a short summary of the point of law in the relevant paragraph, which is placed at the top of the opinion. The headnotes are then collected in the Digests, which exist in both print and electronic forms; in the Digests, all the headnotes from all the cases pertaining to a particular Key Number are collected together and arranged by jurisdiction.

One thing to keep in mind about Digests and the citations found in them: the citations you find in a Digest are in a space-saving format, not a format that is acceptable for citing in a legal research and writing exercise. Moreover, your legal writing professor will know at a glance that you just copied your cite out of the Digest and never looked at the case. Be sure to look up the case itself to get all the necessary information, and use your Bluebook, ALWD manual, or other citation manual to get the proper citation form.

f. Headnotes

Headnotes are short, topical summaries of the points of law in a case written by the legal publisher and inserted at the top of the case in the reporter. Headnotes are not part of the court's opinion for a case and so cannot be cited.

All private legal publishers have their own system of headnotes, though only West's reporters use the Key Number system. If you have a case available in print from two different publishers (or even from the same publisher in two different versions, such as Official California Reports and West's California Reporter, both published by West), compare the headnotes. How are they different? What does one publisher include that the other leaves out? Why would attorneys prefer one version over the other?

g. Indexes

An index can tell you where in a document, volume, treatise, or collection a particular word, phrase, subject, or topic occurs. Indexes in print are usually found at the back of a single volume or in separate volumes at the end of a multi-volume set. Indexes in electronic resources may be an entirely separate database or may be accessible from a document page to find further results. You may find subject indexes, A–Z indexes, or topical indexes. You may find cross-references within an index showing you where to find what you are looking for if you have used an outdated or archaic term, or if the topic is more appropriately indexed under a separate subject heading.

h. Tables

Tables come in many forms and usually provide a map to the contents of a work or a section, or may provide even more basic information.

- **Table of Contents:** Usually found at the beginning of a volume or section, the Table of Contents shows you the contents to be found in the particular volume or section you have in front of you.

- **Table of Authorities:** Briefs filed with a court include a Table of Authorities, which is a listing of all the law and other authorities cited therein and where to find them within the document. Many electronic databases will allow you to generate your own Table of Authorities for a case.

- **Table of Cases:** Usually an alphabetical listing of all the cases, by name, contained in a set of reporters or digest. This finding tool can be very helpful when you have a case name but not a specific citation.

- **Conversion Tables:** Sometimes code sections or Key Numbers are changed, or an act, once codified, is scattered among titles in the code. A conversion table can help you track any such changes and find out where your information can now be found.

- **Popular Name Tables:** You know you have to find the USA PATRIOT Act, or Sarbanes-Oxley, but you do not have the slightest notion where to start looking—and searching for these acts by name is just giving you references to the acts, but not the citations. You can go to the Popular Name Table, look up the acts by their popular names, and get the code sections. (You may have to take the extra step of consulting a conversion table as well).

i.   Annotated Codes and Regulations

As discussed briefly under statutes, annotated codes provide more than just the bare (and sometimes, very brief) text of a statute or administrative regulation. The publishers have added several types of finding aids, including the following:

- Case annotations, which help you find cases that have analyzed your code section or regulation;

- Judges' and practitioners' commentaries, which help you understand how they are used in practice;

- Cross-references to other statutes and rules;

- Legislative history and history of amendments, so you can see how the section may have changed over time (particularly important when you have an older case discussing the statute, or your client's case arose prior to an amendment);

- References to secondary sources; and

- Currency information.

3.   HOW FRESH IS YOUR RESEARCH? UPDATING AND USING CITATORS

As discussed briefly above, citators can be used to help you find the law using the One Good Case/One Good Statute approach, but their chief use is to update your research—to make sure that your authority is still "good law" and has not been overturned, amended, declared unconstitutional, or had its validity otherwise called into doubt.

The one rule you should always follow is to ALWAYS UPDATE YOUR RESEARCH. You do not want to be the one caught relying on a statute that has just been declared unconstitutional, or a case that has been thoroughly overruled. Using a citator as a last-minute check can save you a lot of embarrassment down the road.

If you enjoy using electronic tools, you will be happy to note that for all intents and purposes, the only citators worth using are online citators. Lexis has Shepard's, which was the leading print citator for many decades, and West developed its own online tool, KeyCite. Other systems, such as Bloomberg Law, have their own citators, but for right now, Shepard's and KeyCite are the standard-bearers. And both tools will give you basically the same features: a signal indicating whether any of the cases or statutes citing your authority has affected your authority negatively, and to what degree; the depth of analysis in the citing authority; filters that allow you to sort your results by type of source, jurisdiction, level of court, depth of treatment, topic, type of treatment, date, or a combination of these; cites to your authority in secondary decisions and administrative authority; and other tools that allow you to find other authorities, such as the Table of Authorities feature in Shepard's.

When you are using a citator for validation purposes, the thing you will want to pay most attention to is the visual signal the citator uses to indicate whether there is any negative treatment. No signal *usually* means that there is no negative treatment, and probably no history and no citing references at all. (One major exception is KeyCite for statutes in Westlaw, which does not display a signal on the statute page even if there is negative treatment. Get in the habit of checking the negative treatment tabs regardless of the signaling, because the signaling could be misleading). Each system also has indicators when there are citing references or direct history (such as an appeal, or a petition for review), but the signals you want to watch for are in green, yellow, and red.

A green flag or green circle means that the case has been cited and there is no negative treatment by a later authority. A yellow flag or yellow triangle means that there has been some negative treatment, but it does not affect the validity of the authority—for example, the holding of a case may have been questioned by a court in another jurisdiction, or a statute might have proposed amending legislation. If you see either of those signals, you'll want to look at the citator's report, but you should be able to proceed.

A red flag or red stop sign? That is when you need to sit up and pay attention. Despite what you might think, a red signal does not automatically mean you cannot cite to the authority. It means you need to open up the full report on the citator, pull the negative citing authority, and *read it with care*. It could be that your case has been depublished, or your statute has been rescinded, in which case you absolutely cannot use it. Or it could be that a reviewing court has overturned your case on one point of law but left intact the lower court's ruling that you were relying on. In the case of a statute, there may have been an amendment on one subsection but not another, or part of an act may have been unconstitutional, but not the section relevant to your matter.

Another thing that might happen when you use a citator is that you may find an even better, more recent authority on the same subject. And, yes, you should absolutely take a look at that authority, and then repeat your research steps as necessary.

4.   CLOSING THE LOOP: HOW DO YOU KNOW WHEN TO STOP?

Legal research may seem like an endless process, with stops and starts and returns and do-overs and checking the same ground seemingly forever. And it is hard to know when to walk away. But you will need to figure out when and how to stop your research.

Think of the legal research process as a series of loops, the kind you probably practiced when you were learning cursive, proceeding forward across the page but doubling back on themselves as well. You will have to repeat the process for each new resource you find, but you will also come to a point where you realize that you are seeing the same few cases over and over, you are seeing the same statutes, the annotations are all pointing you to the same few secondary sources, and you do not seem to be making the same kind of progress you did at first. There is a reason you keep seeing the same cases if you are on the right track: when you have a common-law system that builds on precedent, the cases with precedential value tend to be cited a lot.

If you are finding yourself running into the same authority time and again, try adjusting your search terms to broaden or narrow them, and see if your results change markedly. Try a different approach, or a different finding aid or research tool. If your results are substantially different, you probably still have some work to do (and you may want to look back over your notes). If your results look pretty much the same, however, you can start the process of closing the loop.

Before you put your research down, take a few minutes and make some notations on your research plan. What worked? What did not? What might you try differently next time? Sort your research into Yes, No, and Maybe categories. What worked with the Yes pile? What didn't work with the No pile? Take a last pass at the citator to be sure you haven't missed anything.

Congratulations. You have finished your research. Do not be alarmed if it took more time than you wanted it to—that is very common, even with seasoned researchers. The research process by its nature takes a lot of time. What you want to do is make sure that that time is used effectively and productively.

Research Plan Template

Relevant Client Facts:

Legal Question:

Research Plan:

1. **Search Terms:**

    Parties involved:

    Places and things/what is in controversy:

    Potential claims and defenses:

    Relief sought by possible plaintiff:

2. **Jurisdiction/Binding Authority/Timing:**

3. **Preliminary/Secondary Resources:**

4. **Primary Authority:**

5. **Shepardize/Keycite:**

CHAPTER 26

FOREIGN AND INTERNATIONAL LEGAL RESEARCH

■ ■ ■

By Maureen Moran[1]

A. INTRODUCTION

As you have been learning, the American legal system is only one of hundreds in the world. Each of those legal systems has its own rules, sources, and authorities. But these systems do not exist in a vacuum.

What rules govern when two or more States or entities interact? What are the enforcement mechanisms? The study of these questions comprises the fields of foreign law and international law. The purpose of this chapter is not to give you a comprehensive review of all the resources available for researching this vast field of law. Rather, the goal is to give you enough of an overview to get you pointed in the right direction when faced with an issue of foreign or international law.

B. CATEGORIES OF EXTRA-TERRITORIAL LAW

When presented with an issue involving extra-territorial, or non-domestic U.S. law, it is helpful to understand the different categories into which this law is divided.

Foreign Law. The domestic law of any State other than the United States is considered "foreign law." This is the law that applies within the borders of that State, just as domestic U.S. law applies within the United States. However, just as U.S. law may apply in some instances outside of the country's borders, so may foreign law sometimes be applied in U.S. courts.

For example, in a case involving an international shipping contract, the contract may specify that the substantive law of a foreign nation controls in any action brought to enforce the terms of the contract. Where a United States party and a Greek party enter into a shipping contract, which may be adjudicated in any court in either country but which specifies

---

[1] This chapter relies on the research guides written by Paul Howard and Jack Schroeder of the McGeorge School of Law, Law Library. Special thanks to Jennifer Wertkin, formerly of Columbia Law School's Diamond Law Library for her work reviewing the chapter.

that Greek law must apply to any dispute, a U.S. court deciding a case brought under the contract would apply Greek law when making its decision.

International Law. International law is the law governing the interactions between States and between States and private persons, corporations, or organizations based in another State. International law is usually divided into private and public international law. *Private international law* concerns the rules that govern jurisdiction, choice of law, and enforcement of judgments in private disputes involving more than one jurisdiction. *Public international law*, on the other hand, consists of the rules and principles governing the conduct of States and international organizations in the international sphere, as well as the relations between those States and international organizations and natural or legal persons. There are several sources of public international law.

These sources include the following:

- **International Agreements.** These include treaties, accords, and other formal agreements between States and between States and international organizations. These may be bilateral (between two parties) or multilateral (between more than two parties), and may include reservations or other limitations by the signatories. International agreements also include United Nations agreements, as well as agreements generated by the European Union and other multinational organizations, such as the United Nations.

- **Customary Law.** Customary law is the principle that, when a practice or rule becomes a custom—when it is the way things have been or usually are done—that practice or rule takes on the character of law.

  For a practice or rule to become customary law, the States or organizations involved must follow the rule or practice out of a sense of obligation, so that the practice or rule is accepted by the parties involved to be legally binding and not simply a courtesy. Thus, even if a practice is widely followed, it does not necessarily take on the force of law unless there is evidence that the parties are treating the practice as a legal obligation that they are not free to depart from. Evidence that a rule has become customary law may be derived from international judicial and arbitral decisions, national judicial decisions, scholarly writings, and pronouncements by States.

- **General Principles.** These principles are sometimes used as supplementary rules where appropriate; the rules must be common to the major legal systems of the world. General principles differ from customary law in that the rules existed in most legal systems prior to their application to the international context, while customary law refers to rules derived from practices among international entities.

C. WHERE CAN YOU FIND FOREIGN AND INTERNATIONAL LAW?

Before you look up a foreign law, a treaty, or a UN document, you should map out a strategy for research. The strategy you should employ will be remarkably similar to the one you would employ for researching an unfamiliar issue of U.S. law, discussed in Chapter 25. You will first need to define your issue, select your search terms, and choose your sources. You will want to begin with secondary sources to gain an understanding of foreign and international law and of how the issue plays out in the international context (as well as to gain a better understanding of any unfamiliar practices or terms of art).

You will also need to identify which area of law you need to research. Do you have an issue involving the application of a foreign country's law in a U.S. court? Do you have an issue involving evidence of customary international law? Do you need to research a treaty, and if so, is the United States a party to it? Are you looking at a UN convention? Are you researching the decisions of an international tribunal? Which body of law you need to research will ultimately determine where you look to find your answers, but you should always begin the same way you would to research any unfamiliar issue of law: by letting an expert guide you.

D. GENERAL SECONDARY SOURCES

1. RESEARCH GUIDES

Luckily for the novice legal researcher, many guides to researching foreign law and international law are available, both online and in print. These guides can provide assistance in locating sources, an overview of the particular topic and legal context, and guidance on how to approach a particular research problem. The researcher should be aware, however, that while such guides are readily obtainable, not every source cited in them will be easily accessible.

Many foreign and international legal research materials are available in print only, and not every library will have those resources. Moreover, many subscription databases are expensive and may not be part of a particular library's legal research plan. Consult your library to see which resources are available to you, whether in your library or through interlibrary loan. You may also, if you are researching U.S. treaty materials or UN documents, be able to find materials at a library that is a depository for federal materials or UN materials.

The following are some suggested research guides; you can also find research guides by typing a search string such as "research guides international law" or "research guides treaties" or "research guides united nations" into your favorite search engine. Many libraries with large international law collections have excellent research guides, though the materials are unique to their collections; be sure to check your own library's website and catalog for research guides as well.

2. ONLINE RESEARCH GUIDES

- *GlobaLex* contains links to a plethora of research guides to foreign, international, and comparative law.

  - http://www.nyulawglobal.org/globalex/Index.html

- *Foreign and International Law* by the Law Library of Congress provides research guidance for a selection of foreign legal systems.

  - http://www.loc.gov/law/help/foreign.php

- *International Legal Research Tutorial* provides information about foreign, comparative, and international law, as well as research instruction and a resource guide.

  - http://law.duke.edu/ilrt/index-2.html

- *World Legal Information Institute (World LII)* is a global site that includes links to information on foreign, comparative, and international law, as well as conference papers and other materials.

  - http://worldlii.org/

- *International Law Research Guides* provides a wealth of sources, including an extensive list of jurisdiction-specific foreign legal research guides.

  - www.law.columbia.edu/library/research-guides

- *United Nations Collection in the Princeton University Library* provides links to resources for researching United Nations and League of Nations documents.

  - https://libguides.princeton.edu/UnitedNations

- *United Nations Documentation* provides helpful tips on how to use a variety of UN finding aids.

  - http://www.nyulawglobal.org/globalex/UN_Resources_Research_Tools1.html

- *Guide to Treaty Research* provides a guide for researching treaties, whether or not the United States is a party.

  o http://library.law.columbia.edu/guides/Guide_to_Treaty _Research

- *Treaty Research* provides guidance for researching treaties, whether or not the United States is a party.

  o http://guides.ll.georgetown.edu/TreatyResearch

3. PRINT RESEARCH GUIDES

- MARCI B. HOFFMAN & ROBERT C. BERRING, INTERNATIONAL LEGAL RESEARCH IN A NUTSHELL (2008).

- MARCI HOFFMAN & MARY RUMSEY, INTERNATIONAL AND FOREIGN LEGAL RESEARCH: A COURSEBOOK (2008).

- CLAIRE M. GERMAIN, GERMAIN'S TRANSNATIONAL LAW RESEARCH: A GUIDE FOR ATTORNEYS (2006).

- ELLEN G. SHAFFER & RANDALL J. SNYDER, CONTEMPORARY PRACTICE OF PUBLIC INTERNATIONAL LAW (1997).

- GEO. WASH. J. INT'L L. & ECON., GUIDE TO INTERNATIONAL LEGAL RESEARCH (4TH ED. 2002).

4. TREATISES

While research guides can give you an overview of a topic and help you determine which resources you will need to consult to find your answer, treatises can give you an in-depth understanding of a legal topic. Research guides can help you locate the most relevant treatises for your purposes; you should check your library's catalog to see if the treatise is available to you. While there are some international treatises available through commercial databases, you may find that you need to use a print resource because not every treatise is available electronically.

The following are some examples of treatises on international law:

- VOLKER RITTBERGER, GLOBAL GOVERNANCE AND THE UNITED NATIONS SYSTEM (2001).

- MARK W. JANIS, AN INTRODUCTION TO INTERNATIONAL LAW (4TH ED. 2003).

- J.L. BRIERLY, THE LAW OF NATIONS: AN INTRODUCTION TO THE INTERNATIONAL LAW OF PEACE (6TH ED. 1963).

- IAN BROWNLIE, PRINCIPLES OF PUBLIC INTERNATIONAL LAW (7TH ED. 2008).

- STEPHEN C. MCCAFFREY, UNDERSTANDING INTERNATIONAL LAW (2006).

- FRANZ CEDE & LILLY SUCHARIPA-BEHRMANN, THE UNITED NATIONS: LAW AND PRACTICE (2001).

5. DICTIONARIES AND ENCYCLOPEDIAS

Legal dictionaries and encyclopedias of foreign and international law provide definitions of legal terminology and summaries of cases and treaties, biographical information of individuals, and information on international organizations and legal systems. Thus, they are similar to legal dictionaries and encyclopedias of U.S. law.

- JAMES R. FOX, DICTIONARY OF INTERNATIONAL LAW (3D ED. 2003).

- MAX PLANCK INSTITUTE FOR COMPARATIVE PUBLIC LAW AND INTERNATIONAL LAW, DICTIONARY OF PUBLIC INTERNATIONAL LAW (2003).

- JOHN GRANT & J. CRAIG BARKER, PARRY AND GRANT ENCYCLOPAEDIC DICTIONARY OF INTERNATIONAL LAW (2D ED. 2004).

6. LEGAL PERIODICALS

Scholarly articles may not only help a researcher gain an understanding of international law and practice, but they may also provide evidence of international norms in customary law. Articles on international and foreign law may be found in international or domestic law reviews and journals, which may be found through full-text searching on a periodicals database on HeinOnline, Westlaw or Lexis. Some articles may only be available in print. Useful periodical indexes include the following:

- INDEX TO FOREIGN LEGAL PERIODICALS covers worldwide, foreign, and non-Anglo-American legal periodicals. The electronic version has coverage beginning in 1985; the paper version covers the years 1960–2002.

- *LegalTrac* contains over 1.6 million articles from 1,400 domestic and international legal journals and periodicals. The database has articles from 1980–2012.

- INDEX TO LEGAL PERIODICALS & BOOKS AND INDEX TO LEGAL PERIODICALS RETROSPECTIVE index thousands of legal periodicals, including many foreign and international titles. While coverage in the electronic version varies by individual title, INDEX TO LEGAL PERIODICALS & BOOKS covers 1981–

date, while INDEX TO LEGAL PERIODICALS RETROSPECTIVE covers 1908–1981.

- LEGAL JOURNALS INDEX covers journals published in the United Kingdom and Europe as well as journals which pertain to the laws of the European Community and its member States. It is available on Westlaw, and coverage dates from 1986.

7. PORTAL SITES

Portal sites may be useful in finding primary as well as secondary sources of foreign and international law. These sites aggregate and organize websites on a particular topic. As with any website, be sure to evaluate the trustworthiness of the source: who maintains the site? Does the person or institution which has compiled the site have a bias, or an interest in one aspect of international or foreign law, which may result in incomplete coverage of a topic? How complete and recent are the sources linked? Be aware that portal sites may come and go, or links may change or be broken.

- *EISIL*, the Electronic Information System for International Law, is a portal site curated by the American Society for International Law. It contains links to primary and secondary sources of international law, authoritative websites, and research guides, organized by topic and subtopic.

  o   http://www.eisil.org/

- *Foreign and International Law Guide*, Cornell University Law Library. This site provides topical and regional research information, as well as links to foreign law websites and links to world law portals.

  o   http://guides.library.cornell.edu/Foreign_and_Internatio nal_Law_Guide/

- *Guide to Law Online: Nations* by the Law Library of Congress provides links to primary law resources of nearly all legal systems.

  o   http://www.loc.gov/law/help/guide/nations.php

Once you have determined your research approach, based on the particulars of your issue, you will need to find legal authority for the particular area of the law relevant to your research. The following are suggested sources and steps for treaty, customary international law, foreign law, and United Nations and other international organization research.

E. TREATY RESEARCH

Researching treaties and international agreements can be complex, which will require you to look in a variety of sources. Even when the United States has ratified a treaty and it is thus part of the supreme law of the land, researching that treaty is not as simple as looking up a citation on an online database. There are several steps common to treaty research whether or not the United States is a party, and whether the agreement is bilateral or multilateral. The following steps should be taken:

1. CHECKING FOR RELEVANT SECONDARY SOURCES

Secondary sources may include research guides and texts, as well as treatises and law review articles. These may be general, may be jurisdiction-specific, or may be topic-specific. Some examples include:

- ***Research Guides***
  - *Guide to Treaty Research* (general research guide) http://library.law.columbia.edu/guides/Guide_to_Treaty _Research
  - *GlobaLex* (jurisdiction-specific research guides included) http://www.nyulawglobal.org/Globalex/Treaty_Research 1.html
  - International Law of the Sea (topic-specific research guide) https://www.peacepalacelibrary.nl/research-guides /special-topics/law-of-the-sea/

- ***Treatises and Law Review Articles***
  - **U.S. Treaties.** Search for scholarly articles or treatises on treaties to which the United States is a party. You may search by treaty name or topic, but be aware that you may have to look in print sources to find relevant articles, especially for older treaties.
    - Law review articles may be located through the INDEX TO LEGAL PERIODICALS, LEGAL INDEX, and the full-text law review databases on Westlaw, Lexis, and HeinOnline.
    - Treatises may be located through your library's catalog or a research guide.
  - **Non-U.S. Treaties.** Many prominent non-U.S. treaties will be discussed in law review articles or treatises. The two main approaches for researching these treaties are by treaty name or by topic. Paid legal research databases which focus on U.S. law rarely have materials on non-

U.S. treaties, so be aware that you may not find any coverage at all.

- For international law review articles, consult the INDEX TO FOREIGN LEGAL PERIODICALS OR LEGAL JOURNALS INDEX. For articles in U.S. law journals that discuss non-U.S. treaties, try the INDEX TO LEGAL PERIODICALS OR LEGALTRAC.

- For treatises, try a keyword search in your library's catalog or use a source suggested by a treaty research guide.

2. FIND THE AUTHORIZED TEXT OF THE TREATY

The full text of a treaty may be found in a variety of official and unofficial sources, whether that treaty is a U.S. treaty or a non-U.S. treaty. These sources include treaty sets, publications of individual countries or intergovernmental organizations, commercial sources, and free and fee-based electronic resources.

While the U.S. government prints the text of its treaties, the source that contains the text will vary depending on the year the treaty was published. Your approach will depend on whether you have a citation, or at least know the treaty name or date. If you have a citation, you can find it through the citation. If you have a name, or a topic, you might consider using a search engine or a law review database as a starting point. Sometimes, a search engine will lead you to the full text, but you need to determine whether that text is the authorized text.

Here are some places to look:

- *For U.S. Treaty Text*
  - United States Statutes at Large (Stat.) is an official publication that has the text of treaties from 1776–1949. Volume 64, Part 3 (1950–51) has a cumulative list of agreements.

  - United States Treaties and Other International Agreements (U.S.T.) is an official publication that has the text of treaties from 1950–1984.

  - Treaties and Other International Acts Series (T.I.A.S.) is an official publication, published in pamphlet form, which has the text of treaties from 1984–1997.

  - Senate Treaty Documents reproduces the text of treaties presented to the Senate for its advice and consent. Available online through Lexis, Westlaw, HeinOnline, Congress.gov, and in microfiche from the Congressional

Information Service. This service has the text of treaties from 1980–present.

o   Hein's United States Treaties and Other International Agreements Current Service, available on microfiche and on HeinOnline. HeinOnline's Treaties and Agreements Library contains every treaty entered into by the United States, whether in-force, expired, or not yet published.

o   United States Code Service includes the text of dozens of treaties, organized by topic (Intellectual Property, Sale of Goods, Competition Laws, International Civil Litigation, Air Transportation of Passengers and Property, Diplomatic and Consular Relations, Armed Conflict and Human Rights, and Children) in an unnumbered volume entitled "International Agreements." This volume includes annotations and research references. Also available on Lexis.

o   United Nations Treaty Series (U.N.T.S.) is available in print and online (as the United Nations Treaty Collection, https://treaties.un.org/) and includes treaties registered with the UN's Secretariat. Coverage begins in 1946.

o   League of Nations Treaty Series (L.N.T.S.) has international agreements that were registered with the League's Secretariat from 1920–1946.

- *For Non-U.S. Treaty Text*

o   United Nations Treaty Series (U.N.T.S.) is available in print and online (as the United Nations Treaty Collection, https://treaties.un.org/) and includes treaties registered with the UN's Secretariat. Coverage begins in 1946.

o   League of Nations Treaty Series (L.N.T.S.) has international agreements that were registered with the League's Secretariat from 1920–1946.

o   Council of Europe Treaty Series has treaties from 1949 to date negotiated under the auspices of the Council of Europe. This set was known prior to 2004 as the European Treaty Series. Available online at the Council of Europe's website, http://www.coe.int/en/web/conventions.

o   Consolidated Treaty Series, Clive Parry, ed. This set is a collection of multilateral and bilateral treaties entered into between 1648 and 1919. Available in print.

- o Intergovernmental Organizations websites. Intergovernmental organizations, such as the African Union, the European Union, and the Organization of American States often have official treaty texts on their websites.

- o International Legal Materials, a publication of the American Society for International Law published biweekly since 1962, is available on Lexis, Westlaw, JSTOR, and in print. The ASIL website has an index of most of the tables of contents at http://www.asil.org/resources/international-legal-materials. Coverage is limited.

- o Treaty Indexes, such as Flare Index To Treaties (http://193.62.18.232/dbtw-wpd/textbase/treatysearch.htm); M.J. Bowman & D.J. Harris, Multilateral Treaties: Index and Current Status (1984); United Nations Cumulative Treaty Index (http://treaties.un.org/Pages/cumulative indexes.aspx); World Treaty Index (http://worldtreaty index.com/).

- o For individual countries, consult a research guide for resources.

3. VERIFY ITS CURRENT STATUS, INCLUDING PARTIES TO THE AGREEMENT

Has the treaty entered into force? Has it been updated? A multilateral treaty often requires a certain number of signatories to adopt or ratify the treaty in order to enter into force, which may be years or even decades after the treaty is drafted and signed by the first party.

The most useful source to check for the status of a treaty is the treaty depositary, which may be a national government or an international or intergovernmental agency. The UN is the depositary for many important international agreements and maintains a list of over 500 multilateral treaties for which it is the depositary (Multilateral Treaties Deposited with the Secretary-General, http://treaties.un.org/pages/ParticipationStatus. aspx), but the depositary may be an intergovernmental trade organization or national government.

In the case of U.S. treaties, you should determine whether the Senate has ratified the treaty, or whether the status is that of an executive agreement. The U.S. State Department publishes annually *Treaties In Force*, which lists all treaties to which the United States is a party as of January 1 of that year. Because the list is published only once a year, it will not have the most recent information. *Treaties In Force* is available in print, on subscription services, and on the State Department's website at http://www.state.gov/s/l/treaty/tif/index.htm.

4. ASCERTAIN WHETHER THERE ARE ANY RESERVATIONS OR DECLARATIONS TO THE TREATY

Parties to a multilateral agreement often sign with reservations that seek to limit or exclude certain provisions from applying to that party, or with declarations that provide the party's interpretation or understanding of a particular provision or of the treaty in general. Such reservations and declarations are rare in bilateral treaties but common in multilateral treaties. The depositary's website or *Treaties In Force* are good sources for this information. Since the Senate will often add reservations or declarations as part of its advice and consent function during ratification, so that the reservations or declarations are part of domestic law, you should check *Treaties In Force* or Congress.gov for any such reservations or reservations.

5. LOCATING STATUTES AND REGULATIONS THAT IMPLEMENT THE AGREEMENT

A self-executing treaty is one that does not require any legislation to go into effect. A non-self-executing treaty requires some local action to become part of that nation's law. Not every treaty, and not every country, requires implementing legislation. If you can determine that the treaty is not self-executing (for example, if the text itself specifies it is not), you will have to find the implementing legislation. For U.S. treaties, you should consult *United States Code Annotated* or *United States Code Service* for statutes, and the *Federal Register* and the *Code of Federal Regulations* for regulations. For non-U.S. treaties, consult a research guide for the particular individual country.

6. FIND INTERPRETIVE MATERIALS, SUCH AS JUDICIAL DECISIONS AND THE TRAVAUX PRÉPARATOIRES (TREATY NEGOTIATION AND DRAFTING DOCUMENTS)

Just as judicial decisions interpret statutes, judicial decisions interpret treaties. In addition, just as legislative history documents provide guidance as to the intent of the drafters, *travaux préparatoires* provide guidance as to the intent of the drafters to those interpreting or applying a treaty.

- ***For U.S. Treaties***

  o   Judicial decisions may be found in commercial databases or reporters; in addition, if the treaty has been codified or if there is implementing legislation, interpretive decisions may be listed in the notes of cases following the code section. The *United States Code Service* also has volumes entitled "International Agreements" and "Uncodified: Notes to Uncodified Laws and Treaties," which contain such references. In addition, West's Digest and Key Number system has a topic called "Treaties" through which judicial decisions interpreting treaties can be found. Citators may be used for any codified treaties. Where a multilateral treaty to which the United States is a party has been interpreted by an international tribunal, such as the International Court of Justice, check the court's website or a research guide.

  o   *Travaux préparatoires* from the treaty drafting process may be available at the depositary website or through a commercial publisher. Legislative history materials from the Senate's advice and consent process, such as committee reports, floor debates and hearing transcripts, may also be useful.

- ***For Non-U.S. Treaties***

  o   Judicial decisions from international tribunals and implementing legislation from intergovernmental organizations may be found on the websites of those tribunals and organizations. For judicial decisions and legislation from individual countries, consult a research guide particular to that country.

  o   *Travaux préparatoires* may be available at the depositary's website, or through a commercial publisher.

F.   CUSTOMARY INTERNATIONAL LAW

Legal research into customary international law, like treaty research, requires consulting a number of sources, many of which are not available in electronic format. Because customary law derives from consistent practice of nations out of a sense of legal obligation and not from any written agreement, a researcher must look for evidence that a practice has risen to the level of custom and can therefore be considered customary law. The first thing to do is to examine secondary sources and case law for such evidence. If a search of these sources is inconclusive, you should examine documents that reflect State practice. The following are some sources for researching State practice:

- *Sources of State Practice In International Law* (Ralph Gaebler & Maria Smolka-Day 2002) lists sources of treaties and diplomatic documents for 16 States, including the United States.

- Yearbooks and Digests—These are annual or periodic publications that provide information about a country, an issue, an international organization, or a legal system. Yearbooks and digests may contain scholarly articles, book reviews and documents, such as case law, legislation, treaties and statements by government officials, that evidence or illustrate State practices.

  o HeinOnline provides electronic access to some yearbooks in its Foreign & International Law database, but not the most current ones. Search your library's catalog or consult a research guide to find an appropriate yearbook or digest.

  o *Digest of United States Practice in International Law* is available in print, and excerpts are available on the State Department website.

  o Yearbooks for other countries or regions may be found through a search engine or library catalog.

- Voting records in International Organizations—A State's voting record at the UN, the European Union, or another intergovernmental or international organization may provide evidence of State practice. For example, if a State consistently voted in favor of recognition of a particular border or to define its territorial waters in a certain way, that may be seen as evidence of where the border should be or where international waters should begin. See the section on the United Nations (below) for further guidance, or consult the website of the particular organization for information on how to obtain such information.

G. FOREIGN LAW

As noted above, foreign law is the domestic law of a foreign State. While some legal systems have excellent websites, it is rare to find any outside the English-speaking world that are in English. Moreover, even if you can read the website of the country you are researching, ask yourself how much you know about that legal system. You need to consider whether the authority is precedential or, if not, whether it is likely to influence the tribunal hearing your case.

The best practice is to consult a secondary source as well as a foreign law research guide for the particular country whose law you are interested in. It will save you time and give you background that will be helpful in deciding whether you have the right law. If your knowledge of the law of a foreign country is less developed than your knowledge of American law, let an expert in that country's law guide you in your research. *GlobaLex*, the Law Library of Congress' *Foreign and International Law* and *Guide to Law Online: Nations*, Reynolds and Flores' *Foreign Law Guide* (available both in print and online to subscribers), the World Legal Information Institute's website, and Columbia Law Library's *A Selective List of Guides to Foreign Legal Research* are all excellent places to start.

1. UNITED NATIONS AND OTHER INTERNATIONAL ORGANIZATIONS

International organizations, such as the United Nations, Council of Europe, or World Trade Organization, are valuable sources for international law. Not only do these bodies generate resolutions, rules, and regulations themselves, but they are good sources for evidence of State practice through the voting records and comments of member States. The following is a brief list of some resources you may find helpful; as always, consult a research guide or treatise if your particular issue requires a different resource.

- **Research Guides.** In addition to the research guides listed above, the United Nations Dag Hammarskjold Library has an excellent guide to United Nations documents, *United Nations Documentation: Research Guide*. This research guide, found at http://research.un.org/en/docs, provides information about UN document numbers, the structure of the various bodies within the UN, and helpful research tips.

- **Treatises.** There are a number of treatises which have been written about various international organizations and how they operate. You can do a keyword search in your library's catalog or in a search engine for the particular international organization you seek to research.

2. ACCESS TO DOCUMENTS OF INTERNATIONAL ORGANIZATIONS

Many international organizations put their documents online, and many of those resources are in English. These documents may include founding documents, agreements, dispute resolution documents, and governing rules. The following are some helpful databases:

- *AccessUN* is a web-based index to more than 500,000 UN documents, dating back to 1946, as well as the full text of over 35,000 documents. AccessUN is a subscription service through your library.

- Council of Europe—the website for the Council of Europe provides information about the Council, treaties deposited with the Council, and case law through the European Court of Human Rights, among other documents. http://www.coe.int/

- *ODS* is the Official Document System of the United Nations. It provides free access to all types of United Nations documents going back to 1993, and selected documents (resolutions of the Security Council, General Assembly, Economic and Social Council and Trusteeship Council) from 1946. ODS continues to add older documents as they are digitized. https://documents.un.org/prod/ods.nsf/home.xsp

- World Trade Organization—the WTO's website contains the full text of nearly all unrestricted WTO documents and legal texts, as well as podcasts, videos, terminology, and selected GATT documents. http://www.wto.org/english/res_e/res_e.htm

3.   INTERNATIONAL TRIBUNALS

While most international courts and arbitral tribunals do not strictly observe the rule of *stare decisis* as do common law courts, these courts and tribunals often look to prior judicial and arbitral decisions for guidance on international practice or the interpretation of international treaties, rules, and norms.

- **Websites.** Many international courts and arbitral tribunals make their decisions and rules available on their websites. The following is a selected list of such sites:

  o   European Court of Human Rights: http://echr.coe.int/Pages/home.aspx?p=home

  o   European Court of Justice: http://curia.europa.eu/

  o   Inter-American Commission on Human Rights: http://www.oas.org/en/iachr/

  o   International Court of Justice: http://www.icj-cij.org

  o   International Criminal Court: http://www.icc-cpi.int

- **Case Reporters.** You may want to consult a print case reporter to find case law from a tribunal that investigated or adjudicated a particular dispute and has dissolved, or to find older case law that has not yet been digitized. The following are a selection of those you might find in your library or through interlibrary loan:

o   *Annotated Leading Cases of International Criminal Tribunals* is a series which contains documents for the Special Court for Sierra Leone and the criminal tribunals for Rwanda and the former Yugoslavia. The first volume was published in 1998. The accompanying website is at http://www.annotatedleadingcases.com/.

o   University of Nottingham Human Rights Law Centre, *International Human Rights Reports* contains selected cases on the topic of human rights. Published since 1994, with four volumes per year since 1998. This title is also available online to subscribers.

o   Elihu Lauterpach & Christopher Greenwood (eds.), *International Law Reports* (1929) is a publication of Cambridge University Press which contains selected judicial and arbitral decisions from international and national courts. The series was first published in 1929 and contains decisions from as early as 1919. An electronic subscription database is also available.

o   European Court of Human Rights, *Série A: Arrêts et décisions = Series A: Judgments and Decisions* (1960–1996); *Reports of Judgments and Decisions = Recueil des arrêts et décisions* (1996–date). Cases are also available online at HUDOC, http://www.echr.coe.int/echr/en/hudoc/faq/.

o   United Nations, *Reports of International Arbitral Awards*. The first volume appeared in 1948.

o   International Court of Justice, *Reports of Judgments, Advisory Opinions and Orders. Recueil des arrêts, avis consultatifs et ordonnances*. Decisions from 1947 to date.

o   James J. Patton, *World Trade Organization Dispute Settlement Decisions: Bernan's Annotated Reporter* (1998). This is an example of a reporter compiled by a commercial publisher.

• **Commercial Databases.** Lexis and Westlaw both provide access to a variety of international judicial and arbitral decisions and opinions, such as decisions of the International Court of Justice; European Union courts; International Criminal Tribunals from Rwanda and the Former Yugoslavia; Iran-U.S. Claims Tribunal; WTO & GATT Panel; Inter-American Commission for Human Rights; and international arbitration bodies. Not every subscription plan will have access to all these databases, and what you have available to you in law school will most likely be different from what you will have available in practice. It is always a good idea to find out what resources your school's or employer's database subscription plan includes, and how extensive and recent the coverage for each database is.

CHAPTER 27

THE CITATION REQUIREMENT

■ ■ ■

By Stephanie J. Thompson

A. PURPOSE OF CITATION

Legal citations provide more than just a reference to the authority being relied upon. Citations are a form of legal analysis: they show that the analysis is legally supported, they identify if the authority is binding on the court, and they demonstrate where the particular authority sits in the hierarchy of all authority. Furthermore, citations inform whether the analysis is grounded in legal tradition dating back to the 1900s, or maybe that the analysis is a new trend in the law. Recognizing the importance of citation as more than a research reference tool is the first step to using citation effectively.

Additionally, proper citation directly correlates with an attorney's credibility. Judges expect attorneys to cite to relevant legal authority and to use proper citation form. In a number of published opinions, judges have humiliated attorneys, imposed monetary sanctions, and initiated disciplinary actions against attorneys for failure to properly cite legal authority.

For example, in *Hurlbert v. Gordon*,[1] the Court of Appeals of Washington sanctioned attorneys for failure to properly cite their brief, both in form and in substance. The court reasoned that the purpose of citation "is to enable the court and opposing counsel efficiently and expeditiously to review the accuracy of the factual statements made in the briefs and efficiently and expeditiously to review the relevant legal authority." The court criticized the attorneys not only for flawed citation form, but also for citing to cases that did not support the positions for which they were being cited, including references to documents that did not exist. Thus, it is not just the accuracy of the citation form that concerns the court, but also the accuracy and the relevance of the substance to which the citation refers.

In another case, *In re Shepperson*,[2] a State Bar disciplinary action was taken against an attorney because his "briefs contained numerous citation

---

[1]   824 P.2d 1238 (Wash. Ct. App. 1992).

[2]   674 A.2d 1273 (Vt. 1996).

errors that made identification of the cases difficult, cited cases for irrelevant or incomprehensible reasons, made legal arguments without citation to authority, and inaccurately represented the law contained in the cited cases." As a result, the State Bar found that the attorney had "disserved his clients by preparing inadequate and incomprehensible legal briefs."[3] Based on these and other errors, the State Bar stated that the only issue was whether the attorney should be disbarred or suspended indefinitely.

B. CITATION MANUALS

A variety of citation manuals are available. Which one you use will be based on the jurisdiction where you practice or the citation manual assigned by your professor in law school. The goal of learning citation in law school is not to become an expert at using one particular citation manual. Instead, the goal is to understand the purpose of citation, how citation should be used as a part of legal analysis, and how to use any citation manual efficiently and effectively.

While some of the nuances of the manuals are different, they all generally agree on the basic information to be included in citations. For example, when citing to a case, all citation manuals require that the case citation include the case name, the date of the case, reference to the court, and the title and volume of the reporter where the case is published. Similarly, when citing to a statute, the statutory citation must include the title of the statute and the numerical code section where it is codified. Additionally, when citing to a secondary source, the citation must include the title of the secondary source, the author (if applicable), the volume and page number, and the date. Below is a brief summary of the most well-known citation manuals.[4]

1. BLUEBOOK[5]

The Bluebook was created by the Harvard Law Review in 1926 and is updated every few years with the publication of a new edition. The Bluebook is the most widely used citation manual in the United States. It is divided into two sections—the Bluepages and the Whitepages. The Bluepages are known as the "Practioner Pages" or the "how to guide" for citation, and these are the pages used by practitioners or by law students

---

[3] *Id.*

[4] There are numerous web sites that provide research guides on how to use the various citation manuals. A few examples are: http://www.law.cornell.edu/citation/ (last visited Nov. 2012); http://guides.library.cornell.edu/c.php?g=31610&p=200437 (last visited Feb. 2018); http://www.law.georgetown.edu/library/research/bluebook/ (last visited Nov. 2012).

[5] THE BLUEBOOK: A UNIFORM SYSTEM OF CITATION (20th ed. 2015). The Bluebook is compiled by the editors of the COLUMBIA LAW REVIEW, the HARVARD LAW REVIEW, the UNIVERSITY OF PENNSYLVANIA LAW REVIEW, and THE YALE LAW JOURNAL. The Bluebook is published and distributed by the HARVARD LAW REVIEW ASSOCIATION.

during law school for their legal research and writing courses. The Whitepages pages are designed for scholarly writing, such as law review or journal articles. If you work on your school's law review or journal or write a law review or journal article, you will use the Whitepages.

The Bluepages begin with general rules regarding typeface conventions, where to place citations, and signals. Each type of legal source, such as cases, statutes, secondary sources, constitutions, and court documents, also has its own specific citation rules. One of the most useful features of the Bluebook are the Quick Reference guides provided on the inside of the front and back covers of the manual.

2. ALWD[6]

The ALWD Guide was created by the Association of Legal Writing Directors in 2000 and is updated when needed with the publication of a new edition.[7] The goal of the ALWD Guide was to create a more user-friendly citation manual with simplified rules, eliminating the distinction between practitioner citations and scholarly citation. It uses clear explanations and abundant illustrations. The *Guide* contrasts the formats used in practice-based documents with those used in academic footnotes, but in a single set of rules that novice and experienced legal writers can easily consult. While the ALWD Guide does not have the same nation-wide acceptance as the Bluebook, it has been adopted by numerous courts and taught at many law schools.

The ALWD Guide begins with general rules regarding typeface, abbreviations, spelling and capitalization, numbers, page and location numbers, sections and paragraphs, footnotes, and short citations. As in the Bluebook, each type of legal source has its own set of specific citation rules, such as cases, statutes, secondary sources, constitutions, and court documents. Two of the most useful aspects of the ALWD Guide are the Fast Format Locator provided on the inside of the front cover, the Short-Citation Locator for Commonly Used Sources, and the numerous examples of citations provided throughout the manual. Additionally, the ALWD Guide's citation rules are the same as those provided in the Bluebook.[8]

---

[6] ALWD & COLLEEN M. BARGER, ALWD GUIDE TO LEGAL CITATION (6th ed. 2017) and available at http://www.alwd.org/publications/citation-manual/ (last visited Feb. 4, 2018).

[7] As of this writing, the ALWD GUIDE TO LEGAL CITATION was in its 6th Edition.

[8] For more information on the differences between the ALWD Manual and the Bluebook, go to ALWD Publications, available at http://www.alwd.org/wp-content/uploads/2017/09/ALWD_to_BB_6e_correlations.pdf (last visited Feb, 1, 2018).

3. CALIFORNIA STYLE MANUAL (CSM)[9]

The California Style Manual (CSM) was created in 1942 by Bernard E. Witkin, who is best known for the Witkin treatise on California law, and was adopted by the California Supreme Court as the official guide for citations in California courts. While it originally was created as a guide for court staff, it eventually was adopted as the official California citation manual. The CSM citation formats are quite different from those used in either the Bluebook or the ALWD Manual. The manual is also different from the Bluebook and ALWD in its organization. It begins with citation formats for specific legal sources such as cases, statutes, and secondary sources, which are then followed by general rules on style and mechanics. If you plan to practice law in California courts, you will need to know how to use the CSM.

4. NEW YORK LAW REPORTS STYLE MANUAL (THE TAN BOOK)[10]

The New York Law Reports Style Manual, also known as the Tan Book, was created by New York State Law Reporting Bureau in 1983. It is the required citation manual for New York courts. The New York Style Manual begins with general rules for cases, statutes, secondary sources, and other resources, which are then followed by general rules on style and mechanics.

5. THE MAROON BOOK[11]

The Maroon Book was created by the University of Chicago Law Review in 1989. It was created for the purpose of providing a simpler approach to citation. The Maroon Book does not provide a formula for every possible citation situation, but instead offers a general framework for citation guided by four overriding principles: sufficiency, clarity, consistency, and simplicity.

Like the Bluebook and the ALWD Manual, the Maroon Book begins with general rules regarding typeface, abbreviations, spelling and capitalization, numbers, page and location numbers, and other technical rules. Each type of legal source, such as cases, statutes, secondary sources, constitutions, and court documents, has its own set of rules. Even though the Maroon Book has support from Judge Richard Posner and is used in Chicago, it has not been widely adopted.

---

[9] THE CALIFORNIA STYLE MANUAL: A HANDBOOK OF LEGAL STYLE FOR CALIFORNIA COURTS AND LAWYERS (4th ed.2001).

[10] NEW YORK LAW REPORTS STYLE MANUAL (2012); also available at http://www. courts.state.ny.us/reporter/New_Styman.htm (last visited Feb. 16, 2018).

[11] THE MAROON BOOK: THE UNIVERSITY OF CHICAGO MANUAL OF LEGAL CITATION (2013); also available at http://lawreview.uchicago.edu/page/maroonbook (last visited Feb. 16, 2018).

6. THE REDBOOK: A MANUAL ON LEGAL STYLE[12]

The Redbook was created by Bryan A. Garner in 2002. Unlike most of the other citation manuals discussed in this chapter, the Redbook is not solely a citation manual but is a comprehensive legal style manual that was created for the purpose of assembling an exhaustive guide to the "thousands of sentence-level quirks that arise in legal writing."[13] It includes a specific chapter dedicated to citation that provides over twenty general principles on citation regardless of the citation manual being used. It takes a broader view of citation than a manual with nuanced rules for each specific element of a legal citation. It can be used independently, but, most frequently, it is used as a supplement to other citation manuals.

7. OTHER STATE CITATION MANUALS

Several other states also have their own state-specific citation manuals, including Ohio, North Dakota, and Texas.[14] When practicing law, you must check the court rules to determine the authorized citation manual for your jurisdiction.

C. HOW TO USE A CITATION MANUAL

The strategy for using any citation manual is generally the same. First, locate the citation format that applies to the specific source you are citing. Second, consult the general rules of citation addressing typeface, abbreviations, spelling and capitalization, spacing, section and paragraph numbering, footnotes, and other specifics. Third, evaluate how to pin cite your source. Fourth, locate and apply short citation rules if you are citing the source more than once. And, finally, consult your local state and court rules to determine if there are any additional citation requirements or exceptions.

D. FREQUENCY OF CITATION

As a general rule, how often you cite to authority will depend on the rules of the specific citation manual you are using. However, an attorney's ethical obligations to the court and the goals of citation also should guide an attorney's decision-making on when to cite. Specifically, legal citation itself is a part of legal analysis, and proper legal citation demonstrates to the reader that the analysis and arguments presented are legally supported.

Additionally, pinpoint references should be provided for every citation. Judges, and other readers, do not appreciate searching through cases or

---

[12] BRYAN A. GARNER, THE REDBOOK: A MANUAL ON LEGAL STYLE (2d ed. 2006).

[13] THE BLUEBOOK: A UNIFORM SYSTEM OF CITATION ix (19th ed. 2010).

[14] *Id.* at 277–425.

secondary sources to find the cited material. Instead, direct your reader to the specific page or pages that support the proposition you are citing, thereby making the task of finding the cited material much easier for your reader.

E. CITATION CHECKING SOFTWARE

There are a variety of tools that may assist you with your legal citations. They generally come in two forms: citation checking software, where the software checks the format of your citations; and bibliographic software, where the software inserts citations into your document for you. Most of these products, however, are available only by purchasing the software or by a paid subscription.

The most well-known citation checking software products are Drafting Assistant on Westlaw and Lexis for Microsoft Office.[15] In addition to other features, both of these services review the citations in your document and provide suggested changes to the citations you have written. The software does not write the citations for you but only checks them to determine if they are correct according to a variety of citation manuals. Frequently, however, it is more time consuming to use these software products than writing the citations yourself.

In addition, bibliographic software exists that imports citations into a document for you, but those citations are not necessarily in proper citation form. Some examples of these are RefWorks, EndNote, ProCite, Zotero, and Cite Stack, and many more are in development.

WARNING: If you choose to use citation checking software or bibliographic software, be mindful that ultimately you are responsible for the accuracy in form and substance of your cites. Judges, supervising attorneys, and law school professors will be unsympathetic to the excuse that the software erred. It is your responsibility to ensure your citations are correct.

F. CROSS-CULTURAL CONSIDERATIONS

Many of the citation manuals described above include citation rules for foreign and international legal citations. However, several citation manuals are dedicated exclusively to foreign and international legal citations. New York University School of Law, Journal of International Law and Politics created the Guide to Foreign and International Legal Citations in 2009 for the purpose of providing standards for citing foreign laws, treaties, and international organizations. Washington University's Global Studies Law Review created online guides to citation of legal

---

[15] Other citation checking software products include West Cite Advisor on Westlaw, Zotero, and RefWorks.

materials from select countries.[16] The EISIL database, from the American Society of International Law, also includes legal citation format for some treaties and international documents.[17]

Additionally, many countries have their own citation manuals or general rules for citation format.[18] For example, the Oxford Standard for Citation of Legal Authorities (OSCOLA) is the primary citation manual for the main legal sources in the United Kingdom[19] and the Canadian Guide to Uniform Legal Citation is the uniform system of citation for Canada created by the McGill Law Journal in 1986.[20] Thus, it is likely that wherever you may practice law, there will be uniform rules for citation that must be followed.

---

[16] WASHINGTON UNIVERSITY LAW, GLOBAL STUDIES LAW REVIEW, available at http://law.wustl.edu/WUGSLR/index.asp?ID=5513 (last visited Feb. 16, 2018).

[17] ELECTRONIC INFORMATION SYSTEM FOR INTERNATIONAL LAW, available at http://www.eisil.org (last visited Feb. 16, 2018).

[18] THE BLUEBOOK: A UNIFORM SYSTEM OF CITATION, Table 2 (19th ed. 2010).

[19] OXFORD LAW, OXFORD UNIVERSITY STANDARD FOR CITATION OF LEGAL AUTHORITIES, available at https://www.law.ox.ac.uk/sites/files/oxlaw/oscola_2006.pdf (last visited Feb. 1, 2018).

[20] MCGILL LAW JOURNAL, CANADIAN GUIDE TO UNIFORM LEGAL CITATION, available at http://lawjournal.mcgill.ca/en/text/22 (last visited Feb. 1, 2018).

CHAPTER 28

THE LAST CRITICAL TASK: THE "WHITE-GLOVE INSPECTION"

■ ■ ■

By Edward H. Telfeyan

A. INTRODUCTION

After you have completed all the hard work of researching the law, studying the relevant authorities, developing well-reasoned analyses, and drafting your memo or brief, you still have one more critically important task to complete before your document can leave your desk. That task requires you to make sure that your document represents your commitment to professionalism in all of your work, or, to state it in more basic terms, that it is error-free and reader-friendly.

And while simple proofreading may catch some errors (typically typos and misspellings), the best way to ensure that you are providing your reader with a document that is truly error-free and reader-friendly is to submit it to a "white-glove inspection." A "white-gloved" document is one that has been reviewed in a series of steps that are designed to catch all errors and make it an easy, error-free read for your intended reader.

An "error-free" document is one that contains nothing that would cause the reader to lose, even for a moment, the intended thought you as the writer sought to convey. In other words, it is a document that can be read from start to finish without a single mental hiccup by the reader, wherein he has to pause momentarily to mentally correct something that shouldn't have been in the text.

What are mental hiccups? Read the following short paragraph.

> The case establishes that victim who dies in the commission of a robbery. The court in the case used the felony murder rule to satisfy the malice requirement. In the case: defendant drove the getaway car and didn't otherwise participate in the crime.

Did you have trouble getting through this paragraph? Chances are you stumbled briefly over the missing article—a—in the first sentence and then had to re-read it just to verify that it in fact was not a complete sentence. You also probably wondered why the hyphen was missing for felony-murder rule in the second sentence and puzzled over the use of the colon in the third.

All of those errors cause a reader to lose the flow, even momentarily, of the substantive point the writer is trying to make. Each little mental hiccup that results has the potential impact of causing the reader to lose the train of intended thought the writer is trying to convey. And when a document is replete with those errors, or mental hiccups, the reader may give up on it subconsciously, if not intentionally.

A "reader-friendly" document is completely free of errors, such that the reader never experiences those mental hiccups. Beyond that goal, however, a "reader-friendly" document is written in such a way that the reader can receive all of the intended information contained in the document as quickly and effortlessly as possible.

Thus, "reader-friendly" documents provide detailed information in small, easily digestible pieces. As a result, short sentences are preferred, as are short paragraphs. And specific analyses or arguments are also presented in their most finite possible form. Creating a "reader-friendly" document will ensure that your work is actually read, instead of being disregarded, as happens when it ends up in the wrong "pile" on your reader's desk.

1. THE PILES ON YOUR READER'S DESK

Consider the recipients of your thoroughly researched, thoughtfully analyzed, and carefully written memo or brief. If they are typical lawyers or jurists, they invariably receive and continually have far more "stuff" to read every day than they reasonably have time for. As a result, most of them, in one way or another, will divide the wealth of material they receive every day into three separate piles.

The first pile will consist of material that, for one reason or another, they will want—or need—to read immediately, or before the end of the day. Material of this type goes into their "read-now" pile. It gets read before they pack up at the end of the day (or, in some instances, gets taken home in their briefcase, to be read after dinner or in bed before calling it a night).

The second pile is made up of material that they immediately recognize as being unworthy of their time (or just not of interest to them). This material goes into a "read-never" pile, and that pile is quickly dispensed with, usually be being placed directly into the circular file on the floor near the reader's desk.

The third pile is where everything else initially ends up. It is the "read-later" pile. The "read-later" pile consists of things that the reader would really like to read at some point. Perhaps a law review article that looks interesting might go there, or a letter from a professional colleague, or a lengthy newsletter from the county bar association. And, in some instances, something you have written might end up there as well.

Having your document end up in this last of the three piles on your intended reader's desk is a disaster for you. Why? Consider what happens to the "read-later" pile. It doesn't get read that day. It doesn't get taken home with the left-overs from the "read-now" pile at the end of the day. Instead, it just gets left there, soon to be joined by more "read-later" stuff (from the next day's material after the onslaught of new material arrives).

Sooner or later, and often sooner, the material in the "read-later" pile gets moved to the "read-never" pile. And once that happens, your thoroughly researched, thoughtfully analyzed, and carefully written memo is lost forever, its significance never to be understood by your intended reader because she never read it.

Now consider why your document may have ended up in that "read-later" pile in the first place. Maybe the intended reader started to read it and quickly found that it was a "hard" read (i.e. replete with "errors" or just not "reader-friendly"). Or, perhaps, the reader has grown to know what to expect from you and just assumes that anything you submit for his perusal will just be too difficult to get through. In either instance, your document is not going to be read, and you will be the reason. A "white-gloved" document can help your paper get into the "read-now" pile.

2. AVOIDING THE "READ-LATER" AND "READ-NEVER" PILES: THE "WHITE-GLOVE INSPECTION"

The term, "white-glove inspection," derives from military training. Specifically, during the first stages of that training (irrespective of which branch of service—Army, Navy, Air Force or Marines—we are talking about), all of the new recruits are housed in a single structure (the barracks), where they and their living space are regularly inspected by the commanding officer (or someone in authority). Traditionally, that inspection is done with a white glove, which the officer wipes on all areas of the barracks. If any dirt or dust or grime is on the glove, the entire unit will be penalized (usually with a loss of a weekend pass or maybe extra latrine duty).

Most recruits, after they have been humiliated and punished with a failed white-glove inspection learn that the best way to avoid continued humiliation and punishment is to perform their own white-glove inspection before the commanding officer conducts one. The logic is that if you can pass your own white-glove inspection, you are more likely to pass the commanding officer's.

In a sense, the commanding officer's inspection of the new recruits' barracks is comparable to the "inspection" your reader implicitly performs of your documents. If the document is loaded with dirt and dust and grime, it will be "punished" by being placed in the reader's "read-later" pile. If the writer has failed numerous such "inspections" in the past, the current document might automatically get placed there.

In the end, the quality of the documents you write establishes your reputation, not just as a writer, but as a thoroughly competent attorney, because thoroughly competent attorneys recognize the importance of error-free documents, for their clients' sake and for the benefit of their own reputation.

Therefore, for the sake of your professional reputation and, more importantly, for your clients' sake, avoid the "read later" pile, if at all possible. The "white-glove inspection" is the best way to avoid that fate. It ensures that your document is as "error-free" as it can possibly be and as "reader-friendly" as any document on the subject can be.

B. THE "WHITE-GLOVE INSPECTION": TEN STEPS TO ABSOLUTE CLEANLINESS

Merely proofreading your final draft will not catch all the errors, especially if proofreading means "read it once and correct the typos." Polishing it may make it look shiny, but it, too, won't catch all the errors. Too often, polishing is just a less specific way to describe proofreading.

Any serious effort to remove and correct all of the possible errors in your document first requires an understanding of what kinds of errors can—and often do—exist in legal documents. Even when a writer has presented a carefully-considered and well-written legal document, errors can be overlooked in the drafting process.

Errors in a final draft of a legal document can occur in these nine separate and distinct ways:

1. The separate points that are addressed may not be well organized. They may not lay out and explain the overall thesis or message intended by the writer in the most easily-followed logical development or in the most effectively persuasive presentation.

2. Paragraphs may be constructed so as to be overly burdensome for the reader, either because they address more than one topic (a substantive error) or because they appear to be overly long (a presentation error).

3. The flow of the document, from sentence to sentence, may appear illogical to the reader, with too many seemingly unconnected jumps from one idea to the next.

4. Individual sentences may not be crafted as carefully as they need to be so as to impart exactly the meaning intended by the writer.

5. Grammatical and punctuation errors may exist, creating the dreaded mental hiccups for the reader.

6. Case names and party names may be misspelled and citations to legal authorities may be inaccurately indicated or improperly noted.

7. Typographical errors may (and almost assuredly will) exist throughout the document.

8. Words may be misspelled throughout the document, some even to the point of suggesting either an entirely different word (e.g., "not" for "now", "form" for "from").

9. The printed version of the document may not have the final appearance the writer intended or expected.

The ten white-glove steps devote a separate detailed inspection of the document to find and correct each of the nine possible ways that errors may have crept into it. The tenth step is that final read-through that might have been the only step in a traditional proofread. These steps proceed from the "macro" to the "micro," from a gross overview of the look and flow of the document to a literal assessment of every sentence, indeed, of every word. The inspections are demanding and difficult, and because of this reality they should not be done in immediate succession. Rather, after each step, the writer should take a break and do something else so as to be able to commence the next step with refreshed energy and without the mental fatigue that can result from tedious repetition.

Thus, the entire inspection (all ten steps) can take time, in instances of especially long and complex documents perhaps as long as a full work day or even several days. The result, an absolutely error-free and reader-friendly document that represents your complete commitment to professionalism in your written work, makes it well worth the time and effort.

As you review each of the inspection steps detailed below, consider how they cover all of the potential errors that could appear in a document you have written. Then consider how easy it would be to miss any of those errors with a single "proof read" of your document or even with a quick run through each of the steps without taking a break after each one.

1. STEP ONE—LOGICAL CONSISTENCY AND ORGANIZATIONAL FLOW

a. The Format and the Delineation of Substantive Points

Errors in the structure of your document can appear in a number of ways. A common error, one that even seasoned attorneys sometimes make, is to deviate from the accepted numeration of points covered in the brief or memo.

Assume, for example, that a brief addresses two separate issues and that two separate primary assertions are made for each issue. Assume further that those primary assertions are presented in a series of arguments, some of which have sub-arguments contained within them. The proper delineation of the brief, just in terms of the numeration used for each argument, would be as follows:

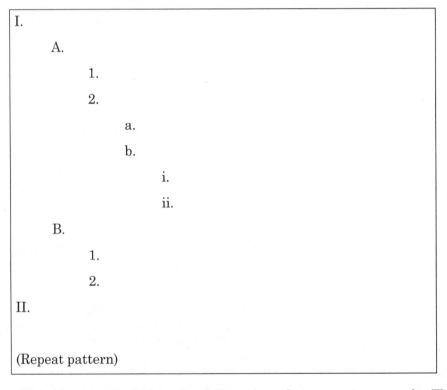

Note the progression as the delineation of arguments proceeds: The first designation is with a capital Roman numeral. The first level of subordinate designations consists of capital letters. Succeeding levels of subordination (and more finitely identified arguments) are shown with Arabic numbers, lower case letters and then, if necessary, with lower case Roman numerals.

Errors can occur in the numeration in a brief when the normal order noted above is not followed, as when a Roman numeral is immediately followed by a lower case letter or when an upper case letter is immediately followed by a lower case Roman numeral.

Another error that can occur in the formatting of the brief is when a single sub-point is noted. The simple rule is "you can't have an A without a B; you can't have a 1 without a 2." Properly understood, sub-points are divisions of main points, and since you can't divide one into less than two parts, you can't have a main point with only one sub-point. In such an instance, one of two things needs to happen in your white-glove work. You either have to figure out what the second sub-point is and label and denominate it as such, or you have to eliminate the sub-point as a separate designation and subsume it into your main point.

Skilled attorneys and judges understand and follow this method of formatting the office memo or brief. These professional colleagues will expect your documents to conform to this method. Evaluate the organization of your document by making sure you have the proper order of numeration for your points (from the most broadly stated to the most finite) and that you always have at least two sub-points under each point if you are dividing broader points into more finite ones. Your table of contents serves as a good way to double-check that you have conformed to these rules.

b.   Headings and Umbrellas

Once you have established the proper format for your document, you need to provide your reader with guideposts to help her appreciate the way the organization lays out. Headings and umbrellas serve as those guideposts.

Headings are signposts for the reader. They tell the reader what she is about to encounter in the reading of the document. Headings should be provided for each separate substantive point in the format of your document. Thus, every time you have a delineation of a separate point, whether it is designated with a capital Roman numeral, an upper case letter, or any of the other format designations noted above, you should have a heading that identifies the topic or subject of the designated substantive point.

As indicated in earlier chapters in this text, in a persuasive document, like a law and motion brief, the headings should be stated persuasively. In a predictive memo, they should present the point to be discussed in more neutral terms, while still perhaps containing the prediction the writer will be explaining in the text that follows. They should state the argument to be made in a concisely written assertion. They should not include authorities or citations, but should rather read as a simple statement of the assertion that will immediately follow with legal support.

Subordinate points should also be noted with headings, and they should also be stated persuasively in a brief, more neutrally in a predictive memo. In all instances, good headings should contain a "because" clause (that part of the heading that gives the basic reason for the assertion or prediction that is made in the text that follows).

Umbrellas serve as introductions to the substantive points that will follow. They should be short, normally a single paragraph, and should be used as roadmaps for what will follow. Thus, if a substantive point will be divided into two or more sub-points in the discussion or arguments that will follow, an umbrella will provide the reader with an understanding of that division and of what each sub-point will concern.

Umbrella paragraphs can also be used to cover basic points that are foundational for the sub-points that will follow. But if you use an umbrella for this purpose, the same basic points should then not be made in each of the sub-points, because doing so would be redundant, and redundancy is another error that a reader-friendly document should not contain.

Inspecting your headings and umbrella paragraphs to make sure they accurately and effectively state the points you then make in the following text will keep your document organized and ensure against redundancy.

c.   Logical Flow and Leading with Your Best

Organizational errors can occur in at least two other ways, both of which can be more troubling in terms of how your reader receives and accepts your document.

The first of these possible errors can occur if you open with an argument or analytical point that isn't particularly compelling. Readers tend to focus the greatest amount of their attention to the beginning of a document. Thereafter, their attention will tend to drift over the succeeding sections, picking up at the end of the document. Therefore, all other things being equal, the best way to begin your document is with your strongest point, and the best way to end it is with your second strongest point.

But you also have to pay attention to the logical flow of the arguments or analytical points you present in your document. Leading with your strongest argument or analytical point won't work well if that particular point can only make sense if it is preceded by a foundational point that needs to be made first.

Thus, the first rule of the substantive organization of your document is that the points you make must be made in a logical sequence. That sequence might be adjustable, depending on the way you decide to make your case or present your analysis, but however you end up structuring your document, the substantive points contained in it must flow logically from one to the next.

And so, in this first of the white-glove steps, you need to read the entire document with that perspective in mind. When specific points seem out of place, you to move them, and, if possible, you want to place your strongest point in the first position.

A well-organized document, with proper numeration of points made, good headings that serve as signposts, umbrella paragraphs that serve as roadmaps, and a logical flow that leads with the strongest of your points and closes with the second strongest, will be a well-received document that will allow your reader to better appreciate the hard work you invested in preparing it.

2. STEP TWO—PARAGRAPH STRUCTURE AND PARAGRAPH LENGTH

Paragraphs serve two important purposes. First, they develop a single idea that is part of the larger point that the entire section of the document addresses. Taken together, a series of paragraphs may constitute a minor thesis that, taken with other minor theses, makes up a complete argument or substantive analysis. For this reason, no paragraph should ever contain more than one substantive point.

Therefore, the first goal of the second white-glove step is to review each paragraph in the document to ensure that it does not violate this first rule. If a paragraph is found that addresses more than one substantive point, that paragraph needs to be divided into separate paragraphs, one for each point. (Of course, paragraphs can also be faulty if they do not address any substantive point, and that kind of paragraph should be quickly identified and eliminated in this white-glove step.)

The second purpose of paragraphs is to give the reader a chance to take a mental breath. Most readers sub-consciously look for the breaks that come at the ends of paragraphs as an opportunity to stop for a brief moment to consider what they have just read and to let the thought thereby obtained register in their mind.

For this reason, overly long paragraphs are not reader-friendly. Think about it. Do you like the sight of an overly long paragraph? If you are like most readers, you do not. And the reason is, essentially, that they appear to require that we have to work too hard to consume the information contained in them.

And so, the second paragraph check that this step of the white-glove work entails is checking for overly long paragraphs. Happily, most long paragraphs can be conveniently split into shorter ones.

The third paragraph check is to ensure that paragraphs are properly constructed. Proper paragraph construction is another aspect of your writing that will be appreciated by your reader.

Ideally, a paragraph will have a topic sentence, followed by several sentences that develop the topic, followed by a sentence that summarizes the topic. That approach to paragraph construction is most definitely the norm. But consider the effect on the reader of a succession of such "ideally-constructed" paragraphs. All those topic and summary sentences are giving the reader a lot more to read and, potentially, making some paragraphs overly long.

Another approach—one that can be more reader-friendly if it also reduces or eliminates a number of overly long paragraphs in your document—is to start a succession of paragraphs that deal with the same topic with a topic sentence, and then to conclude that succession of paragraphs with a summary sentence. Thus a string of shorter paragraphs can replace what would otherwise be one overly long, extremely ponderous, and very reader-unfriendly paragraph.

Consider the following examples, the first being the traditional "ideally-constructed" paragraph and the second being the same exact text in a succession of shorter paragraphs:

First example:

> Malice in support of a murder conviction can be found in a number of ways. It can be found when the defendant clearly and expressly intended to kill the victim and did so with an act that brought about that result. A defendant who aims a loaded gun at a victim and pulls the trigger, intending to thereby kill the victim, exhibits malice. Malice can also be found when a defendant intends to cause severe bodily harm to a victim and does so with death resulting. A defendant who intends to torture an individual by chopping off the victim's hand exhibits malice. And malice can be established when a defendant acts willfully and wantonly so as to create the likely result of death of an individual even when that death may not have been specifically intended. A defendant who fires a loaded gun into a crowded movie theater may exhibit this form of malice even if he claims he didn't intend the death of anyone. And finally, malice can be established by law if a death occurs during the commission of a violent felony that the defendant was committing. Under this form of malice, a defendant will be guilty of murder if he engaged in a robbery of a gas station and the attendant at the gas station died of a heart attack because of the robbery. Thus at least four methods of finding malice exist: by specific intent to kill; by intent to cause serious bodily injury; through willful and wanton misconduct; and by virtue of the felony-murder rule.

Second example:

> Malice in support of a murder conviction can be found in a number of ways. It can be found when the defendant clearly and expressly intended to kill the victim and did so with an act that brought about that result. A defendant who aims a loaded gun at a victim and pulls the trigger, intending to thereby kill the victim, exhibits malice.
>
> Malice can also be found when a defendant intends to cause severe bodily harm to a victim and does so with death resulting. A defendant who intends to torture an individual by chopping off the victim's hand exhibits malice. And malice can be established when a defendant acts willfully and wantonly so as to create the likely result of death of an individual even when that death may not have been specifically intended. A defendant who fires a loaded gun into a crowded movie theater may exhibit this form of malice even if he claims he didn't intend the death of anyone.
>
> And finally, malice can be established by law if a death occurs during the commission of a violent felony that the defendant was committing. Under this form of malice, a defendant will be guilty of murder if he engaged in a robbery of a gas station and the attendant at the gas station died of a heart attack because of the robbery. Thus at least four methods of finding malice exist: by specific intent to kill; by intent to cause serious bodily injury; through willful and wanton misconduct; and by virtue of the felony-murder rule.

Which of the two examples is more likely to be read willingly and will be more likely to be understood fully? Which of the two is reader-friendly? The answers suggest a good rule of thumb for all good legal writers: never let a formalistic rule of construction become a roadblock to a reader-friendly presentation of substance.

The best legal writers understand the preferred rules of construction but are also able to depart from them when necessary to make their documents less burdensome for their readers. Thus, the second white-glove step should include careful consideration of the length as well as the content of every paragraph.

3. STEP THREE—LOGICAL SENTENCE FLOW AND COHESIVENESS

A reader-friendly legal document is one that effectively makes the reader feel as if she is on a smooth ride that gently takes her through a succession of mental tour stops and ends with a sense of both specific highlights (strong arguments and analyses) and an appreciation for the entire trip (recognition of, if not agreement with, the document's principal thesis).

To create that feeling, the writer must be sensitive to how the brain digests information in the process of reading. Essentially, it involves a silent voice in the brain that "hears" the words from the document much as the brain hears words that are spoken in conversations. What is heard or written is then interpreted and, ultimately, understood.

Hiccups, as we have already noted, interrupt this smooth ride. The smooth ride that a well-written document creates for a reader limits one source of these hiccups by allowing the reader to move easily from one paragraph to the next, indeed, from one sentence to the next.

And so, a separate step in the white-glove inspection involves ensuring that each sentence flows logically from the one that precedes it and leads logically to the one that follows it. In part, this result can be attained by using transition words and phrases. Such words and phrases include "therefore," "in that regard," "however," "in furtherance of," "similarly," "on the other hand," and "in this respect."

Each of those words and phrases, and the many others that might be in your document, serve to tie one thought to the next, giving the flow of the document a cohesiveness that makes it easier for the reader to grasp the substance of the text. The best way to find points in your document that would benefit from transition words and phrases is to look for sudden jumps, either substantively or tonally, in the text of your document. The value of the transition word or phrase is that it links the prior sentence to the succeeding one.

In this regard, compare these two examples:

> As the mens rea requirement for murder, malice can be satisfied by less than a specific intent to kill the victim. Courts have held that extreme forms of wanton conduct can suffice.
>
> As the mens rea requirement for murder, malice can be satisfied by less than a specific intent to kill the victim. Thus courts have held that extreme forms of wanton conduct can suffice.

Note how the mere addition of the word "thus" ties the second sentence to the first, thereby making it easier for the reader to comprehend immediately that the second sentence describes a form of malice that is not specific intent to kill.

But the flow of a document can also be affected by the substance of the text. And so, this step of the white-glove work should also include a review of all of the potential bumps in the road for the reader that appear in the document.

One such bump can be quotations. Quoting to legal authorities is a commonly used way to enhance the persuasiveness of an argument or an analytical point. But using quotes carries a risk that every writer should appreciate. That risk is that the quoted passage, assuming the reader actually reads it at all, introduces a new "voice" in the reader's brain, and, therefore, creates the potential for a break in the reader's concentration, i.e., a hiccup.

Therefore, this step of the white-glove work should include careful consideration of each quote in the draft that is being inspected. First, you should ask yourself whether the quote is really necessary to make the point you want to make. If the substance of the quote is desirable, can you paraphrase it, thereby avoiding the break in the reader's internal voice a full quote will be likely to create? If you still deem the actual quote to be necessary, can you shorten it, perhaps with the use of ellipses, so as to make the intrusion on the reader's attention to the flow of the text minimal?

As risky as the use of quotes can be, the inclusion of block quotes in a legal document can be absolutely disastrous. Think about how you react to block quotes in material you read. Do you experience a sense of dread at the mere sight of them? Do you often think to skip them entirely, or if not, to just skim them to gain a quick sense of what information they contain?

Most readers would answer yes to those questions because block quotes are a severe intrusion on the brain as it works on the substance of your text. And so, in this step of your white-glove work, you should seek, if at all possible, to remove those block quotes from your document. At the least, find a way to break up the quote to less than 50 words so that it does not need to be blocked.

Some quotes will survive this step of your white-glove work, but at least your reader will not be burdened with an excessive number of interruptions and possible hiccups that can result from an abundance of quotes. Remember, quotes don't substitute for your reasoning and analysis; at best, they only support them.

Another intrusion on your reader's brain in its attempt to receive and appreciate the information your document seeks to impart can be the placement of citations in mid-text. The importance of citing accurately is covered in a different step (#6) of the white-glove work, but in this step the task is to make the citations as unobtrusive as possible. Placing those cites at the end of sentences rather than in the middle of them is the best way to accomplish that goal.

Placed in mid-sentence, a cite, especially a lengthy one, is an invitation for a mental hiccup, primarily because your reader won't expect to see it there. The key is to construct the sentence requiring the cite so that the cite can appropriately be placed at the end of the sentence.

Consider these two examples, both imparting the same substantive information:

> The location of the warning sign in *Messa v. Sullivan*, 61 Ill.App.2d 386 (1st Dist. 1965) was held to be inadequate to constitute actual notice of the danger.
>
> In one case, the court held that the location of the warning sign was inadequate to constitute actual notice of the danger. *Messa v. Sullivan*, 61 Ill.App.2d 386 (1st Dist. 1965).

Obviously, the second is far less likely to burden the reader since it does not intrude on the reader's attempt to read the sentence and can easily be skipped over by the reader if she is not interested in knowing the name of the case or the court that issued it or where it can be found in the two reporters that have printed versions of it.

An even less obtrusive way to present a citation is with a footnote, and some courts encourage (or at least do not deny) the use of footnotes to note citations (and the cases referred to in the text in some instances). Whether this alternative is acceptable in any particular document and for any particular reader may depend on the rules of the court or the dictates of the firm where you work. Either way, removing case citations from the middle of sentences in this white-glove step will go a long way to making your document reader-friendly.

4. STEP FOUR—SENTENCE ACCURACY, SIMPLICITY, AND BREVITY

Consider the beauty of a well-constructed sentence. Sentences are the basic unit of communication. They are where effective communication starts and where it can end. A well-constructed sentence says what the writer wants to say clearly, concisely, and accurately. A poorly-constructed sentence can leave a reader confused and frustrated, even to the point that he decides to stop reading the document, placing it in that dreaded "read-later" pile, or even worse in that circular file to the side of his desk.

Every sentence in your document should be constructed so as to say precisely what you want it to say in as few words as possible. It should be constructed in such a way as to impart the information you want to impart and to encourage, or at least to entice, your reader to read the sentence that follows it. We aren't talking about creating a page-turner novel here, but you should be trying to create in your reader an impetus to keep reading. And ensuring that each sentence in your document is a separate thing of beauty will accomplish that goal.

Consider the two sentences that follow, each of which is an attempt to say the same thing:

> Attorneys can draft wills, contracts, and partnership agreements, among other documents, in the states where they are licensed.
>
> Attorneys, being licensed by the state where they practice law, can draft, among other documents, wills, contracts, and partnership agreements.

Both sentences contain the critical components of the thought the writer is trying to convey. But the first sentence places those components—the subject, the verb, and the object—at the very start of the sentence, while the second spreads them out over the entire length of the sentence. The first sentence is preferable because it gives the reader all of the essential information right at the start of the sentence.

Readers look for these basics in every sentence: who did what to whom. In essence, everything else is excess, some of it undoubtedly necessary, but none of it as important as the basic component parts of the sentence. If the rest is more important, the sentence should be structured with those items in the position of subject, verb, and object.

Thus one of the first things to check, as to every sentence in your document, is whether you have succeeded in placing the subject, verb and object of each sentence as close to the beginning of the sentence as possible.

A similar rule of sentence construction is to keep the who-did-what-to-whom parts of each sentence close to each other, even if an introductory phrase moves them away from the opening of the sentence.

Consider these examples:

> Even with the best of intentions, a lawyer, despite years of training and practice, might raise, due to the pressure of the moment, an inappropriate objection.
>
> Even with the best of intentions and despite years of training and practice, due to the pressure of the moment, a lawyer might raise an inappropriate objection.
>
> A lawyer might raise an inappropriate objection, even though he had the best of intentions, and had years of training and practice, due to the pressure of the moment.

The first of the examples is made unduly difficult to read because the subject, "lawyer," is separated from the verb, "might raise," which is further separated from the object, "an inappropriate objection." The second example cures that deficiency, but violates the previous rule by putting all three elements at the end of the sentence. The third sentence keeps the three elements together and places them at the start of the sentence.

Now consider these two sentences:

> The witness wept while she recounted the details of the accident.
>
> The witness became overly emotional, even to the point of weeping, as she proceeded with her testimony, which provided the specific details of the incident that was the basis of her lawsuit.

Both of these sentences impart the information the writer wants to convey about the witness's testimony, but the first does it directly and simply, while the second does it in a laboriously long-winded flow of information that forces the reader to digest many more words than may be needed to convey the desired information. There will certainly be occasions when the longer sentence will be justified precisely because it does impart the information with more emotion or sentiment, but if all the reader needs to know is the basic information, keep it short.

The general lesson to be learned is that shorter sentences are better than longer sentences, primarily because they make the task of reading them easier for the reader. But there is another reason to keep your sentences short.

Consider this sentence:

> The attorney tried to conduct a probing cross-examination of the witness, being a skilled debater and an accomplished public speaker, but he couldn't overcome the resistance he encountered, which often seemed to be the result of her coaching by the opposing counsel.

What is wrong with this sentence? Well, for starters, it is certainly too long. Its length alone is enough to frustrate the reader (especially if the document is replete with sentences of similar length and construction). But look at what else has happened in the writer's attempt to squeeze everything possible into the single sentence: the writer has lost track of the subject and has concluded the sentence by shifting the focus from the attorney to the witness and opposing counsel.

Note, too, that the sentence is also imperiled by a misplaced modifier that suggests the witness is "a skilled debater and accomplished public speaker." Thus short sentences are not only reader-friendly, but they are safer from the risk of containing a grammatical error that doubles down on the potential negative impact on the reader.

But as important as all the sentences are in your document, perhaps none are more important than those that state the rules or legal principles on which your arguments or analyses are based. Thus, extra-special care should be given to those sentences. In many instances, they will also constitute the topic or thesis sentences for the paragraphs they start, making their significance even more paramount.

Consider these two rule statements that might be used in a brief opposing a motion to dismiss:

> A motion to dismiss must be denied if facts are alleged that establish a cause of action.
>
> Facts that suggest the existence of a cause of action can be sufficient to make a motion to dismiss inappropriate.

Both rule statements express a rule that would then form the basis for an argument that would presumably focus on the particular facts in the case at hand. But the first is crisply stated and is succinct to the point of the argument that will follow. The second, on the other hand, states the point of the rule far less directly and much less succinctly. It may even leave the reader in some doubt as to exactly what argument it is meant to introduce.

Of course, a longer, less crisply stated rule might be strategically desirable in a particular argument, as when the essence of the rule could be detrimental to your client's case. In such an instance, a less concise rule, one that perhaps suggests ambiguity or uncertainty, may be the more desirable approach. But if the rule you want to apply works in your client's favor, the best approach is to state it as directly and succinctly as you can.

Every sentence in your document should be an easy read for your reader. Even if the subject matter is dense, the sentences that describe and explain that subject matter should be constructed so as to be easy to digest. If your reader has to stop to consider what the sentence means, you risk losing your reader. Some readers may stop reading because they don't have the patience to deal with the subject matter, but no reader should stop because they can't figure out what you're saying.

And so, this step in your white-glove process should consider whether each sentence says exactly what you want to say in as few words as possible. If your document consists of well-tailored sentences, it will be far less likely to end up unread, and far more likely to be appreciated for the writing talent that it represents.

5.   STEP FIVE—GRAMMAR AND PUNCTUATION

Although writers of literary fiction frequently take license with the rules of grammar and punctuation, the legal profession has not followed suit. Grammar and punctuation rules are closely followed, as they must be in the drafting of rule-making documents, where a missing comma can sometimes make a difference between absolutely requiring something and merely permitting it.

Because they are trained to write with precision, lawyers and judges understand the importance of grammar and punctuation and expect what they read to also reflect that understanding. And so, if for no other reason than to establish your bona fides as a member of the profession, you need to submit documents that are without grammar and punctuation errors.

The fifth step of the inspection, then, is to review every sentence for possible grammar and punctuation errors. This is painstaking work, but it can be successfully accomplished if you know what you're looking for.

Without intending to cover all the rules of the mechanics of writing, the following are some of those most commonly violated in poorly written legal documents. (To gain a complete understanding of the mechanical rules of good writing, many excellent sources are available. Your legal writing professor may have a list of recommended texts or may even require one to supplement your assignments in your course.)

a.   The Requisites of a Complete Sentence

A complete sentence requires a subject and a verb. That's it—just a noun or pronoun that is the subject of the sentence and a verb that attaches to the subject to indicate the action the subject took.

Hence, it should be easy to write complete sentences, and, in most instances, it is. In fact, it is hard to compose an incomplete short sentence because we almost always think in terms of someone doing something when we start to write a sentence.

It's when our sentences get longer that problems can arise. Consider this example:

> The attorney, never intending to create the grounds for objection, which the opposing counsel then raised, but instead hoping the question would pass unnoticed. Still, he managed to utter a response before the judge ruled.

The first "sentence" is, of course, incomplete, as it lacks a verb that would attach to the subject "attorney." What happened to cause this error?

Most probably, the writer had in mind to say that the attorney "hoped the question would pass unnoticed," but in the midst of making that point, he thought to add what happened next, which was the opposing attorney's objection. The incomplete sentence could have been written as three short complete sentences that would have told the whole story.

> The attorney never intended to create the grounds for an objection. Instead, he hoped it would pass unnoticed. But the opposing attorney did object as soon as the question was asked.

It could also have been written as one complete sentence, as in this alternative construction:

> The attorney never intended his question to create the grounds for an objection, hoping instead that it would pass unnoticed, but opposing counsel raised one anyway.

The single corrected sentence is long, which may make it less desirable in reader-friendly terms, but it is a correctly composed compound-complex sentence and thus is grammatically correct. Is it more reader-friendly than the three shorter sentences in the previous example? That decision might depend on what surrounds this passage in the entire paragraph or series of paragraphs. Good writing, and good white-glove work, requires careful consideration of whether to construct grammatically-correct longer sentences or simple shorter ones.

But you can't leave incomplete sentences in your document. They will inevitably cause a major mental hiccup for your reader and can, if too many of them appear in your document, lead the reader to place the document in the purgatory of the "read-later" pile.

b.   Commas, Comma Splices, and Run-on Sentences

Commas serve a purpose, but that purpose is not just to indicate a pause, as some may believe. Rather, commas indicate to the reader how to comprehend the sentence she is in the midst of reading.

Perhaps one of the most common uses of commas is to denote the items in a series. Legal writers often have need for serial commas because legal documents often include lists of things. When a list of items is included in a sentence, a comma must precede each item in the list after the first item. In a short list, the comma can be omitted before the last item, but in longer lists, it should be included before the word (usually "and," or "or") that precedes the last item.

Consider these two examples:

Crimes requiring malice include murder, mayhem, and arson.

Malice can be satisfied by a specific intent to kill, by an intent to cause serious bodily injury, by willful misconduct, or by application of the felony-murder rule.

In the first sentence, the last comma can be omitted without risking any confusion for the reader. That said, many writers will include it anyway. The current preference among folks who dwell on this kind of thing is to include it. In the second sentence, leaving the last comma out would make it more difficult for the reader to understand that a fourth form of malice is the felony-murder rule. In both sentences, however, the commas delineate the different items in the series, which is the purpose of serial commas.

Commas are also used to identify for the reader that he is reading a compound or a complex sentence.

Compound sentences are sentences that contain two independent clauses—clauses that contain both a subject and a verb that attaches to the subject—that are joined by a conjunction (e.g., and, but, or). Complex sentences contain one independent clause and one dependent clause—a clause that contains a subject or a verb, but not both. Commas are used in both to note the break from one clause to the other.

Consider, again, the example concerning the attorney who wanted to pose a question without getting an objection.

> The attorney never intended his question to create the grounds for an objection, hoping instead that it would pass unnoticed, but opposing counsel raised one anyway.

The sentence contains two properly placed commas. The first notes the beginning of the dependent clause, "hoping," being the verb that does not have a subject to attach to. The second notes the beginning of the independent clause, the conjunction "but" introducing the subject and verb "counsel raised."

But as valuable as the commas are in that sentence, pulling together essentially three different thoughts in a cohesive single sentence, commas cannot be used to attempt to bring separate thoughts together indiscriminately. Consider this attempt:

> The attorney hoped the question would pass unnoticed, he didn't intend to create the grounds for an objection, but opposing counsel raised one anyway.

The second comma in that attempt at a sentence is fine. It marks the introduction of an independent clause that is preceded by that little conjunction ("but"). But the first comma is an attempt to bring the two independent clauses ("attorney hoped" and "he didn't intend") together in a single sentence. But we can't join independent clauses without a conjunction if we are trying to join them with a comma.

The phrase used to identify this error is a comma splice, where the comma is being used incorrectly to try to "splice" together the two independent clauses. (Splicing is a word that was in vogue in the old days when reel-to-reel tapes—ask your grandparents—were the common recording devices. The tapes would often split, and small pieces of tape were used to "splice" them together.)

The intended joining of the two independent clauses can be accomplished in a single sentence (thereby avoiding a comma splice) in one of two ways. First, a conjunction can be added before the second independent clause, thereby creating a compound sentence. Or, the two independent clauses can be joined with a different punctuation mark: the semi-colon. Or, a third way to cure the comma splice would be to end the first clause with a period, thereby making them two separate sentences.

What we can't do in an attempt to correct a comma splice is just remove the comma. Doing so creates a different problem, one we call a run-on sentence.

> The attorney hoped the question would pass unnoticed he didn't intend to create the grounds for an objection, but opposing counsel raised one anyway.

Run-on sentences, such as the one above, are rarely caused by a lack of knowledge of punctuation rules. Most writers would recognize the need for some form of punctuation after "unnoticed" in the sentence above. That kind of error is more likely the result of hasty writing and poor editing— yet another reason this white-glove step is critical.

Commas have other useful functions, but, again, they must be used correctly. One such instance is to set off a parenthetical phrase that is contained within a complete sentence. Consider this example:

> The attorney asked the question, never intending in so doing to elicit an objection, but opposing counsel made one anyway.

In that sentence, the commas mark off the phrase that is the equivalent of a parenthetical insert. The sentence would be complete without the phrase, but the writer wants to include the added information. The addition is understood as such by the reader because the commas set it off. But it would be an error, one that might well cause a mental hiccup for the reader, if either comma were missing in the sentence.

Commas also serve to tell a reader that the heart of the sentence will follow, as when a lengthy introductory phrase precedes the subject and verb in the sentence.

> Disregarding the possibility of an objection from opposing counsel, the attorney asked the question.

The comma in the preceding sentence tells the reader that the heart of the sentence will follow. Without the comma, the reader will hesitate, if for only an instant, to comprehend the structure of the sentence. The properly placed comma in that instance keeps the reader in the rhythm of the read, as all reader-friendly writing should.

c. Colons and Semi-Colons

For legal writers, these two punctuation marks serve critically important functions. They are used in a most common part of legal writing: the creation of lists.

Lists in the law are ubiquitous. We are always identifying factors or elements or some combination of the two, and almost as often listing series of events that compare favorably or unfavorably to some existing authority or that comprise the key facts in a case we are using in an argument.

Properly used, the colon introduces the list, and properly used, the semi-colon notes the separate items in the list. But there are rules for what constitutes "properly used" for each.

If you introduce the series of items with only a subject and a verb, a colon is not required and would be inappropriate. Thus, if your sentence begins with, "These factors include," you would not use a colon to introduce the series of factors that would follow. The colon introduces the items in the series only when you add an object to the subject and the verb that introduce the series, as in, "These factors include the following:"

Why the different rule depending on whether that third part (the non-essential part) of the sentence is included? The answer is that usually if the list is short or uncomplicated we don't need the object, as in the following example, "These colors include red, green, and yellow."

It would be excessive to say, "These colors include the following: red, green, and yellow."

But if the list is more complicated than a simple list of colors, the introduction to that list might well need to include the object ("the following") as a way to identify for the reader the nature of the list that will follow. In that regard, consider the following example:

> These are the factors that control the decision: whether the defendant knew the victim; whether the defendant had previously engaged in the same kind of conduct; whether the defendant was shown, through expert testimony, to have a mental disease or defect of reason; and, whether the defendant was intoxicated at the time of the act.

The colon in that sentence introduces the series properly. If the sentence had begun with only "These are the factors" we would still use the colon, because we'd still have the required subject, verb, and object introducing the list. But if the list were only preceded with "The factors are" a colon would be improper. But note that for such a long and complicated list, that introduction would not be helpful in terms of alerting the reader to what was about to follow. For reader-friendly purposes, if not out of grammatical necessity, the slightly longer introduction is necessary for longer, more complicated lists, and the colon is the punctuation that accompanies the longer introduction.

Semi-colons are also appropriate punctuation in listing a series of items. They are used to separate the items in a series in two instances: when the items in the series are long and when they include internal commas. In both instances, the purpose of the semi-colon is to identify for the reader where one item ends and another begins. In that regard, let's again look at the example we just used.

> These are the factors that control the decision: whether the defendant knew the victim; whether the defendant had previously engaged in the same kind of conduct; whether the defendant was shown, through expert testimony, to have a mental disease or defect of reason; and, whether the defendant was intoxicated at the time of the act.

Note the placement of the semi-colons in the series. The items in the series are long enough to justify the use of semi-colons, but the third of the items also contains internal commas, thereby justifying the use of semi-colons as well. The alternative would be to separate the items in the series with commas, but it isn't as helpful to the reader to use commas in lengthy and complicated series, and thus isn't as reader-friendly.

But if the list is simple, as in our color example above, commas work just fine. So, just as with the use of colons to introduce a list of items in a series, the use of semi-colons to separate those items should be limited to when the rules call for them.

Semi-colons are also useful as a way to avoid a comma-splice, as noted above. But we need to clarify another form of comma splice that many writers are not cognizant of. These are sentences that separate two independent clauses with conjunctive adverbs: words like "therefore," "however," and "rather."

When you join two independent clauses with these words, as in the example below, you need a semi-colon before the joining word.

> Sentences that consist of two independent clauses can be joined by a comma and a conjunction; however, if they are joined instead by a conjunctive adverb, they must be joined by a semi-colon.

Obviously, to make correct use of the semi-colon in sentences of this type, we need to be able to distinguish between conjunctions and conjunctive adverbs. Fortunately, the distinction is fairly easy to identify. Conjunctions are short, single syllable words (all consisting of only two or three letters) that comprise a relatively short list. The acronym for the list is FANBOYS, as in for, and, nor, but, or, yet, so.

All other joining words are conjunctive adverbs, and they all must be immediately preceded by a semi-colon and immediately followed by a comma (unless it is a single-syllable word like "thus," in which case the following comma is not required).

Admittedly, the rules for these two punctuation marks can seem irksome, but, in truth, they aren't all that complicated. Spending a little time learning the rules for their use will allow you to perform this part of your white-glove work with relative ease.

d. Parallelism in Series

When you have occasion in your document to set out items, they should be constructed in parallel form. Parallelism in series makes what might be a dense set of details easier to read and, therefore, makes it easier for your reader to grasp and appreciate the substantive information contained in the series.

Compare these two examples, both listing the same factors used to summarize the defendant's tortious conduct in a case:

> The commission of the tort in this case is established by these facts: defendant failed to exercise due care; injury of the plaintiff; the act causally related to the injury; absence of a recognized defense.
>
> The commission of the tort in this case is established by these facts: the defendant failed to exercise due care; the plaintiff suffered injury; the defendant's act was causally related to the injury; and, the defendant cannot assert a recognized defense.

Note that both summaries contain four items that the writer lists as the facts that establish the tort. In the first summary, the items are written without regard for the form of any of the others. Thus the entire sentence is difficult to read and the specific facts may be difficult to relate to each other. In the second summary, each item is written in the same form: the subject is preceded by "the" and followed by the verb and the result or occurrence.

When items in a series are listed in random form, the reader is likely to struggle to get through it. When items in a series are written in the same basic form, the reader reads with a rhythm that facilitates understanding.

Writing in parallel form can be more difficult and can take more time than writing in random form, but the consequence for the reader, especially with respect to detailed and complicated lists, can be significant. Writing series in parallel form is reader-friendly and is one way to establish your bona fides as a good legal writer.

e. Quotation Marks and Parentheses

Quotes must be noted with quotation marks. That rule should be easy enough to employ, but it can be the source of a punctuation error if the end of the quote is not noted with the second closing quotation mark. This error can slip into a document because the writer will simply forget to mark the end of the quote.

It can get more complicated, however, when the quote is in a parenthetical, as in the following example:

> The court held that malice could be found by way of the felony-murder rule. (*People v. Smith*, 28 Utop.2d 346 (1946) holding that "in the action by the defendant of starting the fire that spread to the adjoining property . . . even though the fire would not have consumed that property . . . malice existed as a matter of law.)

Obviously the closing quotation marks are missing in the parenthetical, and they were probably overlooked by the writer due to the greater concern of constructing the parenthetical correctly. A lot is involved in constructing this kind of parenthetical, including the proper citation for the case. But the closing quotation marks are not only necessary; they may be essential, especially if the quoted part of the case ended after the second ellipsis, with the writer adding "malice existed as a matter of law" to complete the intended point.

The other area of possible error with respect to quotation marks and parentheses is where the ending punctuation should appear. As to quotation marks, the American rule is that periods and commas must be placed inside the quotation marks, while all other punctuation marks (colons, semi-colons, question marks, and exclamation points) must appear outside of them, unless, of course, those punctuations are part of the original quote, as in these examples:

> She shouted, "Fire!"
>
> The attorney's next question was, "Did you know he hated you when you struck the fatal blow?"

Note that in both examples, the closing punctuation mark within the quote serves as the last punctuation mark in the sentence, even though, theoretically, a period would be expected to note the end of the sentence.

The rule for closing punctuation marks for parentheses is a little easier to understand. A period will always go inside the parentheses if the parenthetical consists entirely of a single sentence that is not within a larger sentence. Otherwise, the closing punctuation is placed after the closing parenthetical mark. Consider these two examples of those rules:

> He concluded his argument by bowing his head. (Whether he was praying or just containing his emotions was not clear.)
>
> He concluded his argument by bowing his head (not thereby revealing whether he was praying or just containing his emotions).

We make ample use of quotation marks and parentheses in legal documents (although the use of quotes should be carefully considered and limited, as noted in Step 4). The rules for when they should appear and how other punctuation marks appear relative to them are not difficult, but they can be tricky and, therefore, must be applied carefully in this white-glove step.

f. Apostrophes

Apostrophes are used in two, and only two, instances. The most common use in a legal document is to indicate a possessive. The other use, less likely in most legal documents, is to show a contraction of two words into one.

Contractions should not be used in most instances in a legal document. Using them is generally considered too casual for a document that may become part of an official transcript or court file. Even for internal file documents in a law firm, the use of contractions will usually be discouraged.

The only time a contraction problem in the use of an apostrophe is likely to be an error is with respect to the distinction between "its" and "it's." (Note, and please remember for all time, that *its'* is not a word, has never been a word, and never will be a word, unless we someday develop a different meaning for the word "it.")

The distinction between *its* and *it's* is simple. "Its" is the possessive form of it. It does not include an apostrophe. "It's" is the contraction for "it is." It always includes the apostrophe. If you use "its," you must be referring to a possessive for the thing that "it" identifies in your document. If you use "it's," you are saying "it is" in the looser, less formal manner. (And, as already noted, that form is not preferred in legal documents.)

As for all other uses of apostrophes, the rules are relatively simple. If you are speaking of someone's or something's possession of something, place an apostrophe at the end of the noun and add the letter "s." If you are speaking of more than one person or thing that possesses something, add an "s" and then add the apostrophe. Consider these two examples:

> The co-conspirator's statements were incriminating.
>
> The co-conspirators' statements were incriminating.

The first example refers to a single individual's comments. The second refers to the statements of a more than one individual. Obviously, placing the apostrophe in the wrong place can create the wrong understanding of whether one or more than one individual's statements were incriminating.

Apostrophes that appear incorrectly in a legal document can create confusion for the reader, but more frequently they lessen the regard the reader will have for the writer's efforts. Incorrectly placed apostrophes, perhaps more than any other punctuation mark, are a sign of sloppy and unprofessional work, something no attorney would ever want as his reputation.

g.   Misplaced Modifiers

A commonly encountered problem for readers occurs when a sentence includes a modifying word or phrase that is unclear with regard to what in the sentence it is supposed to modify. And, because we use modifiers frequently in legal documents, misplaced modifiers need to be found and removed from all legal documents.

Consider the following sentence:

> To determine if he was insane, the judge allowed expert testimony regarding the defendant's psychiatric evaluation.

The modifier in the sentence, "to determine if he was insane," is placed immediately before the subject in the sentence, the judge. A reasonable interpretation by the reader, therefore, would be that the judge wanted to determine if he was insane. Obviously, we know from the rest of the sentence that it is the defendant whose sanity is in issue, but the misplaced modifier runs the risk of creating a mental hiccup (perhaps in the form of an unintended chuckle) by the reader.

The preceding sentence could be corrected in a number of ways, but the best way would be to place the modifier as close to the word it is intended to modify as possible, as in this alternative construction of the sentence:

> The judge allowed expert testimony regarding the psychiatric evaluation of the defendant to determine if he was insane.

h. Pronouns

Pronouns will be used frequently in a legal document, and normally they will not be the source of an error. But there are two instances where pronouns can be used incorrectly. Consider these examples:

> Dogs like the one Mr. Simpson owns can be a danger to others, especially if it attacks friendly visitors.
>
> An attorney is at risk of sanctions if they violate the code of ethical conduct in court.

In the first example, the writer has lost track of the subject of the sentence to which the pronoun is intended to refer. If the subject, "dogs," is plural, the pronoun must be as well. Sentences that include modifiers ("like the one Mr. Simpson owns" in the example) are most at risk of this kind of error and thus must be reviewed with special care in this white-glove step.

The second example is similarly wrong but probably for a different reason. In the bad-old days, it was all too easy to assume that any attorney was a male; thus the pronoun would have defaulted in that sentence to "he." But in modern America, attorneys are just as likely to be women; thus the question becomes what pronoun to use. This issue is not so much one of political correctness as pronoun consistency. In the example above, the writer is using the plural pronoun, "they," where the singular pronouns, "he" or "she," are grammatically required.

Many legal writing instructors are struggling with this problem. Some choose to switch genders (from "he" to "she" and "him" to "her") without thereby intending to create confusion (or, presumably, make a political statement). Others just use the combinations of "he and she," "him and her" whenever a neutral singular pronoun is called for. At some point, a single word, gender-neutral pronoun may enter the lexicon to solve the problem. But until then, none of us can support the erroneous use of the plural pronoun in reference to the singular subject.

Of course, an easy way to cure the error would be to make the subject plural, as in the following alternative construction:

> Attorneys are at risk of sanctions if they violate the code of ethical conduct in court.

Some grammatical errors, like this one, are easily fixed. Others require much more work. But they all command the attention of a writer of a professionally-prepared, error-free, reader-friendly legal document.

One last pronoun usage merits attention, especially since it takes a while for law students to get comfortable with it. The rule is that when referring to a court, any court, the proper pronoun is "it," not "they." The same rule applies for a business.

Consider these examples:

> In the court's opinion, it referred to the long standing rule on willful misconduct as a form of malice.
>
> The business noted its approval of the union contract in a press release it issued.

The point of using the singular pronoun in the first sentence is to indicate that a court, irrespective of the number of judges involved in the hearing of a case, is always identified as if it were a single individual or entity. The same rule applies for a business, as the second sentence reflects.

6.   STEP SIX—CASE AND PARTY NAMES AND CITATIONS

Perhaps no errors in a legal document are more unacceptable than the misspelling of the names of the parties involved in the case you are analyzing. Obviously, misspelling the name of your own client would be beyond embarrassing, but any misspelled names in your document reflect poorly on your overall sense of professionalism and on your specific interest in the particular case you are writing about.

Case names must also be spelled correctly. Many cases consist of names that are easily misspelled. Is it, for example *Schneckloth v. Bustamonte* or *Shneckloth v. Bustomonte*? Spelling them correctly and consistently doing so can be a taxing task, but it is one that a writer committed to professionalism and to providing the reader an error-free document will attend to.

The citations you provide to support your legal arguments are of even greater concern. The purpose of a citation, as is explained in detail in Chapter 27, is to provide your reader with the source for the statement about the law or the assertion based on the law that you include in your document. Citations represent the writer's professional integrity more, perhaps, than any other aspect of the written document. If your citations are inaccurate, you risk not only irritating your reader (should she seek to review the cited authority), but you put your professional reputation (and, if the errors are egregious and numerous, your professional license) in jeopardy.

So, with that concern in mind, this step in the inspection process can be particularly intense, because it requires that every cite in your document be checked. And they must be checked to ensure not just that they conform with the requirements of the citation manual you are required to use for the document, but that they are accurate as to the location of the source, should the reader decide to review it.

Cite checking, as anyone who has done staff work as a law review editor can tell you, is painstakingly time-consuming work. For pinpoint cites, the exact page of the case cited must be accurately stated, and finding that particular point in a case, especially if it was originally noted incorrectly, can be grueling work. But it must be done in this step of your white-glove work.

One way to approach this task that may make it somewhat easier would be to cite check all cites for the same case throughout the document. In this way, the spelling of the name of the case can also be verified for each cite. You may discover other ways to make this step of the inspection process a little less time consuming, but don't treat your goal lightly. Judges and their clerks, as well as senior associates and partners in your firm, will quickly ascertain your commitment to your craft and to your ethical obligations by the accuracy of your citations.

7. STEP SEVEN—TYPOS

Typographical errors are the bane of every writer's existence. How do they occur? Why do even the best writers let them occur? The answers to these questions are best left to psychologists. For our purposes, the task is not to determine why or how they happen, but to make sure they are found and corrected before the document leaves your office.

Can typos be the source of mental hiccups for your readers? Read this typo-laden paragraph and decide for yourself:

> The statue in question has been criticized in any number of treaties, some on which even go so far is to suggest political malfeasance if its passage. Form a review of several similar statues, one commentator has drawn the conclusion that the state's legislature wax lead by corrupt infusions of cash. Others report that now only are legislators subject to corruption, but that many candidates far office succumb to the attraction of the almighty dollar even before them are elected.

Did you get frustrated trying to work through the dozen typos in the paragraph? Now read the corrected version:

> The statute in question has been criticized in any number of treatises, some of which even go so far as to suggest political malfeasance in its passage. From a review of several similar statutes, one commentator has drawn the conclusion that the state's legislature was led by corrupt infusions of cash. Others report that not only are legislators subject to corruption, but that many candidates for office succumb to the attraction of the almighty dollar even before they are elected.

Obviously typos are potential minefields in a document, creating continuous risks of losing your reader (either because of the constant case of mental hiccups she will be suffering with or because she finally gives up and stops reading entirely). And yet, until technology develops a system that allows us to dictate our documents and not have to type them, this part of the entire inspection will remain among the most daunting of the ten white-glove steps.

Various methods might work to catch and correct all of the typos in your final draft. Reading the draft backwards, from last sentence to first, might make spotting the typos easier, since you won't be as likely to focus on the substance of the document by doing so. Reading sections, or even paragraphs, out of order might also help, as might reading the document aloud. Or you can just go line-by-line, word-by-word, studying each one for the otherwise innocuous typo that somehow slipped into your otherwise perfectly written document. No single method is guaranteed to catch them all, which is why many writers use a combination of them.

Of course, as you've probably appreciated by now, by the time you get to this step of the inspection, many of the typos that were in your original final draft should have already been corrected as a bi-product of the earlier steps in the inspection. Many will also have been corrected if you have used the "clean-as-you-go" approach that is discussed more fully at the end of this chapter.

But whatever approach you use, and no matter how long it takes, you must catch and correct all of the irksome typos in your final draft before your document leaves your office. The goal of providing your reader with an error-free, reader-friendly document requires nothing less.

8.   STEP EIGHT—SPELL AND GRAMMAR CHECK

This one is easy, certainly a lot easier than the steps that have preceded it. But with the gift that our modern technology has provided to check our spelling and our grammar, it would be foolish to ignore it. And even though your particular software application may default to indicate a spelling or grammar error where there is none, you should verify each red and green underlining to make sure this isn't one of those rare times when the computer is right and you are wrong.

And beware of the spell check programs that do not work on material that is typed in ALL CAPS, as is required by most courts for point headings in briefs. Other anomalies may exist with your particular software, so be careful not to over-rely on your spell- and grammar-check functions.

Of course, after completing the first seven inspection steps, the expectation would be that there would be few, if any, red and green underlines in the entire document, but on the chance that there may be at least a few spelling and grammar glitches that you haven't caught, this step will provide the opportunity to catch them and correct them.

9. STEP NINE—THE PLEASURE READ AND ONE-VOICING

At this point, the document should be completely clean. And so this step is just that last chance to enjoy your work and to appreciate the effort you have expended to produce a quality legal document that represents your best work and that is error-free and reader-friendly.

So, sit back, relax, and read it one last time, just to enjoy the feeling that comes from achieving perfection. And as you read your document in its pristine state, if you should happen to find one last typo that you somehow didn't catch, or one errant apostrophe that somehow survived your earlier scrubbing, or one case that you misspelled, or one heading that doesn't accurately identify the argument that it introduces, then make the necessary correction and thank yourself for taking the time to read your now perfectly clean document this one last time.

And as you enjoy your work, take the opportunity to consider whether the entire document reads as if it had been written by one person. Look for changes in tone or style that suggest more than one author of the document. One-voicing a document is your last check for a writing glitch that could disrupt the flow of information you want your reader to receive.

10. STEP TEN—THE PRINTED VERSION

Now that you are fully satisfied that your document is as error-free as it can possibly be, you have only one more item to check, and that is what the document will look like to your intended reader. This step requires you to print out a final version of your document and to inspect it one last time, not for content or for typos or for grammatical errors, but for its appearance.

The look of your document can be as important as the substantive points it contains and the writing that communicates those points. And, even though our wonderful computers appear to show our document on our monitor in the exact form we expect to be duplicated in the printed version, sometimes, for whatever reason, the printed version will be slightly different.

Here are a few things to look for in the printed version of your document:

a.   Pagination

Is each page of your document correctly paginated? Do the page numbers all appear in the same place (the place you want them to appear) on each page of your document? Are the pages numbered in proper sequence? If you have non-substantive pages (e.g., a table of contents) that you wanted to have numbered with lower case Roman numerals, do those designations appear on those pages? And finally, do the page numbers on your table of contents match the page numbers in the text of your document?

b.   Widows and Orphans

Widows are single lines that appear at the bottom of a page. Orphans are single lines that appear at the top of a page. Widows and orphans are commonplace in all printed materials, including legal documents. If they are merely the first (in the case of a widow) or last (in the case of an orphan) line of a paragraph, and if page limitation isn't an issue, the better approach is to avoid these single line misfits.

One absolute no-no, however, is when a point- or sub-heading is split into a widow and an orphan. Those instances should be avoided if at all possible, lest the reader suffer a mental hiccup, caused by having to switch back to the previous page to reconsider the significance of the heading. Similarly, entire headings (widowed headings) that show at the bottom of a page can be disconcerting for the reader and potentially less impactful as well.

The preferred approach is to eliminate widowed headings and split headings, assuming that moving the full heading to the top of the next page does not put the entire document at risk of exceeding an imposed page limitation. (Happily, many courts and firms are moving from page limitations to word limitations, thereby removing this concern.)

c.   Skipped or Blank Lines

Every so often, a different kind of typo will appear on the printed version of the document. The skipped line or blank page is an error that may not be evident until the printed version is carefully inspected. Once found, these errors can be corrected, but if they aren't seen, they most certainly won't be.

d.   Italics and Underlines

Did you put all of your case names in italics or underline them? Are they all in italics or underlined in the printed version of your document?

Were you consistent in your use of one or the other of those two alternatives?

Are your headings underlined (or in bold, if required) where you intended them to so be? If you intended to add emphasis to any quotes or textual material in your document, do they so appear in the printed version? And, finally, are there any random italics or underlined portions that you did not intend to appear in that form?

You may think you gave correct instructions to your friendly computer, but this check will allow you to fix any miscommunication between you and your PC (or Mac).

e. Margins

Similarly, the margins you intended may not be as you expected. This last check will give you the opportunity to correct to the court's (or your firm's) requirements. Also related to margins are the sizes of indents for paragraphs. These should always be the same throughout your document.

f. Hard Copy for Mailing

If you are submitting your document by mail (or personal delivery, as when it is just going upstairs to your senior partner), carefully inspect the copy your reader is going to receive. Is the print quality excellent? Nothing less than excellent print quality is acceptable in an error-free document. If your printer needs toner or some other adjustment, make your document the one that forces that matter to be taken care of.

And now look at every page of the document, just to make sure the pages are in proper order and that no page somehow came out cockeyed, another anomaly that can inexplicably occur even with the best of printers.

C. A FINAL POINT—THE VALUE OF CLEANING AS YOU GO

By now you are probably thinking that performing the ten-step inspection is more burdensome than the entire process you went through in researching and writing the document in the first place. At its worst, white-gloving your document can be, depending on its length, an extended task that consumes the better part of a work week (or most of a weekend).

But if you have been diligent and vigilant throughout the process of drafting your document, the ten white-glove steps needn't be as imposing. In the military boot camp scenario, the new recruits quickly learn the value of "cleaning as you go," and you should, too.

To "clean as you go" means that you make corrections (grammatical and otherwise) as you are composing each of the drafts that lead to your final draft. A document that has already been cleaned of its obvious errors before it gets to final-draft status is far less likely to need much polishing in the ten white-glove steps.

So, clean as you go. It's step zero in the "white-glove inspection."

D. CONCLUSION

And so now you are finally finished. The document is on its way to your intended reader. It reflects your best work, the result of your thorough research and your solid analysis of the issues. It is well-written and presents your thesis, prediction, or argument in compelling terms.

And you have subjected it to a thorough "white-glove inspection" that consisted of these ten, fully-completed steps (with breaks, to allow your head to clear, after each step):

1.   You reviewed the document's organization;

2.   You considered the length and content of each paragraph;

3.   You confirmed that each sentence followed logically from the one that preceded it;

4.   You made sure that every sentence said exactly what you wanted it to say and in as few words as possible;

5.   You checked every sentence for grammatical accuracy and correct punctuation;

6.   You ensured that all party names and case names were spelled correctly and that all citations were accurate and correctly positioned;

7.   You corrected all typos;

8.   You re-checked all possible spelling and grammar errors with your computer's software application;

9.   You read the final draft one more time, thereby catching any remaining glitches that you somehow hadn't previously caught; and,

10. You carefully inspected the printed copy your reader will receive to make sure it was as perfect in appearance as you had intended it to be.

Now, take the rest of the day off.

INDEX

References are to Pages